World Combat Aircraft Directory

A Soviet Backfire-B, now in production for Soviet Long-Range Aviation and Naval Aviation. More than fifty had been delivered by early 1976.

World Combat Aircraft Directory

Edited by Norman Polmar

*In association with Floyd D. Kennedy, Jr.
and Macdonald and Jane's*

DOUBLEDAY & COMPANY, INC., Garden City, New York, 1976

Library of Congress Catalog Card Number 76-5340
ISBN: 0-385-12146-6

Doubleday Edition, Updated 1976

Contents

Introduction

The World Combat Aircraft Directory seeks to provide an overview of the world's air forces and a brief description of contemporary combat aircraft in a single, usable volume. This edition appears as a number of significant changes are occurring in the major air forces of the world.

Selection of the General Dynamics F-16 as the Air Combat Fighter (formerly Light-Weight Fighter) by the US Air Force and a number of NATO air arms will lead to one of the largest fighter production runs of the jet era. The comparatively low cost of the single-seat, single-engine F-16 could again place a US fighter in competition with European designs for some of the smaller Asian, African and South American air forces. Ironically, the US Navy has selected the Northrop F-18 — a carrier-capable variant of the YF-17/ Cobra designs — for its advanced light-weight fighter. This, in turn, could provide a similar aircraft for those nations desiring the capabilities provided by a twin-engine aircraft as well as a potential fighter for other navies retaining carriers for fixed-wing aircraft operation.

Fighter aircraft continue to emerge at a regular rate from the USSR design bureaux, providing for continued and impressive modernization of Soviet and bloc air arms. Of special interest are the relatively large and sophisticated MiG-23 *Flogger* and MiG-25 *Foxbat,* with the latter attaining a large number of air records previously held by Western fighters, including some recently set by the McDonnell Douglas F-15 Eagle. Beyond the successive Soviet designs, including several with variable-geometry configuration, the Soviet fighter inventory is noteworthy for its large numbers. On balance, however, the multiplicity of types do present some training, maintenance, and logistic problems.

Another aspect of the modernization of Soviet air forces is the anticipated large-scale production of the Tupolev *Backfire*, a variable-geometry wing, supersonic 'medium' bomber. The aircraft may be used in a 'strategic' role against the continental United States, but for a variety of reasons this appears of lesser probability than the *Backfire's* wide employment as a theatre and anti-shipping aircraft. Armed with stand-off missiles, the *Backfire* will present a credible threat in those roles.

Development of the *Backfire* has been cited, in part, as rationale for the proposed US production of the Rockwell International B-1 strategic bomber. This aircraft is proposed as a successor for the aging Boeing B-52 Stratofortress. However, the availability of other US strategic weapon systems (operational and proposed), the high quality and large quantity of Soviet air defences, the increasing B-1 costs and the availability of alternative aircraft such as modified FB-111 configurations, make the question of B-1 production difficult and controversial. A decision in favour of B-1 production may well be motivated by political factors.

Several other combat aircraft of recent vintage may also impact considerably upon future air force capabilities. The more significant aircraft include the Grumman F-14 Tomcat, the most sophisticated fighter in the West's arsenal; the Dassault-Breguet Mirage F-1, light-weight competitor to the F-16/YF-17/F-18 designs; the SEPECAT Jaguar, proof that multi-national collaboration can produce an outstanding aircraft design; the Israeli Aircraft Industries Kfir, partly indigenous Israeli fighter; the Fair-child-Hiller A-10 close-support aircraft; the Boeing E-3/Airborne Warning and Control System and its Soviet counterpart, the Tu-126 *Moss* (formerly known as the Tu-*114*); and the Yak-36 *Freehand* VSTOL aircraft, which will provide Soviet Naval Aviation with a ship-based, fixed-wing combat aircraft.

The term "combat aircraft" has been broadened in this volume to include certain unarmed reconnaissance and electronic aircraft which have vital roles in combat operations.

An effort has been made to update the air force orders of battle through the fall of 1975, employing information from official and unofficial sources. Obviously, the fall of the governments of Cambodia and South Vietnam to Communist forces during 1975 has made the fate of their air forces highly questionable in view of their combat losses in the final days of fighting, the number of aircraft flown out of those countries immediately prior to their fall, and the lack of spare parts for the surviving aircraft.

This overview of the world's air forces and combat aircraft is necessarily limited in scope and depth. Those who would seek additional unclassified material in these fields are directed to the outstanding efforts of Messrs. William Green, Gordon Swanborough, and John W. R. Taylor, especially the monthly journal *Air International* edited by Green and Swanborough, and the annual *Jane's All the World's Aircraft*, edited by Taylor. The gentlemen have also authored numerous books which, along with the efforts of Kenneth Munson, are also recommended.

The editor of this volume is in debt to a number of individuals, aircraft firms, and government agencies for their assistance with encouragement in this effort, in particular the Beech Aircraft Corporation, Bell Helicopter Company, Boeing Vertol Company, British Aircraft Corporation, Dassault-Breguet, General Dynamics Corporation, Grumman Aerospace Corporation, Hawker Siddeley Aviation, Hughes Helicopters, Kaman Aerospace Corporation, Kawasaki Aircraft Group, Lockheed Aircraft Service Company, McDonnell Douglas Corporation, Northrop Corporation, Rockwell International, Sikorsky Aircraft, and Westland Helicopters.

Much appreciation is owed directly and indirectly to Messrs. Green, Swanborough, and Taylor; also to Dr. D. A. Paolucci, longtime friend and mentor; Mr. Robert Carlisle of the US Navy's Office of Information; Lieutenant Colonel Shirley Bach (USAF) of the US Air Force's Office of Information; Lieutenant Colonel Jack T. Munsey (USA) of the Department of Defense Public Affairs Directorate; Vice Admiral William D. Houser (USN), Deputy Chief of Naval Operations (Air Warfare); Captain Werner Globke (*Bundesluftwaffe*); R. S. Bryden of the Office of Director of Public Relations (Royal Navy); Ken W. Sayers, who prepared an initial draft; Floyd D. "Ken" Kennedy, Jr., who collaborated in the final draft; Paul Ellis for his editorial support; and Miss Geraldine Miller, who typed, and typed, and typed.

NORMAN POLMAR
Alexandria, Virginia

Glossary of Terms

AABNCP Advanced Airborne National Command Post

AAH Advanced Assault Helicopter

AAM Air-to-Air Missile

AAR Air-to-Air Rocket

ACF Air Combat Fighter

ACP Airborne Command Post

ADC Aerospace Defence Command (US)

AEW Airborne Early Warning

AMSA Advanced Manned Strategic Aircraft (now B-1)

ARM Anti-Radiation Missile

ASM Air-to-Surface Missile

ASW Anti-Submarine Warfare

ATDS Airborne Tactical Data System

AWACS Airborne Warning and Control System

BAC British Aircraft Corporation

Be Beriev

B-N Britten-Norman

Bö. Bölkow

Br. Breguet

Bü Bücker

COD Carrier On-board Delivery

COIN Counterinsurgency

DHC De Havilland of Canada

Do. Dornier

ECM Electronic Countermeasures (passive/active)

ehp equivalent horsepower

ELINT Electronic Intelligence (collection)

ESM Electronic Surveillance Measures (passive)

EW Electronic Warfare

FA *Frontovaya Aviatsiya* (Frontal Aviation; Soviet)

FAA Fleet Air Arm (Great Britain)

FLIR Forward-Looking Infra-red

FMA *Fábrica Militar de Aviones* (Argentina)

F + W Swiss Federal Aircraft Factory

FY Fiscal Year

GE General Electric

HAL Hindustan Aeronautics Ltd.

hp horsepower

IAI Israeli Aircraft Industries

IR Infra-red

Il Ilyushin

IV-PVO *Istrebitilnaya Aviatsiya Protivo-vozdushnoi Oborony Strany* (Fighter Aviation of the Air Defence of the Country; Soviet)

Ka Kamov

LAMPS Light Airborne Multi-Purpose System (helicopter)

lb st pounds static thrust

LOH Light Observation Helicopter

LRA Long Range Aviation (Soviet)

LWF Light-Weight Fighter (now ACF)

MAC Military Airlift Command (US)

MAD Magnetic Anomaly Detector
Mi Mil
MiG Mikoyan-Gurevich
Mya Myasishchev
NASA National Aeronautics and Space Administration (US)
NATO North Atlantic Treaty Organization
NOGS Night Observation Gunship
PVO *Protivo-vorzdushnoi Oborony Strany* (Air Defence of the Country; Soviet)
P & W Pratt & Whitney
RAAF Royal Australian Air Force
RAF Royal Air Force (Great Britain)
R & D Research & Development
RDT & E Research, Development, Test & Evaluation
RN Royal Navy (Great Britain)
SAC Strategic Air Command (US)
SAM Surface-to-Air Missile
SAR Search and Rescue
shp shaft horsepower
SLAR Side-Looking Airborne Radar

SRAM Short Range Attack Missile
STOL Short Take-Off and Landing
TAC Tactical Air Command (US)
TRAM Target Recognition Attack Multi-sensor
Tu Tupolev
USAF US Air Force
USMC US Marine Corps
USN US Navy
UTTAS Utility Tactical Transport Aircraft System
VERTREP Vertical Replenishment
VIP Very Important Person (executive configuration)
VVS *Voenno-Vozdushny Sily* (Military Aviation; Soviet)
VSTOL Vertical and Short Take-Off and Landing
VTA *Voyenno-Transportnaya Aviatsiya* (Transport Aviation; Soviet)
Yak Yakovlev

Section 1
Air Order of Battle

Air Order of Battle

Abu Dhabi

Abu Dhabi provides the main air arm of the United Arab Emirates along the Arabian Gulf (the other members of the UAE being Dubai, Umm-al-Qaiwain, Ajman, Fujairah Ras-al-Khaimah and Sharjah). The force originally was established with British assistance, but the primary combat aircraft is now the French Mirage and certain training and support functions are undertaken by the ubiquitous Pakistanis. The Mirages when fully operational will replace the Hunters.

ABU DHABI AIR FORCE

	Personnel	1,200
	Aircraft	
18	Mirage III	fighter
12	Mirage 5-AD/5-RAD	fighter
2	Mirage 5-DAD	fighter
10	Hunter FGA.76	fighter-attack
2	Hunter T.77	fighter-attack
4	B-N Islander	transport
2	C-130H Hercules	transport
4	DHC Caribou	transport
1	Lake LA4	transport-VIP
5	Bell AB.206 Jet Ranger (Kiowa)	helicopter
5	Alouette III	helicopter
5	SA.330 Puma	helicopter

Afghanistan

The Afghanistan air arm is fully trained and equipped by the Soviet Union under the terms of an agreement which dates back to 1955. Some Afghani pilots have received advanced training in India. The Il-28 light bombers are believed not to be fully operational; these aircraft and some MiG-17 fighter-bomber aircraft are expected to be replaced by additional Su-7 *Fitter-As*.

ROYAL AFGHAN AIR FORCE

	Personnel	6,000	
		Aircraft	
60	MiG-17	*Fresco*	fighter (4 squadrons)
12	MiG-19	*Farmer*	fighter (1 squadron)
30	Mig-21	*Fishbed*	fighter (2 squadrons)
24	Su-7	*Fitter-A*	attack
20	Il-28	*Beagle*	attack
few	Mi-1	*Hare*	helicopter
18	Mi-4	*Hound*	helicopter
few	Mi-8	*Hip*	helicopter
10	An-2	*Colt*	transport
25	Il-14	*Crate*	transport
2	Il-18	*Coot*	transport

Albania

Albania's small air force operates mostly Chinese-provided aircraft, although a few of the MiG-15 and MiG-17 fighters provided by the Soviet Union during the mid-1950s may still be operational. After the break in diplomatic relations between Albania and the Soviet Union in late 1961 the former nation relied on China for providing spares and subsequently for aircraft and other technical assistance. The defensive-orientated Albanian air arm is under the control of the Army.

ALBANIAN PEOPLE'S ARMY AIR FORCE

	Personnel	5,000	
		Aircraft	
24	F-2/MiG-15	*Fagot*	fighter (2 squadrons)
24	F-4/MiG-17	*Fresco*	fighter (2 squadrons)
36	F-6/MiG-19	*Farmer*	fighter } (2 squadrons)
12	Mig-21	*Fishbed*	fighter }
20	{ Mi-1	*Hare*	helicopter
	{ Mi-4	*Hound*	helicopter
3	An-2	*Colt*	transport
3	Il-14	*Crate*	transport
few	{ MiG-15UTI	*Midget*	trainer
	{ Yak-18	*Max*	trainer

Algeria

Immediately after attaining independence from France in 1962 Algeria relied on the Soviet Union and Egypt for aircraft and training. Subsequently, French armed trainers and helicopters have been supplied together with a few other Western-produced aircraft.

AIR FORCE *(Force Aérienne Algérienne)*

			Personnel 4,500
		Aircraft	
20	MiG-15	*Fagot*	fighter (2 squadrons)
40	MiG-17	*Fresco*	fighter (4 squadrons)
30	MiG-21	*Fishbed*	fighter (2 squadrons)
24	Il-28	*Beagle*	attack (2 squadrons)
28	Magister		attack-trainer
2	Alouette II		helicopter
few	Mi-1	*Hare*	helicopter
40	Mi-4	*Hound*	helicopter
20	SA.330 Puma		helicopter
8	An-12	*Cub*	transport
few	Il-14	*Crate*	transport
4	Il-18	*Coot*	transport
3	Fokker F.27		transport
1	Beech King Air 100		navigation calibration

Argentina

Argentina is the second largest nation in South America and has the third largest inventory of combat aircraft, after Brazil and Venezuela. There are three separate air arms in Argentina which fly a mixture of aircraft mainly from France, Great Britain, and the United States. In addition, the state aircraft factory has produced twin-engine transports and assembled trainer components manufactured in the United States.

The naval air arm flies both fixed-wing aircraft and helicopters and operates one light aircraft carrier, the *25 de Mayo*. The carrier was built in Britain during the Second World War as HMS *Venerable*; she subsequently served in the Dutch Navy as the *Karel Doorman* from 1948 to 1968, when sold to Argentina.

AIR FORCE *(Fuerza Aérea Argentina)*

	Personnel 17,000

Aircraft		
20	F-86F Sabre	fighter-trainer
2	Mirage III-DA	fighter ⎱
14	Mirage III-EA	fighter ⎰ (1 squadron)
45	A-4P Skyhawk	attack (2 squadrons)
10	Canberra B.62	attack ⎱
2	Canberra T.64	attack ⎰ (1 squadron)
30	FMA IA.58 Oucara	COIN
25	IA.35 Huanqueros	COIN-transport
4	Bell 47G/J	helicopter
14	OH-6A Cayuse	helicopter
2	Sikorsky S-61NR (Sea King)	helicopter
10	UH-1D/H Iroquois	helicopter
6	UH-19 Chickasaw	helicopter
14 ⎧	Aero Commander	transport
⎨	Beaver	transport
⎩	Dove	transport
2	Aeritalia G.222	transport
1	Boeing 707-320B	transport-VIP
7	C-47 Dakota/Skytrain	transport
1	C-118 Liftmaster	transport
7	C-130E/H Hercules	transport
1	Fokker F.28	transport-VIP
22	IA.50	transport
30	MS.760 Paris	trainer
60	T-34 Mentor	trainer

MILITARY AIRLINE *(Lineas Aereas del Estado);* operated by Air Force

7	DHC Twin Otter	transport
2	Douglas DC-6	transport
8	Fokker F.27	transport
5	Fokker F.28	transport

NAVAL AVIATION *(Commando de Aviación Naval)*

Personnel	approx 3,000	
Aircraft		
15	A-4Q Skyhawk	attack*
8	Aermacchi MB.326G	attack-trainer
6	S-2A Tracker	anti-submarine*
3	HU-16B Albatross	maritime patrol-SAR
6	P-2H Neptune	maritime patrol
few	PBY-5A Catalina	maritime patrol-SAR

9	Alouette III	helicopter-ASW
6	Bell 47 (Sioux)	helicopter
6	Hughes 500M (Cayuse)	helicopter
4	Sikorsky S-61D (Sea King)	helicopter-ASW
few	SH-34G Seabat	helicopter-ASW
2	Sea Lynx	helicopter-ASW
5	Sikorsky S-55 (Chickasaw)	helicopter
3	DHC Beaver	transport
8	C-47 Dakota/Skytrain	transport
3	C-54 Skymaster	transport
1	Guarani II	transport
1	HS.125	transport
3	Lockheed L-188 Electra	transport
5	Short Skyvan	transport
28	T-28 Fennec	trainer

* carrier-based aircraft

ARMY AVIATION *(Commando de Aviación Ejercito)*

7	Bell 206 Jet Ranger (Kiowa)	helicopter
7	Fairchild FH-1100 (OH-5A)	helicopter
5	Beech Queen Air	transport
3	DHC-6 Twin Otter	transport

Australia

Australia's air arms are sharing the overall reduction in defence expenditures undertaken by the Australian Labor Party which came to power in 1972 after twenty-three years of Liberal-Country Party control of the government. Accordingly, several squadrons were disbanded and the long-awaited replacement for the Neptune maritime reconnaissance aircraft has been postponed. It is still planned to reconfigure some of the F-111C strike fighters delivered in 1973 for reconnaissance. Foreign-built aircraft are being supplemented with Australian-built helicopters.

There are three separate air arms, with the Navy operating the light aircraft carrier *Melbourne*. The carrier was laid-down during the Second World War as HMS *Majestic*, but not completed until 1956 when she entered Australian service.

ROYAL AUSTRALIAN AIR FORCE

	Personnel	21,500
	Aircraft	
24	F-111C (fighters)	attack (2 squadrons)
100	Mirage III-0 *some in reserve*	fighters (3 squadrons)
8	Canberra B.20	reconnaissance/target tow (1 squadron)
10	P-3B Orion	maritime patrol (1 squadron)
15	SP-2H Neptune	maritime patrol (1 squadron)
12	CH-47C Chinook	helicopter (1 squadron)
35	UH-1B/D/H Iroquois *some in reserve*	helicopter (2 squadrons)
2	BAC-111	transport-VIP
few	C-47 Dakota/Skytrain	transport
24	C-130A/E Hercules	transport (2 squadrons)
30	DHC Caribou	transport (2 squadrons)
2	HS.748	transport-VIP
86	Aermacchi MB.326H *some in reserve*	trainer-attack
37	CT/4 Airtrainer	trainer

FLEET AIR ARM

8	A-4G Skyhawk	attack* ⎫ (1 squadron)
2	TA-4G Skyhawk	attack* ⎭
14	S-2E Tracker	anti-submarine* (1 squadron)
2	Bell 206B Jet Ranger (Kiowa)	helicopter
7	UH-1B Iroquois	helicopter
10	Sea King Mk.50 (replacing Wessex)	helicopter-ASW
20	Wessex HAS.21B	helicopter-ASW
few	C-47 Dakota/Skytrain	transport
2	HS.748	transport
18	Aermacchi MB.326H	trainer-attack

* carrier-based aircraft

ARMY AVIATION CORPS

18	Pilatus Porter	COIN
57	Bell 206B Jet Ranger (Kiowa)	helicopter
11	Nomad	transport

Austria

The diminutive Austrian air force has a small fighter-bomber force plus a few transport and training aircraft, while helicopters are fully integrated into the Army. A replacement fighter-bomber aircraft is being sought for the SAAB-105ÖEs.

AIR FORCE *(Oesterreichische Luftstreitkräfte)*

	Personnel	4,500
	Aircraft	
38	SAAB-105ÖE	attack (3 squadrons + 1 training squadron)
18	0-1A/E Bird Dog	observation
22	AB.204B (Iroquois)	helicopter
13	AB.206 Jet Ranger (Kiowa)	helicopter
20	Alouette III	helicopter
5	OH-13H Sioux	helicopter
2	Sikorsky S-65C (Sea Stallion)	helicopter
3	DHC Beaver	transport
2	Short 3M Skyvan	transport
16	SAAB-91D Safir	trainer

Bangladesh

Following the establishment of Bangladesh in December 1971 after the last Indo-Pakistani War a defence force was organized. Subsequently, an air wing was established using former Pakistani aircraft (Sabres and one Shooting Star) and later, Soviet-supplied aircraft. The former are no longer fully operational because of the lack of spares.

BANGLADESH DEFENCE FORCE AIR WING

	Personnel		500–1,000
	Aircraft		
9	MiG-21MF	*Fishbed*	fighter (1 squadron)
3	F-86F Sabre		fighter
4	Alouette III		helicopter
few	Mi-8	*Hip*	helicopter
1	An-24	*Coke*	transport
few	An-26	*Curl*	transport
2	MiG-21UTI	*Midget*	trainer
1	T-33A Shooting Star		trainer

Belgium

The Belgian Air Force has both NATO and national commitments, the former as part of the 2nd Allied Tactical Air Force. In addition, both the Belgian Army has an air arm while the Navy operates a few helicopters. The Belgian AF will purchase 102 General Dynamics F-16 fighters to replace the F-104G Starfighters which are flown in the all-weather fighter and fighter-bomber roles (two squadrons in each role).

AIR FORCE *(Force Aérienne Belge)*

Personnel	20,000	
Aircraft		
72	F-104G Starfighter	fighter ⎫ (4 squadrons)
few	TF-104G Starfighter	fighter ⎭
60	Mirage 5-BA	fighter ⎫ (3 squadrons + 1 training
15	Mirage 5-BD	fighter ⎭ squadron)
25	Mirage 5-BR	reconnaissance (1 squadron)
11	Sikorsky S-58 (Seabat)	helicopter-SAR
5	Sea King	helicopter-SAR
	(replacing S-58)	
12	BAC Pembroke	transport
12	C-130H Hercules	transport
4	Douglas DC-6B	transport
3	HS.748	transport
2	Falcon 20	transport-VIP
40	Magister	trainer
33	SF.260MB	trainer
21	T-33A Shooting Star	trainer

ARMY AVIATION *(Force Terrestre Belge)*

75	Alouette II	helicopter
11	Dornier Do.27	observation

NAVAL AVIATION *(Force Navale Belge)*

3	Alouette III	helicopter
2	Sikorsky S-58 (Seabat)	helicopter

Bolivia

Bolivia primarily operates aircraft provided by the US Government since the overthrow of the Marxist revolutionary government in November 1964. However, Bolivia has recently gone to neighbouring Brazil for Embraer EMB.326GB Xavantes counterinsurgency aircraft and Aerotec 122 Uirapuru trainers. The former are licence-built Aermacchi MB.326GBs.

AIR FORCE *(Fuerza Aérea Boliviana)*

	Personnel	6,000
	Aircraft	
18	EMB.326GB Xavantes	COIN
10	F-51D Mustang	COIN
12	Hughes 500M (Cayuse)	helicopter-gunship
few	C-45 Expeditor	transport
12	C-47 Dakota/Skytrain	transport
15	Cessna 185 (U-17A)	transport
2	Cessna 210 Turbo-Centurion	transport
few	Cessna 402	transport
5	Convair 440	transport
18	Aerotec 122 Uirapuru	trainer
12	T-6G Harvard/Texan	trainer
4	T-28 Trojan	trainer
13	T-33A Shooting Star	trainer

Brazil

Brazil is the largest nation on the South American continent and operates the largest combat aircraft inventory of the southern American hemisphere. There is an independent air force that controls all of the nation's fixed-wing aircraft, including those operated from the Navy's light aircraft carrier *Minas Gerais*, and a number of helicopters. Naval aviation, instituted as a separate air arm in 1965, flies only helicopters.

Brazil's air arms fly aircraft from a number of nations with major acquisitions from the United States and France. Brazil's own aircraft industry is producing an increasing number of military aircraft of indigenous design and under licence, the latter including the Aermacchi MB.326GB counterinsurgency aircraft.

The Navy's aircraft carrier was built in Great Britain as HMS *Vengeance*, and was completed in 1945. After service in the Royal Navy she served under Australian colours in 1953–1955, and was then purchased by Brazil in 1956, becoming operational in 1960 after extensive reconstruction in a Dutch shipyard. Air Force S-2 Tracker aircraft are regularly embarked in the ship.

AIR FORCE *(Fôrce Aérea Brasileira)*

	Personnel 35,000	
	Aircraft	
6	F-5B Freedom Fighter	fighter-trainer
36	F-5E Tiger II	fighter
4	Mirage III-DBR	fighter
12	Mirage III-ERB	fighter
15	A-4F Skyhawk	attack*
15	B-26K Invader	attack
30	AT-6G Harvard/Texan	COIN
64	AT-26 Xavantes/MB.326GB	COIN
10	P-2E Neptune	maritime patrol
13	S-2A Tracker	anti-submarine*
100	C-42/L-42 Regentes	observation†
4	Bell 206 (Kiowa)	helicopter-gunship
3	Bell 206 (Kiowa)	helicopter-VIP
6	FH-100 (OH-5A)	helicopter
36	H-13J Sioux	helicopter-training (few SAR)
5	UH-1D Iroquois	helicopter-SAR
6	UH-1D Iroquois	helicopter-gunship
22	UH-1 Iroquois	helicopter
2	BAC-111-400	transport-VIP
56	C-47 Dakota/Skytrain	transport
60	C-95 Bandeirante	transport
12	C-119G Packet	transport
14	C-130E/H Hercules	transport (3 SAR and 2 tanker)
24	DHC Buffalo	transport
4	Douglas DC-6	transport
9	HS.125	transport
12	HS.748	transport
13	HU-16A/B Albatross	transport-SAR
12	PBY-5A	transport-SAR
few	Pilatus P-3	transport‡
few	T-28 Trojan	transport‡
3	C-47 Dakota/Skytrain ⎫	
20	C-95 Bandeirante ⎬	navigation calibration/survey
2	HS.125 ⎭	
112	AT-26	trainer
25	Cessna T-37C	trainer
7	Magister	trainer
100	T-23 Uirapuru	trainer
150	T-25 Universal	trainer

* carrier-based aircraft
† operated for Brazilian Army
‡ operated for Brazilian Navy

NAVAL AVIATION *(Aeronaval)*

few	Bell 47G (Sioux)	helicopter
18	Bell 206 Jet Ranger	helicopter (some trainer)
6	SH-3D Sea King	helicopter-ASW
4	Wasp	helicopter
5	Whirlwind Mk.3	helicopter

Brunei

Brunei military aviation was established in 1966 to support the Army and is under command of a Royal Air Force officer.

ROYAL BRUNEI MALAY REGIMENT AIR WING

	Aircraft	
2	Bell 205A (Iroquois)	helicopter
4	Bell 206 Jet Ranger (Kiowa)	helicopter
4	Bell 212 (Iroquois)	helicopter
1	HS.748	transport

Bulgaria

Bulgaria maintains a defensive air force which consists entirely of Soviet-produced aircraft except for the Czech L-29 Delfin (NATO code name *Maya*). In addition, the Bulgarian Navy operates a few helicopters. Bulgaria and Romania possess the smallest air arms of the Warsaw Pact.

AIR FORCE

	Personnel	22,000	
	Aircraft		
60	MiG-17	*Fresco*	fighter (5 squadrons)
36	MiG-19	*Farmer*	fighter (3 squadrons)
72	MiG-19	*Farmer*	fighter-bomber (6 squadrons)
50	MiG-21	*Fishbed*	fighter (4 squadrons)

30 {	Il-28	*Beagle*	reconnaissance (1 squadron)
	MiG-17	*Fresco*	reconnaissance (1 squadron)
40	Mi-4	*Hound*	helicopter
25 {	An-2	*Colt*	transport
	Il-14	*Crate*	transport
4	Il-18	*Coot*	transport
1	Tu-134	*Crusty*	transport
	Delfin L-29	*Maya*	trainer
	MiG-15UTI	*Midget*	trainer
	Yak-18	*Max*	trainer

NAVAL AVIATION

6	Mi-4	*Hound*	helicopter

Burma

The Union of Burma operates a small air arm which flies primarily US and British aircraft in support of police and counterinsurgency operations.

AIR FORCE

Personnel	7,000	
Aircraft		
12	F-86F Sabre	fighter
5	AT-33 Shooting Star	COIN
6	Vampire T.55	COIN
13	Alouette III	helicopter
12	HH-43B Huskie	helicopter
13	Kawasaki-Bell 47G (Sioux)	helicopter
2	Bristol 170	transport
4	C-45 Expeditor	transport
6	C-47 Dakota/Skytrain	transport
10	Cessna 180	transport
6	DHC Otter	transport
10	DHC Chipmunk	trainer
30	Provost T.53	trainer

Cambodia (Khmer Republic)

This Indochinese nation has been fully re-equipped with US-provided aircraft, having previously flown Chinese and French aircraft. The Peoples Republic of China also provided advisers and training during the early 1960s. Numerous aircraft were lost during the 1974–1975 fighting. The number of operational aircraft that remain is unknown, but the types are listed below.

AIR FORCE

Personnel	9,500
Aircraft	
A-37B Dragonfly	COIN
AC-47 Dragon Ship	COIN
AU-24A Helio Stallion	COIN
T-28D Trojan	COIN
0-1 Bird Dog	observation
Alouette II/III	helicopter
UH-1H Iroquois	helicopter (some gunships)
C-47 Dakota/Skytrain	transport
C-54 Skymaster	transport
C-123 Provider	transport
DHC Otter	transport
T-41 Mescalero	trainer

Canada

The Canadian Forces were fully integrated in 1964 with six functional commands being established (listed below, plus a Communications Command). Five of the functional commands operated aircraft. In addition, Canadian Forces Europe functioned as a separate command with an aviation component. However, in early 1975 the decision was made to revert to a conventional force structure with an Air Force being re-established.

Canadian military aircraft are largely of domestic production with several produced under license.

The Canadian "Navy" no longer operates an aircraft carrier, but its Tracker fixed-wing aircraft and ASW helicopters periodically fly from US aircraft carriers during exercises. A decision was made in November 1975 to replace the CP-107 Argus maritime patrol aircraft, which is unique to Canadian service, with the Lockheed P-3 Orion; 18 Orions will be delivered in 1979–80. Replacements also are being considered for the CF-100 and CF-101 fighter aircraft.

MOBILE COMMAND

	Aircraft	
27	CF-5 Freedom Fighter	fighter (2 squadrons)
5	CH-113A Voyageur (Sea Knight)	helicopter
8	CH-147 Chinook	helicopter
25	CH-135 Twin Huey (Iroquois)	helicopter
47	CH-136 Kiowa	helicopter
	some assigned to NATO	

MARITIME COMMAND

32	CP-107 Argus	maritime patrol (4 squadrons)
16	CP-121 Tracker	anti-submarine* (1 squadron)
35	CH-124 Sea King	helicopter-ASW

* carrier-based aircraft

AIR DEFENCE COMMAND

	Personnel	8,500
	Aircraft	
63	CF-101B/F Voodoo	fighter (3 squadrons + 1 training squadron)
several	CF-100 Canucks (Super Sabre)	trainer (1 squadron)
few	T-33 Shooting Star	trainer

AIR TRANSPORT COMMAND

	Personnel	6,500
	Aircraft	
7	CC-109 Cosmopolitans	transport ⎫ (1 squadron)
7	Jet Falcon	transport ⎭
23	CC-130E Hercules	transport (2 squadrons)
5	CC-137 Stratoliner	transport (1 squadron)
few	C-47 Dakota/Skytrain	transport
15	DHC/CC-115 Buffalo	transport-SAR
8	DHC/CC-138 Twin Otter	transport-SAR
9	CH-113 Labrador	helicopter-SAR

TRAINING COMMAND

25	Beech Musketeer	trainer
5	C-130H Hercules	trainer
26	CF-5B Freedom Fighter	trainer
several	Canadian Tutor	trainer
several	TH-58 Kiowa	helicopter-trainer

CANADIAN FORCES EUROPE COMMAND

50 +	CF-104D Starfighter	fighter-bomber (3 squadrons)

Central African Republic

This former French colony has developed a small air force under a defence agreement between the two countries.

AIR FORCE *(Force Aérienne Centrafricaine)*

Aircraft		
few	A-1D Skyraider	attack
1	Alouette II	helicopter
few	H-34 Choctaw	helicopter
10	Aermacchi AL.60	transport
1	Dassault Falcon 20	transport
few	Nord Noratlas	transport

Chad

A small air force has also been provided by France to this former African colony.

AIR FORCE *(Escadrille Tchadienne)*

	Aircraft	
5	A-1D Skyraider	attack
few	Alouette II	helicopter
few	H-34 Choctaw	helicopter
10	Nord Noratlas	transport

Chile

Following the overthrow of the Allende government in 1973, Chile has again been able to obtain US aircraft for the modernization of its air arms. As of early 1975 a total of 15 F-5E and 3 two-seat F-5F Tiger II aircraft were on order to replace the B-26 Invader attack aircraft, with deliveries due to start in mid-1976. Additional A-37 Dragonfly aircraft were on order to replace the T-33 Shooting Star trainers.

AIR FORCE *(Fuerza Aérea de Chile)*

	Personnel	10,000
	Aircraft	
34	Hunter FGA.71	attack
42	A-37B Dragonfly	attack
12	A-4B Skyhawk	attack
15	B-26 Invader	attack
2	HF-1100 (OH-5A)	helicopter
6	Hiller SL-4	helicopter
6	Hiller 12E (Raven)	helicopter
6	Sikorsky S-55 (Chickasaw)	helicopter
2	UH-1H Iroquois	helicopter
few	0-1 Bird Dog	observation
few	Cessna 180	observation
9	Beech 99	transport
5	Beech Twin Bonanza	transport
4	C-118 Liftmaster	transport
2	C-130E Hercules	transport
25	C-47 Dakota/Skytrain	transport
20	DHC Beaver	transport
12	DHC Otter	transport
8	DHC Twin Otter	transport
1	HS.748	transport
30	Cessna T-37	trainer
4	Hunter T.22/55	trainer
8	T-33A Shooting Star	trainer
45	T-34 Mentor	trainer

NAVAL AVIATION

4	SP-2 Neptune	maritime patrol
14	Bell 47G (Sioux)	helicopter
4	Bell 206 Jet Ranger (Kiowa)	helicopter
2	UH-1D Iroquois	helicopter-SAR
4	UH-19 Chickasaw	helicopter-SAR
few	Beech D18S	transport
3	C-45 Expeditor	transport
3	C-47 Dakota/Skytrain	transport
3	PBY-6A Catalina	transport-SAR
few	T-34 Mentor	trainer

ARMY AVIATION

2	Bell 206 Jet Ranger (Kiowa)	helicopter
5	SA-330 Puma	helicopter
3	UH-1H Iroquois	helicopter

China (People's Republic of China)

There are a large number of unknown aspects of the Chinese air forces which currently operate over 4,500 combat aircraft. Principal among the questions are the reasons for cessation of production of certain combat aircraft during the last few years. PRC production of the Tu-16 *Badger* medium-range jet bomber began in 1968 but apparently halted after some 60 aircraft were built; Chinese production of the F-8 (MiG-21 *Fishbed*) ceased abruptly about 1971 after a reported 75 were built; and the long-range, all-weather F-9 Shenyang fighter appears to have remained in a development status into 1975 and had not entered operational service as had been predicted. Production is continuing on the F-6 (MiG-19SF *Farmer*) at the Chinese State Aircraft Factory. This aircraft is probably substituting for the F-8/MiG-21 until the problems in the F-9 project can be corrected.

Chinese military aircraft have been provided to Albania, Cambodia, Pakistan, Tanzania, and North Vietnam. A number of Soviet-produced aircraft delivered prior to the Russo-Chinese break in the mid-1950s remain in PRC service; the only recent foreign military aircraft acquisition by China has been the SA.321-J Super Frelon helicopter from France for civil defence and SAR missions.

There is a separate and distinct Naval Air Force within the PRC armed forces although most of its aircraft are fighters assigned to national air defence. The following aircraft mission groupings are provided for mission assignment of aircraft and do not necessarily reflect the PRC service organization.

AIR FORCE OF THE PEOPLE'S LIBERATION ARMY

	Personnel	over 200,000	
	Strategic aircraft		
60	Tu-16	*Badger*	bomber
	Air defence aircraft*		
3,500 +	F-4/MiG-17	*Fresco*	fighter
	F-6/MiG-19	*Farmer*	fighter
	F-8/MiG-21	*Fishbed*	fighter
	Tactical aircraft*		
400	II-28	*Beagle*	attack
approx **600**	F-6/MiG-19	*Farmer*	
	and other types		fighter-bomber
	Transport aircraft		
500 +	Mi-4 *Hound* and other types		helicopter
13	SA.321-J Super Frelon		helicopter-SAR
approx **400**	An-2	*Colt*	transport
	II-14	*Crate*	transport
	II-18	*Coot*	transport
	Li-2	*Cab*	transport
	Training aircraft		
	several hundred of various types		

*   includes 400 to 500 fighter aircraft operated by Naval Aviation

NAVAL AVIATION

	Personnel	30,000	
	Aircraft		
approx **100**	II-28	*Beagle*	attack (torpedo)
several	Be-6	*Madge*	maritime patrol
several	Mi-4	*Hound*	helicopter

Colombia

Colombia's air force has joined other South American air arms in acquiring French-built Mirage aircraft following United States reluctance to provide them with high-performance aircraft. In the Colombian situation the Mirages replace US and Canadian F-86 Sabres. All military aircraft are flown by the Colombian Air Force in support of all the military services including some 30 *Satena* transports.

AIR FORCE *(Fuerza Aérea Colombiana)*

	Personnel	6,000	
		Aircraft	
14	Mirage 5-COA	fighter	
2	Mirage 5-COD	fighter	
2	Mirage 5-COR	fighter	
8	B-26K Invader	attack	
	RB-26C Invader	attack-reconnaissance	
16	Bell 47 (Sioux)	helicopter	
1	Bell 212 (Iroquois)	helicopter-VIP	
4	H-23 Raven	helicopter	
6	HH-43 Huskie	helicopter	
12	OH-6A Cayuse	helicopter	
6	TH-55 Osage	helicopter-trainer	
6	UH-1B Iroquois	helicopter	
few	AT-33A Shooting Star	trainer	
10	Cessna T-37	trainer	
30	T-34 Mentor	trainer	
30	T-41D Mescalero	trainer	

MILITARY AIRLINE *(Satena)*

few	Aero Commander	transport
6	C-47 Dakota/Skytrain	transport
10	C-54 Skymaster	transport
5	C-130B/E Hercules	transport
10	DHC Beaver	transport
4	DHC Otter	transport
1	Fairchild F-28	transport
6	Fairchild Porter	transport
4	HS.748	transport

Cuba

This nation, which occupies the largest island in the Caribbean, continues to receive essentially all of its military assistance from the Soviet bloc. None of the US aircraft provided prior to the Castro takeover of the government on January 1st, 1958, can be considered operational. Current aircraft availability is severely restricted by limitations in support and fuel as well as personnel shortcomings.

AIR FORCE *(Fuerza Aérea Revolucionaria)*

	Personnel	20,000*	
	Aircraft		
75	MiG-17	*Fresco*	fighter-bomber (4 squadrons)
40	MiG-19	*Farmer*	fighter-bomber (2 squadrons)
80	MiG-21	*Fishbed*	fighter-bomber (5 squadrons)
30	Mi-1	*Hare*	helicopter
25	Mi-4	*Hound*	helicopter
	⎧ An-2	*Colt*	transport
50	⎨ An-24	*Coke*	transport
	⎩ Il-14	*Crate*	transport
20	MiG-15		trainer

* includes personnel manning an estimated 25 battalions of SAM launchers, primarily SA-2 Guideline, and anti-aircraft artillery

Czechoslovakia

Czechoslovakia operates one of the major air forces of the Warsaw Pact. The fighter-orientated Czech air force is large and continues to be updated with Soviet-built aircraft. However, the nation's own Aero Vodochody National Corporation has built more than 3,000 Delfin L-39 jet trainers which are flown by a number of nations and has developed the improved Albatross L-39 trainer. Basic training is undertaken in the various light piston aircraft produced by the Czech firm Zlin Aircraft Moravan National Corporation. More sophisticated military aircraft can be expected from the Czech aircraft industry in the coming years.

AIR FORCE *(Ceskoslovenské Letectvo)*

	Personnel	45,000		
	Aircraft			
80	MiG-15	*Fagot*	fighter-bomber*	
40	MiG-17	*Fresco*	fighter-bomber	
40	MiG-17	*Fresco*	fighter	
100	MiG-19	*Farmer*	fighter	
150	MiG-21	*Fishbed*	fighter	
157	Su-7B	*Fitter-A*	fighter-bomber	
60	Il-28	*Beagle*	attack	
	⎧ Delfin L-29	*Maya*	reconnaissance ⎫	
80	⎨ Il-28	*Beagle*	reconnaissance ⎬	(6 squadrons)
	⎩ MiG-21	*Fishbed*	reconnaissance ⎭	

100 +	Mi-1	*Hare*	helicopter
	Mi-4	*Hound*	helicopter
	Mi-8	*Hip*	helicopter
50	An-24	*Coke*	transport
	Il-14	*Crate*	transport
	Il-18	*Coot*	transport
100–200	Delfin L-29	*Maya*	trainer
few	L-39		trainer
few	MiG-15UTI	*Midget*	trainer
150	Zlin F 226/326		trainer

* reportedly the *Letectvo* operates 18 fighter squadrons and 12 ground support squadrons which fly fighter-bomber and attack aircraft

Denmark

The Royal Danish Air Force—generally known as *Flyvevaaben*—is fully committed to NATO's Allied Forces Northern Europe, providing a small but highly competent air arm to that sector of the alliance. Advanced Swedish-built combat aircraft have replaced some British and US-supplied aircraft in first-line roles. The Danish Army and Navy both have small air arms flying primarily helicopters. Thirty-two SAAB Supporter aircraft are replacing the Piper L-18 and DHC Chipmunk aircraft.

The General Dynamics F-16 has been selected as replacement for the aging F-104G Starfighters.

AIR FORCE *(Kongelige Danske Flyvevaaben)*

	Personnel	9,500
	Aircraft	
20	F33XD Draken	fighter ⎫ (1 squadron)
few	TF33XD Draken	fighter ⎭
46	F-100D/F Super Sabre	fighter
49	F-104G/CF-104G Starfighter	fighter (2 squadrons)
20	RF33XD Draken	reconnaissance ⎫ (1 squadron)
few	TF33SC Draken	reconnaissance ⎭
8	Sikorsky S-61A (Sea King)	helicopter-SAR
few	C-47 Dakota/Skytrain	transport
few	C-54 Skymaster	transport
2	C-130H Hercules	transport
26	DHC Chipmunk	trainer

ARMY AVIATION

few	Piper L-18	observation
12	Hughes 500M (Cayuse)	helicopter

NAVAL AVIATION

8	Alouette III	helicopter

Dominican Republic

The Dominican Republic, which occupies the eastern half of the Caribbean island of Hispaniola, operates a small number of obsolete combat aircraft. The government is currently investigating options to modernize its air arm and probably will do so with equipment from the United States.

AIR FORCE *(Aviación Militar Dominicana)*

	Personnel	3,000
	Aircraft	
20	F-51D Mustang	fighter-bomber
10	Vampire F.1/FB.50	fighter
7	B-26K Invader (in reserve)	attack
2	PBY-5A Catalina	maritime patrol-SAR
3	Alouette II/III	helicopter
2	H-19 Chicasaw	helicopter
7	OH-6A Cayuse	helicopter
2	Hiller 12E (Raven)	helicopter
3	Cessna 170	transport
6	C-46 Commando	transport
6	C-47 Dakota/Skytrain	transport
3	DHC Beaver	transport
30	T-6 Harvard/Texan	trainer
	BT-13 Valiant	trainer
	PT-17 Kaydet	trainer

Dubai

Dubai is a member of the United Arab Emirates on the Persian Gulf and with Abu Dhabi provides the military aircraft available to the UAE.

AIR FORCE

	Aircraft	
5	Aermacchi MB.326K	COIN
2	Aermacchi MB.326G	COIN-trainer
1	Aermacchi MB.326L	COIN-trainer
2	Bell AB.206 Jet Ranger (Kiowa)	helicopter
1	SIAI-Marchetti SF.260	trainer

Ecuador

This South American nation, also facing a requirement for upgrading its military air arm, has decided on the Anglo-French Jaguar for the fighter/attack role and the BAC Strikemaster for the attack/trainer role. Being phased out for the ten single-seat and two two-seat Jaguars are the nine F-80C Shooting Stars, and the T-33A aircraft for the Strikemasters, while the Canberras and Meteors can be expected to be discarded in the near future.

AIR FORCE *(Fuerza Aérea Ecuatoriana)*

	Personnel 3,500	
	Aircraft	
12	SEPECAT Jaguar	fighter-bomber
14	BAC-167 Strikemaster	attack-trainer
5	Canberra B.6	attack
7	Meteor FR.9	reconnaissance
2	PBY-5A Catalina	maritime patrol-SAR
6	Alouette III	helicopter
3	Bell 47G (Sioux)	helicopter
1	Fairchild FH-1100 (OH-5A)	helicopter
4	SA.315B Lama	helicopter
2	SA.330 Puma	helicopter
6	C-45 Expeditor	transport
12	C-47 Dakota/Skytrain	transport
4	Douglas DC-6B	transport
4	HS.748	transport
1	Gates Learjet 25B	survey

24	Cessna 150 Aerobat	trainer
10 +	T-6 Harvard/Texan	trainer
10 +	T-41 Mescalero	trainer

ARMY AVIATION

10	IAI Arava	transport
1	Short Skyvan 3M	transport

NAVAL AVIATION

1	Cessna 177	transport

Egypt (United Arab Republic)

Egypt operates the largest air force of any Arab nation and has been able to consistently replace losses suffered to the Israelis primarily through Soviet aid and, of late, third-party transfer of British and French aircraft. During the winter of 1974–1975 the Sadat government reportedly negotiated the direct transfer of 50 Mirage F-1 fighters from France and up to 50 of the MiG-23 *Flogger-B* "swing-wing" fighters from the Soviet Union. Previously Egypt received a number of Mirage fighters as well as Commando and Sea King helicopters from other Arab states, primarily Libya and Saudi Arabia. Early in 1975 Egypt acquired rights to build Hawker-Siddeley Hawk fighters under license.

The Egyptian air force is supported in part by advisers, technical personnel, and possibly pilots from North Korea, Pakistan, the Soviet Union, and North Vietnam.

AIR FORCE

	Personnel	over 30,000	
	Aircraft		
38	Mirage III series		fighter
38	Mirage 5-D series		fighter
200	MiG-17	*Fresco*	fighter/fighter-bomber
200 +	MiG-21	*Fishbed*	fighter
few	MiG-23	*Flogger-B*	fighter
120	Su-7	*Fitter-A*	fighter-bomber
10	Tu-16	*Badger*	bomber (with ASM)
25	Il-28	*Beagle*	attack

15	Tu-16	*Badger*	reconnaissance
few	An-12	*Cub*	reconnaissance (ELINT)
200	Mi-4	*Hound*	helicopter
	Mi-6	*Hook*	helicopter
	Mi-8	*Hip*	helicopter
20	An-12	*Cub*	transport
40	Il-14	*Crate*	transport
150	Delphin L-29	*Maya*	trainer
	MiG-15UTI	*Midget*	trainer
	Yak-11	*Moose*	trainer
	Yak-18	*Max*	trainer

Eire (Ireland)

Eire's small air arm has only lately attained a limited combat capability with a few armed Super Magister aircraft. All other aircraft are dedicated to support missions.

IRISH ARMY AIR CORPS

	Personnel 600	
	Aircraft	
6	Super Magister CM-170	COIN
8	Alouette III	helicopter
4	BAC Provost	transport
8	DHC Chipmunk	transport
2	HS Dove	transport
8	Reims Rocket	transport

El Salvador

This Central American republic has a small air arm which flies piston-engined F-51D Mustang and F4U Corsair fighter-bombers. The latter aircraft remain in service with Honduras as well as El Salvador. The Mustangs are of the type modified by Cavalier for counterinsurgency operations.

AIR FORCE *(Fuerza Aerea Salvadoreña)*

	Personnel	1,000
	Aircraft	
6	F4U-4 Corsair	fighter-bomber
6	F-51D Mustang	COIN
6	Super Magister CM-170	COIN
1	Fairchild FH-1100 (OH-5A)	helicopter
4	C-47 Dakota/Skytrain	transport
10	T-6 Harvard/Texan	trainer
3	T-34 Mentor	trainer

Ethiopia

The internal turmoil in Ethiopia following the 1974 downfall of Emperor Haile Selassie has reduced the effectiveness of the nation's air arm and halted a modernization programme to acquire 12 A-37B Dragonfly and 12 F-5E Tiger II combat aircraft from the United States.

ETHIOPIAN AIR FORCE

	Personnel	over 2,000
	Aircraft	
10	F-5A Freedom Fighter		fighter
11	F-86F Sabre		fighter
4	Canberra		attack
6	T-28 Trojan		COIN
6	AB.204B (Iroquois)		helicopter
5	Alouette III		helicopter
2	Mi-8	*Hip*	helicopter
2	HS Dove		transport
1	Il-14	*Crate*	transport
20	SAAB Safir		trainer
few	T-28 Trojan		trainer
11	T-33A Shooting Star		trainer

Finland

Finland's air force is limited under the terms of the 1947 Treaty of Paris to a combat strength of 60 aircraft and 3,000 personnel. The Finns shop in a number of nations for their aircraft and have in the past borrowed aircraft from Sweden as well as purchasing aircraft outright.

AIR FORCE *(Ilmavoimat)*

	Personnel	3,000	
		Aircraft	
12	J35XS Draken		fighter-bomber (1 squadron)
38	MiG-21F	*Fishbed*	fighter (2 squadrons)
1	Bell AB.206 Jet Ranger (Kiowa)		helicopter
1	Alouette II		helicopter
3	Mi-4	*Hound*	helicopter
5	Mi-8	*Hip*	helicopter
1	B-N Islander		transport
8	C-47 Dakota/Skytrain		transport
5	Piper Cherokee Arrow		transport
1	Piper Navajo		transport
50	Magister		trainer
4	MiG-15UTI	*Midget*	trainer
4	MiG-21UTI	*Mongol*	trainer

France

The Republic of France has the largest number of combat aircraft of any western European nation. These aircraft include a small strategic bomber force (*force de dissuasion*) as well as a most capable tactical air arm and naval air arm. The last is based both ashore and afloat, with two aircraft carriers of post Second World War construction in service, the *Clémenceau* and *Foch*, as well as several ships with a helicopter capability. The French Navy is constructing a nuclear-propelled light carrier that will operate VSTOL aircraft and helicopters. In addition, the French Army operates a large number of light aircraft and helicopters.

Most combat aircraft of the French armed forces are of French design and manufacture, with many of the Mirage fighters being the equal of their US and Soviet contemporaries. The most significant foreign contributions to French military aviation are Boeing KC-135F Stratotankers which support the strategic bomber force, LTV F-8E Crusader carrier-based fighters and North American F-100D Super Sabre fighter-bombers. Several American-built transport and training aircraft also are in service as well as the Anglo-French Jaguar.

The number of tactical aircraft in the French Air Force will increase during the next few years with the deliveries of 160 Mirage F-1s and 170 Jaguars. In addition, delivery of 200 Alpha Jet trainers will begin in 1977. *Aéronavale* will receive Super Etendards to replace the Etendard fighters and 80 Lynx helicopters for shipboard operation.

AIR FORCE *(L'Armée de l'Air)*

Personnel	over 100,000

Tactical Air Command
(Commandement des Forces Aériennes Tactiques — FATAC)

56	F-100D Super Sabre	fighter-bomber (4 squadrons)
45	SEPECAT Jaguar	fighter-bomber (3 squadrons)
120	Mirage III-E	fighter-bomber (8 squadrons)
30	Mirage 5-F	fighter-bomber (2 squadrons)
45	Mirage III-R/RD	reconnaissance (3 squadrons)
few	Mirage IIIB/BE	trainer (1 squadron)

Air Defence Command
(Commandement des Forces de Defense Aérienne — CAFDA)

45	Mirage III-C	fighter (3 squadrons)
45	Mirage F-1	fighter (3 squadrons)
45	Super Mystére B.2	fighter (3 squadrons)

Strategic Air Command
(Commandement des Forces Aériennes Stratégiques — COFAS)

36	Mirage IV-A	bomber (9 squadrons)
	plus approx 40 aircraft in reserve	
11	KC-135F Stratotanker	tanker (3 squadrons)

Air Transport Command
(Commandement du Transport Aérien Militaire — COTAM)

2	Breguet 763	transport
9	Douglas DC-6/6B	transport
3	Douglas DC-8	transport
2	Falcon 10	transport
24	Nord Frégates	transport
100 +	Nord 2501 Noratlas	transport
50	Transall C-160F	transport
numerous	Alouette II/III	helicopter
100	H-34 Choctaw	helicopter
9	SA.330 Puma	helicopter

Air Training Command
(Commandement des Escoles de l'Armée de l'Air)

Broussard	trainer
Cessna 310N	trainer
Cessna 411	trainer
Dassault Flamant	trainer
Magister	trainer
MS.733	trainer
Mystére IV-A	trainer
T-33A Shooting Star	trainer

NAVAL AVIATION *(Aéronautique Navale)*

Personnel 13,000		
Aircraft		
36	Etendard IV-M	fighter-bomber* (2 squadrons)
36	F-8E (FN) Crusader	fighter* (2 squadrons)
12	Etendard IV-P	reconnaissance* (1 squadron)
36	Br.1050 Alizé	anti-submarine* (2 squadrons)
34	Br.1150 Atlantic	maritime patrol (4 squadrons)
27	SP-2H Neptune	maritime patrol (1 squadron)
17	Alouette II	helicopter
25	Alouette III	helicopter
16	HSS-1/CH-34 Choctaw	helicopter
12	HSS-1/SH-34 Seabat	helicopter-ASW
16	SA.321 Super Frelon	helicopter-ASW
few	CM.175	trainer
15	MS.760	trainer
10	Rallye 100	trainer
2	Falcon 10	transport-trainer
21	Nord Frégates	transport
10	Piper Navajo	transport

* carrier-based aircraft

ARMY AVIATION *(Aviation Légère de l'Armée de Terre)*

Personnel 3,700		
Aircraft		
300 +	Alouette II/III	helicopter
140	SA.330B Puma	helicopter
100	SA.341 Gazelle	helicopter
150	0-1 Bird Dog / Broussard	observation / utility

East Germany (German Democratic Republic)

The East German Air Force flies mainly Soviet aircraft, as do most Warsaw Pact air arms. The force is predominantly a fighter and fighter-bomber organization supplemented by a small number of transport and trainer aircraft, and helicopters. The GDR Army operates a number of gunship helicopters and the GDR Navy has a few helicopters for communication purposes. The following aircraft strengths are estimated.

AIR FORCE *(Luftstreitkräfte)*

	Personnel	30,000*	
		Aircraft	
90 { MiG-17		*Fresco*	fighter-bomber
{ MiG-19		*Farmer*	fighter-bomber
300	MiG-21	*Fishbed*	fighter
few	MiG-23	*Flogger*	fighter
90	Su-7	*Fitter-A*	fighter-bomber
few	Il-28	*Beagle*	attack
80 + { Mi-1		*Hare*	helicopter
{ Mi-2		*Hoplite*	helicopter
{ Mi-4		*Hound*	helicopter
{ Mi-8		*Hip*	helicopter
35 { An-2		*Colt*	transport
{ An-14		*Clod*	transport
{ Il-14		*Crate*	transport
	Delphin L-29	*Maya*	trainer
	MiG-15UTI	*Midget*	trainer
	Yak-11	*Moose*	trainer
	Yak-18	*Max*	trainer
	Zlin Z 226		trainer

* includes personnel manning two battalions of SA-2 Guideline SAM launchers plus anti-aircraft artillery

ARMY AVIATION

Mi-24	*Hind*	helicopter-gunship

NAVAL AVIATION

Mi-1	*Hare*	helicopter
Mi-4	*Hound*	helicopter
Mi-8	*Hip*	helicopter

West Germany (Federal Republic of Germany)

The West German air arms are currently undergoing a major aircraft modernization. The FRG Air Force is receiving 260 F-4 Phantoms to replace approximately 600 F-104 Starfighters that remain operational; from 1976 onward 200 Alpha Jet attack-trainer aircraft will replace the 350 Fiat G.91 aircraft now flying; and beginning in the late 1970s the FRG plans to purchase 322 Panavia 200 MRCA multi-purpose aircraft for Air Force and Navy service. A large number of transport aircraft and helicopters are flown by the Air Force. The Navy flies a variety of aircraft while the Army has a large number of helicopters as well as a small number of fixed-wing aircraft. About 300 Bö.105 helicopters will be procured to replace currently operated Army helicopters plus about 30 to the Air Force for training.

AIR FORCE *(Luftwaffe)*

Personnel	106,000*	
Aircraft		
approx **75**	F-4F Phantom	fighter (4 squadrons
approx **100**	F-4F Phantom	fighter-bomber (4 squadrons)
approx **460**	F-104G Starfighter	fighter-bomber (4 squadrons)
approx **290**	Fiat G.91R3	attack (8 squadrons)
88	RF-4E Phantom	reconnaissance (4 squadrons)
	28 in reserve	
24	Alouette II	helicopter
125	UH-1D Iroquois	helicopter
9	BAC Pembroke	transport
4	Boeing 707-320C	transport
3	Boeing 727	transport
87	C.160D Transall	transport
10	Do.27	transport
65	Do.28 Skyservant	transport
8	HFB.320 Hansajet	transport
3	Lockheed Jet Star	transport
5	Nord Noratlas	transport
55	Fiat G.91T.3	trainer
few	Piaggio P. 149D	trainer
43	Cessna T-37B	trainer†
45	T-38A Talon	trainer†
110	TF-104G Starfighter	trainer

* includes personnel manning 60 missile batteries with Nike-Hercules and Hawk SAM launchers

† based in the United States for pilot training

NAVAL AVIATION *(Marineflieger)*

130	{F-104G/TF-104G Starfighter	fighters	(4 squadrons)
	{RF-104G Starfighter	reconnaissance	
20	Br.1150 Atlantic	maritime patrol	
	8 in reserve		
22	Westland Sea King HAR.41	helicopter-SAR	
20	Do.28D Skyservants	transport	

ARMY AVIATION *(Heeresflieger)*

230	Alouette II	helicopter
110	CH-53DG Sea Stallion	helicopter
190	UH-1D Iroquois	helicopter
18	OV-10Z Bronco	utility-target tow
18	Do.27	transport

Ghana

Ghana's air arm is primarily a transport force but does fly six combat aircraft. The air force, founded in 1959, has recently phased out of service a number of older transport aircraft.

AIR FORCE

	Personnel over 1,000	
	Aircraft	
6	Aermacchi MB.326F	attack-trainer
4	Alouette III	helicopter
2	Bell 212 (Iroquois)	helicopter
8	B-N Islander	transport
6	Fokker F.27	transport
6	Skyvan 3M	transport
13	Bulldog 120	trainer

Great Britain

The Royal Air Force continues to undergo reductions in aircraft strength while at the same time modernizing its inventory. One hundred and sixty-three Jaguar strike aircraft are being procured for the tactical role (permitting the transfer of tactical Phantoms to the air defence role in place of aging Lightnings); from 1977 onward 385 MRCA strike aircraft will be obtained to replace the Buccaneers and Vulcans in maritime reconnaissance and strike roles. Another 200 MRCAs will be employed in the tactical strike and reconnaissance roles in the 1980s, meaning that this aircraft in its several variants will comprise some two-thirds of the RAF combat strength during the next decade.

The Royal Navy's Fleet Air Arm continues to phase out its fixed-wing air strength with the decline of the Navy's carrier force. The sole remaining carrier, HMS *Ark Royal,* of wartime construction but not completed until 1955, will be discarded in the late 1970s. Under construction is HMS *Invincible,* the first of a class of anti-submarine cruisers (formerly through-deck cruisers). When completed in 1980, the ship will operate Sea King ASW helicopters and fixed-wing VSTOL Harriers. In addition, the Navy flies large numbers of helicopters from surface warships, amphibious ships (including the helicopter carriers *Bulwark* and *Hermes*), and fleet auxiliaries. The Royal Marines do not have an air-arm, but Marines fly FAA troop helicopters and Marine markings are on liaison helicopters assigned to Marine Commandos. The FAA also has a few fixed-wing aircraft for specialized training and communications work.

The British Army's air arm now has the status of a corps similar to the Armoured Corps, etc. The Army Aviation Corps has a large number of helicopters that fly in direct support of ground units. Lynx helicopters will replace the current inventory of Scouts and SA.341 Gazelles are now being phased into service. Both of the new helicopter types can be armed for support missions. The army also flies light training aircraft.

ROYAL AIR FORCE

Personnel	96,500*	

Strike Command/1 Group (bomber)

30 +	Vulcan B.2	bomber (4 squadrons)
100 +	Buccaneer S.2/S.2B	attack (3 squadrons)
few	Canberra PR.7/PR.9	reconnaissance ⎰ (2 squadrons)
3	Nimrod R.1	reconnaissance ⎱
7	Vulcan SR.2	reconnaissance (1 squadron)
28	Victor K.2	tanker (3 squadrons)
	replacing Victor K.1	
few	Canberra E.15/T.17	trainer
7	Hasting C.1A/T.5	trainer
9	Argosy E.1	radar calibration (1 squadron)
few	Vulcan B.2	development

Strike Command/11 Group (air defence)

100	Lightning F.3/F.6	fighter (5 squadrons)
20	Phantom FG.1 (F-4K)	fighter (1 squadron)
few	Phantom FGR.2 (F-4M)	fighter (1 squadron)
	replacing Lightnings	
12	Shackleton AEW.2	early warning (1 squadron)
35 +	Canberra B.2/T.4/TT.18/T.19	utility-target tow (3 squadrons)

Strike Command/18 group (maritime)

30 +	Nimrod MR.1	maritime patrol (4 squadrons)
20 +	Whirlwind HAR.10	helicopter-SAR (2 squadrons)

Strike Command/38 Group (tactical)

several	Hunter FGA.9	fighter-bomber (2 squadrons)
12	Phantom FGR.2 (F-4M)	fighter-bomber (1 squadron)
several	Harrier GR.1	attack (1 squadron)
several	Jaguar GR.1	attack (2 squadrons)
24	Puma HC.1	helicopter (2 squadrons)
20	Wessex HC.2	helicopter (1 squadron)

* includes personnel in 11 RAF ground defence and air defence squadrons with SAM launchers and anti-aircraft artillery

Strike Command/46 Group (transport)†

2	Wessex HCC.4	helicopter-VIP
few	Whirlwind HC	helicopter
few	Andover C.1	transport
3	Andover CC.2	transport-VIP
20	Basset CC.1	transport
10	Belfast C.1	transport
22	Britannia C.1/C.2	transport
5	Comet C.4	transport
few	Devon	transport
50	Hercules C.1 (C-130K)	transport
6	HS.125−400/−600	transport-VIP
14	Pembroke C.1	transport
13	VC 10 C.1	transport

† organized into 15 squadrons plus several VIP aircraft and helicopters in the Queen's Flight

RAF Germany/2nd Allied Tactical Air Force

approx 40	Lightning F.2A	fighter (2 squadrons)
approx 60	Phantom FGR.2 (F-4M)	fighter (3 squadrons)
approx 60	Buccaneer S.2	attack (2 squadrons)
36	Harrier GR.1	attack (3 squadrons)
approx 20	Phantom FGR.2 (F.4M)	reconnaissance (1 squadron)
15	Wessex HC.2	helicopter (1 squadron)

Near East Air Force

14	Lightning F.6	fighter (1 squadron)
15 +	Vulcan B.2	bomber (2 squadrons)
few	Nimrod MR.1	maritime patrol (1 squadron)

few	Canberra PR.7/PR.9	reconnaissance (1 squadron)
	Wessex HC.2	helicopter (2 squadrons)‡
	Whirlwind HAR.10	helicopter-SAR (1 squadron)
2	Argosy C.1	transport } (1 squadron)
5	Hercules C.1 (C-130K)	transport

‡ 1 squadron based at Hong Kong and 1 squadron at Singapore

	Training Command	
few	Gazelle HT.3	helicopter-trainer
16	Whirlwind	helicopter-trainer
40	Bulldog T.1	trainer
170	Chipmunk T.10	trainer
95	Dominie	trainer
65	Gnat	trainer
22	Hunter T.7	trainer
195	Jet Provost T.3/T.5	trainer
several	Jetstream T.1	trainer
54	Varsity	trainer

FLEET AIR ARM

	Aircraft	approx 150
12	Phantom FG.1 (F-4K)	fighter (1 squadron) §
14	Buccaneer S.2	attack (1 squadron) §
4	Gannet AEW.3	early warning §
	Gazelle	helicopter-trainer
	Hiller HT.2	helicopter-trainer
	Sea King	helicopter-ASW (3 squadrons)
	Sea King	helicopter-trainer
100 +	Wasp HAS.1	helicopter-ASW (1 squadron)
	Wasp	helicopter-trainer
	Wessex HU.5	helicopter-transport (2 squadrons)
	Wessex HAR.1	helicopter-ASR (1 squadron)
	Wessex	helicopter-trainer
	Whirlwind	helicopter-trainer
	Devon	transport
	Sea Heron	transport
	Canberra T.22	trainer
	Chipmunk T.10	trainer
	Hunter GA.11	trainer
8	Sea Prince T.1	trainer

§ carrier-based aircraft

ARMY AIR CORPS

Aircraft			
few	Alouette II (AH.2)	helicopter	
159	Gazelle AH.1	helicopter	(18 squadrons) ¶
140	Scout AH.1	helicopter	
250	Sioux AH.1	helicopter	
24	Chipmunk	trainer	
42	DHC Beaver	trainer	

¶ 1 squadron based at Hong Kong and flights at other overseas bases

Greece

The Greek air arm suffered several aircraft losses in combat against the Turkish Air Force during the 1974 invasion of Cyprus by Turkish forces. However, more significant was the potential impact of the war on the NATO alliance with both antagonists threatening inimical actions against other members of the alliance for their positions on the Cyprus issue. The Greek Air Force contracted for several aircraft types, with 60 LTV A-7H Corsair IIs, 18 Lockheed C-130 Hercules, and 40 North American-Rockwell T-2C Buckeyes being ordered from the United States, and 40 Mirage F-1s from France.

The Greek Army operates a small number of helicopters and fixed-wing aircraft.

AIR FORCE *(Elliniki Aeroporia)*

	Personnel	23,000	
	Tactical Air Command		
36	F-4E Phantom	fighter (2 squadrons)	
60	F-5A Freedom Fighter	fighter-bomber (4 squadrons)	
20	F-5B Freedom Fighter		
54	F-84F Thunderstreak	fighter-bomber (3 squadrons)	
18	F-102A Delta Dagger	fighter (1 squadron)	
31	F-104G Starfighter	fighter-bomber (2 squadrons)	
few	A-7H Corsair	attack	
18	RF-5A Freedom Fighter	reconnaissance (1 squadron)	
8	HU-16B Albatross (amphibian)	maritime patrol (1 squadron)	
	Air Material Command		
10	Bell 47G (Sioux)	helicopter	
6	Bell AB.205 (Iroquois)	helicopter	
12	H-19D Chickasaw	helicopter	

30	C-47 Dakota/Skytrain	transport
few	C-130H Hercules	transport
1	Grumman Gulfstream I	transport-VIP
36	Nord Noratlas	transport

Training Command

	Cessna T-37	trainer
	T-2E Buckeye	trainer
60 +	T-33 Shooting Star	trainer
	T-41 Mescalero	trainer
	TF-102A Delta Dagger	trainer
	TF-104G Starfighter	trainer

ARMY AVIATION

Bell 47G (Sioux)	helicopter
Cessna 185 (U-17)	observation
Piper L-21	observation
Aero Commander 500	transport

Guatemala

Guatemala's air arm is increasing its limited combat and transport-supply capabilities with a number of aircraft provided by the United States. Guatemala maintains one of the largest military forces in Central America.

AIR FORCE *(Fuerza Aérea de Guatemala)*

Personnel	approx 1,000	
Aircraft		
8	A-37B Dragonfly	COIN
6	UH-1D Iroquois	helicopter
3	H-19 Chickasaw	helicopter
1	OH-23G Raven	helicopter
2	Cessna U206C Super Skywagon	observation
6	C-47 Dakota/Skytrain	transport
1	C-54 Skymaster	transport
6	Cessna 170	transport
3	Cessna 180	transport
7	T-6G Harvard/Texan	trainer
5	T-33A Shooting Star	trainer
3	Cessna T-37C	trainer

Guinea

The Guinea Air Force is equipped with Soviet aircraft and provides a base for Soviet reconnaissance aircraft on the coast of the west African "bulge". Only about half of the MiG fighter force is considered operational.

AIR FORCE *(Force Aérienne de Guinée)*

	Personnel	300	
		Aircraft	
8	MiG-21	*Fishbed*	fighter
1	Bell 47G (Sioux)		helicopter
4	An-14	*Clod*	transport
4	Il-14	*Crate*	transport
2	Il-18	*Coot*	transport
few	Delfin L-29	*Maya*	trainer
7	Yak-18	*Max*	trainer

Haiti

The government of this Caribbean country, which shares the island of Hispaniola with the Dominican Republic, has a small air arm of obsolescent aircraft.

HAITIAN AIR CORPS *(Corps d'Aviation d'Haiti)*

	Personnel 250	
	Aircraft	
6	F-51D Mustang	fighter-bomber
4	H-34 Choctaw	helicopter
2	C-45 Expeditor	transport
3	C-47 Dakota/Skytrain	transport
few	T-6 Harvard/Texan	trainer
few	T-28 Trojan	trainer

Honduras

This Central American state has undertaken a limited modernization programme in acquiring four ex-Venezuelan F-86K Sabre fighters to supplement the six F4U Corsair fighters of Second World War vintage. These gull-wing Corsairs and the few flown by El Salvador are believed to be the oldest combat aircraft type still in service by any nation.

AIR FORCE *(Fuerza Aérea Hondureña)*

	Personnel	1,200	
		Aircraft	
4	F-86K Sabre		fighter
6	F4U-4 -5 Corsair		fighter-bomber
3	T-33A Shooting Star		reconnaissance-trainer
few	Cessna 180/185 (U-17)		observation
3	H-19 Chickasaw		helicopter
4	C-47 Dakota/Skytrain		transport
1	C-54 Skymaster		transport
few	T-6 Harvard/Texan		trainer
few	AT-11 Bombardier		trainer
5	T-41 Mescalero		trainer

Hungary

The Hungarian Air Force is one of the smaller Warsaw Pact air arms and is fully dependent upon the Soviet Union for its aircraft.

AIR FORCE *(Magyar Légierö)*

		Personnel	13,000*		
			Aircraft		
100 +	{ MiG-19	*Farmer*	fighter	} (6 squadrons)	
	{ MiG-21	*Fishbed*	fighter		
few	MiG-17	*Fresco*	fighter-bomber	} (3 squadrons)	
50	Su-7	*Fitter-A*	fighter-bomber		
25	{ Mi-4	*Hound*	helicopter		
	{ Mi-8	*Hip*	helicopter		
5	An-2	*Colt*	transport		
10	Il-14	*Crate*	transport		
10	Il-2	*Cab*	transport		

* includes personnel in two battalions operating SA-2 Guidline SAM launchers

India

After China, India currently operates the largest air force on the Asian continent with some 800 combat aircraft in service. However, by the late 1970s Iran will unquestionably overtake India in combat capabilities if not actual number of aircraft. The Indian Air Force flies aircraft from a number of nations, with Soviet-provided equipment predominating in the combat category. About 50 MiG-23 Flogger-B fighters are believed to be on order. There is a reported shortage of spare parts for several aircraft types, especially those of British origin.

The Indian aircraft industry has both assembled and fully produced combat aircraft although the latter have apparently not met quantity and possibly quality requirements. The primary aircraft now being produced by Hindustan Aeronautics Ltd. (HAL) are 150 MiG-21MF *Fishbed* fighters as well as the first of the improved MiG-21PFMA. About 50 of the latter have been provided already by the Soviet Union. Also in production are improved Gnat fighters known as Ajit and the HF-24 Marut fighters.

Both the Indian Army and the Navy have separate air arms. The Navy operates the light aircraft carrier *Vikrant*. The ship was laid down in Britain during the Second World War as HMS *Hercules*, but was abandoned before completion and did not enter service until commissioned by the Indian Navy in 1961. New fixed-wing aircraft, including the Harrier VSTOL, are being considered for the *Vikrant*. No other warships are configured for operating fixed-wing aircraft or helicopters except the few *Leander*-class frigates, hence most Indian naval aircraft are based ashore. The Soviet Il-38 *May* appears to be the replacement for the former Air India Super Constellations used for open-water reconnaissance.

AIR FORCE

	Personnel	100,000	
	Aircraft		
250	Gnat F.1		fighter (8 squadrons)
approx **175**	MiG-21FL	*Fishbed*	fighter ⎫ (10 squadrons
approx **50**	MiG-21PFMA	*Fishbed*	fighter ⎬
few	MiG-21MF	*Fishbed*	fighter ⎭
80	HF-24 Marut		fighter-bomber (2 squadrons)
130	Hunter F.56/T.66		fighter-bomber (6 squadrons)
30	Mystére IV-A		fighter-bomber (2 squadrons)
90	Su-7BKL	*Fitter*	fighter-bomber (6 squadrons)
80	Canberra B.12(B.58/T.13		attack (4 squadrons)
12	Canberra PR.57		reconnaissance (1 squadron)
6	Super Constellation		maritime patrol (1 squadron)
120	Alouette III		helicopter
15	Bell 47G (Sioux)		helicopter
80–100	Mi-4	*Hound*	helicopter
35	Mi-8	*Hip*	helicopter
100	SA.315B Cheetah		helicopter
2	Sikorsky S-62C (HH-52)		helicopter

34	An-12 *Cub*	transport
55	C-47 Dakota/Skytrain	transport
60	C-119G Packet	transport
20	DHC Caribou	transport
30	DHC Otter	transport
65	HS.748 Andover	transport
3	Tu-124 *Cookpot*	transport
50	HJT-16 Kiran	trainer
numerous	HT-2	trainer

NAVAL AVIATION

	Personnel	1,500
approx 35	Seahawk	fighter-bomber (1 squadron)*
12	Alizé	anti-submarine (1 squadron)*
18	Alouette III	helicopter (2 squadrons)
4	Hughes 300 (Osage)	helicopter-trainer
12	Sea King	helicopter (1 squadron)
2	Devon	transport
15	HJT-16 Kiran	trainer
2	Vampire T.55	trainer

* carrier-based aircraft

ARMY AVIATION

15	Alouette III	helicopter
30	Auster	observation
60 +	Krishak	observation

Indonesia

The Indonesian Air Force was built up on Soviet-supplied aircraft during the 1960s. However, the subsequent break in relations between the two nations has left the majority of Indonesia's military aircraft inoperative from a lack of spares. Subsequently, Australia has provided former RAAF Sabres and the United States a number of F-51D Mustangs to Indonesia with more advanced A-7 Corsair II and OV-10F Bronco attack aircraft following. There is a small, shore-based naval air arm.

AIR FORCE *(Angkatan Udara Republik Indonesia)*

Personnel 30,000

Aircraft

16	CA-27 Sabre		fighter
19	F-51D Mustang		fighter-bomber
40	{ MiG-15	*Fagot*	fighter*
	{ MiG-17	*Fresco*	fighter*
35	MiG-19	*Farmer*	fighter*
15	MiG-21	*Fishbed*	fighter*
22	Tu-16	*Badger*	bomber(ASM)*
16	A-7 Corsair II		attack
10	Il-28	*Beagle*	attack*
12	OV-10F Bronco		COIN
4	Alouette III		helicopter
2	Bell 204B (Iroquois)		helicopter
20	Mi-4	*Hound*	helicopter*
6	Mi-6	*Hook*	helicopter*
1	Sikorsky S-61A (Sea King)		helicopter
few	An-24	*Coke*	transport*
several	C-47 Dakota/Skytrain		transport
8	C-130B Hercules		transport
7	Cessna 401/402		transport
5	Cessna T207		transport
7	DHC Otter		transport
few	Fokker F.27 Mk. 400M		transport
10	Il-14	*Crate*	transport*
3	Skyvan 3M		transport

several types of trainer aircraft

NAVAL AVIATION *(Angkatan Laut)*

20	{ MiG-19	*Farmer*	fighter*
	{ MiG-21	*Fishbed*	fighter*
4	Nomad		maritime patrol-SAR
few	HU-16 Albatross		maritime patrol-SAR
few	PBY-5A Catalina		maritime patrol-SAR
3	Alouette II		helicopter
3	Alouette III		helicopter
4	Bell 47G		helicopter
few	Sikorsky S-58 (Choctaw)		helicopter
few	C-47 Dakota/Skytrain		transport

* few if any of the Soviet-built aircraft remain operational

Iran

Iran continues to modernize all of its armed forces, largely with United States equipment. By the late 1970s the Imperial Iranian Air Force will operate more than 700 modern tactical aircraft complemented by a large number of support aircraft. Similarly, the Army will have some 500 helicopters plus light fixed-wing aircraft by 1978. The most sophisticated aircraft now on order are 80 Grumman F-14A Tomcat fighters which will be delivered from 1976 onward with interest expressed in the purchase of some 250 Air Combat Fighters (ACF), now the General Dynamics F-16. Some reports indicate that the Iranian government still favours the twin-engine Northrop YF-17-F-18 for the light-weight fighter role.

The Navy's small air arm is currently shore based; however, Iran has expressed interest in possibly adding a VSTOL aircraft carrier to its naval forces which are undergoing a thorough modernization. The ill-fated US "sea control ship" had been a candidate, but interest now centres on the British "light carrier" (HMS *Invincible*). The Imperial Iranian Navy is already looking into the feasibility of operating Harrier VSTOL aircraft which could eventually be carrier based, as would the SH-3D Sea Kings. The Navy also will acquire six RH-53 Sea Stallion helicopters for minesweeping.

Iran has provided considerable aviation assistance to Oman and has transferred a squadron of F-5A Freedom Fighters to Jordan. Additional, highly selective military assistance to Arab states can be expected to include aircraft.

IMPERIAL IRANIAN AIR FORCE

	Personnel	over 50,000
	Aircraft	
32	F-4D Phantom	fighter-bomber (2 squadrons)
200 +	F-4E Phantom	fighter-bomber (10 + squadrons)
100	F-5A/B Freedom Fighter	fighter-bomber (6 squadrons)
140	F-5E Tiger II	fighter-bomber (8 squadrons)
16	RF-4E Phantom	reconnaissance (1 squadron)
16	RF-5A Freedom Fighter	reconnaissance (1 squadron)
6	P-3F Orion	maritime patrol (ASM)
45	Bell AB.205 (Iroquois)	helicopter
70	Bell AB.206 (Kiowa)	helicopter
38	CH-47C Chinook	helicopter
10	HH-43F Huskie	helicopter
16	SA.321 Super Frelon	helicopter
3	Aero Commander 790	transport
6	Boeing 707-320C	transport-tanker
12	Boeing 747	transport*
56	C-130E/H Hercules	transport
14	Fokker F.27 Mk.400M	transport
4	Fokker F.27 Mk. 600	transport-VIP
45	Beech Bonanza	trainer
30	T-33 Shooting Star	trainer
30	T-41 Mescalero	trainer

* Aircraft employed in both civil and military cargo-transport roles.

ARMY AVIATION

45	Cessna 185 Skywagon	observation
10	Cessna 337 Skymaster O-2A	observation
202	AH-1J Sea Cobra	helicopter-gunship
287	Bell 214A Isfahan	
	(Iroquois mod.)	helicopter

NAVAL AVIATION

4	Bell 205 (Iroquois)	helicopter
14	Bell 206 Jet Ranger (Kiowa)	helicopter
6	Bell AB.212 (Iroquois)	helicopter-ASW
10	SH-3D Sea King	helicopter-ASW
2	Fokker F.27 Mk.400M	transport
2	Fokker F.27 Mk.600	transport
6	Shrike Commander	transport

Iraq

The Iraqi Air Force flies a combination of Soviet and British aircraft in the combat role, with France joining these nations in providing helicopters and support aircraft. Iraq is one of the most militant of the Arab states and is a prime antagonist of Israel although the two nations do not share a common border. Iraqi aircraft are engaged in fighting Turkish rebels in northern Iraq and are a prime factor in the confrontation with certain Persian Gulf states and neighbouring Iran. Losses to the rebels and other causes has reduced the strengths listed below in several categories.

The Tu-22 *Blinder* bombers in Iraq are apparently flown by Soviet crews.

AIR FORCE

	Personnel	over 10,000	
	Aircraft		
9	Tu-16	*Badger*	bomber
12	Tu-22	*Blinder*	bomber
10	Il-28	*Brewer*	attack
90	Hunter FGA.9/FR.10		fighter-bomber
30	MiG-17	*Fresco*	fighter-bomber
few	MiG-19	*Farmer*	fighter
90	MiG-21	*Fishbed*	fighter
50	MiG-23	*Flogger*	fighter
50	Su-7	*Fitter-A*	fighter-bomber

20	Jet Provost T.52		COIN
60 +	Alouette III		helicopter
4	Mi-1	*Hare*	helicopter
35	Mi-4	*Hound*	helicopter
few	Mi-6	*Hook*	helicopter
30	Mi-8	*Hip*	helicopter
9	Wessex		helicopter
12	An-2	*Colt*	transport
6	An-12	*Cub*	transport
10	An-24	*Coke*	transport
2	B-N Islander		transport
3	Bristol Freighter		transport
2	Heron		transport
13	Il-14	*Crate*	transport
2	Tu-124	*Cookpot*	transport
	Delphin L-20	*Maya*	trainer
	L-39Z		trainer
	MiG-15UTI	*Midget*	trainer
	Yak-11	*Moose*	trainer
	Yak-18	*Max*	trainer

Israel

Israel has largely replaced the combat aircraft lost in the Yom Kippur War of October 1973. Those losses constituted about a quarter of the nation's air strength at that time. However, qualitative improvements since the 1973 war have been limited and it is expected that Israel will procure light-weight fighter aircraft from the United States, probably the General Dynamics F-16 which was selected as the Air Combat Fighter (ACF) for the US Air Force. The Israelis have expressed interest in the Grumman E-2C AEW aircraft and the Grumman EA-6B Prowler electronics countermeasures aircraft, but their acquisition seems unlikely because of the cost of the former and US sensitivity about the electronic equipment in the latter. Israel is procuring a new "heavy" fighter from the United States in the McDonnell Douglas F-15 Eagle.

Long dependent upon the French aircraft industry, Israel has shifted almost completely to the United States as its primary source. The fledgling Israeli aircraft industry has developed the Kfir (Young Lion) fighter, previous known as the Barak, and based on the Mirage V, re-engined and otherwise improved. Extensive reconstruction of aircraft and production of transport aircraft is also undertaken internally.

The single Israeli air arm provides aircraft to specific commands and to support naval operations as required.

AIR FORCE *(Heyl Ha'Avir)*

Personnel	15,000 to 20,000 (varies with degree of mobilization)	
Aircraft		
several	F-15 Eagle	fighter
approx **25**	Kfir	fighter
approx **200**	F-4D/E/RF-4E Phantom	fighter-reconnaissance
50 +	Mirage IIIBJ/CJ	fighter
approx **160**	A-4E/F/H/M/N Skyhawk	attack
6	Super Mystére B.2	attack *(in storage)*
10	Vautour IIA	attack *(in storage)*
few	OV-1 Mohawk	observation
few	Cessna U206C Super Skywagon	observation
few	Do.27	observation
few	Piper Super Cub	observation-trainer
few	Alouette II/III	helicopter
several	Bell AH-1 HueyCobra	helicopter-gunship
20 +	Bell 205 (Iroquois)	helicopter
few	Bell 206 (Kiowa)	helicopter
8	CH-47C Chinook	helicopter
9	SA.321K Super Frelon	helicopter
12	Sikorsky S-61R (Sea King)	helicopter
10 +	Sikorsky S-65C (Sea Stallion)	helicopter (some ELINT)
few	Beech Queen Air	transport
5	Boeing 707	transport
several	C-47 Dakota/Skytrain	transport
12	KC-97 Stratofreighter	transport-tanker
19	C-130E Hercules	transport
few	IAI Arava	transport
35	Nord Noratlas	transport
85	Magister	trainer-attack
45	Mystére IV	trainer-attack†
30	Ouragan	trainer-attack *(in storage)*

* these aircraft are in storage
† phasing out of service

Italy

Italy maintains a large Air Force which contributes most of the combat aircraft for the 5th Allied Tactical Air Force in the NATO southern region. Italian-produced aircraft are being flown in increasing numbers with the main tactical aircraft being Lockheed F-104 Starfighters of US and Italian manufacture, and Fiat G.91 fighter-bombers. Italy will procure the Panavia MRCA as at least a partial replacement for the aging Starfighters. Also on order are 44 Fiat G.222 transports to replace the C-47 and C-119 transports.

The Italian Navy operates a large number of helicopters, some of which fly ASW missions from cruisers fitted with large flight decks, as well as smaller destroyers and frigates. Army aviation provides a large number of helicopters and light aircraft for the support of ground troops. One hundred SM-1019 light observation aircraft are being delivered to replace the older Cessna (0-1E) and Piper types.

AIR FORCE *(Aeronautica Militare Italiana)*

	Personnel	70,000
	Aircraft	
60 +	F-104G Starfighter	fighter (1 squadron)
	F-104G Starfighter	fighter-bomber (3 squadrons)
90 +	F-104S Starfighter	fighter (5 squadrons)
	F-104S Starfighter	fighter-bomber (1 squadron)
60	Fiat G.91R	attack-reconnaissance (4 squadrons)
75	Fiat G.91Y	attack
25 +	RF-104G Starfighter	reconnaissance (2 squadrons)
12	Atlantic	maritime patrol* (2 squadrons)
18	S-2 Tracker	anti-submarine* (1 squadron)
2	EC-47 Dakota/Skytrain	ECM-trainer
3	EC-119 Packet	ECM-trainer
1	EC-130 Hercules	ECM-trainer (1 squadron)
2	Fokker F.27	ECM-trainer
few	Piaggio PD-808	ECM-trainer
90	Bell AB.47G/J (Sioux)	helicopter
60	Bell AB.204B (Iroquois)	helicopter
60	Bell AB.206 (Kiowa)	helicopter
few	C-47 Dakota/Skytrain	transport
'30	C-119G/J Packet	transport
14	C-130H Hercules	transport
few	Convair 440	transport
few	Douglas DC-6	transport
few	Douglas DC-9	transport
2	Fokker F.28	transport-VIP
50	Piaggio P.166M	transport
25	Piaggio PD-808	transport
44	SIAI S.208M	transport
90	Aermacchi MB.326	trainer
145	Fiat G.91T	trainer
100	SIAI SF.260	trainer

* these aircraft operate under the operational control of the Navy

NAVAL AVIATION *(Marinavia)*

12	Bell AB.47G/J (Sioux)	helicopter
30	Bell AB.204AS (Iroquois)	helicopter-ASW
28	Bell AB.212AS	helicopter-ASW
	to replace AB.204AS	
24	SH-3D Sea King	helicopter-ASW
5	SH-34J Seabat	helicopter-ASW

ARMY AVIATION

150 {	0-1E Bird Dog	observation
	Piper L-18/21	observation
120	Bell AB.47G/J (Sioux)	helicopter
50	Bell AB.204B (Iroquois)	helicopter
30	Bell AB.205 (Iroquois)	helicopter
50	Bell AB.206 (Kiowa)	helicopter

Japan

The Japanese Air Self-Defence Force operates a large combat force of primarily fighter-type aircraft based on the North American F-86 Sabre and the Lockheed F-104 Starfighter. The former are being replaced by 128 Mitsubishi-built F-4EJ and 14 RF-4EJ Phantoms. However, further modernization of the air arm is being retarded by budget constraints. The first Mitsubishi FS-T2 supersonic attack aircraft developed from the T-2 trainer are being delivered, but programmes for both variants are being reduced. Similarly, a number of Kawasaki C-1A transports are on order to replace the aging C-46 Commando transports which date from the Second World War. Note the absence of bomber aircraft in the listings below.

The Air Self-Defence Force has three principal components, the Air Command which operates the combat aircraft through three regional organizations, the Air Transport Wing, and the Air Training Command. Large numbers of aircraft are operated by the Maritime Self-Defence Force (Navy) and Ground Self-Defence Force (Army) with 112 UH-1H Iroquois on order by the latter. The Shin Meiwa PS-1 flying boat, the only aircraft of this configuration now in production, is replacing the 30 S-2A tracker aircraft flown by the Navy.

AIR SELF-DEFENCE FORCE

Personnel over 40,000		
Aircraft		
80 +	F-4EJ Phantom	fighter
283	F-86F Sabre	fighter (7 squadrons)
188	F-104J Starfighter	fighter (7 squadrons)
16	RF-86F Sabre	reconnaissance (1 squadron)
18	Boeing-Vertol KV-107 (Sea Knight)	helicopter-SAR
8	Sikorsky S-62A (HH-52)	helicopter-SAR
11	C-46 Commando	transport
few	Kawasaki C-1A	transport
16	Mitsubishi MU-2	transport-SAR
13	Nihon YS-11	transport
6	Beech C90 King Air	trainer
18	F-104DJ Starfighter	trainer
57	Fuji T-1A/B	trainer
20	Mitsubishi T-2	trainer
187	T-33A Shooting Star	trainer
107	T-34A Mentor	trainer

MARITIME SELF-DEFENCE FORCE

70 +	P-2J Neptune	maritime patrol
18	Shin Meiwa PS-1	maritime patrol
9	Bell 47G (Sioux)	helicopter
1	Boeing-Vertol KV-107 (Sea Knight)	helicopter
12	Boeing-Vertol KV-107 (Sea Knight)	helicopter-minesweeper
50 +	SH-3 Sea King	helicopter-ASW
5	OH-6J Cayuse	helicopter
11	SH-34 Seabat	helicopter-ASW
2	Sikorsky S-61A (Sea King)	helicopter
9	Sikorsky S-62 (HH-52)	helicopter
1	Beech C90 King Air	trainer
30 +	Fuji KM-2	trainer
several	T-34 Mentor	trainer
3	Shin Meiwa US-1	transport-SAR

GROUND SELF-DEFENCE FORCE

6	Mitsubishi LR-1	reconnaissance
87	0-1 Bird Dog	observation

50	Boeing-Vertol KV-107 (Sea Knight)	helicopter
40	H-13 Sioux	helicopter-trainer
100 +	OH-6J Cayuse	helicopter
35	TH-55 Osage	helicopter-trainer
100 +	UH-1B/H Iroquois	helicopter
22	Fuji LM-1	transport
4	Mitsubishi MU-2C	transport
5	T-34 Mentor	trainer

Jordan

The small Kingdom of Jordan continues to obtain its military aircraft from the West, being one of the few Arab states to avoid using Soviet equipment. While awaiting deliveries of 36 Northrop F-5E Tiger II fighters, the Jordanian Air Force has received 20 earlier F-5A Freedom Fighters from Iran. Pakistani personnel are used for training and maintenance of Jordan's aircraft. During the 1973 war Pakistani pilots apparently flew missions for Jordan and two were reported to have been shot down and captured by the Israelis.

ROYAL JORDANIAN AIR FORCE

	Personnel	4,500
	Aircraft	
20	F-5A Freedom Fighter	fighter (1 squadron)
18	F-104A Starfighter	fighter (1 squadron)
40	Hunter FGA.76/T.77	fighter-bomber (2 squadrons)
6	Alouette III	helicopter
3	C-119K Packet	transport
2	C-130B Hercules	transport
2	Dove	transport
1	Fan Jet Falcon	transport-VIP
5	Bulldog	trainer

Kenya

Kenya's small air arm continues to reflect British influence.

AIR FORCE

	Aircraft	
8	Hunter FGA.9/T.77	fighter-bomber (1 squadron)
6	BAC-167 Strikemaster	attack-trainer (1 squadron)
2	Bell 47G (Sioux)	helicopter
7	DHC Beaver	transport
6	DHC Caribou	transport
5	Bulldog	trainer

North Korea (Democratic People's Republic of Korea)

The North Korean Air Force remains a large combat force with a moderate degree of modernization provided from the Soviet Union and China. Many of the older MiG-type aircraft listed below may no longer be operational.

AIR FORCE

		Personnel	40,000
		Aircraft	
300 +	MiG-17	*Fresco*	fighter-bomber
50	MiG-19	*Farmer*	fighter-bomber
100 +	MiG-21	*Fishbed*	fighter
28	Su-7	*Fitter-A*	fighter-bomber
70	Il-28	*Beagle*	attack
20	Mi-4	*Hound*	helicopter
approx 50	An-2	*Colt*	transport
	Il-14	*Crate*	transport
approx 50	Il-28U	*Mascot*	trainer
	MiG-15UTI	*Midget*	trainer
	Yak-11	*Moose*	trainer
	Yak-18	*Max*	trainer

South Korea (Republic of Korea)

South Korea's Air Force is built on US equipment with 98 Northrop F-5E and 28 two-seat F-5F Tiger II fighters on order to increase the combat strength of the ROK air arm, which is smaller than that of the antagonistic North Korean Air Force.

Late in 1975 the planned transfer of an additional 18 F-4D and 18 F-4E Phantom fighters to South Korea was announced.

AIR FORCE

	Personnel 25,000	
	Aircraft	
18	F-4C Phantom	fighter (1 squadron)
18	F-4D Phantom	fighter (1 squadron)
20	F-86D Sabre	fighter (1 squadron)
100	F-86E Sabre	fighter (3 squadrons)
10	RF-86F Sabre	reconnaissance (1 squadron)
several	0-1 Bird Dog	observation
2	Bell 212 (Iroquois)	helicopter
5	UH-1D Iroquois	helicopter
6	H-19 Chickasaw	helicopter
30	Aero Commander	transport
	C-46 Commando	transport
	C-47 Dakota/Skytrain	transport
	C-54 Skymaster	transport
2	HS.748	transport-VIP
	F-5B Freedom Fighter	trainer
	T-6 Harvard/Texan	trainer
	T-33A Shooting Star	trainer

Kuwait

This oil-rich Persian Gulf state relies on several Western nations for military aircraft to equip its small air arm. Having previously flown British combat aircraft, Kuwait has now ordered some 20 Mirage F-1 fighters. In addition, Douglas A-4M Skyhawks have been acquired from the United States (the first Arab nation to buy the diminutive Skyhawk which is flown in large numbers by Israel).

AIR FORCE

	Personnel 2,000	
	Aircraft	
14	Lightning F.53/T.55	fighter (1 squadron)
6	Hunter FGA.57/T.67	fighter-bomber (1 squadron)
30	A-4M Skyhawk	attack (3 squadrons)
6	TA-4KU Skyhawk	attack-trainer
12	BAC-167 Strikemaster	attack (1 squadron)
6	Bell AB.204B (Iroquois)	helicopter
20	Gazelle	helicopter
10	SA.330 Puma	helicopter
2	Whirlwind	helicopter
1	Argosy	transport
1	Devon	transport
2	DHC Caribou	transport
2	Lockheed L-100-20	transport
8	Bulldog	trainer
6	Jet Provost T.51	trainer

Laos

United States military assistance to Laos has included most aircraft of the government's air arm. The number of these aircraft that are operational is highly questionable.

ROYAL LAOTIAN AIR FORCE

	Personnel over 2,000	
	Aircraft	
10	AC-47D Dragon Ship	gunship
approx 60	T-28 Trojan	COIN
4	Cessna 185	observation
few	0-1 Bird Dog	observation
6	Alouette II/III	helicopter
approx 40	UH-34 Seahorse	helicopter
2	Aero Commander	transport
approx 20	C-47 Dakota/Skytrain	transport
6	T-41D Mescalero	trainer

Lebanon

Lebanon's half-Christian, half-Muslim government looks to the West for military equipment. Lebanon's precarious proximity to Israel limits the effectiveness of its air arm.

AIR FORCE *(Force Aérienne Libanaise)*

	Personnel 1,000	
	Aircraft	
12	Hunter F.6/FGA.9/T.66	fighter-bomber (1 squadron)
11	Mirage III-EL/BL	fighter (1 squadron)
4	Alouette II	helicopter
6	Alouette III	helicopter
2	Bell AB.212 (Iroquois)	helicopter
1	Dove	transport
10	Chipmunk	trainer
4	Fouga Magister	trainer
3	Vampire T.55	trainer

Libya

The revolutionary government of Libya has equipped its Air Force with several squadrons of high-performance aircraft of French design and reportedly has subsequently negotiated for 32 Soviet MiG-23 *Flogger-B* fighter aircraft. A number of Mirage 5 aircraft have periodically been placed at Egypt's disposal and several flew missions against Israel in the 1973 war (with several losses).

Libya's lack of qualified pilots and maintenance personnel have limited the number of aircraft that are operational and have forced the Libyan Air Force to make extensive use of Pakistani personnel. Reportedly, Pakistan pilots flew Libyan aircraft that participated in the 1973 war, several being shot down.

Several Lockheed C-130H Hercules transports have been ordered by the Libyan Air Force but their delivery has been delayed at least into 1975 by the US Department of State.

AIR FORCE

		Personnel	5,000	
		Aircraft		
few	MiG-23	*Flogger-B*	fighter
30	Mirage III-E		fighter
approx 60	Mirage 5D-series		fighter-bomber
10	Mirage III-R		reconnaissance
3	Alouette II		helicopter
10	Alouette III		helicopter
9	SA.321 Super Frelon		helicopter
9	C-47 Dakota/Skytrain		transport
6	C-130E Hercules		transport
1	Lockheed Jet Star		transport-VIP
12	Fouga Magister		trainer
10	Mirage IIIB		trainer
2	Mystére 20		trainer
3	T-33A Shooting Star		trainer

Malaysia

Malaysia's small air arm operates a variety of Western aircraft including Northrop F-5E Tiger IIs from the United States, CA-27 Sabres from Australia, and Canadair CL-41G Tebuan attack-trainers. Similarly, Malaysia's security requirements have been underwritten in treaties with Australia, Great Britain, New Zealand, and Singapore.

ROYAL MALAYSIAN AIR FORCE *(Tentera Udara Diraja Malaysia)*

		Personnel	5,000
		Aircraft	
16	CA-27 Sabre		fighter
16	F-5E Tiger II		fighter
20	Canadair CL-41G Tebuan		attack-trainer
25	Alouette III		helicopter
6	Bell 47G (Sioux)		helicopter-trainer
15	Sikorsky S-61A (Sea King)		helicopter
16	DHC Caribou		transport
5	Dove		transport
2	Fokker F.28		transport-VIP
8	Herald 401		transport
3	Heron		transport
2	HS. 125 Dominie		transport-VIP
15	Bulldog		trainer

Mali

This former French African Colony has been provided with several aircraft by the Soviet Union to supplement the few Western transports obtained when it achieved independence as the Sudanese Republic (1958–1960). The country has only a limited ability to support the MiG aircraft.

AIR FORCE *(Force Aérienne du Mali)*

	Aircraft		
6	MiG-17	*Fresco*	fighter
2	Mi-4	*Hound*	helicopter
2	An-2	*Colt*	transport
1	Broussard		transport
2	C-47 Dakota/Skytrain		transport
	In addition a few Soviet-provided trainer aircraft are also in service		

Mexico

The Mexican Air Force flies a variety of older combat aircraft with an emphasis on light attack capabilities. Most aircraft operated by the Air Force are transports and SAR planes as are the few aircraft flown by the naval air arm.

AIR FORCE *(Fuerza Aérea Mexicana)*

	Personnel	6,000
	Aircraft	
15	Vampire F.3/T.11	fighter
15	AT-33A Shooting Star	attack-trainer
15	AT-11 Kansan	reconnaissance
6	Alouette III	helicopter
14	Bell 47 (Sioux)	helicopter
5	Bell 206A Jet Ranger (Kiowa)	helicopter
1	Bell 212 (Iroquois)	helicopter
1	Hiller H-12E (Raven)	helicopter
3	SA.330 Puma	helicopter

6	C-47 Dakota-Skytrain	transport
5	C-54 Skymaster	transport
2	C-118 Liftmaster	transport
5	IAI Arava	transport
1	Lockheed Jet Star	transport
20	Beech Bonanza F33C	trainer
20	Beech Musketeer	trainer
45	T-6 Harvard/Texan	trainer*
30	T-28 Trojan	trainer*

* some armed for COIN operations

NAVAL AVIATION

5	PBY-5 Catalina	maritime patrol
4	Alouette II	helicopter
5	Bell 47G/J (Sioux)	helicopter

Mongolia (Mongolian People's Republic)

Mongolia's small air arm is totally equipped with Soviet aircraft, reflecting that country's close relationship with the Soviet Union. The Mongolian Air Force recently received its first combat aircraft, having previously flown only transports and helicopters plus a few trainers.

AIR FORCE

	Personnel	1,000	
	Aircraft		
10	MiG-15	*Fagot*	fighter
10	Mi-1	*Hare*	helicopter
	Mi-4	*Hound*	helicopter
30	An-2	*Colt*	transport
	An-24	*Coke*	transport
	Il-14	*Crate*	transport
few	Yak-11	*Moose*	trainer
few	Yak-18	*Max*	trainer

Morocco

Morocco has accepted US and Soviet military and economic assistance on the basis of non-interference with the African state's internal affairs. Both superpowers have provided aircraft for the Royal Moroccan Air Force as has France, which has agreements with Morocco for economic, technical, and cultural co-operation.

Reportedly, 25 Mirage F-1 fighter-bombers were ordered in 1975 as replacements for the F-5 aircraft.

AIR FORCE *(Aviation Royale Chérifienne)*

	Personnel	4,000

	Aircraft	
20	F-5A Freedom Fighter	fighter-bomber ⎫ (2 squadrons)
4	F-5B Freedom Fighter	fighter-bomber ⎭
12	MiG-17 *Fresco*	fighter *(in storage)*
24	Fouga Magister	attack (2 squadrons)
4	Alouette II	helicopter
4	Bell 47G (Sioux)	helicopter
24	Bell AB.205 (Iroquois)	helicopter
4	HH-43B Huskie	helicopter
6	Beech King Air 100	transport
10	C-47 Dakota/Skytrain	transport
8	C-119G Packet	transport
6	C-130H Hercules	transport
1	Do.28D Skyservant	transport-VIP
2	MiG-15UTI *Midget*	trainer *(in storage)*
35	T-6 Harvard/Texan	trainer
25	T-28 Trojan	trainer

Netherlands

The Royal Netherlands Air Force provides a major contribution to NATO's 2nd Allied Tactical Air Force as well as fulfilling national missions. The large number of F-5 Freedom Fighters were manufactured in Canada with basic training for Dutch pilots also provided in that country. The Freedom Fighters as well as the Lockheed F-104 Starfighters will be replaced by the General Dynamics F-16. The Air Force operates Alouette III helicopters and Piper L-21 observation aircraft for the Dutch Army, with the latter being replaced by 30 Bö.105C helicopters.

The Dutch Air Force is organized into a Tactical Air Command which operates the combat aircraft, and a Logistics and Training Command which operates the transport and trainer aircraft.

There is a separate Naval Air Service which maintains an overseas detachment of Lockheed P-2 Neptune patrol aircraft at Curaçao in the Dutch Antilles. Naval helicopters fly from Dutch destroyers and frigates. The Dutch light carrier *Karel Doorman* was sold to Argentina in 1968 and the Grumman S-2 Trackers that she operated have been phased out of service. The first of an estimated 24 Lynx helicopters were to be delivered to the Navy in mid-1976.

AIR FORCE *(Koninklijke Luchtmacht)*

Personnel	22,000	
Aircraft		
75	NF-5A Freedom Fighter	fighter-bomber } (3 squadrons)
30	NF-5B Freedom Fighter	fighter-bomber }
120	F-104G/TF-104G Starfighter	fighter (2 squadrons) / fighter-bomber (2 squadrons) / fighter-reconnaissance (1 squadron)
60	Piper L-21	observation (1 squadron)
72	Alouette III	helicopter (2 squadrons)
few	Bö.105C	helicopter
8	DHC Beaver	transport
2	F.27 Friendship	transport
9	F.27M Troopship	transport
several	Piper L-21	trainer

NAVAL AVIATION *(Loninklijke Marine Luchtvaartdienst)*

Personnel	2,000	
Aircraft		
16	SP-2H Neptune	maritime patrol (1 squadron + 1 detachment)
8	SP-13H Atlantic	maritime patrol (1 squadron)
7	Bell AB.204B (Iroquois)	helicopter-SAR
12	Wasp	helicopter-ASW

New Zealand

New Zealand has a small air arm flying US and British aircraft to undertake national defence requirements and to support Singapore under a multi-nation agreement for security of that "city-state". Additional BAC Strikemasters and New Zealand-manufactured CT/4 Airtrainers were being acquired. The Navy flies two Wasp helicopters from frigates.

ROYAL NEW ZEALAND AIR FORCE

Personnel over 4,000		
Aircraft		
10	A-4K Skyhawk	attack (1 squadron)
4	TA-4K Skyhawk	attack-trainer ⎫
10	BAC-167 Strikemaster Mk.88	attack-trainer ⎭ (1 squadron)
8	Bell 47G (Sioux)	helicopter
13	UH-1D/1H Iroquois	helicopter
4	OH-13H Sioux	helicopter-trainer
6	Bristol Freighter	transport
6	C-47 Dakota/Skytrain	transport
5	C-130H Hercules	transport
4	Airtourer 150	trainer
14	Devon	trainer
2	T-6 Harvard/Texan	trainer

NAVAL AVIATION

2	Wasp	helicopter-ASW

Nicaragua

This Central American nation operates an air arm of US-provided aircraft of limited capability plus one or more Israeli-built Arava STOL light transports.

AIR FORCE *(Fuerza Aérea Guardia Nacional de Nicaragua)*

Personnel 1,500		
Aircraft		
6	B-26 Invader	attack
12	F-51D Mustang	attack
6	T-33A Shooting Star	attack
4	OH-6A Cayuse	helicopter
1	Hughes 269 (Osage)	helicopter

4	C-45 Expeditor	transport
3	C-47 Dakota/Skytrain	transport
10	Cessna 180	transport
1	IAI Arava	transport
15 {	T-6 Harvard/Texan	trainer
	AT-11 Kansan	trainer
	T-28 Trojan	trainer

Nigeria

The African state of Nigeria has been improving the transport capabilities of its air force and can be expected to acquire COIN-type aircraft. Few, if any, of the Soviet aircraft, provided during the late 1960s, are considered operational.

FEDERAL NIGERIAN AIR FORCE

	Personnel 5,000		
	Aircraft		
40	MiG-17	*Fresco*	fighter
4	Il-28	*Beagle*	attack
several	Do.27		observation
10	Alouette II		helicopter
4	Bö.105		helicopter
3	Whirlwind		helicopter
3	C-47 Dakota/Skytrain		transport
8	Do.28 Skyservant		transport
1	Douglas DC-6		transport
6	Fokker F.27		transport
6	Nord Noratlas		transport
2	Piper Navajo		transport
1	Piper Navajo Chieftain		transport
20	Bulldog 123		trainer
8	Delfin L-29	*Maya*	trainer
4	MiG-15UTI	*Midget*	trainer

Norway

The Royal Norwegian Air Force is a component of Allied Forces Northern Europe and has a large force of fighter aircraft, a small anti-submarine component, and a number of support aircraft and helicopters. Army pilots fly the light observation aircraft which are "owned" by the Air Force. Replacements for the fighter aircraft will be required by the end of the decade with the F-16.

AIR FORCE *(Kongelige Norske Flyvaapen)*

Personnel	**9,000**	
Aircraft		
48	F-5A/5B Freedom Fighter	fighter-bomber (3 squadrons)
16	F-104G Starfighter	fighter-bomber (1 squadron)
22	CF-104G Starfighter	fighter-bomber (1 squadron)
16	RF-5A Freedom Fighter	reconnaissance (1 squadron)
5	P-3B Orion	maritime patrol (1 squadron)
25	⎧ 0-1E Bird Dog	observation
	⎩ Piper L-18C Super Cub	observation
32	UH-1B Iroquois	helicopter
10	Sea King HAS.43	helicopter-ASW
6	C-130H Hercules	transport
4	DHC Twin Otter	transport
2	Fan Jet Falcon	transport-VIP
	SAAB Safir	trainer
	T-33A Shooting Star	trainer

Oman

The Sultanate of Oman occupies the strategically important eastern tip of the Arabian peninsula where the Persian Gulf and Gulf of Oman meet. The concern of Iran for keeping this waterway open for super tankers has led to it providing direct support to the Sultan of Oman's battle against Chinese-trained Dhofari guerrillas. This support includes the loan of Bell AB.205 helicopters, and flight and support personnel. The few pilots now qualified in Oman have necessitated the use of British RAF and contract personnel to operate the country's air arm.

Deliveries of a reported 12 SEPECAT Jaguar combat aircraft to Oman were to begin in 1976.

SULTAN OF OMAN'S AIR FORCE

	Aircraft	
20	BAC-167 Strikemaster	attack
25 +	Bell AB.205 (Iroquois)	helicopter
4	Bell AB.206 (Kiowa)	helicopter
3	BAC 111-475	transport
8	B-N Defender	transport
2	DHC Caribou	transport
16	Short Skyvan 3M	transport
1	VC 10	transport
5	Viscount	transport

Pakistan

The Pakistani Air Force is undergoing a major re-equipment programme from a number of sources. Technical support is being provided by the United States and Iran. Specific aircraft deliveries since the 1971 war between Pakistan and India have included Northrop F-5A Freedom Fighters from Iran and Libya, some Lockheed C-130E Hercules from the former nation, Breguet Atlantics from France, and apparently some Chinese-built F-6 (MiG-19 *Farmer*) fighters. Mirage 5 aircraft are being procured to replace the aging Canadair Sabre 6 fighters which have been outfought by Indian aircraft. The SAAB Supporters are replacing T-6 Harvard/Texan trainers and some will be flown by the Army.

Pakistan's surplus pilots have found employment as instructors and reportedly as combat pilots in the air forces of Egypt, Jordan, and Libya.

AIR FORCE

	Personnel	17,000
	Aircraft	
40 +	F-5A Freedom Fighter	fighter
100 +	F-6/MiG-19 *Farmer*	fighter-bomber (4-6 squadrons)
10	F-104A/B Starfighter	fighter (1 squadron)
24	Mirage IIIEP/RP	fighter (2 squadrons)
30	Mirage 5	fighter-bomber (1 squadron)
60	F-86F/CL-13 Sabre Mk.6	fighter-bomber (4 squadrons)
15	B-57B Canberra	attack (1 squadron)
3	Br.1150 Atlantic	maritime patrol

14	Alouette III	helicopter
12	Bell 47G (Sioux)	helicopter
10	HH-43B Huskie	helicopter
few	Beech L-23	transport
approx **15**	C-130B/E Hercules	transport
1	Falcon 20	transport-VIP
1	Fokker F.27	transport
45	SAAB MFI-17 Supporter	trainer

NAVAL AVIATION

6	Sea King	helicopter-ASW
few	UH-19 Chicasaw	helicopter

ARMY AVIATION

50 +	0-1E Bird Dog	observation
20	Alouette III	helicopter
20	Bell 47G (Sioux)	helicopter
12	Mi-8 _Hip_	helicopter

Paraguay

This small South American nation's air arm has the least combat capability of any air force on the continent, with armed T-6 Harvard/Texan trainers being the only aircraft capable of being used against insurgents.

AIR FORCE _(Fuerza Aérea del Paraguay)_

	Personnel	2,000
	Aircraft	
12	H-13 Sioux	helicopter
3	Hiller 12E (Raven)	helicopter
10	C-47 Dakota/Skytrain	transport
2	C-54 Skymaster	transport
1	DHC Twin Otter	transport
few	MS.760	trainer
12	T-6 Harvard/Texan	trainer-COIN

NAVAL AVIATION

2	H-13 Sioux	helicopter

Peru

The Peruvian Air Force is one of the best-equipped and most-efficient air arms of South America. Recent acquisitions from Great Britain, the United States, and the Soviet Union have demonstrated that Peru has a pragmatic approach to aircraft procurement. (Recent purchases from the USSR have been five Mil Mi-8 *Hip* helicopters, one being lost in September of 1974.)

AIR FORCE *(Fuerza Aérea del Peru)*

	Personnel 7,000	
	Aircraft	
20	F-5E Tiger II	fighter
4	F-5F Tiger II	fighter-trainer
12	F-86F Sabre	fighter
16	Hunter F.52/T.12	fighter
22	Mirage 5SP/DP	fighter
24	A-37B Dragonfly	attack
21	Canberra B.2/B.8/B.56	attack
4	PV-2 Harpoon	maritime patrol
4	HU-16B Albatross	maritime patrol
12	Alouette III	helicopter
20	Bell 47G (Sioux)	helicopter
17	Bell 212 (Iroquois)	helicopter
6	Mi-6 *Hook*	helicopter
4	Mi-8 *Hip*	helicopter
2	Canberra T.4	trainer
26	Cessna T-37B	trainer
7	Pilatus Turbo Porter	trainer
8	T-33A Shooting Star	trainer-attack
6	T-34 Mentor	trainer
19	T-41 Mescalero	trainer

ARMY AVIATION

8	Bell 47G (Sioux)	helicopter
2	Nomad	transport

NAVAL AVIATION

2	Alouette III	helicopter

Philippines

The Philippine Air Force, like the other Philippine armed services, is based on US military organization and operates almost entirely with US-provided equipment. The older US-built trainers are being phased out with the introduction of the SIAI-Marchetti SF.260 aircraft.

AIR FORCE

	Personnel	9,000
	Aircraft	
20	F-5A/B Freedom Fighter	fighter-bomber (1 squadron)
30	F-86F Sabre	fighter (2 squadrons)
38	Bö.105	helicopter
8	Fairchild FH-1100 (OH-5A)	helicopter
2	H-34 Choctaw	helicopter
2	Sikorsky S-62 (HH-52)	helicopter
12	UH-1D Iroquois	helicopter
5	CH-19 Chickasaw	helicopter
30	C-47 Dakota/Skytrain	transport
9	Fokker F.27 Mk 100	transport
1	Fokker F.27 Mk 200	transport
4	Lockheed L-100-20	transport
12	Nomad	transport
4	YS-11	transport
32	SF.260MP	trainer
16	SF.260WP Warrior	trainer-attack
12	T-28 Trojan	trainer
10	T-33 Shooting Star	trainer

Poland

Poland has the largest air force of any Warsaw Pact nation except, of course, the Soviet Union. Most Polish-flown aircraft are of Soviet manufacture although a number of Polish-built trainers, Polish-built LIM-5 variants of the MiG-17, and Polish-built variants of Mil helicopters are in wide use.

The Polish naval air arm is unique among all Warsaw Pact navies in that it operates land-based fighters. The more than 600 combat aircraft and helicopters with Polish markings are supplemented by some 250 Soviet combat aircraft based on Polish airfields.

AIR FORCE *(Polskie Lotnictwo Wojskowe)*

Personnel	60,000			
Aircraft				
240	LIM-5/MiG-17	*Fresco*	fighter	(36 squadrons)
	MiG-19	*Farmer*	fighter	
	MiG-21	*Fishbed*	fighter	
200	LIM-5/MiG-17	*Fresco*	fighter-bomber	(12 squadrons)
	Su-7	*Fitter-A*	fighter-bomber	
	Su-20	*Fitter-C*	fighter-bomber	
30	II-28	*Beagle*	attack (4 squadrons)	
50	II-28	*Beagle*	reconnaissance	(6 squadrons)
	MiG-21	*Fishbed*	reconnaissance	
50 +	Mi-2	*Hoplite*	helicopter	
	Mi-4	*Hound*	helicopter	
	Mi-8	*Hip*	helicopter	
40 +	An-2	*Colt*	transport	
	An-12	*Cub*	transport	
	An-26	*Curl*	transport	
	II-14	*Clod*	transport	
	II-18	*Coot*	transport	
	PZL-104 Wilga		transport	
	Tu-134	*Crusty*	transport	
	Yak-12	*Creek*	transport	
numerous	TS-11 Iskra		trainer	

NAVAL AVIATION *(Morskie Wojskowe Lotnictwo)*

40	LIM-5/MiG-17	*Fresco*	fighter
8	II-28	*Beagle*	attack-reconnaissance
30	Mi-2	*Hoplite*	helicopter
	Mi-4	*Hound*	helicopter
few	An-2	*Colt*	transport

Portugal

The change in government in Portugal during 1974 makes that nation's commitment to the Atlantic Alliance extremely tenuous. At the time of writing only the maritime patrol aircraft were assigned to NATO operations. The aging equipment of the Portuguese Air Force will require replacement in the next few years, but the quality and quantity of new military aircraft is again unknown because of the tribulations of the government.

AIR FORCE *(Forca Aera Portugesa)*

Personnel		18,000*
Aircraft		
25	F-84G Thunderjet	fighter bomber (1 squadron)
18	F-86F Sabre	fighter (1 squadron)
36	Fiat G.91R/4	fighter-bomber (2 squadrons) †
6	B-26 Invader	attack (1 squadron)
20 +	T-6G Harvard/Texan	COIN (1 squadron) †
8	P-2E Neptune	maritime patrol (1 squadron)
	Auster D.5/160	observation
	Do.27	observation
20 +	Alouette II	helicopter †
60 +	Alouette III	helicopter †
12	SA.330 Puma	helicopter
2	Boeing 707	transport
15	C-45 Expeditor	transport
20	C-47 Dakota/Skytrain	transport
5	C-54 Skymaster	transport
28	Casa C.212	transport
10	Douglas DC-6	transport
24	Nord Noratlas	transport
30	Cessna T-37	trainer
few	DHC Chipmunk	trainer
15	T-33A Shooting Star	trainer
few	Vampire T.55	trainer

* includes a parachute regiment with more than 3,000 troops
† 1 Fiat G.91 squadron and the T-6G Harvard/Texan squadron as well as some helicopters and transports are based in Mozambique and Guinea

Qatar

This Persian Gulf state has equipped its small Defence Force with British aircraft. In addition, a few helicopters are operated by the police.

AIR FORCE

Aircraft		
12	Hunter F.78	fighters
2	Whirlwind	helicopters

Rhodesia

This Central African state primarily operates European-built aircraft acquired before United Nations sanctions were applied to inhibit Western trade.

AIR FORCE

Personnel	1,200	
Aircraft		
12	Hunter FGA.9	fighter-bomber
12	Vampire FB.9	fighter-bomber
9	Canberra B.2/T.4	attack
13	Provost T.52	reconnaissance
8	Alouette III	helicopter
7	Aermacchi AL 60F5	transport
1	Beech Baron	transport
4	C-47 Dakota/Skytrain	transport
8	Vampire T.55	trainer

Romania

Romania contributes a small, primarily fighter air arm to the Warsaw Pact combat inventory.

AIR FORCE *(Aviatia Română)*

	Personnel 21,000		
	Aircraft		
few	MiG-17	*Fresco*	fighter-bomber
	MiG-19	*Farmer*	fighter-bomber
approx **200**	MiG-21F/PF	*Fishbed*	fighter
	Su-7	*Fitter-A*	fighter-bomber
47	Alouette III		helicopter
few	Mi-2	*Hoplite*	helicopter
10	Mi-4	*Hound*	helicopter
few	Mi-8	*Hip*	helicopter
	Il-14	*Crate*	transport
	Il-18	*Coot*	transport
	L-200 Morava		transport
	Delfin L-29	*Maya*	trainer
	MiG-15UTI	*Midget*	trainer
	MiG-21UTI	*Mongol*	trainer

Saudi Arabia

This oil-rich monarchy is increasing the size and capabilities of its air arm with Anglo-American aircraft. Thirty-eight Mirage III fighter-bombers previously ordered have been transferred to Egypt. It can be expected that Saudi Arabia will acquire a small number of advanced Mirage-type aircraft to supplement the lesser-capability of F-5 Tiger IIs and BAC-167 Strikemasters of recent purchase.

ROYAL SAUDI AIR FORCE

	Personnel over 5,000	
	Aircraft	
70	F-5E Tiger II	fighter
20	F-5F Tiger II	fighter-trainer
37	Lightning F.52/F.53/F.54	fighter
6	Lightning T.55	fighter
30	BAC-167 Strikemaster Mk.80	attack-trainer
2	Alouette III	helicopter
25	Bell AB.205 (Iroquois)	helicopter
16	Bell AB.206 Jet Ranger (Kiowa)	helicopter

1	Boeing 707-320C	transport-VIP
9	C-130H Hercules	transport
12	KC-130 Hercules	transport-tanker
4	Cessna 172G	trainer
few	Cessna 310K	trainer
20	F-5B Freedom Fighter	trainer

Singapore

This Asian city-state is developing a relatively large air arm primarily based on US and British aircraft.

SINGAPORE AIR DEFENCE COMMAND

	Personnel	over 1,500
	Aircraft	
34	Hunter FGA.74/FGA.74B	fighter-bomber
4	Hunter FR.74	fighter-reconnaissance
9	Hunter T.75/T.75A	fighter-trainer
40	A-4S Skyhawk	attack
15	BAC-167 Strikemaster Mk.84	attack-trainer
7	Alouette III	helicopter
6	Short Skyvan 3M	transport (3 fitted for SAR)
14	SF.260MS	trainer-attack

Somalia (Somali Democratic Republic)

The air arm of this northeast African state is being equipped with Soviet aircraft. The country has a long coastline on the Indian Ocean and on the Gulf of Aden, the latter having strategic importance with respect to southern entry to the Suez Canal. Soviet personnel provide technical assistance to the air arm and additional transfers of Soviet aircraft can be expected.

AIR FORCE *(Cuerpo Aeronautica della Somalia)*

	Personnel over 2,000		
	Aircraft		
few	MiG-15	*Fagot*	fighter
40 + {	MiG-17	*Fresco*	fighter
	MiG-19	*Farmer*	fighter
7	MiG-21	*Fishbed*	fighter
few	Il-28	*Beagle*	attack
few	Mi-4	*Hound*	helicopter
few	Mi-8	*Hip*	helicopter
few	An-24	*Coke*	transport
few	An-26	*Curl*	transport
1	C-45 Expeditor		transport
3	C-47 Dakota/Skytrain		transport
7	MiG-15UTI	*Midget*	trainer
8	Piaggio P.148		trainer
20	Yak-11	*Moose*	trainer

South Africa

The large South African Air Force is becoming increasingly independent of European sources for combat aircraft. The indigenous Atlas Aircraft Corporation will deliver Mirage F-1 fighter aircraft from 1977 onward. Initial planning provided for 16 Mirage F-1CZ interceptors and 32 F-1AZ fighter-bombers. The existing Air Force strength is of primarily Anglo-French manufacture with Atlas-built Aermacchi MB.326 aircraft being produced in large numbers. Pressing aircraft replacement requirements include maritime patrol planes, a significant requirement because of the close passage to the Cape of Good Hope of super tankers from the Persian Gulf to Europe and the United States.

The South African Navy's frigates can operate Wasp ASW helicopters.

There also is a reserve component known as the Active Citizen Force which flies some 150 Harvards and MB.326M Impalas, and a number of civilian-operated light aircraft are organized for use in civil emergencies.

AIR FORCE

	Personnel 5,500		
	Aircraft		
50	Mirage III-CZ/DZ/EZ	fighter	}
7	Mirage III-BZ/DZ	fighter-trainer	} (3 squadrons)
4	Mirage III-RZ	fighter-reconnaissance	}

13	Buccaneer S.50	attack (1 squadron)
6	Canberra B.12	attack } (1 squadron)
3	Canberra T.4	attack }
	MB.326K Impala	COIN
18	Piaggio P.166S	maritime patrol
7	Shackleton MR.3	maritime patrol
40	Aermacchi AM.3C	observation
18	Cessna 185 (U-17)	observation
few	Alouette II	helicopter-trainer
40	Alouette III	helicopter
15	SA.321L Super Frelon	helicopter
20	SA.330 Puma	helicopter
11	Wasp	helicopter-ASW
1	BAC Viscount 781	transport-VIP
9	C.160Z Transall	transport
26	C-47 Dakota/Skytrain	transport (3 fitted as VIP)
7	C-130B Hercules	transport
5	Douglas DC-4	transport
4	HS.125	transport
few	C-47 Dakota/Skytrain	trainer
80	MB.326K Impala	trainer
100	T-6 Harvard/Texan	trainer
few	Vampire FB.6/T.55	trainer

Soviet Union (Union of Soviet Socialist Republics)

The Soviet armed forces are organized into five combat services: Strategic Rocket Forces, Air Defence Forces, Ground Forces, Air Forces, and Navy. Within these services there are five separate and distinct "air forces": The Fighter Aviation of the Air Defence of the Country is part of the Air Defence Forces, and Naval Aviation is a part of the Navy; Frontal Aviation, Transport Aviation, and Long-Range Aviation as well as certain training and support activities are generally considered administratively subordinate to the Soviet Air Forces (*Voenno-Vozdushnii Sily*, VVS). However, Frontal Aviation is operationally subordinate to Ground Forces or regional commands, while Transport Aviation and Long-Range Aviation appear to have some direct subordination to the Minister of Defence. Significantly, the Long-Range Aviation or strategic bomber force is separate from the Strategic Rocket Forces, unlike the US Strategic Air Command which controls land-based strategic bombers and land-based ICBMs.

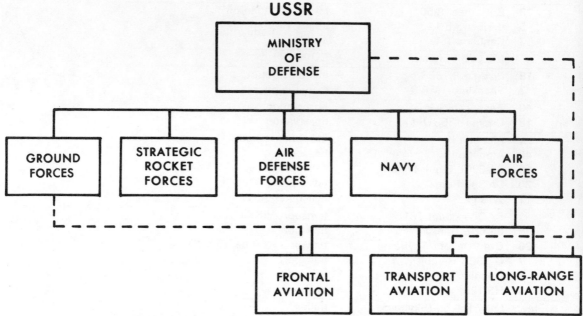

USSR

The Soviet Union's Civil Air Fleet (*Grazhdanskii Vozdushnii Flot*) is under the Ministry of Civil Aviation, which was separated from the Ministry of Defence in 1948. However, the Minister of Civil Aviation generally is a military officer and the large national airline *Aeroflot* has an obvious capability of supplementing regular military airlift resources with 1,200 aircraft configured for inter-theatre movement of troops and cargo.

The Soviet "air forces" have undergone a slight reduction in fixed-wing aircraft numbers during the past few years. The medium bomber force of Long-Range Aviation (LRA) has decreased by about 100 aircraft per year and a similar drop has been seen in the fighter aircraft of the Air Defence Forces (PVO). In both categories as well as in other aircraft types the Soviet Union has had considerable increases in the quality of aircraft to offset the decline in numbers.* The most significant increase in Soviet aircraft quality of late has been introduction of the variable-geometry *Backfire* bomber. This aircraft, under testing since late 1969, apparently began entering the operational inventory in 1974. The *Backfire* is believed to carry free-fall bombs and air-to-surface missiles. The Soviet Union continues to place high priority on ASMs and the current inventory includes five basic missiles, the AS-2, AS-5, and AS-6 carried by the Tu-16 *Badger*, AS-3 carried by the Tu-20 *Bear-B/C,* and AS-4 carried by the Tu-22 *Blinder-B.*

Within the PVO the older, largely gun-armed interceptors such as the MiG-17 *Fresco* and MiG-19 *Farmer* are being rapidly replaced by all-weather, missile-armed aircraft such as the MiG-25 *Foxbat* and Su-15 *Flagon-E.* The variable-geometry MiG-23 *Flogger* with a gun/missile armament is also expected to enter the PVO inventory.

Also in the tactical category, the Soviet Union recently began deployments of the Su-19 *Fencer,* a variable-geometry aircraft that appears to be the first

---

* In addition, the number of SAM launchers has increased during the past few years and there are now some 12,000 in the USSR with an increase in weapon quality.

Soviet fighter specifically designed for ground attack missions. Several production aircraft have been upgraded, notably the MiG-23 *Flogger* and widely flown MiG-21 *Fishbed,* and since about 1970 a significant number of specialized electronic warfare aircraft have appeared, primarily the Yak-28 *Brewer-E* and the An-12 *Cub-C* variants.

Despite the deployment of new fighter variants and the large scale production of several different fighter aircraft, there has been a hiatus in the development of new Soviet fighters. No new fighter prototypes have been observed since 1970. However, US defence officials do expect the Soviet Union to develop and deploy an entirely new fighter-interceptor by the late 1970s.

Also being predicted is an increase in Soviet tanker aircraft, possibly to support the *Backfire* bomber in the strategic role. The current force of 50 Mya-4 *Bisons* configured as tankers for LRA could be supplemented by the conversion of additional *Bison* bombers. There is some evidence that a tanker variant of the Il-76 *Candid* jet transport is being developed. (Soviet Naval Aviation has some 75 Tu-16 *Badgers* employed as tankers.)

Helicopter support of the Ground Forces (i.e., Army) is being improved with a buildup of Mi-24 *Hind* gunships and Mi-8 *Hip* troop carriers. Again, the older units of this category are being phased out.

The Soviet Navy operates two large helicopter carriers of the *Moskva* class, completed in 1967 and 1969, and the larger, angled-deck VSTOL carrier *Kiev,* which was to complete late 1975. The earlier ships normally operate 20 Ka-25 *Hormone* helicopters in the ASW role while the *Kiev* can accommodate an estimated 25 of the Yak-36 *Freehand* VSTOL aircraft or 35 *Hormone* helicopters. A mix of 30-plus *Freehands* and *Hormones* was expected to be embarked. A second of the large VSTOL carrier, the *Minsk,* was under construction in 1975 and there were reports of at least two additional ships of this type to be completed by the end of the decade. In addition, several classes of Soviet cruisers embark *Hormone*-A helicopters for ASW or *Hormone*-B variants for reconnaissance and missile guidance.

Soviet military aircraft are based primarily in the USSR and member nations of the Warsaw Pact. A *Blinder* bomber squadron is in Iraq and reconnaissance aircraft fly from bases in Iraq, Egypt, and Libya, while Soviet Naval Aviation flies maritime patrol and reconnaissance aircraft from bases in Egypt, Guinea, Somalia and Cuba.

LONG-RANGE AVIATION *(Aviatsiya Dalnovo Deistviya,* ADD [LRA])

		Aircraft	over 900
35	Mya-4	*Bison*	long-range bomber
110	Tu-20	*Bear*-B/C	long-range bomber (ASM)
approx **500**	Tu-16	*Badger*	medium bomber (some ASM)
approx **200**	Tu-22	*Blinder-*	
		A/B/C	medium bomber (some ASM)
few		*Backfire*	medium bomber (ASM)
few	Mya-4	*Bison*	reconnaissance
few	Tu-20	*Bear*	reconnaissance
50	Mya-4	*Bison*	tanker

FIGHTER AVIATION OF THE AIR DEFENCE OF THE COUNTRY
(Istrebitilnaya Aviatsiya Protivo-vorzdushnii Oborony Strany, IA-PVO)

		Aircraft	approx 2,700
few	Tu-126	*Moss*	AWACS
over **600** {	MiG-17	*Fresco*	fighter
	MiG-19	*Farmer*	fighter
few	MiG-23	*Flogger*	fighter
	MiG-25	*Foxbat*	fighter
approx	Su-15	*Flagon-A/E*	fighter
1,300	Tu-28P	*Fiddler*	fighter
	Yak-28P	*Firebar*	fighter
approx **600** {	Su-9	*Fishpot-B*	fighter
	Su-11	*Fishpot-C*	fighter

FRONTAL AVIATION *(Frontoyaya Aviatsiya, FA)*; also referred to in the West as the TACTICAL AIR FORCE

		Aircraft	over 4,500*
approx	MiG-17	*Fresco*	fighter-bomber
1,000 {	MiG-19	*Farmer*	fighter-bomber
approx			
1,500	MiG-21	*Fishbed*	fighter
	MiG-23	*Flogger*	fighter-bomber
over **1,500** {	MiG-25	*Foxbat*	fighter
	Su-17	*Fitter-C*	fighter-bomber
	Su-19	*Fencer*	fighter-bomber
approx **600** {	Il-28	*Beagle*	attack
	Yak-28	*Brewer*	attack

Several hundred of the fighter and attack aircraft listed above are fitted for a primary or secondary tactical reconnaissance role.

* Organized into 16 air armies with one air army in each of the 12 military districts of the Soviet Union and one each assigned to the Groups of Soviet Forces in Czechoslovakia, East Germany, Hungary, and Poland. Composition of these air armies varies with major emphasis against Central and Southern NATO, and in the Far East. Helicopters from Transport Aviation are normally assigned to these air armies for troop lift, communications, logistics, and close weapons support of the Ground Forces.

TRANSPORT AVIATION *(Voyenno-Transportnaya Aviatsiya, VTA)*

		Aircraft	approx 3,500
	Mi-6	*Hook*	helicopter
	Mi-8	*Hip*	helicopter
approx	Mi-10	*Harke*	helicopter
2,000	Mi-12	*Homer*	helicopter
	Mi-24	*Hind*	helicopter

approx **30**	An-22	*Cock*	transport
	An-8	*Camp*	transport
	An-12	*Cub*	transport
approx **1,500**	An-24	*Coke*	transport
	Il-14	*Crate*	transport
	Il-18	*Coot*	transport
few	Il-76	*Candid*	transport

NAVAL AVIATION *(Morskaya Aviatsiya)*

		Aircraft over 1,200	
several	Tu-16	*Badger-A*	bomber-trainer
290	Tu-16	*Badger-C/G*	bomber (ASM)
50	Tu-22	*Blinder-A*	bomber
several	Il-28	*Beagle*	attack-trainer
75	Tu-16	*Badger*	tanker
20+	Tu-16	*Badger*	electronic
50	Tu-16	*Badger-D*	reconnaissance
50	Tu-20	*Bear-D*	reconnaissance
75+	Be-12	*Mail*	maritime patrol
30 to **50**	Il-38	*May*	maritime patrol
few	Tu-20	*Bear-F*	maritime patrol
160	Ka-25	*Hormone-A*	helicopter-ASW
	Ka-25	*Hormone-B*	helicopter-reconnaissance
50+	Mi-4	*Hound*	helicopter-ASW
few	Mi-8	*Hip*	helicopter-minesweeper

Approx 300 transport, training, and utility aircraft also are operated by Soviet Naval Aviation.

TRAINING ESTABLISHMENT

The training establishment of the Soviet Air Forces operates approximately 3,000 tactical fighter and attack aircraft in addition to a large number of primary and specialised training aircraft.

Spain

The Spanish air arms, long obsolescent, have been largely re-equipped with Western-built aircraft during the past few years. Spain is not a member of the Atlantic Alliance but the current government has a "western" position on the defence of Europe and Spanish forces regularly exercise with US and other NATO services. Understandably, the Spanish air arms are largely dependent upon the West for modern aircraft supplemented by the small Spanish aircraft industry. Twenty-four F-4E/RF-4E Phantoms were being transferred to Spain during 1975.

The United States provides technical support to the Spanish air arms with the US Air Force operating three air bases and the US Navy operating a large base-air station complex at Rota.

The Spanish Navy has the light aircraft carrier *Dédalo*, transferred from the US Navy in 1967 (having been completed in 1943 as the USS *Cabot*). The carrier operated helicopters exclusively until the transfer of Harrier-type aircraft from the United States (the aircraft being built in Britain). Some Spanish destroyers can accommodate helicopters. The Spanish army flies a number of helicopters and light observation aircraft.

AIR FORCE *(Ejército del Aire Español)*

Personnel over 35,000		
Air Defence Command *(Mando Defensa Aerea)*		
36	F-4C(S) Phantom	fighter (2 squadrons)
24	Mirage III-EE	fighter ⎫
6	Mirage III-DE	fighter-trainer ⎬ (2 squadrons)
15	Mirage F-1C	fighter (1 squadron)
3	KC-97L Stratofreighter	tanker
few	T-33A Shooting Star	trainer

Tactical Command *(Mando de la Aviación Tactica)*		
16	F-4E Phantom	fighter (1 squadron)
18	SF-5A Freedom Fighter	fighter ⎫ (1 squadron)
4	SF-5B Freedom Fighter	fighter ⎬
6	RF-4E Phantom	reconnaissance
10	SRF-5A Freedom Fighter	reconnaissance (1 squadron)
40	HA-200D Saeta	attack (2 squadrons)
11	HU-16B Albatross	maritime patrol ⎫ (1 squadron)
3	P-3A Orion	maritime patrol ⎬
few	Do.27	observation
few	0-1E Bird Dog	observation
few	C-47 Dakota/Skytrain	transport
few	T-6D Harvard/Texan	trainer

Transport Command *(Mando de la Aviación de Transporte)*		
several	C-47 Dakota/Skytrain	transport
	C-54 Skymaster	transport
6	C-130H Hercules	transport
29	CASA-212 Aviacar	transport
20	CASA-207 Azor	transport
few	Convair CV-440	transport-VIP
12	DHC Caribou	transport

	Piper Navajo	trainer
	T-6D/G Harvard/Texan	trainer

Training Command (*Mando de la Aviación de Entrenamiento*)

few	Bell AB.47G (Sioux)	helicopter-trainer
12	AISA I-115	trainer
few	Beech Aztec-E	trainer
11	Beech Baron	trainer
8	Beech King Air	trainer
23	Bü.131	trainer
30	SF-5B Freedom Fighter	trainer
30	HA-200A Saeta	trainer
20	T-6G Harvard/Texan	trainer
25	T-34A Mentor	trainer
few	CASA-127 (Do. 27)	SAR
10	HU-16A/B Albatross	SAR
	HA-220 Super Saeta	development

NAVAL AVIATION (*Arma Aéreadela Armada Española*)

6	AV-8A Harrier	attack
2	TAV-8A Harrier	attack-trainer
2	AH-1G HueyCobra	helicopter-gunship
12	Bell 47D/G/AB.47 (Sioux)	helicopter-trainer
4	Bell AB.204AS (Iroquois)	helicopter
4	Bell AB.212AS (Iroquois)	helicopter-ASW
12	Hughes 500M (Cayuse)	helicopter-ASW
24	SH-3D Sea King	helicopter-ASW
2	Piper Commanche	transport
2	Piper Twin Commanche	transport

ARMY AVIATION (*Arma España*)

	CASA-127 (Do. 27)	observation
	0-1E Bird Dog	observation
6	Bell 47G (Sioux)	helicopter
16	Bell AB.206 Jet Ranger (Kiowa)	helicopter
12	UH-1B Iroquois	helicopter
8	UH-1H Iroquois	helicopter
6	CH-47C Chinook	helicopter

Sri Lanka (Ceylon)

This island nation's air force has a limited combat capability and operates a mixture of aircraft provided by the Soviet Union and Western nations.

AIR FORCE

	Personnel 2,000		
	Aircraft		
5	MiG-17	*Fresco*	fighter-bomber
6	Bell 47G (Sioux)		helicopter
7	Bell 206 Jet Ranger (Kiowa)		helicopter
2	Ka-26	*Hoodlum*	helicopter
4	Cessna 337		transport
1	Convair CV-440		transport
5	Dove		transport
2	Heron		transport
2	Riley Heron		transport
6	Cessna 150		trainer
9	DHC Chipmunk		trainer
8	Jet Provost T.51		trainer
1	MiG-15UTI	*Midget*	trainer

Sudan

The Sudanese Air Force has been equipped largely with Soviet aircraft although this Arab country may be unique in flying fighters of both Soviet and Chinese manufacture.

AIR FORCE

	Personnel 3,000		
	Aircraft		
17	F-4/MiG-17	*Fresco*	fighter
20	MiG-21	*Fishbed*	fighter
4	Mi-4	*Hound*	helicopter
10	Mi-8	*Hip*	helicopter
6	An-12	*Cub*	transport
5	An-24	*Coke*	transport
3	Pembroke		transport
13	Jet Provost T.51/T.52/T.55		trainer-COIN

Sweden

Neutralist Sweden has a large air force with the main combat strength in fighter and light attack squadrons. The SAAB national aircraft industry is producing 150 basic AJ37 Viggens and 25 two-seat Viggens for the light attack role, eventually replacing A32 Lansens flown in ten squadrons. The next Viggen variants to enter service are the SH37 reconnaissance aircraft. Beginning in 1978 the JA37 Viggen all-weather fighter will replace the surviving J35 Drakens. There are also small Army and Navy air arms.

AIR FORCE *(Svenska Flygvapnet)*

Personnel	14,000	
Aircraft		
approx **500**	J35A/D/F Draken	fighter (19 squadrons)
125 +	A32 Lansen	attack (7 squadrons)
50 +	AJ37 Viggen	attack (3 squadrons)
20	SAAB-105	attack (1 squadron)
35 +	S32 Lansen	reconnaissance (2 squadrons)
1	Hkp-2/Alouette II	helicopter
6	Hkp-3/Bell AB.204 (Iroquois)	helicopter
17	Hkp-4/Boeing-Vertol 107	helicopter
7	C-47 Dakota/Skytrain	transport
4	C-130E Hercules	transport
58	Bulldog	trainer
150	SAAB-105	trainer
80	SAAB Safir	trainer
3	Caravelle	research

NAVAL AVIATION *(Kungl. Svenska Marinen)*

10	Hkp-2/Alouette II	helicopter
10	Hkp-4/Boeing-Vertol 107	helicopter
10	Hkp-61/Bell AB.206 Jet Ranger (Kiowa)	helicopter

Switzerland

Switzerland has a tradition of neutrality and non-alignment with major powers. For their military aircraft, the Swiss rely on Britain and France, although other nations provide support aircraft. The Swiss Air Force is the only military service still flying German-built Junkers Ju52/3m transports, the three remaining being valuable for operations in mountainous terrain. Replacement of the large number of Venom fighter-bombers that remain in service will be accomplished by the acquisition of 60 to 90 F-5E Tiger IIs from the United States.

AIR FORCE

Personnel	9,000 + Militia Personnel*	
Aircraft		
approx **150**	Hunter F.58/T.68	fighter-bomber (7 squadrons)
38	Mirage III-S	fighter ⎫ (2 squadrons)
3	Mirage III-BS	fighter-trainer ⎭
approx **150**	Venom FB.50	fighter-bomber (7 squadrons)
16	Mirage III-RS	reconnaissance (1 squadron)
approx **100**	Alouette II/III	helicopter
3	Beech Twin Bonanza	transport
6	Do.27	transport
3	Ju52/3m	transport
20	Pilatus Porter	transport
20	C-3605	target tow
few	Bü.131	trainer
120	Pilatus P-2/P-3	trainer
100 +	Vampire Mk.6/T.55	trainer

* Militia personnel man some operational aircraft while maintenance is undertaken largely by civilians; Air Force personnel also provide 2 battalions with Bloodhound SAM launchers, 37 battalions with AA guns, and a single parachute company.

ARMY AVIATION

20	Bulldog	observation
5	Do.27	observation
12	Piper Super Cub	observation
few	Hkp-2/Alouette II	helicopter
12	Hkp-3/Bell AB.204B (Iroquois)	helicopter
22	Hkp-6/Bell AB.206A Jet Ranger (Kiowa)	helicopter
7	Hughes 269A (Osage)	helicopter

Syria

Syria, which borders on Israel's northeast frontier, is believed to have replaced the estimated 185 fixed-wing aircraft and helicopters lost during the October 1973 war in the Middle East. Flying almost exclusively Soviet-built aircraft, the Syrian Air Force is fighter-attack orientated and these aircraft continue to be involved in periodic skirmishes in the disputed Golan Heights area of Syria which is partially occupied by Israeli forces. Technical assistance is provided by Soviet, North Korean, and North Vietnamese personnel.,

AIR FORCE

		Personnel	10,000
		Aircraft	
80	MiG-17	*Fresco*	fighter (some fitted as fighter-bomber)
120	MiG-21	*Fishbed*	fighter
45–50	MiG-23	*Flogger-B*	fighter
40–50	Su-7	*Fitter-A*	fighter-bomber
9	Ka-25	*Hormone*	helicopter-ASW
8	Mi-4	*Hound*	helicopter
22	Mi-8	*Hip*	helicopter
6	C-47 Dakota/Skytrain		transport
8	Il-14	*Crate*	transport
4	Il-18	*Coot*	transport
	Delphin L-29	*Maya*	trainer
	MiG-15UTI	*Midget*	trainer
	Yak-11	*Moose*	trainer
	Yak-18	*Max*	trainer

Taiwan (Republic of China)

The Chinese Nationalist Air Force consists of combat aircraft acquired from the United States plus licenced production of F-5E Tiger II fighters and UH-1H Iroquois helicopters by the state-owned Aero Industry Development Centre. In addition, the Centre produces training aircraft of indigenous design.

The National Air Force is primarily an air defence organization with limited fighter-bomber, maritime patrol, and reconnaissance capabilities. The Army has a helicopter troop lift force and a few aircraft are flown by the Marine Corps.

CHINESE NATIONALIST AIR FORCE

	Personnel	80,000
	Aircraft	
70	F-5A Freedom Fighter	fighter (4 squadrons)
100	F-5E Tiger II	fighter (4–6 squadrons)
90	F-100 A/D Super Sabre	fighter-bomber (3 squadrons)
63	F-104A/G Starfighter	fighter (3 squadrons)
4	RF-101C Voodoo	reconnaissance ⎱ (1 squadron)
8	RF-104G Starfighter	reconnaissance ⎰
9	S-2A Tracker	anti-submarine (1 squadron)
10	Bell 47G (Sioux)	helicopter
6	Hughes 500 (Cayuse)	helicopter
50 +	UH-1D Iroquois	helicopter
7	CH-19 Chickasaw	helicopter
2	Sikorsky S-62C (HH-52)	helicopter
1	Boeing 720B	transport-VIP
30	C-46 Commando	transport
50	C-47 Dakota/Skytrain	transport
40	C-119 Packet	transport
10	C-123 Provider	transport
10	HU-16 Albatross	transport-SAR
	F-5B Freedom Fighter	trainer
	F-86F Sabre	trainer
	F-100 Super Sabre	trainer
approx 150	TF-104G Starfighter	trainer
	PL-1B Chienshous	trainer
	T-6 Harvard/Texan	trainer
	T-28 Trojan	trainer
	T-33A Shooting Star	trainer

ARMY AVIATION

50 +	UH-1H Iroquois	helicopter
few	CH-34 Choctaw	helicopter

MARINE AVIATION

few	O-1E Bird Dog	observation
few	UH-1H Iroquois	helicopter
few	few OH-13 Sioux	helicopter

Tanzania

This East African state is building its armed forces with Chinese assistance and has a fighter arm of Chinese-provided MiG fighters. However, most transport and trainer aircraft are of Western origin. The majority of the estimated 1,000 Chinese advisors and technicians in Africa are in Tanzania.

TANZANIAN PEOPLE'S DEFENCE FORCE AIR WING
(Jeshi la Wananchi la Tanzania)

	Personnel	1,000	
	Aircraft		
12	F-4/MiG-17F	*Fresco*	fighter
8	F-6/MiG-19SF	*Farmer*	fighter
16	F-8/MiG-21	*Fishbed*	fighter
1	An-2	*Colt*	transport
2–3	DHC Buffalo		transport
12	DHC Caribou		transport
1	HS.748		transport-VIP
2	Bell 47G (Sioux)		helicopter
2	Bell AB.206A (Kiowa)		helicopter
few	Cessna 310		trainer
6	Piper Cherokee		trainer

Thailand

Thailand, which provided bases for the United States in the air war over Vietnam, is building up a large tactical air force with US assistance. In addition to the aircraft listed below, Thai National Police fly nine AU-23A Peacemakers as well as helicopters and fixed-wing liaison aircraft.

Late in 1975 plans to acquire 13 F-5E and 3 two-seat F-5F Tiger II fighters were announced.

ROYAL THAI AIR FORCE

	Personnel	over 40,000
	Aircraft	
20	F-5A/B Freedom Fighter	fighter-bomber
20	F-86F Sabre	fighter
30	A-4B Skyhawk	attack
33	AU-23A Peacemaker	COIN
32	OV-10C Bronco	COIN
20	T-6 Harvard/Texan	COIN
45	T-28D Trojan	COIN
5	RT-33A Shooting Star	reconnaissance
4	Boeing-Vertol 107 (Sea Knight)	helicopter
50	UH-1H Iroquois	helicopter
13	CH-19 Chickasaw	helicopter
20	CH-34C Choctaw	helicopter
3	HH-43 Huskie	helicopter
4	CH-47 Chinook	helicopter

5	C-45 Expeditor	transport
20	C-47 Dakota/Skytrain	transport
13	C-123 Provider	transport
2	HS.748	transport-VIP
few	Cessna T-37B	trainer
24	CT-4 Airtrainer	trainer
12	SF.260MT	trainer
few	T-6 Harvard/Texan	trainer
few	T-33A Shooting Star	trainer

NAVAL AVIATION

2	HU-16B Albatross	maritime patrol
5	S-2 Tracker	maritime patrol

ARMY AVIATION

3	Bell 206 Jet Ranger (Kiowa)	helicopter
16	Fairchild FH-1100 (OH-5A)	helicopter
20	UH-1B/D Iroquois	helicopter
6	OH-23F Raven	helicopter

Tunisia

A small Air Force is maintained by Tunisia, which uses Western military equipment.

AIR FORCE *(Aermée de l'Air Tunisienne)*

Personnel	over 1,000	
Aircraft		
12	F-86F Sabre	fighter
8	Aermacchi MB.326B	attack-trainer
2	Alouette II	helicopter
6	Alouette III	helicopter
3	Flamant	transport
12	SF.260 Warrior	trainer
12	T-6 Harvard/Texan	trainer

Turkey

The Turkish invasion of Cyprus in 1974 strained the nation's relations with other NATO members, and resulted in a cutback of weapon shipments from the United States. Turkey is an important member of the NATO Alliance, sharing a common land border with the Soviet Union as well as being a Black Sea power and controlling the straits that connect that body of water with the Mediterranean. The Turkish Air Force contributes to the Sixth Allied Tactical Air Force as well as performing national missions. The Turkish Army and Navy also have small air arms.

AIR FORCE *(Türk Hava Kuvvetleri)*

	Personnel	over 35,000*
	Aircraft	
18	F-4E Phantom	fighter (1 squadron + 1 forming)†
140	F-5A Freedom Fighter	fighter (2 squadrons) / fighter-bomber (2 squadrons)
75	F-84F/FQ Thunderstreak	fighter-bomber (3 squadrons)
100 +	F-100C/D/F Super Sabre	fighter-bomber (5 squadrons)
36	F-102A Delta Dagger	fighter (2 squadrons)
68	F-104G/S Starfighter	fighter-bomber (4 squadrons)
30 +	RF-84F Thunderflash	reconnaissance (2 squadrons)
few	Bell AB.204 (Iroquois)	helicopter
6	C-45 Expeditor	transport
10	C-47 Dakota/Skytrain	transport
3	C-54 Skymaster	transport
10	C-130E Hercules	transport
20	C.160 Transall	transport
9	Do.28D Skyservant	transport
3	Viscount 794	transport
23	Cessna T-37	trainer
15	MBB-223 Flamingo	trainer
few	TF-102A Delta Dagger	trainer
few	TF-104G Starfighter	trainer
40	T-6J Harvard/Texan	trainer
30	T-33A Shooting Star	trainer
few	T-34 Mentor	trainer
5	T-42 Cochise	trainer

* Air Force personnel operate two battalions of Nike-Hercules SAM launchers.
† delivery of an additional 22 Phantoms was halted by the US Government in 1975.

ARMY AVIATION

few	Cessna 185 (U-17)	observation
few	Do.27	observation
	Bell 47G (Sioux)	helicopter
50 +	Bell AB.205 (Iroquois)	helicopter
	Bell AB.206 Jet Ranger (Kiowa)	helicopter

2	Do.28B Skyservant	trainer

NAVAL AVIATION

12	S-2E Tracker	anti-submarine
3	Bell AB.205 (Iroquois)	helicopter

Uganda

This African nation has a small air arm based on Soviet combat aircraft and receives technical assistance from the Soviet Union, Libya, and apparently Pakistan, with Soviet-built MiG-21s being assembled in Uganda. The Magisters were manufactured in Israel.

AIR FORCE

	Personnel	1,000	
	Aircraft		
approx **30** {	MiG-15	*Fagot*	fighter
	MiG-17	*Fresco*	fighter
few	MiG-21	*Fishbed*	fighter
8	Magister		attack
1	Bell 212 (Iroquois)		helicopter
6	Bell AB.205 (Iroquois)		helicopter
4	Bell AB.206 Jet Ranger (Kiowa)		helicopter
2	Scout		helicopter
6	C-47 Dakota/Skytrain		transport
2	IAI Commodore Jet		transport
1	DHC Caribou		transport
1	DHC Twin Otter		transport
4	Delfin L-29	*Maya*	trainer
4	Piaggio P.149D		trainer

United States

The US Army, Navy, Air Force, and Marine Corps all operate military aircraft. In addition, the US Coast Guard has a small air arm, orientated primarily toward search and rescue missions, which supports the other services in peacetime and can be placed under Navy control at the direction of the President.

The US Air Force operates the largest number of aircraft of any service. Recent USAF reorganizations have placed the large force of C-130 Hercules transports under the Military Airlift Command (MAC) and USAF units in the Pacific under the Tactical Air Command (TAC) with the abolishment of a separate USAF Pacific Command. In the following listings those tactical squadrons under the Alaskan Air Command and USAF in Europe are listed with the Tactical Air Command.

The Strategic Air Command (SAC) is a specified command directly under the Joint Chiefs of Staff. In addition to land-based bombers, SAC operates the nation's 1,000 land-based Minuteman and 54 Titan ICBMs. Three B-1A advanced bomber test aircraft are flying and a decision was to be taken by 1976 on the procurement of 241 bombers to replace the aging B-52 Stratofortresses. Also under consideration are various modifications of the FB-111 for the strategic role.

The USAF Aerospace Defense Command (ADC) also is directly under the Joint Chiefs of Staff with the Commander ADC serving as Commander-in-Chief North American Air Defense Command (NORAD). The NORAD organization includes early warning radars, control centres, Army-operated Nike-Hercules and Hawk SAM batteries (in Alaska and Florida), and the six active USAF fighter-interceptor squadrons and six similar squadrons in the Air National Guard, all flying F-106 Delta Darts. In addition, one TAC F-4 Phantom squadron in Alaska and one Air National Guard F-4 Phantom squadron in Hawaii have primary air defence roles.

Already in production for the USAF are the McDonnell Douglas F-15 Eagle fighter, of which 729 (plus 20 development aircraft) are being built to replace the F-4 Phantom and some A-7 Corsair IIs; the General Dynamics F-16 Air Combat Fighter, of which some 650 are planned (plus extensive NATO sales of at least 350); and the Fairchild-Hiller A-10 close support aircraft, of which 733 (plus eight development aircraft) are planned to replace the remaining A-7 Corsair IIs.

The US Navy's air arm flies from ashore and from 14 aircraft carriers of various classes (see Appendix B). The Navy has selected the Northrop F-18 as its Air Combat Fighter (previously designated VFX/VFAX) to replace about half of the F-4 Phantom IIs flown by the Navy and Marine Corps. Already in production are the Grumman F-14 Tomcat variable-geometry fighter to replace Phantoms in 14 Navy carrier-based squadrons (with a total procurement of 390 aircraft). Also in production for the Navy and Marine Corps are the Grumman A-6E Intruder, LTV A-7E Corsair II, and McDonnell Douglas A-4M Skyhawk attack aircraft; EA-6B Prowler electronic warfare aircraft; Grumman E-2C Hawkeye early warning/surveillance aircraft; and Lockheed P-3C Orion maritime patrol and S-3A Viking anti-submarine aircraft.

The US Marine Corps is the world's only "naval infantry" with its own air arm. There are three Marine aircraft wings associated with the three active Marine divisions (with two wings based on the contiguous United States and the third divided between bases in Japan and on Oahu, Hawaii). There are no aircraft directly subordinate to the Marine divisions. All Marine fliers are "naval aviators" with the fighter and attack aircraft capable of operating from aircraft carriers. (The Navy trains Marine and Coast Guard aviators.)

Navy and periodically Marine tactical squadrons operate from the Navy's aircraft carriers while Marine AV-8A Harriers and helicopters fly from the several helicopter carriers in service. Also based at sea are SH-2D LAMPS (Light Airborne Multi-Purpose System) helicopters in cruisers, destroyers, and frigates, while utility helicopters are carried in several warships, amphibious and auxiliary ships.

The US Army with over 6,000 helicopters operates more rotary-wing aircraft than the remainder of the world's military services combined. In addition, Army aviators fly some 750 fixed-wing liaison, observation, light cargo, light reconnaissance, and training aircraft. Trials involving fitting rockets and machineguns to Army recon aircraft during the Vietnam War were not pursued and no Army fixed-wing aircraft are armed.

There are four reserve air organizations: USAF Reserve, Air National Guard, Naval Air Reserve, and Marine Corps Reserve. These organizations all operate combat and support aircraft, with a few units maintained in active service by rotating personnel on active duty training time.

Helicopters and light aircraft are also flown by the Army Reserve and Army National Guard.

The US Civil Reserve Air Fleet (CRAF) consists of 243 long-range cargo and passenger aircraft in commercial service. During an emergency situation they could be acquired to support military requirements. The US commercial air fleet also has about 2,300 cargo and passenger aircraft with an unrefuelled radius of some 2,800 statute miles.

The US Coast Guard air arm, with a few helicopters based aboard the larger ocean patrol ships or "cutters', is under the Department of Transportation.

(In the tables below where aircraft strengths are given in both bold face and light numbers, the former indicates the total number of aircraft in that category, including pipeline and training units, while the latter is the number of a specific aircraft type or the total strength of the first-line squadrons).

AIR FORCE

	Personnel	590,000*
	Strategic Air Command (SAC)	
	Aircraft	approx 1,000
80	B-52D Stratofortress	bomber (5 squadrons)
151	B-52G Stratofortress	bomber ⎫ (17 squadrons)
90	B-52H Stratofortress	bomber ⎬
66	FB-111A	bomber (4 squadrons)
37	EC-135 Stratolifter	command and control
16	RC-135 Stratolifter	reconnaissance
9	SR-71 Blackbird	reconnaissance
few	U-2	reconnaissance
610	KC-135 Stratotanker	tanker (38 squadrons)*

* Nine squadrons with 72 aircraft flown by USAF Reserve.

Tactical Air Command (TAC)

Aircraft approx 2,700†

1,300	F-4C/D/E Phantom	fighter (45 squadrons)
several	F-5A/B Freedom Fighter	fighter-trainer
20	F-5E Tiger II	fighter-trainer
24	F-15/TF-15 Eagle	fighter (1 squadron)
350	F-111A/D/E/F	fighter-bomber (12 squadrons)
280	A-7D Corsair	attack (10 squadrons)
260	RF-4C Phantom	reconnaissance (13 squadrons)
36	F-4C Phantom	electronic (2 squadrons)‡
36	F-105G Thunderchief	electronic (2 squadrons)‡
7	C-130E Hercules	communications-ABCCC
80	0-2	observation
85	OV-10 Bronco	observation

Aerospace Defence Command (ADC)

Aircraft approx 225

140	F-106 Delta Dart	fighter (6 squadrons)
10	EC-121 Constellation	AEW (1 squadron)
20	EB-57 Canberra	trainer (1 squadron)
50	T-33A Shooting Star	trainer

Military Airlift Command (MAC)

Aircraft approx 1,000

73	C-5A Galaxy	transport (4 squadrons)
19	C-9A Nightingale	transport
137	T-39 Sabreliner	transport
325	C-130E Hercules	transport (17 squadrons) §
30	C-135 Stratolifter	transport
5	VC-137B/C Stratoliner	transport-VIP
11	VC-140B Jet Star	transport-VIP
274	C-141A Stratolifter	transport (13 squadrons)
several	WB-57 Canberra	weather reconnaissance
	RC-130/WC-130 Hercules	weather reconnaissance
	WC-135 Stratolifter	weather reconnaissance
122	UH-1H/N Iroquois	helicopter-SAR
29	CH-3E Sea King	helicopter
23	HH-3E Jolly Green Giant	helicopter-SAAR
12	HH-43F Huskie	helicopter-SAR
54	HH-53B/C Super Jolly	helicopter-SAR

Air Training Command (ATC)

Aircraft approx 1,700

743	T-37	trainer
856	T-38 Talon	trainer
104	T-41 Mescalero	trainer
19	T-43A	trainer

* Air Force personnel man the 1,054 US land-based ICBMs
† includes Alaskan Air Command, Pacific Air Force, USAF Europe
‡ these are "Wild Weasel" aircraft
§ all C-130E except 16 C-130A/D assigned to Alaskan Air Command

ARMY AVIATION

	Aircraft approx 6,800	
12	RU-8 Seminole	reconnaissance
1	RU-9D Aero Commander	reconnaissance
46	RU-21 Ute	reconnaissance
206	OV-1 Mohawk	observation
700	AH-1G/Q/S Huey Cobra	helicopter-gunship
34	TH-1G Huey Cobra	helicopter-trainer
350	UH-1C/M Iroquois	helicopter-gunship
2,350	UH-1B/D/H Iroquois	helicopter
76	OH-6 Cayuse	helicopter-observation
16	OH-13 Sioux	helicopter-observation
148	TH-13 Sioux	helicopter-trainer
350	CH-47 Chinook	helicopter
54	CH-54 Tarhe	helicopter
653	TH-55 Osage	helicopter-trainer
1,350	OH-58 Kiowa	helicopter-observation
9	U-1 Otter	transport
11	U-6 Beaver	transport
152	U-8 Seminole	transport
4	U-10A Helio-Courier	transport
112	U-21 Ute	transport
20	U-25A Huron	transport
125	T-41B Mescalero	trainer
61	T-42A Cochise	trainer

ARMY NATIONAL GUARD

	Aircraft 2,263	
49	OV-1 Mohawk	observation
5	AH-1G Huey Cobra	helicopter-gunship
1,135	UH-1 Iroquois	helicopter (some gunship)
349	OH-6 Cayuse	helicopter-observation
50	CH-47 Chinook	helicopter
22	CH-54 Tarhe	helicopter
587	OH-58 Kiowa	helicopter-observation
7	U-1 Otter	transport
24	U-6 Beaver	transport
29	U-8 Seminole	transport
6	U-10A Helio-Courier	transport

ARMY RESERVE

	Aircraft 474	
9	RU-8 Seminole	reconnaissance
286	UH-1 Iroquois	helicopter (some gunship)
31	CH-47 Chinook	helicopter
122	OH-58 Kiowa	helicopter-observation

	23	U-6 Beaver	transport
	1	U-8 Seminole	transport
	2	U-9C Aero Commander	transport

NAVAL AVIATION

		Aircraft approx 7,200*	
		14 Carrier Air Wings	
600	216	F-4B/J/N Phantom II	fighter (18 squadrons)
	few	F-5E Tiger II	fighter
	48	F-8J Crusader	fighter (4 squadrons) †
	100	F-14A Tomcat	fighter (6 squadrons)
1,000	42	A-4F Skyhawk ·	attack (3 squadrons) †
	324	A-7A/B/C/E Corsair II	attack (27 squadrons)
	144	A-6A/B/C/E Intruder	attack (12 squadrons)
150	9	E-1B Tracer	AEW (3 squadrons) †
	32	E-2A/B Hawkeye	AEW (8 squadrons)
	16	E-2C Hawkeye	AEW (4 squadrons)
	few	EA-3B Skywarrior	electronic †
	32	EA-6B Prowler	electronic (8 squadrons)
	21	RA-5C Vigilante	reconnaissance
	15	RF-8G Crusader	reconnaissance
130	30 +	S-2E Tracker	anti-submarine (4 squadrons) †
	50 +	S-3A Viking	anti-submarine (5 squadrons)
	few	KA-3B Skywarrior	tanker †
	48	KA-6D Intruder	tanker
	72	SH-3A/D/G/H Sea King	helicopter-ASW (9 squadrons)
		Navy land-based aircraft	
275	220	P-3B/C Orion · ·	maritime patrol (24 squadrons)
	few	RA-3B Skywarrior	reconnaissance.
	12	EP-3E Orion	electronic-reconnaissance
	few	EC-121 Warning Star	electronic-reconnaissance
	13	EC-130G/Q Hercules	communication (2 squadrons)
	few	UH-1N Iroquois	helicopter
	62	TH-1 Iroquois	helicopter-trainer
	few	UH-2 Seasprite	helicopter
	105	SH-2D/F LAMPS	helicopter-ASW (7 squadrons)
	few	UH-46 Sea Knight	helicopter
	21	RH-53 Sea Stallion	helicopter-minesweeper
	31	TH-57 Sea Ranger	helicopter-trainer
	30	C-1A Trader	transport
	12	C-2A Greyhound	transport
	8	C-9B Skytrain II	transport

* includes US Navy and Marine Corps aircraft; when bracketed numbers are given for a type of
aircraft they include units in overhaul, assigned to readiness training squadrons, etc.

† F-8J Crusader and A-4F Skyhawk being phased out with decommissioning of carriers
Hancock and *Oriskany* in 1976; various A-3 Skywarrior variants being phased out as newer
aircraft become available.

100 {		CT-39G Sabreliner	transport
		C-118 Liftmaster	transport
		C-130 Hercules	transport
		C-131 Samaritan	transport
	218	A-4/T4-4J Skyhawk	trainer
	79	TS-2A/US-2B Tracker	trainer
	233	T-2B/C Buckeye	trainer
	182	T-28B/C Trojan	trainer
	6	Flying Classroom	trainer
	134	T-34B Mentor	trainer
	25	T-39 Sabreliner	trainer

3 Marine Aircraft Wings

200 {	144	F-4B/J Phantom II	fighter (12 squadrons)
300 {	80	A-4E/F/M Skyhawk	attack (5 squadrons)
	60	A-6 Intruder	attack (5 squadrons)
	110	AV-8A/TAV-8A Harrier	attack (3 squadrons)
{	21	RF-4B Phantom II	reconnaissance } (3 squadrons)
{	21	EA-6A Intruder	electronic
50	36	OV-10 Bronco	observation (3 squadrons)
490 {	72	AH-1G/J Sea Cobra	helicopter-gunship (3 squadrons)
	126	UH-1E/N Iroquois	helicopter (6 squadrons)
	numerous	CH-46 Sea Knight	helicopter (12 squadrons)
	numerous	CH-53 Sea Stallion	helicopter (6 squadrons)
{		C-9 Skytrain II	transport
	19 {	C-47/C-119 Dakota/Skytrain	transport
		CT-39 Sabreliner	transport
	20	KC-130 Hercules	transport-tanker

AIR NATIONAL GUARD

	Personnel	approx 95,000	
	Aircraft	approx 1,500	
10	F-4C Phantom II	fighter (1 squadron)	
423	F-100 Super Sabre	fighter (18 squadrons)	
134	F-101 Voodoo	fighter (7 squadrons)	
38	F-102 Delta Dagger	fighter (2 squadrons)	
19	F-104 Starfighter	fighter (1 squadron)	
105	F-105 Thunderchief	fighter (4 squadrons)	
90	F-106 Delta Dart	fighter (6 squadrons)	
101	A-7D Corsair II	attack (5 squadrons)	
40	A-37B Dragonfly	attack (2 squadrons)	
75	RF-4C Phantom II	reconnaissance (4 squadrons)	
64	RF-101 Voodoo	reconnaissance (3 squadrons)	
25	EB-57 Canberra	electronic (2 squadrons)	
4	EC-121 Constellation	electronic (1 squadron)	
155	O-2A/B Super Skymaster	observation (7 squadrons)	
5	HH-3 Jolly Green Giant	helicopter-rescue	

75	KC-97L Stratofreighter	tanker (8 squadrons)
4	KC-135 Stratotanker	tanker (1 squadron)
17	C-7A Caribou	transport (1 squadron)
10	C-119L Flying Boxcar	transport (2 squadrons)
8	C-123J Provider	transport (1 squadron)
107	C-130 Hercules	transport (13 squadrons)
8	HC-130H Hercules	rescue (2 squadrons)

AIR FORCE RESERVE

	Personnel	approx 53,000
	Aircraft	approx 300
50	F-105 Thunderchief	fighter (3 squadrons)
51	A-37 Dragonfly	attack (4 squadrons)
4	EC-121 Constellation	AEW & control (1 squadron)
16	HH-1H Iroquois	helicopter-SAR (4 squadrons)
	CH-3E	helicopter-special operations (1 squadron)
26	C-7A Caribou	transport (2 squadrons)
47	C-123K Provider	transport (4 squadrons)
100	C-130 Hercules	transport (16 squadrons)

NAVAL AIR RESERVE

	Aircraft	approx 360
48	F-8 Crusader	fighter (4 squadrons)*
28	A-4 Skyhawk	attack (2 squadrons)
48	A-7 Corsair II	attack (4 squadrons)
36	SP-2H Neptune	maritime patrol (3 squadrons)
81	P-3A Orion	maritime patrol (9 squadrons)
16	S-2 Tracker	ASW (2 squadrons)
32	SH-3 Sea King	helicopter-ASW (4 squadrons)
8	RF-8 Crusader	reconnaissance (2 squadrons)
12	EA-3/EKA-3 Skywarrior	electronics (2 squadrons)
8	E-1B Tracer	AEW (2 squadrons)
30	C-118 Liftmaster	transport (4 squadrons)
16	A-4 Skyhawk	training-liaison

* being phased out of service; all Naval Air Reserve aircraft are carrier capable except the maritime patrol and transport types

MARINE AIR RESERVE

	Aircraft	165
9	F-4 Phantom	fighter-bomber (1 squadron)
24	F-8 Crusader	fighter (2 squadrons)
9	OV-10 Bronco	observation (1 squadron)

6	AH-1 Sea Cobra	helicopter-gunship (1 squadron)
18	UH-1E Iroquois	helicopter (1 squadron)
40	CH-46 Sea Knight	helicopter (3 squadrons)
18	CH-53 Sea Stallion	helicopter (2 squadrons)
4	C-119 Flying Boxcar	transport (1 squadron)
1	C-131	transport
4	TA-4 Skyhawk	training-liaison

COAST GUARD AVIATION

	Aircraft	175
38	HH-3F Pelican	helicopter-SAR
88	HH-52A	helicopter-SAR
26	HU-16A Albatross	transport-SAR
1	VC-4A Gulfstream I	transport-VIP
1	VC-11A Gulfstream II	transport-VIP
20	HC-130 Hercules	transport-SAR
1	EC-130E Hercules	navigation calibration

Uruguay

This South American nation has a small air arm of relatively outdated aircraft provided by the United States. There is a separate naval air arm. The acquisition of more modern COIN-type aircraft can be expected.

AIR FORCE *(Fuerza Aérea Uruguaya)*

	Personnel	2,000
	Aircraft	
8	F-80C Shooting Star	fighter-bomber
6	T-33A Shooting Star	fighter-bomber
6	Cessna 185 (U-17)	observation
2	UH-1H Iroquois	helicopter
2	Hiller H-12 (Raven)	helicopter
2	Beech Queen Air	transport
12	C-47 Dakota/Skytrain	transport
3	Fairchild FH-227	transport
2	Fokker F.27	transport
15	T-6 Harvard/Texan	trainer
10	AT-11 Kansan	trainer

NAVAL AVIATION *(Aviación Naval)*

3	S-2A Tracker	anti-submarine

2	Bell 47G (Sioux)	helicopter
3	SNB-5 Kansan (AT-11)	transport-trainer
few	T-6 Harvard/Texan	trainer
1	T-34B Mentor	trainer

Venezuela

Venezuela maintains one of the more modern South American air arms, purchasing aircraft from the United States, Britain, Canada, West Germany, and France. The Air Force is responsible for offshore surveillance of the super tankers servicing Venezuela's oil production as well as patrol of the country's long land borders. The Venezuelan Army operates a number of helicopters.

AIR FORCE *(Fuerzas Aérea Venezulanas)*

	Personnel	8,000
	Aircraft	
20	CF-5A/B Freedom Fighter	fighter
38	F-86K Sabre	fighter
9	Mirage IIIEV	fighter
4	Mirage 5V	fighter
2	Mirage 5DV	fighter
40	Canberra B.2/B.8/T.4	attack*
16	OV-10E Bronco	COIN
2	Canberra PR.3 (Mk.83)	reconnaissance
15	Alouette III	helicopter
12	UH-1D/H Iroquois	helicopter
10	CH-19 Chickasaw	helicopter
few	Beech Queen Air 65/80	transport-trainer
20	C-47 Dakota/Skytrain	transport
18	C-123 Provider	transport
6	C-130H Hercules	transport
12	Cessna 182N	transport
1	Cessna Citation 500	transport
12	Jet Provost T.52	trainer
24	T-2D Buckeye	trainer
20	T-34 Mentor	trainer

* Canberra Mk. 82, 88, and 84, respectively, the higher numbers designating modernized aircraft

ARMY AVIATION

approx 20	{ Alouette III	helicopter
	{ Bell 47G (Sioux)	helicopter

North Vietnam (Democratic Republic of Vietnam)

The Vietnam People's Air Force is defence orientated. It unsuccessfully challenged the US air war against North Vietnam from 1964 to 1972 and was largely destroyed with the surviving aircraft finding refuge on Chinese airfields. Subsequently, it has been built up with Soviet and Chinese aircraft.

AIR FORCE

Personnel		10,000	
Aircraft			
100 { MiG-15	*Fagot*	fighter-bomber	
MiG-17	*Fresco*	fighter-bomber	
30 F-6/MiG-19	*Farmer*	fighter	
60 MiG-21F/PF	*Fishbed*	fighter	
10 Il-28	*Beagle*	attack	
12 Mi-4	*Hound*	helicopter	
5 Mi-6	*Hook*	helicopter	
20 An-2	*Colt*	transport	
4 An-24	*Coke*	transport	
12 Il-14	*Crate*	transport	
20 Li-2	*Cab*	transport	
approx **50** trainers of various types			

NAVAL AVIATION

10	Mi-4	*Hound*	helicopter-SAR

North Yemen (Yemen Arab Republic)

This small Arab state has an air arm almost completely equipped with Soviet aircraft.

AIR FORCE

Personnel		over 1,000	
Aircraft			
12	MiG-17	*Fresco*	fighter
15	Il-28	*Beagle*	attack
few	Mi-4	*Hound*	helicopter
few { C-47 Dakota/Skytrain			transport
Il-14		*Crate*	transport
few	Yak-11	*Moose*	trainer

South Yemen (South Yemen People's Republic)

Like North Yemen, this small Arab state also flies Soviet aircraft along with the surviving Western aircraft previously acquired.

AIR FORCE

Personnel		over 2,000	
Aircraft			
15	MiG-17F	*Fresco*	fighter
6	Il-28	*Beagle*	attack
few	Mi-4	*Hound*	helicopter
	Mi-8	*Hip*	helicopter
few	An-12	*Cub*	transport
	An-24	*Coke*	transport
	Il-14	*Crate*	transport
2	Skyvan 3M		transport
few	MiG-15UTI	*Midget*	trainer

Yugoslavia

Although a Communist nation, Yugoslavia has a unique east-west relationship and its Air Force reflects purchases from both blocks. The Soviet and US fighter and reconnaissance aircraft are supplemented by a large number of Yugoslav-built light attack aircraft. The MiG-21 Fishbed and F-86 Sabres are organized into eight fighter squadrons, the F-84 Thunderjets and light attack aircraft into 12 ground attack squadrons, and the reconnaissance aircraft into two squadrons.

AIR FORCE

Personnel		20,000	
Aircraft			
60	F-84G Thunderjet		fighter-bomber
70	F-86D/E Sabre		fighter
few	CL-13B Sabre Mk.6		fighter
60	MiG-21	*Fishbed*	fighter
150	Jastreb		attack
30	Kraguj		attack
few	RF-86F Sabre		reconnaissance
30	RT-33A Shooting Star		reconnaissance

20	Alouette III	helicopters
few	Bell AB.205 (Iroquois)	helicopter
18	Mi-4 *Hound*	helicopter
12	Mi-8 *Hip*	helicopter
122	SA.341 Gazelle	helicopter
	to replace some earlier types	
10	Whirlwind	helicopter
1	Caravelle	transport
15	C-47 Dakota/Skytrain	transport
4	Douglas DC-6B	transport
13	Il-14 *Crate*	transport
1	Il-18 *Coot*	transport
3	Yak-40 *Codling*	transport
60	Galeb	trainer
few	MiG-15UTI *Midget*	trainer

Zaïre

The Republic of Zaïre is building a substantial air arm based on aircraft from a number of Western nations.

AIR FORCE *(Force Aérrienne Zaïroise)*

	Aircraft	
17	Mirage 5	fighter
23	Aermacchi MB.326GB	attack-trainer
8	T-6 Harvard/Texan	attack-trainer
5	T-28D Trojan	attack-trainer
15	Alouette III	helicopter
7	Bell 47 (Sioux)	helicopter
23	SA.330 Puma	helicopter
10	C-47 Dakota/Skytrain	transport
4	C-54 Skymaster	transport
6	C-130H Hercules	transport
15	Cessna 310	transport
6	DHC Buffalo	transport
1	Douglas DC-6	transport
2	MU-2	transport
24	SF.260M/MC/W	trainer

Zambia

Zambia's Air Force is being developed as a modern, effective service with French and Italian combat aircraft.

AIR FORCE

	Aircraft	
15	Mirage 5	fighter
18	Aermacchi MB.326GB	attack-trainer
4	Jastreb	COIN
8	Alouette III	helicopter
7	Bell 47 (Sioux)	helicopter
28	Bell AB.205 (Iroquois)	helicopter
1	Bell AB.212	helicopter
30	SA.330 Puma	helicopter
10	C-47 Dakota/Skytrain	transport
6	DHC Beaver	transport
7	DHC Buffalo	transport
4	DHC Caribou	transport
10	Do.28 Skyservant	transport
1	HS.748	transport
2	Pembroke	transport
2	Galeb	trainer
24	SF.260MZ	trainer
8	T-6 Harvard/Texan	trainer

Section 2
Aircraft Data

Fighters

Crusader F-8 LTV Aerospace Corporation

The F-8 Crusader is a single-seat, supersonic fighter flown from aircraft carriers of the US and French navies. The Crusader was the US Navy's standard carrier-based day fighter prior to the entry of the F-4 Phantom II into squadron service. Subsequently, the Crusader was retained to operate from the US Navy's *Hancock*-class carriers because of operational limitations of the Phantom aboard smaller carriers. Thus, the Crusader was to disappear from US service when the carriers *Hancock* and *Oriskany* are decommissioned in 1976.

The Crusader is a swept-wing aircraft with the entire wing pivoting upwards seven degrees during landing and take-off to provide the lift coefficient necessary for carrier landing speeds and still permit the fuselage to be in a near-horizontal attitude for maximum pilot visibility. The Crusader life was extended when 448 aircraft were "remanufactured" between 1965 and 1970; the updating included structural reinforcement, the fitting of boundary layer control, new landing gear and improved avionics. The outer wing panels fold for carrier storage. The RF-8 aircraft is an unarmed photo reconnaissance variant employed on older US carriers.

Status: *Operational.* First flight March 25, 1955; squadron delivery March 1957; 1,261 aircraft produced from 1954 to 1965 of which 448 remanufactured 1965 to 1970.

RF-8G Crusader photo-recon-naissance aircraft of the US Navy (US Navy)

*F-8E(FN)
Crusader of the
French Navy
(French Armed
Forces)*

SPECIFICATIONS (F-8J)

Crew: 1 (F-8 and RF-8 variants)
Engine: 1 P & W J-57-P-20A turbojet (18,000 lb, 8,165 kg st with afterburner)
Dimensions: span 35 ft 8 in (10·87 m), length 54 ft 6 in (16·61 m), height 15 ft 9 in (4·80 m), wing area 375 sq ft (34·88 m²)
Max level speed: 1,200 mph (1,930 km/hr) at 36,000 ft (11,000 m) (Mach 1·8)

Ceiling: 38,400 ft (11,712 m)
Range: combat radius 440 miles (708 km)
Weights: 27,550 lb (12,500 kg) loaded; 34,000 lb (15,420 kg) max
Armament: 4 × 20-mm Mk-12 Colt cannon (84 rpg) and 4 × Sidewinder AIM-9 AAMs
or 8 × Zuni rockets ("cheek" rails) plus 2 × Bullpup AGM-12 ASMs
or 2 × 1,000-lb bombs (wing pylons)

VARIANTS

XF-8A formerly XF8U-1; prototype with J57-P-12 turbojet; 2 built.

F-8A formerly F8U-1; J57-P-4A engine; initial production version; 4 × 20-mm guns plus belly pack with 32 × 2·75-inch rockets, and 2 × Sidewinder AAMs on "cheek" rails; first flight September 20, 1955; 318 built from 1956 to 1958.

DF-8A F-8A configured to control Regulus guided missiles; 2 aircraft built.

QF-8A F-8A configured as drone.

RF-8A formerly F8U-1P; photo reconnaissance version of F-8A with five cameras in place of guns; first flight December 17, 1956; 144 built; 73 remanufactured to RF-8G configuration.

TF-8A J57-P-20 engine; two-seat armed trainer; first flight February 6, 1962; 1 converted from F-8A.

F-8B formerly F8U-1E; F-8A with improved APS-67 radar; first flight September 3, 1958; 130 built from 1957 to 1959; see F-8L.

F-8C formerly F8U-2; J57-P-16 engine and fixed ventral fins; "cheek" rails modified to each carry 2 × Sidewinder AAMs; first flight in December 1957; 187 built; see F-8K.

F-8D formerly F8U-2N; J57-P-20A engine; improved all-weather capability with APQ-83 radar; first flight February 16, 1960; 152 built; see F-8H.

F-8E formerly F8U-2NE; similar to F-8D with APQ-94 radar; first flight on June 30, 1962; 286 built; see F-8J.

F-8E(FN) F-8E produced for French Navy incorporating boundary layer control, new wing leading edge, and provision for Matra R.530 AAMs and

Sidewinder AAMs; first flight on February 26, 1964; 36 single-seat and 6 two-seat aircraft built.

DF-8F F-8A reconfigured to control drones.

RF-8G remanufactured RF-8A with J57-P-22 engine; length 54 ft 6 in (16·62 m); wing hard points for external stores; 73 remanufactured 1965 to 1970.

F-8H remanufactured F-8D with J57-P-20A engine; first flight on July 17, 1967; 89 remanufactured 1967 to 1968.

F-8J remanufactured F-8E with J57-P-20A engine; refitted with PAQ-124 radar; first flight January 31, 1968; 136 remanufactured 1968–1969.

F-8K remanufactured F-8C with J57-P-16/16B engine; 87 remanufactured 1968–1969.

F-8L remanufactured F-8B retaining J57-P-4A engine; 63 remanufactured.

F-8M design for remanufactured F-8A retaining J57-P-4A engine.

OPERATIONAL

France, United States (Navy)

Delta Dagger F-102 General Dynamics/Convair

The F-102 Delta Dagger is a supersonic, delta-wing interceptor. The aircraft normally carries Falcon AAMs (nuclear or conventional warhead); no guns are installed. The Delta Dagger was developed as part of Weapon System 201A, a programme that integrated the aircraft, missiles, and an all-weather search and fire control radar in an advanced bomber intercept system. The F-102s flown by the US Air National Guard squadrons were to be phased out of service in 1976. As many as 200 aircraft will be converted to target drones to simulate high-performance Soviet aircraft.

The Delta Dagger is unusual as an all-weather interceptor in having a one-man crew (the TF-102A has side-by-side seating). The "Dagger" has a delta-wing design with aft fuselage speed brakes which serve as doors for the drag chute compartment.

Status: *Operational.* First flight on October 24, 1953; squadron delivery in June 1955; 875 F-102A and 111 TF-102A produced through 1958.

F-102A Delta Dagger of the US Air Force (US Air Force)

SPECIFICATIONS

Crew: 1
Engine: 1 P & W J57-P-23A turbojet (11,200 lb, 5,085 kg st dry; 17,200 lb, 7,809 kg st with afterburner)
Dimensions: span 38 ft $1\frac{1}{2}$ in (11·62 m), length 68 ft 3 in (20·81 m), height 21 ft $2\frac{1}{2}$ in (4·46 m), wing area $661\frac{1}{2}$ sq ft (61·52 m²)
Max level speed: 825 mph (1,327 km/hr) at 36,000 ft (11,000 m)
Ceiling: 54,000 ft (16,460 m)

Range: combat radius 385 miles (619 km); ferry range 1,500 miles (2,413 km)
Max take-off weight: 32,000 lb (14,515 kg)
Armament: 3 × Falcon AIM-4A/E AAMs (weapons bay) plus 3 × Falcon AIM-4C/F AAMs (wing pylons) or 2 × Falcon AIM-26A AAMs plus 2 × 230-gal fuel tanks

VARIANTS

YF-102 prototype with J57-P-11 engine; 10 built.

F-102A standard interceptor; 875 built 1954 to 1958.

QF-102A F-102A modified as drone for use as full-scale manoeuvring target for F-15 Eagle fighter.

TF-102A two-seat trainer; retains weapons capability; speed 646 mph (1,040 km/hr) at 38,000 ft (11,590 m); first flight on November 8, 1955; 111 built through 1958.

YF-102A second prototype series with J57-P-23 engine; modified canopy; lengthened nose; first flight December 20, 1954; 4 built.

PQM-102A F-102A modified as drone for use in Pave Deuce programme to provide a full scale, high-performance target for use in air-to-air missile training; first drone flight August 13, 1974; 24 planned.

OPERATIONAL

Greece, Turkey, United States (Air National Guard)

Delta Dart F-106 General Dynamics/Convair

The F-106 Delta Dart is an all-weather, delta-wing supersonic interceptor. The aircraft was initiated as an improved version of the F-102 Delta Dagger and resembles the earlier aircraft which it succeeded as the principal fighter of the US Air Force Aerospace Defence Command (ADC). The F-106 will remain in service through the 1970s.

The Delta Dart closely resembles the Delta Dagger in size and configuration, with the former aircraft having engine intakes farther back (behind the canopy), a redesigned tail, and a more powerful engine providing greater performance. The Delta Dart is equipped with the MA-1' electronic guidance and fire control system. Originally armed only with missiles; a 20-mm cannon has been retrofitted in the surviving aircraft. Missiles are carried in an internal weapons bay.

F-106A Delta Dart of the US Air Force (US Air Force)

Status: *Operational.* First flight December 26, 1956 (F-106A); squadron delivery in June 1959; 337 aircraft produced.

SPECIFICATIONS (F-106A)

Crew: 1

Engine: 1 P & W J75-P-17 turbojet (17,200 lb, 7,809 kg st dry; 24,500 lb, 11,113 kg st, with afterburner)

Dimensions: span 38 ft 3½ in (11·67 m), length 70 ft 8¾ in (21·56 m), height 20 ft 3 in (6·18 m), wing area 661½ sq ft (61·52 m²)

Max level speed: 1,525 mph (2,455 km/hr) at 36,000 ft (11,000 m)

(Mach 2·3)

Ceiling: 57,000 ft (17,375 m)

Range: radius 365 miles (587 km), ferry range 1,800 miles (2,896 km)

Weights: 24,038 lb (10,913 kg) empty, 34,510 lb (15,668 kg) loaded

Armament: 1 × 20 mm M61A1 cannon, 1 × Genie AIR-2A AAM or Super Genie plus 4 × Falcon AIM-4F/G AAMs (weapons bay)

VARIANTS

F-106A standard interceptor; 17 prototype and preproduction aircraft and 257 production aircraft delivered 1956 to 1961.

F-106B two-seat trainer with full armament retained; first flight on April 9, 1958; 63 aircraft built through 1961.

F-106X proposed interceptor component of advanced US air defence programme; basic F-106 airframes with improved avionics and advanced Falcon AAM; programme cancelled.

OPERATIONAL

United States (Air Force, Air National Guard)

Draken SAAB-35 SAAB

The SAAB-35 Draken (Dragon) was developed to provide the Swedish Air Force with a first-line interceptor for the 1960s and 1970s. The single-seat, delta-wing, all-weather aircraft was initiated as a bomber-defence weapon, but also has been employed in the photographic reconnaissance and ground attack roles.

Designed by a team lead by Erik Bratt, the Draken configuration was flight tested in a flying scale model known as the SAAB-210, which first flew on January 21, 1952. The delta-wing Draken is similar in profile to the larger Convair F-102/F-106 interceptors, but the Swedish aircraft possesses a wing planform of double-delta configuration.

Status: *Operational*. First flight on October 25, 1955; squadron delivery in March 1960; more than 600 aircraft produced including 12 assembled in Finland.

SPECIFICATIONS (SAAB 35S)

Crew: 1

Engine: 1 Svenska Flygmotor RM6C (licenced Rolls-Royce RB.146 Avon 300 series) turbojet (13,220 lb, 6,002 kg st dry; 17,500 lb st, 7,945 kg with afterburner)

Dimensions: span 30 ft 10 in (9·40 m), length 50 ft 4 in (15·35 m) overall, height 12 ft 9 in (3·89 m), wing area 529¾ sq ft (49·20 m²)

Max level speed: 1,320 mph (2,124 km/hr) at 36,000 ft (11,000 m) (Mach 2·0)

Ceiling: 55,000 ft (16,775 m)

Range: Internal fuel only, 395 miles (635 km); ferry range 2,020 miles (3,250 km)

Take-off weight: 25,130 lb (11,400 kg) clean; 33,070 lb (15,000 kg) max

Armament: 2 × 30-mm Aden M55 cannon and 4 × Sidewinder AIM-9 AAMs or 4 × 550-lb bombs (wing pylons)

SAAB 35F Draken of the Swedish Air Force, armed with four Swedish-built Falcon AAMs (SAAB)

VARIANTS

SAAB-35 prototypes with British-built Rolls-Royce Avon 200 engines; 3 built (first two without armament).

SAAB-35A production aircraft with RM6B engine rated at 15,190 lb st with afterburner; built for Swedish Air Force (designated J-35A); many converted to SAAB-35B or SAAB-35C.

SAAB-35B improved avionics; first flight on November 29, 1959; alternative external loads include 2 launchers each with 19 × 75-mm Bofors air-to-air rockets or 9 × 220-lb (100 kg) bombs; built as -35B and converted from -35A for Swedish Air Force (J-35B).

SAAB-35C two-seat trainer; unarmed; first flight on December 30, 1959; all converted from -35A for Swedish Air Force (SK-35C).

SAAB-35D basic 35A with RM6C engine; improved avionics; first flight on December 27, 1960; for Swedish Air Force (designated J-35D).

SAAB-35E SAAB-35D fitted for day/night photographic reconnaissance first flight June 27, 1963; for Swedish Air Force (S-35E).

SAAB-35F SAAB-35D fitted with improved avionics and armed with 4 × Falcon AIM-4 missiles; first flight in October 1965; 2 prototypes were converted -35D followed by additional aircraft built for Swedish Air Force (J-35F).

SAAB-35H company-sponsored prototype with Ferranti Airpass II radar; not produced.

SAAB-35XD/XS long-range fighter/attack aircraft designed for export; similar to SAAB-35F with increased internal fuel and increased external payload (up to 9,000 lb, 4,086 kg) for maximum loaded weight of 35,270 lb, 16,010 kg; 20 fighter-bombers (F-35XD) and 20 photographic reconnaissance aircraft (RF-35XD) produced for Denmark; 12 fighters (SAAB-35XS) produced for assembly in Finland.

SAAB-35XT two-seat trainer variant of SAAB-35X series; 6 aircraft produced for Denmark (TF-35XD).

OPERATIONAL

Denmark, Finland, Sweden

Eagle F-15 McDonnell Douglas

The F-15 is a single-seat, high-performance aircraft developed to succeed the F-4 Phantom as the basic US Air Force fighter. The F-15 has been touted as the first air superiority fighter developed by the US Air Force specifically for the air-to-air combat role since the F-86 Sabre entered production in 1948. However, officials have stated that a limited attack capability was considered from the initiation of the aircraft's design. The Eagle is a contemporary of the US Navy's multi-purpose F-14 Tomcat fighter.

The Eagle has a fixed, swept-back wing, with two advanced technology engines providing high speed, altitude, and manoeuvrability to counter late-model Soviet high-performance fighters. The aircraft is fitted with the Hughes APG-63 attack radar system and carries air-to-air missiles as well as a single, rapid-fire internal General Electric Vulcan 20-mm M-61A1 six-barrel gun.

F-15 Eagle air-superiority fighter of the US Air Force (McDonnell Douglas)

TF-15 Eagle, two-seat variant, of the US Air Force (McDonnell Douglas)

Status: *Operational.* First flight July 27, 1972; squadron delivery in November 1974; 729 operational aircraft for US Air Force with deliveries scheduled through 1980; 25 have been ordered by Israel, some being rehabilitated USAF R&D aircraft.

SPECIFICATIONS

Crew: 1
Engines: 2 P & W F100-PW-100 turbofans (23,500 lb, 10,670 kg st each with afterburner)
Dimensions: span 42 ft 9¾ in (13·05 m), length 63 ft 9¾ in (19·45 m), height 18 ft 7½ in (5·68 m), wing area 608 sq ft (56·54 m²)
Speed: sustained Mach 2·3; maximum dash exceeds Mach 2·5

Absolute ceiling: 66,900 ft (20,390 m)
Range: approx 2,000 miles (3,200 km)
Weight: gross approx 40,000 lb (18,145 kg)
Armament: 1 × 20-mm M61A1 cannon (1,000 rpg) and 4 × Sparrow AIM-7F AAMs and 4 × Sidewinder AIM-9L AAMs

VARIANTS

F-15A basic fighter aircraft.
F-15N proposed carrier-based version for US Navy.

TF-15 two-seat trainer; first flight in July 1973.

OPERATIONAL

United States (Air Force), Israel

Étendard IV-M/IV-P Dassault

The Étendard IV-M is a fighter-interceptor/ground attack aircraft developed specifically for operation from the French Navy's aircraft carriers *Clémanceau* and *Foch.* The single-seat fighter is the only supersonic aircraft developed outside of the United States specifically for shipboard operation.

The swept-wing Étendard IV-M/P design is noted for excellent manoeuvrability. The IV-P can carry up to 3,000 lb (1,362 kg) of external stores on four wing pylons; 2 × 30-mm cannon are fitted. The IV-P is a dual-purpose tanker and reconnaissance variant with fixed refuelling probe, centre-line mounted refuelling drogue, three OMERA cameras in the nose, and two OMERA cameras in ventral position in place of 30-mm gun housing (Aida 7 fire control radar deleted). The IV-M has retractable refuelling probe. Outer wing panels of both types fold for carrier operation. The Étendard is scheduled for replacement by the Super Étendard.

Status: *Operational.* First flight on July 24, 1956; squadron delivery in January 1962; 97 aircraft produced from 1956 to 1965.

SPECIFICATIONS (Étendard IV-M)

Crew: 1

Engine: 1 SNECMA Atar 08B turbojet (9,700 lb, 4,400 kg st)

Dimensions: span 31 ft 6 in (9·60 m), length 47 ft 3 in (14·40 m), height 14 ft 2 in (4·30 m), wing area 312 sq ft (29·0 m²)

Speed: 673 mph (1,085 km/hr) at 36,000 ft (11,000 m) maximum (Mach 1·02), 683 mph at sea level (Mach 0·9)

Ceiling: 49,200 ft (15,000 m)

Range: 185-mile (300 km) radius at sea level

Max take-off weight: 22,650 lb (10,275 kg)

Armament: 2 × 30-mm DEFA cannon and 2 Sidewinder AAMs plus 2 AS.30 ASMs or 2 × 500-lb bombs plus 2 × 1,000-lb bombs

Étendard IV-P refuelling an Étendard IV-M (French Armed Forces)

VARIANTS

IV-01 prototype; developed as private venture; first flight on July 24, 1956.

IV-B third production aircraft; fitted with Rolls-Royce Avon 51 turbojet rated at 11,200 lb, 5,085 kg st.

IV-M standard carrier-based fighter; Aida 7 fire control radar; first flight in July 1961; 1 prototype, 6 preproduction and 69 production aircraft built 1958 to 1962.

IV-M-01 special prototype; first flight May 21, 1958; 1 built.

IV-P unarmed tanker-reconnaissance aircraft; five OMERA cameras; fixed refuelling probe; first flight November 19, 1960; 21 built 1962 to 1965

OPERATIONAL

France (Navy)

F-16 General Dynamics

The F-16 was the successful entry in the US Air Force Air Combat Fighter (ACF) programme, formerly known as the Light-Weight Fighter (LWF) programme. The F-16 competed with the Northrop YF-17 for US sales and also with the Dassault Mirage F-1 and SAAB Viggen for NATO sales. The principal F-16/YF-17 design difference is that the General Dynamics design is a single-engined aircraft.

The F-16 has a slightly swept-back, fixed-wing configuration, with long root extensions to improve supersonic manoeuvring. In addition to carrying two AAMs (500 lb) on wingtips, production F-16 aircraft will carry 7,200 lb (3,270 kg) of additional external stores on four wing pylons and a centreline station. The F-16 engine is the same as that used by the F-15 Eagle fighter.

F-16, successful entry in the US Air Force ACF competition armed with two Sidewinder AAMs (General Dynamics)

Status: Two YF-16 prototypes in flight test. First flight February 2, 1974 (with inadvertent six-minute flight on January 20, 1974). USAF procurement of 650 production aircraft planned.

SPECIFICATIONS

Crew: 1

Engine: 1 Pratt & Whitney F100-PW-100 turbofan; (about 25,000 lb, 11,340 kg st with afterburner)

Dimensions: span 30 ft (9·14 m), length 46 ft 6 in (14·18 m), height 16 ft 3 in (4·95 m)

Speed: 1,400 mph (2,250 km/hr) at 40,000 ft (12,200 m) (Mach 2)

Ceiling: 60,000 ft (18,300 m)

Range: 550 miles (885 km) combat radius; 2,500 miles (4,000 km) ferry range

Weights: 17,500 lb (7,938 kg) normal take-off; 27,000 lb (12,260 kg) maximum take-off

Armament: 1 × 20-mm M-61 cannon and 2 × Sidewinder AIM-9 AAMs (wingtips)

VARIANTS

YF-16 competitive prototype with Northrop YF-17; 2 built.

F-16A production aircraft; first flight in December 1976.

F-16B fitted with special electronics.

YF-17 Northrop

The Northrop YF-17 was the unsuccessful competitor in the US Air Force's Air Combat Fighter (ACF) programme. Northrop still hopes for NATO sales and possibly a carrier-based variant for the US Navy.

YF-17 armed with Sidewinder AAMs (US Air Force)

The YF-17 is a twin-engine aircraft with fixed, slightly swept wings, distinguished by long, curved, leading-edge extensions at the wing roots and twin vertical stabilizers, canted outward from the vertical. In addition to wingtip missile stations (for 400 lb), production F-17 aircraft would have two wing pylons and a centreline station for 9,400 lb (4,265 kg) of additional external stores. The design is based in part on the Northrop P-530 Cobra and was the basis for the F-18.

Status: Two YF-17 prototypes built. First flight June 9, 1974.

SPECIFICATIONS

Crew: 1
Engines: 2 General Electric YJ101-GE-100 (15,000 lb, 6,804 kg st each with afterburners)
Dimensions: span 35 ft (10·67 m), length 55 ft 6 in (16·93 m), height 14 ft 6 in (4·42 m), wing area 350 sq ft (32·5 m²)
Speed: 1,320 mph (2,125 km/hr) at 40,000 ft (12,200 m) (Mach 2)
Ceiling: 60,000 ft (18,300 m)
Range: 500 miles (927 km) combat radius
Weight: 21,000 lb (9,500 kg) normal take-off
Armament: 1 × 20-mm M-61 cannon and 2 × Sidewinder AIM-9 AAMs (wingtips)

F-18 McDonnell Douglas/Northrop

The Northrop-designed F-18 is a derivative of that company's YF-17 programme and was selected by the US Navy as its Navy Air Combat Fighter, formerly designated VFAX (Aircraft, Fighter Attack Experimental). The Northrop/McDonnell Douglas collaboration provides that the latter company will act as prime contractor for all naval variants of the original YF-17 because of that firm's extensive experience in the manufacture of carrier aircraft.

The Navy will supplement its F-14 squadrons with the F-18 while the Marine Corps will entirely replace its F-4 strength with the F-18 and delete all F-14 acquisition. The F-18 is also planned to replace the A-7 in Navy light attack squadrons.

The F-18 has slightly larger exterior dimensions than the YF-17 with provision for nine store stations under the wings and fuselage. Its engines are turbofan developments of the original J101 turbojets, providing an increase in thrust to approximately 16,000 lb st each. This increase is necessary to offset the added weight necessitated by Navy's attack mission and range requirements. More than 13,000 lb (5,900 kg) of external weapons can be carried on nine wing and fuselage hardpoints and pylons.

Status: Development.

Artist's concept of the proposed F-18 for the US Navy's Air Combat Fighter (McDonnell Douglas)

SPECIFICATIONS

Crew: 1

Engines: 2 General Electric F404-GE-400 turbofans (16,000 lb, 7,265 kg st each with afterburners)

Dimensions: span 37 ft 6 in (11·44 m), length 55 ft 7 in (16·96 m), height 14 ft 6 in (4·42 m)

Speed: Mach 1·5 +

Ceiling: 45,000 + ft (13,725 m)

Range: 400 + mile (645 km) combat radius; 2,000-mile (3,220 km) ferry range

Weights: 33,000 lb (14,982 kg) fighter mission take-off; 44,000 + lb (19,976 kg) maximum

Armament: 1 × 20-mm cannon and 2 × Sidewinder AIM-9 AAMs plus 2 × Sparrow AIM-7 AAMs plus various combinations of missiles, bombs, rockets, fuel tanks

F-111 General Dynamics

The F-111 is a variable-geometry strike fighter in service with the US Air Force and the Royal Australian Air Force. The aircraft has an internal bomb bay for conventional or nuclear bombs and can carry air-to-air or air-to-surface missiles on wing pylons. Although designed as a multi-mission tactical fighter (TFX) for use by the US Air Force, Navy, and Marine Corps as well as the Royal Air Force, it has entered service only with the USAF and RAAF.

The F-111 variable-geometry wings sweep from a fully extended position (16-degree sweep) for landing, take-off, and cruise, to a "tucked in" position (72·5-degree sweep) for high-speed flight. The aircraft is powered by twin engines and has side-by-side crew seating. A 20-mm multi-barrel cannon or bombs can be carried in a weapons bay with additional weapons on eight wing pylons, four of which are retained when the wings are swept back. Normal weapons load is up to 20,000 lb (9,080 kg) on short-range missions. A carrier-based version (F-111B) was rejected for service by the US Navy.

*F-111D of the
US Air Force with
wings extended
(General
Dynamics)*

Status: *Operational.* First flight December 21, 1964; squadron delivery (USAF) August 1968; a total of 506 F-111 aircraft have been ordered with the last USAF deliveries scheduled for July 1976 (this includes all "F" series aircraft but not the FB-111 strategic bomber aircraft which is listed separately).

SPECIFICATIONS (F-111A)

Crew: 2
Engines: 2 Pratt & Whitney TF30-P/-3 turbofans (12,500 lb, 5,675 kg st dry; 21,000 lb, 9,525 kg st with afterburners)
Dimensions: span 63 ft (19·20 m), length 73 ft 6 in (22·40 m), height 17 ft 1 in (5·22 m)
Speed: 1,650 mph (2,655 km/hr) at 49,000 ft (15,000 m) (Mach 2·5); 915 mph (1,472 km/hr) at sea level (Mach 1·2)

Ceiling: 60,000 + ft (18,300 m)
Range: 3,800 miles + (6,100 km)
Max take-off weight: 91,500 lb (41,500 kg)
Armament: 1 × 20-mm M-61A1 cannon
or 2 × 750-lb bombs (weapons bay) plus 48 × 750-lb bombs
or 24 × 1,000-lb bombs (wing pylons)

VARIANTS

F-111A original USAF version; equipped with Mark I avionics; 158 built including 18 prototypes.

FB-111 strategic bomber variants; listed under Bombers.

EF-111A electronic jamming aircraft converted from F-111A; ALQ-99 jammer in weapons bay and faired signal receiver pod under fuselage; 2 prototypes and 40 standard conversions planned to equip 2 squadrons with 18 aircraft each.

RF-111A reconnaissance version; 1 built.

F-111B Grumman-built carrier variant for US Navy; TF30-P-1A/-12 engines; programme cancelled in 1968; 7 built.

F-111C RAAF version similar to F-111A; TF30-P-3 engine; 24 built.

F-111D TF30-P-3 engine and Mark II avionics; 96 built.

RF-111D TF30-P-3/-9 engines; planned reconnaissance version; none built

F-111E TF30-P-3/-9 engines; modified F-111A with Mark I avionics and modified engine intakes; 94 built.

F-111F similar to F-111E with Mark IIB avionics; first 30 aircraft delivered with TF30-P-100 engine; 126 built through mid-1976.

YF-111A designation of 2 ex-F-111K assigned to USAF for research and development.

F-111K RAF version cancelled in 1968; 2 built (redesignated YF-111A)

F-111X General Dynamics proposed alternative to F-111B.

F-111X-7 proposed stretched F-111 (length approx 81 ft 10 in) for Improved Manned Interceptor role.

OPERATIONAL

Australia, United States (Air Force)

Fagot MiG-15 Mikoyan-Gurevich

The MiG-15 was the first Soviet swept-wing fighter and fought history's first jet-versus-jet duel when four MiG-15 fighters fought four US Air Force F-80C Shooting Stars over Korea on November 1, 1950; one MiG was lost in the encounter. After the Korean War the MiG-15 became the standard fighter of most Communist nations and, although obsolescent, it is still flown by more than 20 air forces.

The aircraft has a barrel-like fuselage and the original production aircraft were powered by a single RF-45 turbojet engine, designed by Tschelomyey from the British-developed Rolls-Royce Nene. The aircraft's 37-mm Nudelmann and two 23-mm Nudelmann-Suranov cannon are fitted in a pack or "cradle" that can be lowered for maintenance. Two wing tanks (160 US gallons each) can be carried to supplement the internal 330-gallon fuel capacity. MiG-15 aircraft have been produced under licence in China, Czechoslovakia, and Poland.

MiG-15UTI
Midget *two-seat trainer (Flight International)*

Status: *Operational.* First flight on December 30, 1947; squadron delivery in 1948; between 15,000 and 18,000 produced (the largest production run of any jet-propelled aircraft; the most widely used Western jet fighter was the contemporary F-86/CL-13 Sabre, with approximately 7,000 being manufactured).

SPECIFICATIONS (MiG-15bis *Fagot*)

Crew: 1
Engine: 1 Klimov VK-1 turbojet (5,952 lb, 2,700 kg st)
Dimensions: span 33 ft 1 in (10·09 m), length 36 ft 4 in (11·10 m), height 11 ft 1 in (3·39 m)
Speed: 668 mph (1,075 km/hr) max at sea level
Ceiling: 51,000 ft (15,500 m)

Range: 560 miles (900 km); 675 miles (1,085 km) with wing tanks
Weights: 8,320 lb (3,777 kg) empty; 14,238 lb (6,463 kg) loaded
Armament: 1 × 37-mm N-37 cannon (40 rpg), 2 × 23-mm NS-23 cannon (160 rpg) and 2 × 550-lb bombs or 2 × 1,100-lb bombs (wing pylons)

VARIANTS

MiG-15 basic fighter powered by RD-45 engine; prototype first flight December 30, 1947; licenced production in Czechoslovakia (as S-102) and Poland (as LIM-1).

MiG-15bis VK-1 turbojet; first flight in November 1948; some units adapted as fighter-bombers with cannon armament plus 2 × 550-lb (250 kg) or 1,100-lb (500 kg) bombs; others converted to reconnaissance aircraft;

licenced production in China, Czechoslovakia (as S-103), and Poland (as LIM-2).

MiG-15UTI *Midget*; two-seat trainer powered by RD-45 engine; length 36 ft 4 in (11·08 m); licenced production in Czechoslovakia (as CS-102) and Poland (as LIM-3); some LIM-3 armed with 2 × 23-mm cannon; MiG-15UTI and CS-102 variants are unarmed.

OPERATIONAL

Afghanistan, Albania, Algeria, Bulgaria, Ceylon, China, Cuba, Czechoslovakia, Egypt, Finland, Guinea, Indonesia,

Iraq North Korea, Mali, Mongolia, Nigeria, Poland, Romania, Somalia, Syria, Uganda, North Vietnam

Farmer MiG-19 Mikoyan

The MiG-19 *Farmer* was the first production Soviet aircraft to achieve supersonic speed in level flight. The single-seat, twin-engine, swept-wing fighter is the direct follow-on to the similarly configured MiG-17 *Fresco*. Developed as a day fighter for the Soviet air forces, the *Farmer* subsequently has been employed in all-weather missions and is flown today by 15 nations.

In addition to the large numbers of MiG-19 fighters built in the USSR, Soviet-provided plans and production data has enabled China to produce the aircraft (under the designation F-6).

Status: *Operational.* First flight late in 1953; squadron delivery in 1955.

SPECIFICATIONS (*Farmer*-C)

Crew: 1
Engines: 2 Klimov RD-9F turbojets (6,170 lb, 2,800 kg st each dry; 7,850 lb, 9,560 kg st each with afterburners)
Dimensions: span 29 ft 6 in (9·00 m), length 41 ft 4 in (12·54 m), height 12 ft 5 in (3·80 m), wing area 285 sq ft (26·51 m²)
Max level speed: 845 mph (1,360 km/hr) at 35,000 ft (10,675 m)
(Mach 1·28); 740 mph (1,190 km/hr) at 50,000 ft (15,250 m) (Mach 1·12)
Ceiling: 55,000 ft (16,775 m)
Range: combat radius 280 miles (450 km)
Weights: 18,000 lb (8·170 kg) loaded clean; 22,500 lb (10,200 kg) max overload
Armament: 3 × 30-mm cannon and 2 × *Atoll* AAMs

VARIANTS

Farmer-C early aircraft fitted with Klimov AM-5 engine (designated MiG-19S) and subsequent aircraft with RD-9F engine; (designated MiG-19SF); standard day fighter.

Farmer-D RD-9F engine; all weather fighter (designated MiG-19PF); aircraft armed with 4 × *Alkali* AAMs designated MiG-19PM.

Farmer-E day fighter similar to MiG-19PM armed with 4 × *Alkali* AAMs.

F-6 Chinese-built variant flown by China, Albania, and Pakistan.

MiG-19 Farmer-E armed with four Alkali AAMs

Farmer-A Klimov VK-5 engine; initial production day fighter; armed with 1 × 37-mm and 2 × 23-mm cannon plus wing pylons for rocket pods.

Farmer-B Klimov RD-9B engine; all-weather and night fighter version; same armament as *Farmer*-A.

OPERATIONAL

Afghanistan, Albania, Bulgaria, China, Czechoslovakia, East Germany, Hungary, Indonesia, North Korea, Pakistan, Poland, Romania, Soviet Union (PVO, FA), Tanzania, North Vietnam

Fencer Su-19 Sukhoi

The *Fencer*, believed designated Su-19 by the Soviet Union, was publicly identified for the first time in early 1974 by the Chairman of the US Joint Chiefs of Staff who described the aircraft as "the first modern Soviet fighter to be developed specifically as a fighter-bomber for the ground attack mission". The aircraft has a variable-geometry wing configuration.

Status: *Operational.*

SPECIFICATIONS

Crew: 2
Engines: 2 turbojets, type not known (approx 17,000 lb, 7,720 kg st each dry; 24,700 lb, 11,215 kg st each with afterburner)
Dimensions: span 39 ft 4 in (12 m) swept, 65 ft 7 in (20 m) extended, length 78 ft 9 in (24 m), height 15 ft 1 in (4·6 m)
Speed: Mach 2·3

Ceiling: 52,500 ft (16,015 m)
Range: 800-mile combat radius (1,290 km)
Weights: approx 35,000 lb (15,890 kg) empty, 75,000 lbs (34,050 kg) loaded
Armament: internal cannon and various combinations of bombs, rockets, and ASMs

OPERATIONAL

Soviet Union (FA)

Fiddler Tu-28P Tupelov

The Tu-28P *Fiddler* is the world's largest fighter aircraft to attain operational status. The Soviet two-seat, twin-engine aircraft is employed as a long-range, all-weather fighter and as a reconnaissance platform.

The *Fiddler* is a swept-wing aircraft with large turbojet housings faired into the fuselage just aft of the cockpit. External fuel tanks are faired into the wings. There may be a small internal weapons bay in addition to wing pylons for air-to-air missiles.

Status: *Operational.* Squadron delivery in 1966.

SPECIFICATIONS

Crew: 2
Engines: 2 turbojets, type not known (approx 27,000 lb, 12,250 kg st each with afterburner)
Dimensions: span 64 ft 11 in (19·81 m), length 90 ft (27·45 m), height 22 ft 11 in (7·00 m)
Speed: 1,150 mph (1,850 km/hr) at 36,000 ft (11,000 m) (Mach 1·75)
Ceiling: 65,620 ft (20,000 m)
Range: 3,100 miles (5,000 km)
Weight: approx 100,000 lb (45,400 kg) loaded
Armament: 4 × *Ash* AAMs (wing pylons)

OPERATIONAL

Soviet Union (PVO)

Tu-28P Fiddler-*B armed with four* Ash *AAMs*

Fishbed MiG-21 Mikoyan

The MiG-21 represents the ultimate stage of Soviet short-range, light-weight, fighter-interceptor aircraft. Conceived during the Korean War and first flown only two years after the end of that conflict, the MiG-21's numerous variants are today flown by more than a score of nations. Finland and India received the first export version in 1963; the MiG-21 was the first non-Western combat aircraft to be flown by the Indian Air Force. A few MiG-21s went to China before the Sino-Soviet break and apparently the first Chinese copy was produced late in 1964.

MiG-21 Fishbed of the Yugoslav Air Force, armed with Atoll AAMs (US Navy)

The basic MiG-21 is a single-seat, single-engine fighter with a distinctive delta wing. Although sometimes cited for armament, weapons, and avionics limitations as well as short combat radius, the MiG-21 has achieved considerable popularity because of its manoeuvrability, ability to operate from unimproved airfields, ease of maintenance, and comparatively low cost. Armament includes internal cannon in some variants and various combinations of wing pylons and a ventral attachment point for external stores, with some aircraft being assigned primarily ground support roles.

MiG-21 Fishbed

Status: *Operational*. First flight in 1955; squadron delivery late in 1959; also built in China, Czechoslovakia, and India.

SPECIFICATIONS (MiG-21MF *Fishbed*-J)

Crew: 1

Engine: 1 Tumansky RD-11-300 turbojet (11,244 lb, 5,100 kg st dry; 14,550 lb, 6,600 kg st with afterburner)

Dimensions: span 23 ft 5½ in (7·15 m), length 51 ft 8½ in (15·76 m), height 14 ft 9 in (4·50 m); wing area 247 sq ft (22·98 m²)

Speed: 1,386 mph (2,230 km/hr) at 36,000 ft (11,000 m) (Mach 2·1);

810 mph (1,300 km/hr) at sea level (Mach. 1·06)

Ceiling: 59,050 ft (18,000 m)

Range: combat radius 350 miles (560 km)

Weights: 18,078 lb (8,200 kg) loaded with 4 × AAMs; 20,723 lb (9,400 kg) maximum

Armament: 2 × 23-mm cannon (Gsh-23 two-barrel gun pack) and 4 × *Atoll* AAMs (wing pylons)

VARIANTS

Fishbed-A prototype MiG-21 with Tumansky RD-11 engine; armed with 2 × 30-mm NR cannon; produced in limited numbers; Ye-5 was test aircraft.

Fishbed-B probably aerodynamic test aircraft; sighted in 1956.

Fishbed-C MiG-21F day fighter armed with 1 × 30-mm cannon and 2 × *Atoll* AAMs (on wing pylons); first major production aircraft; early export recipients included Finland (MiG-21F-12), Indian and Iraq (both MiG-21F-13); Ye-66/Yo 66A were test aircraft.

Fishbed-D MiG-21PF/-21PFM all-weather fighter; RD-11-F2S-300 engine; armed with 2 × *Atoll* AAMs (on wing pylons; no internal gun); prominent fixed conical centre-body in air intake to house Spin Scan search-and-track radar; major production aircraft.

Fishbed-E existence questionable; reported similar to *Fishbed*-C; Ye-76 may have been test aircraft.

Fishbed-F MiG-21 PFM; modified *Fishbed*-D; major production aircraft; large numbers transferred to other nations and manufactured in India

under licence.

Fishbed-G experimental STOL variant of *Fishbed*-D; two vertical lift engines fitted in fuselage, increasing length to approx 55 ft (16·78 m); first observed in 1967.

Fishbed-H reconnaissance variant fitted with cameras and electronic countermeasure devices; derived from *Fishbed*-D.

Fishbed-J MiG-21 MF; multi-mission fighter armed with 2 × 23-mm cannon, 4 × *Atoll* (on wing pylons), plus centreline pylon for 23-mm cannon pod, fuel or cameras; dorsal fairing enlarged; major production aircraft still in production in USSR and India (Hindustan Aeronautics Ltd.).

Fishbed-K MiG-21SMT; similar to *Fishbed*-J with improved electronics and back-looking radar.

Mongol-A MiG-21UTI; two-seat trainer derived from *Fishbed*-C/D fighters; Ye-33 was test aircraft.

Mongol-B MiG-21UTI; two-seat trainer derived from later fighter variants.

OPERATIONAL

Afghanistan, Albania, Algeria, Bangladesh, China, Cuba, Czechoslovakia, Egypt, Finland, East Germany, Hungary, India, Indonesia, Iraq, North Korea, Poland, Romania, Somalia, Soviet Union (FA, PVO), Sudan, Syria, Uganda, North Vietnam, Yugoslavia

Fishpot-B Su-9 Sukhoi
Fishpot-C Su-11

The Su-9 is a single-seat, all-weather fighter that bears some resemblance to the smaller MiG-21 *Fishbed.* Although developed at the same time as the MiG-21, the Su-9 was designed from the outset as an all-weather aircraft. The Su-9 and its trainer variant, the *Maiden,* are used only by the Soviet Air Forces. The Su-11 is an improved aircraft with a lengthened nose and other modifications.

The aircraft has a delta-wing configuration that can be easily distinguished from the somewhat similar MiG-21 by the Mikoyan aircraft's fixed ventral fin. The Su-9 shares many components with the Su-7 Fitter ground-attack fighter. The Su-9 has no internal gun; air-to-air missiles are carried on four wing pylons. A conical radome is mounted in the centre of the circular air intake.

Status: *Operational.* First flight about 1955; squadron delivery in 1960.

SPECIFICATIONS (*Fishpot*-B)

Crew: 1

Engine: 1 Lyulka AL-7F-1 turbojet (15,432 lb, 7,000 kg st dry; 22,046 lb, 10,000 kg st with afterburner)

Dimensions: span 27 ft 8 in (8·45 m), length 55 ft (16·75 m), height 16 ft (4·90 m)

Speed: 1,190 mph (1,915 km/hr) clean at 36,000 ft (11,000 m) (Mach 1·8); 990 mph (1,600 km/hr) with 4 × AAMs at 36,000 ft (11,000 m) (Mach 1·5)

Ceiling: 55,700 ft (17,000 m)

Weights: 18,300 lb (8,308 kg) empty; 30,000 lb (13,620 kg) maximum

Armament: 4 × *Alkali* AAMs or 2 × *Anab* AAMs (wing pylons)

Su-9 Fishpot-*B*
all-weather fighter

VARIANTS

Fishpot-A prototype; armed with 2 × 30-mm cannon plus 4 × AAMs.

Fishpot-B Su-9; production aircraft, cannon deleted.

Fishpot-C Su-11; improved produc-

tion aircraft; span 26 ft (7·90 m), length 56 ft (17·00 m) (over probe).

Maiden two-seat trainer variant.

T-431 test aircraft.

OPERATIONAL

Soviet Union (PVO)

Fitter-A Su-7B Sukhoi

The Su-7B is a swept-wing, ground-attack fighter that was the standard aircraft in this role with the Soviet Air Forces and is now in the air arms of several Warsaw Pact and other nations. The Su-7B superficially resembles the MiG-19 *Farmer*. Listed separately is the Su-17, known as the *Fitter*-B under the US-NATO designation system, which is a variable-geometry wing modification of the Su-7. A two-seat trainer variant of the earlier aircraft is the Su-7UTI *Moujik*.

The Su-7B has a sharply swept mid-wing configuration with a small cone extending from the nose air intake. Some components are common to the Su-9 *Fishpot*-B fighter which was developed at the same time as the Su-7. Two internal guns are fitted in the wing roots (a location which provides a stable platform during firing); external stores are carried on two ventral pylons and two wing pylons, each of which can carry 1,000 lb (454 kg) of bombs or rockets with the fuselage pylons often used for auxiliary fuel tanks.

Status: *Operational*. First flight about 1955; squadron delivery in 1959–1960.

SPECIFICATIONS

Crew: 1

Engine: 1 Lyulka AL-7F turbojet (15,432 lb, 7,000 kg st dry; 22,046 lb, 10,000 kg st with afterburner)

Dimensions: span 29 ft 3½ in (8·93 m), length 57 ft (17·37 m) (over probe); height 15 ft (4·57 m)

Speed: 1,055 mph (1,700 km/hr) clean at 36,000 ft (11,000 m) (Mach 1·6); 788 mph (1,270 km/hr) at 36,000 ft (11,000 m) with external

stores (Mach 1·2)

Ceiling: 49,700 ft (15,150 m)

Range: 900 miles (1,450 km)

Weights: 19,000 lb (8,625 kg) empty; 26,450 lb (12,000 kg) normal; 29,750 lb (13,500 kg) maximum

Armament: 2 × 30-mm NR-30 cannon (70 rpg) and up to 4,000 lb (1,815 kg) of bombs, rockets (fuselage and wing pylons)

Su-7 Fitter-*A*
ground-attack
fighter

VARIANTS

Fitter-A Su-7B; production ground
attack fighter; Su-78M has modified
nosewheel door to accommodate

low-pressure tyre.
   Moujik Su-7UTI; two-seat trainer.

OPERATIONAL

Afghanistan, Algeria, Cuba, Czechoslovakia, Egypt, East Germany,
Hungary, India, Iraq, North Korea,

Poland, Soviet Union (FA), Syria,
North Vietnam

Fitter-B Su-17 Sukhoi
Fitter-C Su-20

The Su-17 is a variable-geometry derivative of the Su-7 *Fitter*-A. The aircraft
has been described as the Soviet Union's first aircraft with a variable-geometry
wing. The outer, 13-ft wing panels can adjust sweep angle, improving take-off
performance and range when in the forward (extended) position; the panels
are swept back for high-speed flight. The Su-20 is believed to be an improved
variant of the aircraft and is designated *Fitter*-C by US-NATO officials.
   The Su-17 is similar in dimensions and performance to the Su-7 with a
span of 41 ft when the wing panels are extended and 29 ft 6 in when swept
back. In addition, four wing pylons are provided as against two in the Su-7
(plus ventral pylons in both aircraft) with a maximum weapons load of
almost 8,000 lb (3,630 kg).

Status: *Operational; Fitter*-C squadron delivery in 1971.

Su-20 Fitter-*C of the Polish Air Force*

SPECIFICATIONS (*Fitter*-C)

Crew: 1

Engine: 1 Lyulka AL-21F-3 turbojet (17,195 lb, 7,800 kg st dry; 24,700 lb, 11,200 kg st with afterburner)

Estimated dimensions: span 41 ft (12·50 m) spread; 29 ft 6 in (9·00 m) swept; length 56 ft (17·00 m) (over probe), height 15 ft 5 in (4·71 m)

Speed: 1,430 mph (2,300 km/hr) at 39,370 ft (12,000 m) (Mach 2·17); 808 mph (1,300 km/hr) at sea level (Mach 1·06)

Ceiling: 57,415 ft (17,500 m)

Range: combat radius 375 miles (600 km)

Weight: 39,000 lb (17,700 kg)

Armament: 2 × 30-mm NR cannon (70 rpg) and various combinations of bombs, rockets, and missiles

OPERATIONAL

Poland, Soviet Union (FA)

Flagon **Su-15** Sukhoi

The Su-15 is a single-seat, high-performance, all-weather fighter which is relatively new to Soviet service. There are several variants of the twin-engine aircraft, one of which (*Flagon*-B) has a short-field (STOL) capability. The *Flagon* was first observed in 1967 and entered production a short time later.

The standard Su-15 has a modified delta wing and tail assembly similar to the Su-9/Su-11 *Fishpot* fighters. However, the twin-engine Su-15 has air intakes on both sides of the fuselage alongside the cockpit and an elongated nose housing a large radar. The STOL *Flagon*-B variant is a slightly larger aircraft with three lift-jet engines fitted behind the cockpit and hinged doors over their air intakes. No internal guns are fitted.

Status: *Operational.* More than 600 aircraft of this series are believed to have been produced.

SPECIFICATIONS (*Flagon*-A)

Crew: 1
Engines: 2 Lyulka A1-9 turbojets
Dimensions: span 30 ft (9·15 m), length 68 ft (20·50 m), height 16 ft 5 in (5·00 m)
Speed: Mach 2·5 clean; Mach 2·3 with external stores

Ceiling: 80,000 ft (24,400 m)
Range: combat radius 450 miles (725 km)
Weight: 35,275 lb (16,000 kg) maximum
Armament: 2 × *Anab* AAMs (wing pylons)

VARIANTS

Flagon-A basic production aircraft.
Flagon-B STOL variant with three lift-jet engines; span approx 36 ft (11·00 m), length approx 75 ft (23·00 m)

Flagon-C two-seat trainer.
Flagon-D/E similar to *Flagon*-A with modified wingtips; *Flagon*-E entered service in late 1973.

OPERATIONAL

Su-15 Flagon-*B*
STOL fighter

Soviet Union (PVO)

Flogger MiG-23 Mikoyan

The MiG-23 is a variable-geometry Soviet fighter, apparently designed primarily for ground attack missions. The aircraft resembles the US F-111, but with air intakes further forward and more squared as in the F-4 Phantom II series. The Soviet aircraft has a single turbojet engine whereas both the F-111 and F-4 are twin-engine fighters.

The MiG-23 wings sweep out to an extended position for landing, take-off, and cruise, and sweep back for high-speed flight. The aircraft has a small ventral fin that retracts upward for landing and take-off. There is a twin-barrel GP-9 gun pod fitted under the fuselage and four pylons for missiles or bombs, two under the fuselage and two on the inboard (fixed) wing panels. The rear crewman in the *Flogger*-C sits slightly higher than the pilot and uses a retractable periscope.

Status: *Operational.* Squadron delivery in 1971–1972.

SPECIFICATIONS

Crew: 1 (2 in *Flogger*-C)
Engine: 1 turbojet (estimated 14,330 lb, 6,500 kg st dry; 20,500 lb, 9,300 kg st with afterburners)
Dimensions: span 46 ft 9 in (14·25 m) fully spread; 26 ft 9½ in (8·17 m) fully swept; length 55 ft 1½ in (16·80 m) (over probe)
Speed: Mach 2·5 maximum at altitude; Mach 1·1 at sea level
Ceiling: 59,000 ft (18,000 m)
Range: combat radius 600 miles (960 km)
Approximate weight: 35,000 lb (15,890 kg) loaded
Armament: 2 × 23 mm Gsh-23 cannon plus 4 × AAMs or ASMs (wing pylons)

VARIANTS

Flogger -A prototype.
Flogger-B MiG-23B; leading edge slats on outer wing sections; production model; six-barrel semi-recessed cannon.
Flogger-C MiG-23U two-seat trainer/attack variant.

OPERATIONAL

Egypt, Iraq, Libya, Soviet Union, Syria

MiG-23 Flogger-A *variable-geometry aircraft*

MiG-25 Foxbat *(Flight International)*

Foxbat MiG-25 Mikoyan

The MiG-25 is a high-performance, all-weather, air-superiority and reconnaissance fighter. The aircraft is a contemporary of the US F-14 Tomcat and F-15 Eagle (resembling the latter), but the Soviet aircraft is significantly heavier and faster than either US fighter.

A single-seat aircraft, the MiG-25 design has a high swept-back wing, box-like intakes flared into the fuselage; and twin vertical stabilizers canted outward. The aircraft is believed to have been designed primarily for all-weather bomber intercept and may have a "look-down" scanning radar. No internal gun is provided.

Status: *Operational.* First flight in 1965; squadron delivery in 1968.

SPECIFICATIONS (F-5A)

Crew: 1
Engines: 2 Tumansky RD-31 turbojets (24,200 lb, 11,000 kg st each with afterburners)
Dimensions: span 40 ft (12·20 m), length 69 ft (21·00 m), height 19 ft 7 in (5·96 m)
Speed: Mach 3 + at altitude; Mach 1·8

at sea level
Ceiling: 80,000 ft (24,400 m)
Range: combat radius 700 miles (1,125 km)
Weight: approx 64,200 lb (29,120 kg) loaded
Armament: 4 × *Ash* or *Atoll* AAMs (wing pylons)

VARIANTS

Foxbat-A basic production aircraft; E-266 is test aircraft.

Foxbat-B MiG-25R; reconnaissance variant with improved ECM capabilities.

OPERATIONAL

Soviet Union (FA, PVO)

Freedom Fighter F-5A/B Northrop

The F-5 Freedom Fighter is a light-weight, supersonic fighter provided in large numbers to the air forces of US allies and third world nations. Designed specifically to meet the needs of small air forces, the aircraft's relatively low cost, ease of maintenance and high performance have made it a most successful fighter. It is flown in various configurations by 20 nations (including the F-5E/F Tiger II variants, listed separately). However, it has had little US Air Force squadron service because of an American preference for and the availability of larger, more-capable fighter aircraft.

The F-5 is similar in design and construction to Northrop's T-38 Talon, a supersonic trainer. The F-5 has twin engines, short, straight wings, five pylons for external stores, and two wingtip points for air-to-air missiles with a total capacity of 6,200 lb (2,800 kg) of ordnance.

Status: *Operational.* First flight July 30, 1959; squadron delivery (USAF) in 1964. Assembled or built under licence in Canada (Canadair) and Spain (CASA).

SPECIFICATIONS (F-5A)

Crew: 1 (2 for F-5B)
Engines: 2 GE J85-GE-13 turbojets (2,720 lb, 1,235 kg st each dry; 4,080 lb, 1,850 kg st with afterburners)
Dimensions: span 25 ft 3 in (7·70 m), length 47 ft 2 in (14·38 m), height 13 ft 2 in (4·01 m), wing area 170 sq ft (15·79 m²)
Speed: 924 mph (1,488 km/hr) clean at 36,000 ft (11,000 m) (Mach 1·4); 870 mph (1,400 km/hr) with 2 × AAMs at 36,000 ft (Mach 1·32)

Ceiling: 50,500 ft (15,390 m)
Range: combat radius on air intercept mission 195 miles (314 km); radius on attack mission 635 miles (1,020 km); ferry range 1,865 miles (3,000 km)
Weights: 8,085 lb (3,667 kg) empty; 20,677 lb (9,379 kg) max take-off
Armament: 2 × 20-mm M-39 cannon (280 rpg) and 2 Sidewinder AIM-9 AAMs (wingtips) plus 4 × Bullpup AGM-12 ASMs or 4 × 1,000-lb bombs (wing pylons)

VARIANTS

F-5A Freedom Fighter of the US Air Force configured for photo-reconnaissance (Northrop)

F-5A standard fighter aircraft.
RF-5A reconnaissance variant with four KS-92 cameras; full cannon armament retained.
F-5B two-seat trainer; full armament capability; first flight February 24, 1964; length 46 ft 4 in (14·12 m).
F-5C proposed model for US Air Force; J85-GE-15 engines.

CF-5A/D F-5A/B aircraft, respectively, produced by Canadair for Canadian Forces; J85-CAN-15 engines; some fitted with reconnaissance nose housing three 70-mm Vinten camera; additional armour, improved avionics, and jettisonable pylons; also provided to Venezuela.

NF-5A/D F-5A/B aircraft, respectively, produced by Canadair for the Netherlands; modified wing and fuselage; leading edge manoeuvring slats on wings.

SF-5A/B F-5A/B aircraft, respectively, produced by CASA for Spanish Air Force; identical to Northrop configurations.

YF-5B-21 prototype F-5E with J85-GE-21 turbojets fitted in F-5B airframe.

F-5-21 Northrop designation for F-5E.

F-5E/F advanced F-5 configuration known as Tiger II; listed separately.

OPERATIONAL

Brazil, Canada, Ethiopia, Greece, Iran, Jordan, South Korea, Libya, Malaysia, Morocco, Netherlands, Norway, Pakistan, Philippines, Saudi Arabia, Spain, Taiwan, Thailand, Turkey, United States (Air Force), Venezuela

Freehand Yak-36 Yakovlev

The Yak-36 is a Soviet V/STOL fighter aircraft, apparently developed for use aboard the Soviet Navy's aircraft carriers of the *Kiev* class. The single-seat, twin-engine aircraft has a barrel-like fuselage and swept wings similar to the MiG-15 and its derivatives. However, the Yak-36 is a distinct design. The aircraft has been observed operating from the Soviet helicopter cruiser *Moskva*, apparently in at-sea evaluation for use from the *Kiev*-class ships.

First observed in July 1967, the Yak-36 has an elliptical cross-section fuselage and employs two vectored-thrust turbojet engines for both vertical and horizontal thrust. This is the same arrangement used by the Hawker-Siddeley Harrier V/STOL aircraft. The aircraft also has a long in-flight refuelling probe protruding above the large, elliptical air intake.

Yak-36 Freehand flown by the Soviet Navy and apparently developed for use on board Kiev *class carriers*

Status. *Operational.*

SPECIFICATIONS

Crew: 1
Engines: 2 vectored-thrust turbojets
   (7,000–9,000 lb, 3,180–4,085 kg st
   each)
Dimensions: span 27 ft (8·25 m),
   length overall 57 ft 6 in (17·5 m)
Speed: approx Mach 0·85 at altitude

Range: combat radius approx 175
   miles (280 km)
Weight: approx 18,000 lb (8,170 kg)
   loaded
Armament: 2 × 16 unguided rocket
   pods (wing pylons)

OPERATIONAL

Soviet Union (Navy)

Fresco MiG-17 Mikoyan-Gurevich

A refinement of the Mig-15 *Fagot*, the MiG-17 was developed as a day
fighter-interceptor. The single-seat, single-engine, swept-wing aircraft has
probably been adopted by more nations than any other Soviet aircraft and
remains in service with 25 air forces.

The MiG-17 was the first Soviet service aircraft to exceed the speed of
sound in level flight (in December 1949). The basic aircraft retains the
barrel-like fuselage of the MiG-15, but a slightly shorter wing span gives the
illusion of a longer aircraft. The *Fresco*-D and-E variants can be distinguished
by the cone-shaped radome in the centre of the intake and the smaller
radome on the upper lip of the radome. The *Fresco*-C was the major production variant and is capable of ground attack as well as interceptor missions.
Four wing pylons can carry tandem loads (e.g., 8 bombs or 8 rocket pods).
Soviet production of the MiG-17 has been supplemented by aircraft built in
China, Czechoslovakia, and Poland. The aircraft was developed with the
designation Type S.I.

Status: *Operational.* First flight in 1949; squadron delivery in 1952.

SPECIFICATIONS

Crew: 1
Engine: 1 Klimov VK-1A turbojet
   (5,952 lb, 2,700 kg st dry; 6,990 lb,
   3,173 kg st with afterburner)
Dimensions: span 31 ft 6 in (9·60 m),
   length 36 ft 4 in (11·10 m), height
   11 ft (3·36 m), wing area 233 sq ft
   (21·67 m²)
Speed: 635 mph (1,020 km/hr) at
   39,370 ft (12,000 m) (Mach 0·96);

700 mph (1,125 km/hr) at sea level
   (Mach 0·92)
Ceiling: 57,500 ft (17,538 m)
Range: combat radius 465 miles (750
   km)
Weight: 11,000 lb (4,995 kg) loaded
Armament: 3 × 23-mm cannon and
   4 pods × 55-mm rockets plus
   4 × 550-lb bombs (wing pylons)

MiG-17 Fresco

VARIANTS

Fresco-A day fighter with VK-1 turbojet; armed with 2 × 23-mm NR-23 cannon and 1 × 37-mm N-37 cannon; produced in large numbers.

Fresco-B MiG-17P; modified with repositioned dive brakes; produced in limited numbers.

Fresco-C MiG-17F; day fighter with repositioned dive brakes and VK-1A engine; slow-firing (400 rpm) 37-mm cannon replaced by third 23-mm weapon; produced in large numbers in USSR, China, Czechoslovakia (S-104), and Poland (LIM-5).

Fresco-D MiG-17PF; limited all-weather fighter with VK-1A or VK-1FA engine; cannon deleted on some aircraft; 4 × *Alkali* AAMs plus two drop tanks carried under fuselage.

Fresco-E MiG-17PFU; similar to *Fresco*-D with afterburning VK-1 engine.

OPERATIONAL

Afghanistan, Albania, Algeria, Bulgaria, Cambodia, China, Cuba, Czechoslovakia, Egypt, East Germany, Guinea, Hungary, Indonesia, Iraq, North Korea, Morocco, Nigeria, Poland, Romania, Somalia, Soviet Union (FA, PVO), Syria, Uganda, North Yemen, South Yemen

XFV-12 Rockwell International

Artist's concept of the XFV-12 V/STOL aircraft being developed for the US Navy (Rockwell International)

The XFV-12 is a high-performance V/STOL aircraft being developed for operation from US Navy warships. The aircraft will have a thrust-augmented wing design for both high-speed in level flight and vertical/short take-off and landing capabilities. Two prototypes have been constructed.

The XFV-12 design features near-delta wings aft and small canards forward with engine exhaust being directed through large lateral nozzles located in the wings and canards to provide vertical lift capability. A runout of 300 ft (92 m) will add an additional 5,000 lb (2,270 kg) to the maximum gross vertical take-off weight of over 19,000 lb (8,626 kg). The single-seat, single-engine aircraft employs the forward fuselage and landing gear of the diminutive A-4 Skyhawk and the air intakes and wing box of the F-4 Phantom II aircraft. (In size the XFV-12 is comparative to the A-4 Skyhawk.) The advanced technology engine is derived from that developed for the F-14 Tomcat. The service variants of the XFV-12 would carry external weapon stores on pylons and pallets mounted under the fuselage.

Status: *Development.* First flight in 1976.

SPECIFICATIONS

Crew: 1
Engine: 1 Pratt & Whitney F401-PW-400 turbofan (14,070 lb, 6,388 kg st; 21,800 lb, 9,900 kg st in lift configuration)
Dimensions: span 28 ft 10 in (8·80 m), length 43 ft 10 in (13·30 m), height 10 ft 5 in (3·19 m)
Speed: Mach 2·2 to 2·4 at altitude

Range: combat radius 575 miles (925 km)
Weights: 13,800 lb (6,259 kg) empty; 19,500 lb (8,845 kg) VTOL gross; 24,250 lb (11,000 kg) STOL gross
Armament: 1 × 20-mm M-61A1 cannon and gun pods, bombs, missiles (fuselage attachment points)

G.91 Aeritalia

The G.91 is a multi-purpose fighter design with a swept-wing configuration that resembles the F-86 Sabre design. The G.91 was developed in response to a NATO requirement for a light-weight fighter; although the G.91 design won the competition, it has entered service with only three air forces.

The basic single-engine fighter variants have been followed by twin-turbojet reconnaissance and ground attack aircraft. The combat aircraft are single-seat (there is a two-seat training variant); fitted with cameras, internal guns, and wing pylons for external stores. Design produced in Italy by Fiat (now Aeritalia) and in Germany under licence by Dornier.

Status: *Operational.* First flight August 9, 1956; squadron delivery in August 1958; 739 aircraft of all G.91 variants produced.

SPECIFICATIONS (G.91R)

Crew: 1

Engine: 1 Fiat-built Bristol Siddeley Orpheus 803 turbojet (5,000 lb, 2,270 kg st)

Dimensions: span 28 ft 1 in (8·56 m), length 33 ft 9½ in (10·30 m), height 13 ft 1½ in (4·00 m), wing area 176¾ sq ft (16·42 m²)

Max level speed: 650 mph (1,045 km/hr) at 5,000 ft (1,500 m) (Mach 0·87)

Ceiling: 40,000 ft (12,200 m)

Range: combat radius 200 miles (320 km); ferry range 1,150 miles (1,850 km)

Weights: 8,130 lb (3,688 kg) empty; 11,880 lb (5,390 kg) normal loaded; 12,125 lb (5,500 kg) maximum take-off

Armament: 4 × 0·50-cal Colt-Browning MG (300 rpg) in G.91R.1/R.4
or 2 × 30-mm DEFA cannon (125 rpg) in G.91R.3/R.6 and 2 pods × 2·75-in rockets
or 2 500-lb bombs
or 2 AS.20 or AS.30 ASMs (4 wing pylons in G.91R.1B and later variants)

VARIANTS

G.91 of the German Air Force (Bundesminesterium der Verteidigung)

G.91 3 prototype and 27 pre-production aircraft; 16 of latter subsequently modified for use by Italian national aerobatic team (designated G.91 PAN for *Pattuglid Acrobatica Nazionali*).

G.91R.1 initial production aircraft; three Vinten cameras in nose; 4 × MG and two wing pylons; 25 aircraft produced for Italy.

G.91R.1A improved avionics; 25 aircraft produced for Italy.

G.91R.1B improved avionics and four underwing pylons; 50 aircraft produced for Italy.

G.91R.3 similar to G.91R.1B with 2 × 30-mm DEFA cannon in place of MG; 74 produced by Fiat for Germany (with 12 assembled by Dornier) and 270 produced under licence in Germany.

G.91R.4 similar to G.91R.3 with R.1 armament; 50 aircraft produced for Greece and Turkey, but delivered instead to Germany with 40 aircraft subsequently being transferred to Portugal.

G.91T two-seat training variant; first flight on May 31, 1960; armed with 2 × 0·50-cal MG and two wing pylons; 76 T.1 type produced for Italy and 66 T.3 type for Germany (44 by Fiat and 22 by Dornier).

G.91T.4 proposed G.91T.1 fitted with F-104G Starfighter electronics; none built.

G.91Y long-range reconnaissance variant with 2 GE J-85-GE-13A turbojets (with afterburners); armed with 2 × 30-mm cannon and four weapon pylons; first flight on December 27, 1966; 75 produced for Italy.

G.91YS proposed G.91Y modified to meet Swiss specifications for ground-attack role; none built.

G.91YT proposed two-seat trainer variant of G.91Y; none built.

G.291 proposed advanced fighter-attack aircraft developed from G.91Y; new wing with leading-edge slats; four weapon pylons; improved bomb-aiming system.

OPERATIONAL

West Germany, Italy, Portugal

Gnat Hawker Siddeley

The Gnat is a single-seat, swept-wing, transonic aircraft developed as a low-cost, light-weight fighter. It has been compared to the US-developed F-5 Freedom Fighter. The Gnat's combat capabilities were demonstrated in Indian use against Pakistani Sabres and Starfighters in the 1965 and 1971 conflicts, with the Gnat's record in the former war being responsible for extension of the aircraft's production beyond a planned 1966 halt.

Developed as a private venture by Folland Aircraft (subsequently absorbed by Hawker Siddeley), the aircraft was produced by the British firm and under licence as the Ajit by Hindustan Aeronautics Ltd. (HAL) in India. The prime user of the Gnat is India, with the limited number flown by Great Britain (as a two-seat trainer) and Finland being phased out. The aircraft is noted for simplicity of avionics and maintenance, and for high manoeuvrability.

Status: *Operational.* First flight July 18, 1955; squadron delivery in 1959.

SPECIFICATIONS

Crew: 1
Engine: 1 Bristol Siddeley Orpheus 701 turbojet (4,520 lb, 2,050 kg st)
Dimensions: span 22 ft 2 in (6·75 m), length 29 ft 9 in (9·06 m), height 8 ft 10 in (2·68 m), wing area $136\frac{1}{2}$ sq ft (12·69 m²)
Max level speed: 695 mph (1,118 km/hr) clean at 20,000 ft (6,100 m); 647 mph (1,040 km/hr) at 36,000 ft (11,000 m) (Mach 0·98)
Ceiling: 50,000 + ft (15,250 m)
Range: combat radius 500 miles (805 km)
Weight: 9,145 lb (4,150 kg) loaded
Armament: 2 × 30-mm Aden cannon (115 rpg) and 2 × 500-lb bombs or 12 × 3-inch rockets (wing pylons)

VARIANTS

Fo.141 prototype built as private venture by Folland Aircraft; Orpheus B.Or.1 engine; 6 pre-production aircraft with B.Or.2 engine produced for Royal Air Force evaluation.

F.1 production aircraft; 10 fighter and 2 reconnaissance variants with three Vinten cameras produced for Finland; over 200 produced for India (15 by Hawker Siddeley and about 200 by HAL); first HAL delivery in 1962.

Gnat T.1s flown by the Royal Air Force (Ministry of Defence)

F.2 improved fighter variant; none built.

T.1 originally designated Fo.144; two-seat trainer; 14 pre-production aircraft built by Folland; 91 built by Hawker Siddeley with Orpheus 101 turbojet; first flight on August 31, 1959; all for RAF.

OPERATIONAL

Finland, Great Britain, India

Kfir Israel Aircraft Industries

The Kfir (Young Lion) is a Mach 2.2 fighter built by Israel Aircraft Industries that first saw combat in the 1973 Yom Kippur War, performing well against Egyptian and Syrian MiG-21s. Israeli designers based the Kfir upon the airframe of the Mirage 5, combining that with the engine from the F-4E Phantom, thereby producing this versatile fighter-bomber. Mirage IIICJs used in the 1967 war were modified to accept the General Electric turbojets of the Phantom to increase their performance and extend their useful life, but the Kfir is not a modification but a "new" Israeli-produced aircraft. It was initially referred to as the Barak (Lightning). There is an Israeli requirement for 200 aircraft.

The aircraft has a delta platform with low wing loading for optimum manoeuvrability and ordnance payload. The Kfir has two fuselage intakes and a third air intake at the base of the vertical stabilizer to provide additional cooling during reheat to the J79 engine. It also differs from the French Mirage 5 in having stronger landing gear, a fly-by-wire system, Israeli-produced avionics, high-lift devices, a new wing leading edge, a longer nose, and a shorter, thicker tail cone.

Status: *Operational*. First flight 1972; approximately 70 operational in 1973 Yom Kippur war.

SPECIFICATIONS

Crew: 1

Engine: 1 General Electric J79-GE-17 (17,900 lb, 7,876 kg st with afterburner)

Dimensions: span 26 ft 11½ in (8·22 m), length 50 ft 10¼ in (15·50 m), height 13 ft 11½ in (4.25 m),

wing area 375 sq ft (34·85 m²)

Speed: Mach 2·2

Ceiling: 50,000 + ft (15,250 m)

Weight: 31,980 lb (14,519 kg) loaded

Armament: 1 × 30-mm DEFA cannon and various combinations of rockets, bombs, missiles

OPERATIONAL

Israel

Two views of the Kfir (Young Lion) (IAI)

Lightning BAC

The Lightning is a supersonic, swept-wing, fighter-interceptor in service with the Royal Air Force and two Middle Eastern air forces. Although it is a relatively old aircraft, having been developed in the late 1950s, the Lightning will be used through the mid-1970s as a first-line RAF fighter.

Powered by two turbojets in the unusual arrangement of one above the other in the fuselage, the Lightning can fly at Mach 2 speeds and cruise on one engine.

Status: *Operational.* First flight August 4, 1954; squadron delivery July 1960; more than 230 aircraft produced through 1972.

SPECIFICATIONS (F Mk 53)

Lightning F.6 of the RAF, armed with Red Top AAMs and carrying two 260-gallon overwing fuel tanks (BAC)

Crew: 1
Engines: 2 Rolls-Royce Avon 302-C turbojets (16,300 lb, 7,393 kg st each with afterburners)
Dimensions: span 34 ft 10 in (10·61 m), length 55 ft 3 in (16·84 m), height 19 ft 7 in (5·97 m)

Max level speed: More than 1,320 mph (2,124 km/hr) (Mach 2 +)
Ceiling: 60,000 ft (18,300 m)
Weight: 49,000 lb (22,250 kg) loaded
Armament: 2 × Red Top or Firestreak AAMs (wing pylons)

VARIANTS

P.1A research aircraft with Sapphire ASSa.5 engine; first flight August 4, 1954; 3 built.

P.1B operational prototype aircraft powered by Avon 200 engines; first flight April 4, 1957; 3 built.

F.1 production version with Avon 201 engine; armed with 2 × 30-mm Aden cannon; first flight October 29, 1959; 20 built plus 28 as F.1A with in-flight refuelling capability.

F.2 F.1A with Avon 210 engine; 2 × 30-mm Aden cannon plus Red Top or Firestreak AAMs; first flight July 11, 1961; 40 or 50 built for RAF with 30 updated as F.2A; 4 transferred to Saudi Arabia as F.52.

F.3 Avon 301 engine; first flight June 16, 1962; armed only with Red Top or Firestreak AAMs; F.3A with modified wing configuration; most F.3 aircraft converted to F.6 configuration.

F.6 final production version; first flight April 17, 1964; more than 60 built.

F.53 multi-mission variant; 12 built for Kuwait and 35 for Saudi Arabia.

T.4 two-seat unarmed trainer, first flight May 6, 1959; approximately 15 built; 2 transferred to Saudi Arabia as T.54.

T.5 two-seat training variant of F.3 with provision for AAMs; first flight March 29, 1962; more than 20 built.

T.55 two-seat trainer; 2 built for Kuwait and 6 for Saudi Arabia.

OPERATIONAL

Great Britain (RAF), Kuwait, Saudi Arabia

Mirage III Dassault

The Mirage III is one of the most successful and widely used French-built aircraft. The single-seat, single-engine fighter was developed for high-altitude, all-weather combat, but has been employed in the ground attack, nuclear strike, reconnaissance, and training roles.

Mirage IIIEA of the Argentine Air Force (Dassault)

The Mirage III has a delta-wing configuration with fuselage engine intakes alongside the cockpit featuring pronounced half-cones in the intake openings. Two cannon are mounted internally and external stores can be carried on a ventral pylon and two wing pylons.

Status: *Operational.* First flight November 17, 1956; squadron delivery in 1962. Through 1974 approximately 1,000 aircraft produced by Dassault plus 98 aircraft built under licence in Australia and 32 aircraft in Switzerland.

SPECIFICATIONS (Mirage III-E)

Crew: 1

Engine: 1 SNECMA Atar 09C turbojet (13,670 lb, 6,200 kg st with afterburner); optional and jettisonable SEPR 844 rocket motor (3,300 lb, 1,500 kg st)

Dimensions: span 27 ft (8·22 m), length 49 ft 3½ in (15·03), height 13 ft 11½ in (4·25 m)

Max level speed: 1,460 mph (2,350 km/hr) at 40,000 ft (12,000 m) (Mach 2·1); maximum stabilized speed 1,188 mph (1,911 km/hr) (Mach 1·8)

Ceiling: 55,775 ft (17,000 m) at Mach 1·8; 75,450 ft (23,000 m) using rocket motor

Range: combat radius in ground attack role, 745 miles (1,200 km)

Weights: 15,540 lb (7,050 kg) empty; 29,760 lb (13,500 kg) maximum take-off

Armament: 2 × DEFA 30-mm cannon and 2 × 1,000-lb bombs (wing pylons)

or 1 × AS.30 ASM (ventral pylon) plus 2 × Sidewinder AIM-9 AAMs (wing pylons) plus 1 × Matra R.530

VARIANTS

III-001 prototype with Atar 101G turbojet (9,900 lb, 4,495 kg st, with afterburner).

III-A preproduction aircraft with Atar 09B turbojet; first flight May 12, 1958; 10 built.

III-B two-seat training variant of III-A; strike capability provided; length 50 ft 6 in (15·40 m); first flight October 20, 1959; flown by Argentina (III-BA); Brazil, Lebanon (III-BL); South Africa (III-BZ); France, Israel, Libya, Peru, Spain, Switzerland; 77 built.

III-C all-weather interceptor with day ground-attack capability; powered with Atar 9B3 turbojet; length 43 ft 10 in (13·36 m); first flight October 9, 1960; flown by Israel (III-CJ); South Africa (III-CZ); France, Lebanon, Switzerland; 196 built.

III-D two-seat trainer based on III-0 built in Australia for Royal Australian Air Force powered by Atar 9C; length 51 ft (15·56 m); also flown by Brazil (III-DBR), Pakistan (III-DP), South Africa, Spain (III-DE).

Mirage IIIS of the Swiss Air Force (Dassault)

III-E long-range multi-purpose fighter; first flight April 5, 1961; flown by Argentina (III-EA); Brazil (III-BR); France, Libya, Pakistan (III-EP); South Africa (III-EZ); Spain (III-EE); Venezuela.

III-O Australian-built version of III-E with different navigation equipment; first 2 aircraft built in France and delivered to RAAF in 1963 with additional 98 aircraft built in Australia.

III-R reconnaissance aircraft; retains armament with five cameras in nose; length 50 ft 10 in (15·49 m) first flight November 1961; 2 units converted from III-A; flown by France (III-R and improved III-RD); Libya, Pakistan (III-RP); South Africa (III-RZ); Switzerland.

III-S Swiss-built III-E aircraft; different fire control and weapon systems; nose section hinges to facilitate storage in underground hangers; first 2 aircraft built in France with additional 32 aircraft built in Switzerland.

III-T experimental VSTOL aircraft powered with SNECMA TF-106 turbofan rated at 19,840 lb, 9,000 kg st; first flight June 1964.

OPERATIONAL

Argentina, Australia, Brazil, Colombia, France, Israel, Lebanon, Libya, Pakistan, Peru, Saudi Arabia, South Africa, Spain, Switzerland, Venezuela

Mirage F-1 Dassault-Breguet

The Mirage F-1 or "Super Mirage" is a single-seat, multi-mission fighter, being offered to NATO and Middle East air forces in the F-1/M53 variant as a competitor to the General Dynamics F-16 and Northrop F-17. The Mirage F-1 was developed as a replacement for the Mirage III.

The swept-wing aircraft has large engine intakes just behind the cockpit with pronounced half-cones in the intake openings. The aircraft has a ventral pylon and four wing pylons for ordnance and two air-to-air missiles can be fitted to the wingtips; maximum external ordnance capacity is 8,200 lb (3,723 kg).

Status: *Operational.* First flight December 23, 1966; squadron delivery 1973. Through 1974 a total of 168 aircraft ordered (105 for French Air Force, 48 for South Africa, 15 for Spain) plus a reported 100 ordered by Egypt and Kuwait (for retransfer to Egypt).

Mirage F-1E of the French Air Force, armed with Matra 550 Magic AAMs (Dassault)

SPECIFICATIONS

Crew: 1
Engine: 1 SNECMA Atar 09K-50 turbojet (11,090 lb, 5,035 kg st dry; 15,875 lb, 7207 kg st with afterburner) F-1/M53 variant has SNECMA M53 turbofan of 18,000 lb, 8,170 kg st with afterburner
Dimensions: span 27 ft $6\frac{3}{4}$ in (8·40 m), length 49 ft $2\frac{1}{2}$ in (15·00 m), height 14 ft 9 in (4·50 m), wing area 269 sq ft (25 m²)
Speed: 1,450 mph (2,334 km/hr) above 36,000 ft (11,000 m) (Mach 2·2)
Ceiling: 65,600 ft (20,000 m)

Endurance: 3 hr 45 min
Weights: 16,314 lb (7,400 kg) empty; 24,030 lb (10,900 kg) loaded clean; 32,850 lb (14,900 kg) max; F-1/M53 17,120 lb (7,772 kg) empty; 24,555 lb (11,148 kg) loaded clean; 33,070 lb (15,014 kg) max
Armament 2 × 30-mm DEFA 553 cannon (125 rpg) and 8 × 882-lb bombs
or 3 × Matra R530 or Super 530 (wing pylons) plus 2 × Sidewinder AIM-9 AAMs or Matra 550 Magic (wingtips).

VARIANTS

Mirage F.1 of the French Air Force, armed with Matra 530 AAMs and AIM-9 Sidewinder AAMs (Dassault)

F-1-01 prototype Mirage F-1 with Atar 9K engine; first flight December 23, 1966 (crashed May 18, 1967).

F-1-02 pre-production aircraft with Atar 9K-31 engine; refitted with Atar 9K-50 engine; first flight March 20, 1969.

F-1-03 pre-production aircraft with Atar 9K-50 engine.

F-1-04 pre-production aircraft with Atar 9K-50 engine.

F-1C production all-weather fighter with Atar 9K-50 engine; limited ground attack capability; first flight February 15, 1973.

F-1A proposed day interceptor with some avionics deleted and additional fuel capacity.

F-1B proposed two-seat trainer with limited combat capability.

F-1E proposed all-weather interceptor and ground-attack aircraft.

F-1/M53 improved multi-purpose fighter with M53 engine.

OPERATIONAL

Egypt, France, South Africa, Spain

MRCA Panavia Aircraft

The MRCA is a two-seat, variable-geometry aircraft being developed for the air forces of Great Britain, West Germany, and Italy by a co-operative effort of aerospace firms in those three nations. The designation MRCA is an abbreviation for Multi-Role Combat Aircraft; it is intended to perform (1) close air support, (2) interdiction, (3) air superiority, (4) interceptor, (5) naval strike, and (6) reconnaissance.

The MRCA is a product of Panavia Aircraft, a co-operative company formed by the British Aircraft Corporation, Messerschmitt-Bölkow-Blohm, and Aeritalia. Similarly, the engines are produced by Turbo-Union, a joint venture of Rolls-Royce, MTV, and Fiat. Nine MRCA prototypes are being built: 4 in Great Britain, 3 in Germany, and 2 in Italy. A trainer variant is planned. The MRCA is fitted with internal cannon and three weapons attachment points under the fuselage and two under each outer wing panel.

Status: *Flight test.* First flight August 14, 1974; estimated squadron delivery in 1977. Planning provides for 385 aircraft to be ordered by the Royal Air Force (to replace Vulcan, Buccaneer, and Phantom aircraft); 202 by the Luftwaffe (to replace F-104G Starfighter and, in part, G.91; 120 by the West German Navy; and 100 by the Italian Air Force (to replace Phantom and G.91Y).

SPECIFICATIONS

Crew: 2

Engines: 2 Turbo-Union RB.199-34R turbofans (8,500 lb, 3,855 kg st each (dry 14,500 lb, 6,577 kg st each with afterburning)

Dimensions: span 45 ft 7¼ in (13·90 m) extended and 28 ft 2½ in (8·60 m) swept, length 54 ft 9½ in (16·70 m), height 18 ft 8½ in (5.70 m)

Speed: more than 1,320 mph (2,125 km/hr) at 36,000 ft (11,000 m)

Weights: approx 22,000 lb (10,430 kg) empty; approx 38,000 lb (17,240 kg) maximum

Armament: 2 × 27-mm Mauser cannon and various combinations of bombs, ASMs and AAMs

Panavia MRCA which is due to enter service with the air forces of Britain, West Germany and Italy in 1977

Mystère IV-A Dassault

The Mystère IV-A is a single-seat, swept-wing fighter-bomber and interceptor aircraft. The aircraft has been used extensively in air combat by the Israeli Air Force and the Indian Air Force. Although now obsolescent, it remains in limited service with those air forces.

The aircraft has a straightforward, swept-wing design, somewhat resembling the contemporary F-86 Sabre and MiG fighter designs of the 1950s. The first 50 Mystère IV-A aircraft had the Hispano-Suiza Tay 250A turbojet with the subsequent 371 aircraft having the more powerful Verdon 350 engine. Two internal cannon are fitted and external stores can be carried on four wing attachment points.

Status: *Being phased out of service.* First flight September 28, 1952; 421 aircraft produced through 1958 with 110 being delivered upon completion to India and 60 to Israel.

SPECIFICATIONS

Crew: 1
Engine: 1 Hispano-Suiza Verdon 350 turbojet (7,716 lb, 3,500 kg st)
Dimensions: span 36 ft 5$\frac{1}{2}$ in (11·12 m), length 42 ft 1$\frac{1}{2}$ in (12·85 m), height 15 ft 1 in (4·61 m), wing area 344$\frac{1}{2}$ sq ft (32 m²)
Speed: 696 mph (1,118 km/hr) at sea level (Mach 0·91); 615 mph (990 km/hr) at 39,370 ft (12,000 m) (Mach 0·94)

Ceiling: 45,000 ft (13,725 m)
Endurance: 1 hr 10 min on internal fuel
Weights: 12,950 lb (5,880 kg) empty; 16,530 lb (7,505 kg) loaded clean; 20,050 lb (9,103 kg) max take-off
Armament: 2 × 30-mm DEFA cannon and 2 × 1,000-lb bombs
or 4 × 500-lb bombs
or 4 pods × 37-mm rockets

*Mystère IV-A of
the Israeli
Defence Force
(Israeli Defence
Force)*

VARIANTS

IV-A production aircraft.
IV-B 3 prototype and 16 pre-production aircraft with Avon RA-7R

engine.
IV-N two-seat, all-weather prototype with Avon RA-7R engine; 1 built.

OPERATIONAL

India, Israel (phasing out)

Phantom II F-4 McDonnell Douglas

The F-4 Phantom II is a two-seat, multi-purpose fighter which is considered to be one of the most successful combat aircraft of the post-Second World War era. Originally developed for US Navy carrier service, the aircraft subsequently has served in the air arms of 10 nations. The aircraft is flown from most US Navy aircraft carriers and the surviving British aircraft carrier *Ark Royal*. The Phantom is scheduled for replacement in the US Navy and Marine Corps by the F-14 Tomcat and F-18, and in the US Air Force by the F-15 Eagle and the F-16 Air Combat Fighter (ACF).

The Phantom is a twin-engine, swept-wing fighter with box-like "cheek" air intakes. The aircraft has a large nose radar housing with a distinctive infra-red sensor fitted in a pod directly beneath the radar. Four air-to-air missiles can be carried semi-recessed under the fuselage with various combinations of external ordnance on six multiple wing pylons plus two fuselage attachment points (when the semi-recessed AAM positions are not used); maximum external payload is approximately 12,000 lb (5,450 kg) (i.e., 24 × 500-lb bombs in three-bomb clusters have been carried in tests). Only the F-4E has an internal cannon. Some F-4C and F-4D in US Air Force modified to "Wild Weasel" electronic jamming configuration. Wings fold on navalized variants for carrier operation.

Status: *Operational.* First flight May 27, 1958; squadron delivery in July 1961; approximately 5,000 aircraft produced by McDonnell Douglas and under licence in Japan by Mitsubishi.

SPECIFICATIONS (F-4J)

Crew: 2 (1 pilot, 1 radar intercept officer [RIO])

Engines: 2 GE J/79-GE-10 turbojets (17,900 lb, 18,127 kg st each with afterburning)

Dimensions: span 38 ft 5 in (11·71 m), length 58 ft 3 in (17·76 m), height 16 ft 3 in (4·96 m), wing area 530 sq ft (49·2 m²)

Speed: 1,450 mph (2,333 km/hr) at 36,000 ft (11,000 m) (Mach 2·2)

Ceiling: 71,000 ft (21,655 m)

Range: approx 900-mile (1,510 km) combat radius with AAMs; approx 1,000-mile (1,610 km) combat radius in ground attack configuration: 2,300-mile ferry range

Weights: 28,000 lb (12,710 kg) empty; 46,000 lb (20,885 kg) loaded clean; 54,600 lb (24,788 kg) maximum

Armament: 4 × Sidewinder AIM-9 AAMs and 4 × Sparrow III AIM-7 AAMs
or 6 × Sparrow III AIM-7 AAMs plus 18 × 750-lb bombs
or 11 × 1,000-lb bombs
or 4 × Bullpup AGM-12 ASMs

VARIANTS

F-4A formerly F4H-1F; initial Phantom II with J79-GE-2/2A engines; 23 preproduction and 24 production aircraft built.

TF-4A similar to F-4A but not carrier deployable nor combat capable.

F-4B formerly F4H-1; standard US Navy and Marine Corps fighter with J79-GE-8 engines; DF-4B modified for drone control and QF-4B as target drone.

QF-4B target drone configuration; 44 converted for use as supersonic target by Navy.

RF-4B unarmed photographic and electronic reconnaissance aircraft flown by US Marine Corps; J79-GE-15 engines; length 62 ft 10 in (19·15 m).

F-4C formerly F-110A; US Air Force version of F-4B with dual controls, heavier landing gear; first flight May 27, 1963; 583 built through 1966 for US Air Force plus 36 flown by Spanish Air Force.

RF-4C formerly RF-110A; multi-sensor reconnaissance aircraft flown by US Air Force; length 62 ft 10 in (19·17 m); fitted with cameras, forward-looking radar, and side-looking radar; first flight (YRF,4C) on August 9, 1963; 505 built.

F-4D similar to F-4C with improved avionics for ground attack for US Air Force; 843 built including 32 for Iran and 18 for South Korea.

F-4E similar to F-4D with improved intercept capability for US Air Force; J79-GE-17 engines; length 63 ft (19·22 m); fitted with internal 20-mm M61A1 multi-barrel cannon (640 rpg); flown by USAF, Australia, Greece, Iran, Israel, Japan, and Turkey.

F-4EF single-seat variant proposed for export to West Germany.

F-4EJ Mitsubishi-produced variant configured for Japanese air defence; 158 built.

RF-4E reconnaissance variant of F-4E flown by Israel and West Germany.

F-4F F-4E configured for West Germany with J79-GE-17 engines; leading edge wing slats; modified avionics; 175 being built.

F-4G F-4B fitted with data link; reduced fuel capacity; first flight March 20, 1963; 12 built for US Navy; most modified to standard F-4B configuration.

F-4J improved long-range aircraft for US Navy and Marine Corps; first flight May 27, 1966; 518 built through 1971.

F-4K/FG.1 carrier-based version for Royal Navy with Rolls-Royce RB.168-25R Spey turbofans; 52 built.

F-4M/FGR.2 similar to F-4K/FG.1 for Royal Air Force; modified electronics and communications; provision for reconnaissance pod; 118 built through 1970.

F-4N updated F-4B for US Navy; 178 aircraft modified.

F-4S updated F-4B for US Marine Corps.

F-4VG proposed variable-geometry variant intended as alternative to F-111B advanced carrier fighter.

F-4X proposed variable-geometry variant for US Air Force air defence mission.

OPERATIONAL

West Germany, Great Britain (RAF, Navy) Greece, Iran, Israel, Japan, South Korea, Spain, Turkey, United States (Air Force, Navy, Marine Corps)

F-4J Phantom of the US Navy carrying six AIM-7 Sparrow AAMs (US Navy)

F-4F Phantom of the German Air Force (Bundesminesterium der Verteidigung)

Sabre F-86 North American

The Sabre was the first operational US Air Force swept-wing fighter and the primary US and NATO fighter during the latter 1950s. The aircraft remains in limited service with a score of nations. The Sabre is a single-seat, single-engine fighter evolved from the Navy's straight-wing FJ-1 Fury. The aircraft was adopted by the Air Force in a swept-wing configuration. The US Navy also flew the swept-wing aircraft in the FJ-2 and later Fury variants as a carrier-based light attack aircraft.

The Sabre has been flown in a number of variants with certain models being optimized for air superiority, all-weather interception, ground attack, carrier operations, and even tactical nuclear strike. Approximately 4,400 produced by North American Aviation and 1,815 produced by Canadair, plus 68 built in Australia. This was the largest production of any Western combat aircraft after the Second World War. The Navy XFJ-1 Fury first flew in November 1946; three prototypes and 30 production FJ-1s were built. The Navy later took delivery of 200 FJ-2 (basic F-86E) for the Navy and Marine Corps followed by 149 FJ-3s and 222 FJ-4s (included in above North American totals). The surviving Furies were redesignated F-1 in 1962. CL-13 is the Canadair company designation for the Sabre and CA-27 for Australia's Commonwealth Aircraft Corp.

Status: *Operational.* First flight October 1, 1947 (XP-86); squadron delivery early 1949.

SPECIFICATIONS (F-86F)

Crew: 1

Engine: 1 General Electric J47-GE-27 turbojet (5,970 lb, 2708 kg st)

Dimensions: span 39 ft 1 in (11.91 m), length 37 ft 6½ in (11·44 m), height 14 ft 8 in (4·48 m)

Max level speed: 687 mph (1,105 km/hr) at sea level (Mach 0·9); 600 mph (965 km/hr) at 36,000 ft (11,000 m) (Mach 0·9)

Ceiling: 49,600 ft (15,130 m)

Range: combat radius 460 miles (740 km; ferry range 1,525 miles (2,454 km)

Weight: 20,610 lb (9,350 kg) maximum loaded

Armament: 6 × ·50-cal M3 machine-guns (267 rpg) and 2 × Sidewinder AIM-9 AAMs.

or 2 × 1,000-lb bombs

or 8 × 5-inch rockets (wing pylons)

VARIANTS

XP-86 experimental aircraft initially fitted with J35-C-3 engine; 3 built.

F-86A-1 formerly P-86A; initial production version with J47-GE-1 engine; first flight on May 20, 1948; 33 built.

F-86A formerly P-86B; production aircraft initially fitted with J47-GE-3 and later J47-GE-13 engine; 521 built through 1950.

F-86C originally YF-93A; proposed bomber escort fighter; 2 built.

F-86D originally F-95; all weather fighter with J47-GE-17/17B/33 engine with afterburner; armed with guns and rocket packs; first flight December 22, 1949; 2,504 built through 1955; flown by US Air Force, Denmark, Greece, Japan, South Korea, Philippines, Taiwan, Turkey, Yugoslavia.

F-86E similar to F-86A with movable horizontal tail surface; J47-GE-13 engine; first flight on September 23, 1950; 336 built through 1952 including 60 F-86E(M) by Canadair; flown by US Air Force, Greece, Italy, Turkey, Yugoslavia.

F-86F multi-purpose aircraft; first flown March 19, 1952; 1,539 built through 1956 with some assembled by Mitsubishi; flown by US Air Force, Japan, South Korea, Norway, Pakistan, Peru, Philippines, Portugal, Spain, Taiwan, Thailand, Venezuela.

RF-86F photographic reconnaissance variant; 16 converted from F-86F by Mitsubishi in 1961; 6 flown by Japan, 10 by South Korea.

TF-86F two-seat trainer; 2 built.

F-86H fighter-bomber variant, with J79-GE-3/30 engine; 60 armed with 4 × 20-mm cannon; 473 built for US Air Force.

F-86J test aircraft with Avro Orenda engine; 1 built.

F-86K all-weather interceptor with J47-GE-17B engine; armed with 4 × 20-mm cannon and 2 × Sidewinder AAMs; 2 converted from F-86D; North American built 120 for the Netherlands (later to Turkey); Fiat assembled 211 for Italy (later to France and West Germany).

F-86L improved avionics including data link for bomber defence role; 981 converted from F-86D; flown by US Air Force, Thailand.

CA-27 Australian-built variants; first flight July 13, 1954; 68 built for Royal Australian Air Force.

CL-13A Sabre Mk. 5 of the Canadian Armed Forces (Canadair)

CL-13 Canadian-built variants: Mk 1 was F-86A assembled and flown at Canadair; Mk 2 with J-47 engine (350 built); Mk 3 was prototype Mk 4 with Orenda 10 engine (1 built); Mk 4 with Orenda 10 engine and modified electronics (438 built); CL-13A Mk 5 with Orenda 10 engine and extended wing leading edge (370 built); CL-13B Mk 6 with Orenda 14 engine and 40 ft 1 in span (655 built); first flight August 9, 1950; produced through 1958; flown by US Air Force, Canada, Colombia, West Germany, Great Britain, Italy, South Africa, Yugoslavia.

OPERATIONAL

Bangladesh, Burma, Colombia, Ethiopia, Japan, South Korea, Malaysia, Pakistan, Peru, Philippines, Saudi Arabia, South Africa, Taiwan, Thailand, Tunisia, Turkey, Venezuela, Yugoslavia

Sea Hawk Hawker

Sea Hawk FGA.6 of the Indian Navy

The Sea Hawk is a single-seat, straight-wing, turbojet fighter developed for operation from British aircraft carriers. During the mid-1950s the Sea Hawk was the most numerous aircraft in the Fleet Air Arm (FAA), being employed in the fighter and ground attack roles, and seeing combat in the November 1956 invasion of Suez. The Sea Hawk remains in service with the Indian Navy, being flown in the Mk.50 variant from the light aircraft carrier *Vikrant*

and from ashore. The Indian Navy is seeking a replacement with the McDonnell-Douglas A-4 Skyhawk and Hawker-Siddeley AV-8 Harrier being the principal candidates. (The last FAA squadron flying Sea Hawks disbanded in December 1960; the aircraft also was flown in squadron strength by the Dutch and West German navies.)

The basic Sea Hawk design was developed from the first Hawker jet fighter, the P.1040. Most Sea Hawks, however, were built by Armstrong Whitworth. The aircraft has a single turbojet engine with the intakes in the wing roots; the bubble-type canopy is located completely forward of the wings, and the horizontal tail surfaces are mounted midway on the relatively small tail fin with an "acorn" fairing at their junction. The carrier arresting hook protrudes beyond the tail when in the retracted position and the wings fold upward for carrier operation.

Status: *Operational.* First flight November 1951; squadron delivery in March 1953.

SPECIFICATIONS (FGA.6/Mk.50)

Crew: 1

Engine: 1 Rolls-Royce Nene 103 turbojet (5,400 lb, 2,450 kg st)

Dimensions: span 39 ft (11·90 m), length 39 ft 8 in (12·10 m), height 8 ft 8 in (2·64 m), wing area 278 sq ft (28·85 m²)

Speed: 600 mph (965 km/hr) at sea level clean; 530 mph (853 km/hr) at 40,000 ft (12,200 m) clean; 524 mph (843 km/hr) at 10,000 ft (3,050 m)

with 2 × 500-lb bombs and external fuel

Ceiling: 44,500 ft (13,572 m)

Range: 288-mile (463 km) radius with external stores

Weights: 13,200 lb (5,992 kg) loaded clean; 16,000 + lb (7,264 kg) loaded

Armament: 4 × 20-mm cannon and 2 × 500-lb bombs plus 10 × rockets (wing pylons)

VARIANTS

P.1040 prototype with Rolls-Royce Nene 1 engine; span 36 ft 6 in (11·13 m).

N.7/46 prototype built to Royal Navy specification with Rolls-Royce Nene II engine; span 36 ft 6 in (11·13 m).

F.1 initial production aircraft with Rolls-Royce Nene RN.4 (Mk.101) engine; 35 built by Hawker and 60 by Armstrong Whitworth.

F.2 similar to F.1 with power-boosted ailerons; 40 built by Armstrong Whitworth.

FB.3 similar to F.1 with strengthened wings for fighter-bomber role; 116 built by Armstrong Whitworth; subsequently re-engined with Rolls-Royce Nene RN.4 (Mk.103) as FB.5.

FGA.4 similar to F.1 configured for close support role; 97 built by Armstrong Whitworth.

FGA.6 similar to F.1 with Rolls-Royce Nene RN.4 (Mk.103); 86 built by Armstrong Whitworth for FAA plus 30 built for Holland (Mk.50), 64 for West Germany (Mk.100 and 101); approximately 35 subsequently transferred to India.

OPERATIONAL

India

Shenyang F-9

The Shenyang F-9 is a large, Chinese-built fighter derived from the MiG-19/F-6 aircraft. The F-9 is a twin-engine aircraft with air intakes in the wing roots and a rose radome. The aircraft may have a nuclear weapons delivery capability in the ground support role.

Status: *Development—possibly operational.* First flight in early 1970s.

SPECIFICATIONS

Crew: 1
Engines: 2 turbojets with afterburners
Dimensions: span 33 ft 5 in (10·20 m), length 50 ft (15·25 m)

Speed: Mach 2
Weight: 22,050 lb (10,000 kg) loaded
Armament: air-to-air and air-to-surface weapons

OPERATIONAL

China

Super Étendard Dassault

The Super Étendard is being developed as a carrier-based fighter and strike aircraft for service aboard the French aircraft carriers *Clémenceau* and *Foch*. The Super Étendard has a superficial resemblance to the Étendard which it will replace. This is the only non-V/STOL carrier aircraft now under development outside of the United States.

With a swept-wing configuration, the single-seat Super Étendard will be a transonic aircraft. Two internal guns will be fitted and external stores will be carried on four wing pylons. Provision for in-flight refuelling and folding outer wing panels for carrier operation.

Status: *Development.* First flight in 1976 and squadron delivery in 1977–1978.

SPECIFICATIONS

Crew: 1
Engine: 1 SNECMA Atar 8K-50 turbojet (no afterburner)
Dimensions: span 31 ft 6 in (9·60 m), length 46 ft 11½ in (14·31 m), height 12 ft 8 in (3·85 m), wing area 305¾ ft (28·4 m²)
Speed: Mach 1 at 36,000 ft (11,000 m)

Range: combat radius more than 400 miles (650 km)
Weights: 13,780 lb (6,250 kg) empty; approx 25,000 lb (11,350 kg) maximum
Armament: 2 × 30-mm cannon and bombs, rockets, missiles (wing pylons)

*Super Étendard
under develop-
ment for the French
Navy (Dassault)*

Starfighter F-104 Lockheed

Conceived as a day fighter-interceptor, this single-seat, single-engine aircraft has a unique configuration among American-developed fighters and has evolved into a widely used and versatile aircraft. The Starfighter's design emphasizes flight performance at the expense of range and all-weather capability; these features plus engine problems and other troubles made the aircraft relatively unpopular and it served as a first-line fighter-interceptor with the US Air Force only from 1958 to 1960. Subsequently, the aircraft underwent a design metamorphosis that has made it one of the most popular aircraft in Western air forces.

The Starfighter has a long, needle-nose fuselage, exceptionally small anhedralled trapezoidal wings, and a small T-shape tail. The engine intakes are mounted well aft of the cockpit but still forward of the wing leading edges and feature small half cones in the intake openings. An internal, rapid-fire cannon is fitted and various weapons can be carried on fuselage and wing pylons; drop tanks or Sidewinder AAMs can be fitted on the wingtips. In addition to Lockheed production, Starfighters have been built under licence by Canadair, Fiat, Arge Sud, Arge Nord, SABCA and Avions Fairey, and Mitsubishi.

Status: *Operational.* First flight February 7, 1954; squadron delivery in January 1958; more than 2,400 built by all manufacturers.

*F-104G Star-
fighters of the
German Air
Force (Bundes-
minesterium der
Verteidigung)*

SPECIFICATIONS (F-104G)

Crew: 1

Engine: 1 GE J79-GE-11A turbojet
(10,000 lb, 4,540 kg st dry; 15,800
lb, 7,165 kg st with afterburner)

Dimensions: span 21 ft 11 in (6·68
m), length 54 ft 9 in (16·69 m),
height 13 ft 6 in (4·11 m), wing area
196 sq ft (18·22 m²)

Speed: 1,450 mph (2,338 km/hr) at
36,000 ft (11,000 m) (Mach 2.35)

Ceiling: 58,000 ft (17,680 m)

Range: combat radius 745 miles (1,200
m)

Weights: 14,088 lb (6,387 kg) empty;
28,779 lb (13,054 kg) maximum

Armament: 1 × 20-mm M61 Vulcan
rotary cannon and 4 × Sidewinder
AIM-9 AAMs

or 2 × Bullpup AGM-12 ASMs

or 2 × 1,000-lb bombs and 1   2,000-lb
bomb

VARIANTS

XF-104 prototype with J79-W-6
engine; 2 built.

YF-104A preproduction aircraft with
J79-GE-3 engine; 17 built.

F-104A day interceptor aircraft with
J79-GE-3A engine; first flight February
17, 1956; 153 built for US Air Force;
subsequently transferred to Jordan,
Pakistan, Taiwan.

NF-104A F-104A fitted with AR-2
auxiliary rocket (6,000-lb, 2,725 kg st)
for training; 3 converted from F-104A.

QF-104A formerly ZQF-104A; target
drone; 24 converted from F-104A.

F-104B two-seat trainer; same
dimensions and engine as F-104A; first

flight February 7, 1957; 26 built for US
Air Force; subsequently transferred to
Jordan, Pakistan.

F-104C fighter-bomber variant with
J79-GE-7 engine; fixed flight refuelling
probe; 77 built.

F-104D two-seat trainer variant of
F-104C; cannon deleted; 22 built for
US Air Force, 38 for Canada (CF-113
later CF-104D), 30 for West Germany
(F-104F), 1 for Japan (F-104DJ) plus
19 assembled by Mitsubishi for Japan
(F-104DJ); some CF-104D transferred
to Denmark and upgraded to F-104G
standard.

F-104G multi-mission aircraft also known as Super Starfighter; fitted with NASAAR F-15A-41B radar system; first flight October 5, 1960; 180 built by Lockheed, 110 by Canadair, and 977 by consortiums of Belgian, Dutch, German, and Italian companies; flown by Belgium (100), Denmark, West Germany (750), Greece, Italy (155), Netherlands (130), Norway, Spain, Taiwan, Turkey. Some German aircraft were fitted as RF-104G reconnaissance aircraft.

TF-104G two-seat variant with cannon deleted; first flight in October 1962; 180 built including some as RTF-104G fitted with cameras and side-looking radar; flown by Belgium, Denmark, West Germany, Italy, Netherlands.

F-104J F-104G for Japanese Air Self-Defence Force; first flight June 30, 1961; Lockheed built 3 and Mitsubishi assembled 207 including 20 two-seat TF-104J.

F-104N aircraft modified for astronaut proficiency training (US National Aeronautics and Space Administration).

F-104S all-weather interceptor aircraft with J79-GE-17 engine; fitted with 2 × AIM-7 Sparrow AAMs in addition to 2 × AIM-9 Sidewinder AAMs; Aeritalia built 205 F-104S for Italy plus 36 for Turkey.

CF-111 single-seat strike/reconnaissance variant of F-104G with improved fire control and navigation system, 4 cameras; cannon deleted; first flight May 26, 1961; Canadair built 200 for Canada (Canadair designation is CL-90 and US designation CF-104A).

CL-901 Lockheed proposal for improved F-104 with J79-GE-17 engine providing Mach 2·4 speed; provision for AIM-7 Sparrow AAM; variations include CL-981, CL-984, CL-1010.

CL-1200 Lockheed proposal for an advanced Starfighter (named Lancer) for foreign transfer; CL-1200-1 powered by J79-GE-19 and CL-1200-2 by P & W TF30-P-100 engine.

F-104J Star-fighter of the Japanese Air Self Defence Force (Lockheed)

OPERATIONAL

Belgium, Canada, Denmark, West Germany, Greece, Italy, Japan, Jordan, Netherlands, Norway, Pakistan, Spain, Taiwan, Turkey, United States (Air National Guard)

Super Mystère Dassault

The Super Mystère is a single-seat, swept-wing interceptor with a limited attack capability. The aircraft, derived from the Mystère IV-B, was the first aircraft to reach production status in Western Europe that could attain supersonic speeds in level flight. Procurement was cut back because of the development of the Mirage III; flown only by France and Israel.

The aircraft has a superficial resemblance to the larger F-100 Super Sabre because of the "flattened" fuselage, oval engine intake, and low, swept-wing configuration. Internal cannon are fitted and external stores are carried on two wing pylons; a fuselage rocket pack is also provided.

Status: *Operational.* First flight March 2, 1955; squadron delivery in 1957; approximately 190 built.

SPECIFICATIONS (B.2)

Crew: 1

Engine: 1 SNECMA Atar 101G turbojet (9,700 lb, 4,400 kg st with afterburning)

Dimensions: span 34 ft 5¾ in (10·51 m), length 46 ft 1 in (14·04 m), height 14 ft 10¾ in (4·51 m), wing area 377 sq ft (35·06 m²)

Speed: 743 mph (1,195 km/hr) at 36,000 ft (11,000 m) (Mach 1·125)

Ceiling: 55,775 ft (17,000 m)

Range: tactical radius 270 miles (435 km) clean; range 730 miles (1,175 km) with external fuel tanks

Weights: 15,400 lb (6,992 kg) empty; 19,840 lb (9,007 kg) loaded; 22,046 lb (10,000 kg) maximum

Armament: 2 × 30-mm DEFA cannon, 35 × 68-mm rockets (fuselage pack) and 2 × 1,100-lb bombs (wing pylons)

VARIANTS

B.1 prototype aircraft with Rolls-Royce Avon RA.7R engine.

B.2 pre-production aircraft; first flight May 15, 1956; 5 built.

B.2 production aircraft; first flight February 26, 1957; approx 180 built.

B.4 high-speed (Mach 1·4) test aircraft for SNECMA Atar 09 engine; 2 built.

OPERATIONAL

France, Israel

Super Mystère of the Israeli Defence Force (Stephen Peltz)

Super Sabre F-100 North American

The F-100 Super Sabre initiated the US Air Force "century series" fighter aircraft and was probably the world's first fighter fully capable of sustained supersonic performance. The single-seat, swept-wing aircraft served during the latter 1950s and the 1960s as a principal aircraft of the USAF Tactical Air Command and with several NATO air forces, and was employed extensively in the Vietnam War as a fighter bomber.

The single-engine Super Sabre was initiated early in 1949 as a re-design of the F-86 Sabre to produce a fighter with sustained supersonic speed in level flight. Subsequently produced in both single-seat and two-seat variants, the Super Sabre has performed as both a "heavy" fighter and as a ground-attack/strike aircraft with up to 7,500 lb (3,405 kg) of ordnance carried on six wing pylons in addition to internal cannon.

Status: *Operational.* First flight May 25, 1953; squadron delivery in 1954; 2,286 aircraft built.

SPECIFICATIONS (F-100D)

Crew: 1

Engine: 1 Pratt & Whitney J57-P-21A turbojet (11,700 lb, 5,310 kg st dry; 16,950 lb, 7,695 kg st with afterburner)

Dimensions: span 38 ft 9 in (16·54 m), length (over probe) 54 ft 3 in (16·54 m), height 16 ft $2\frac{2}{3}$ in (4·95 m), wing area 385 sq ft (35·81 m²)

Speed: 864 mph (1,390 km/hr) at 36,000 ft (11,000 m) (Mach 1·3); 810 mph (1,300 km/hr) at 8,000 ft (2,440 m) (Mach 1·1)

Ceiling: 50,000 + ft (15,250 m)

Range: combat radius (clean) 550 miles (885 km)

Weights: 21,000 lb (9,534 kg) empty; 29,762 lb (13,510 kg) normal load; 34,832 lb (15,814 kg) maximum

Armament: 4 × 20-mm M-39E cannon (200 rpg) and 4 × Sidewinder AIM-9 AAMs

or 6 × 1,000-lb bombs

or 2 × 1,000-lb bombs plus 2 × Bullpup AGM-12 ASMs (wing pylons)

VARIANTS

YF-100A prototype aircraft; 2 built.

F-100A first production aircraft with J57-P-7 engine (except J-57-P-39 in last 36 aircraft); first flight October 29, 1953; 203 built; 80 subsequently reconfigured to F-100D for Nationalist Chinese service.

F-100C fighter-bomber aircraft with J57-P-21 engine, six wing pylons, air-refuelling capabilities, improved radar, additional internal fuel; first flight January 17, 1955; 476 built; some

fitted as DF-100C for drone control.

F-100D similar to F-100C with autopilot; first flight January 24, 1956; 1,274 built.

F-100F two-seat derivative of F-100D with full combat capability except for deletion of 2 × 20-mm cannon; length 55 ft 3 in (16·85 m); 22,300 lb (10,125 kg) empty; 30,700 lb (13,938 kg) normal loaded; first flight March 7, 1957; 333 built.

OPERATIONAL

Denmark, France, Taiwan, Turkey, United States (Air National Guard)

*F-100 Super
Sabre of the US
Air Force (US
Air Force)*

Thunderchief F-105 Fairchild Republic

The F-105 Thunderchief was designed specifically as a tactical strike aircraft with an internal weapons bay for carrying nuclear weapons. The "Thud" was used extensively in the Vietnam War by the US Air Force as both a strike fighter carrying conventional ordnance and in the two-seat configuration as a "Wild Weasel" (F-105G) electronic jamming aircraft. The Thunderchief now serves only with USAF reserve units.

The Thunderchief is the world's largest and heaviest single-engine fighter. The single-seat, swept-wing aircraft can exceed Mach 2 in level flight and has a relatively large combat radius. When employed in the delivery of conventional weapons during the Vietnam War the internal bay was fitted with fuel tanks. Up to 12,000 lb (5,450 kg) of external ordnance and fuel can be carried on 17 pylons and attachment points.

Status: *Operational.* First flight October 22, 1955; squadron delivery May 1958; 831 aircraft built through 1965.

SPECIFICATIONS (F-105D)

Crew: 1

Engine: 1 Pratt & Whitney J75-P-19 turbojet (16,100 lb, 7,310 kg st dry; 24,500 lb, 11,125 kg st with afterburner)

Dimensions: span 34 ft $11\frac{1}{4}$ in (10·66 m), length 67 ft $\frac{1}{3}$ in (20·43 m), height 19 ft $8\frac{1}{3}$ in (6·01 m), wing area 385 sq ft (35·81 m²)

Speed: 1,390 mph (2,235 km/hr) at 36,000 ft (11,000 m) (Mach 2·1); 1,122 mph (1,805 km/hr) at 50,000 ft (15,250 m) (Mach 1·7); 855 mph (1,375 km/hr) at sea level (Mach 1·1)

Ceiling: 50,000 ft (15,250 m)

Range: 920-mile (1,480 km) tactical radius with 2 × Bullpup ASMs and external fuel; 230-mile (370 km) tactical radius with 16 × 750-lb bombs; 2,400-mile (3,860 km) ferry range

Weights: 28,000 lb (12,710 kg) empty; 38,034 lb (17,265 kg) loaded clean; 52,546 lb (23,855 kg)

maximum

Armament: 1 × 20-mm M-61 Vulcan rotary cannon (1,029 rpg) and 16 × 750-lb bombs
or 9 × 1,000-lb bombs
or 4 × Bullpup AGM-12 ASMs
or 3 × 3,000-lb bombs (plus centreline tank)

VARIANTS

YF-105A prototype aircraft with J57-P-25 engine; 2 built.

F-105B redesigned pre-production aircraft with J57-P-3/-5/-19 engines; first flight May 22, 1956; 75 built.

RF-105B reconnaissance variant with three nose-mounted cameras; redesignated JF-105B; 3 built.

F-105D all-weather aircraft; first flight June 9, 1959; 610 built with some modified to F-105G configuration.

F-105F two-seat derivative of the F-105D; length 69 ft 7 in (21·23 m),

height 20 ft 2 in (6·15 m); 40,073 lb (18,190 kg) normal loaded (clean); 54,027 lb (24,528 kg) maximum; first flight June 11, 1963; employed as "Wild Weasel" electronic jamming aircraft; 143 built.

F-105G two-seat missile suppression aircraft converted from F-105F; first flight August 7, 1967; normally armed with Shrike AGM-45 or Standard-ARM AGM-78 anti-radiation missiles (ARMs); 48 converted.

OPERATIONAL

United States (Air Force Reserve, Air National Guard)

F-105G Thunderchief flown by the US Air Force (Republic)

Thunderstreak F-84F Republic

The F-84F Thunderstreak is the swept-wing variant of the F-84 Thunderjet, the first post-Second World War fighter aircraft to enter production for the US Air Force. The F-84F and its RF-84F reconnaissance derivative are still flown by three NATO air forces although all F-84 variants have been phased out of US service.

   The Thunderstreak was conceived on the eve of the Korean War to increase the speed of the straight-wing F-84 fighter by fitting swept-back wings to the F-84E fuselage. The resulting YF-84F was not particularly successful, but after the Korean War began additional funding was available and with minor fuselage redesign and a more powerful engine the F-84F soon achieved acceptance as a first-line combat aircraft. Four machineguns are mounted in the fuselage and two in the wing roots; up to 6,000 lb (2,725 kg) of weapons and fuel can be carried externally. Now largely replaced in NATO air arms by the American-built F-5 Freedom Fighter and F-104 Starfighter, the remaining Thunderstreaks can be expected to be phased out by the end of 1976.

F-84F Thunder-
streak

Status: *Operational.* First flight June 3, 1950 (YF-84F); squadron delivery in December 1952; 3,428 F-84F/RF-84F built through 1957.

SPECIFICATIONS (F-84F)

Crew: 1

Engine: 1 Wright J65-W-3 turbojet (7,220 lb, 3,278 kg st)

Dimensions: span 33 ft $7\frac{1}{4}$ in (10·26 m), length 43 ft $4\frac{3}{4}$ in (13·21 m), height 14 ft $4\frac{3}{4}$ in (4·36 m), wing area 325 sq ft (30·32 m²)

Speed: 695 mph (1,118 km/hr) at sea level clean (Mach 0·91); 658 mph (1,058 km/hr) at 20,000 ft (6,100 m) (Mach 0·94)

Ceiling: 46,000 ft (14,030 m)

Range: combat radius 450 miles (725 km) clean; combat radius with external tanks 800 miles (1,285 km); ferry range 2,140 miles (3,443 km)

Weights: 19,340 lb (8,780 kg) loaded clean; 26,000 lb (11,800 kg) loaded; 28,000 lb (12,710 kg) maximum

Armament: 6 × ·50-calibre M-3 machineguns and 2 × 1,000 lb bombs plus 8 × 5-inch rockets (wing pylons) and centreline fuel tanks

VARIANTS

YF-84F prototype aircraft originally designated YF-96A; 1 with J35-A-29 engine and 1 with J65-W-1 engine and other modifications.

F-84F production fighter initially with J65-W-1 engine and subsequently J65-W-3; 2,711 built with 1,301 ordered specifically for Belgium, France, Greece, Italy, Netherlands, West Germany, and Turkey.

RF-84F Thunderflash reconnaissance variant initially with J65-W-3 engine and subsequently J65-W-7 engine; six cameras in nose bay; length 47 ft 6 in (14·49 m); 4 × ·50-cal MG retained; 715 built; flown by USAF, Belgium, Denmark, France, West Germany, Greece, Italy, Norway, Taiwan, and Turkey.

F-84G straight-wing aircraft similar to F-84E.

YF-84J prototype Super Thunderstreak with J73-GE-7 engine; first flight May 7, 1954; 2 built.

OPERATIONAL

Greece, Portugal, Turkey

Tiger II F-5E/F Northrop

The F-5E Tiger II is a lightweight, supersonic aircraft developed as an inexpensive, easily maintained fighter capable of operating from rough airfields. The US Air Force expects that over 1,000 F-5E and two-seat F-5F aircraft will be procured for other air forces with a limited number retained by the USAF and US Navy for training, including the simulation of high-performance MiG fighters. A total of 476 F-5E/F aircraft have been ordered through Fiscal Year 1975.

The Tiger II was the winner of a 1970 US government fighter competition for an international fighter aircraft. The design was a follow-on to Northrop's highly successful F-5A/B Freedom Fighter with an advanced engine, modified flaps to increase manoeuvrability, extension of wing leading edges,

*F-5E Tiger II
flown by US Navy
(US Navy)*

and a wider fuselage. Nose cannon are fitted, up to 7,000 lb (3,178 kg) of weapons and fuel can be carried on one fuselage and four wing pylons, and two Sidewinders on the wingtips. The designation suffix "II" was added to the name Tiger to avoid possible confusion with the now-discarded US Navy F11F/F-11 Tiger. Being built under licence by the Aero Industry Development Centre in Taiwan.

Status: *Operational.* First flight 11 August 1972; squadron delivery early 1973.

SPECIFICATIONS (F-5E)

Crew: 1 (2 in F-5F)
Engines: 2 General Electric J85-GE-21 turbojets (5,000 lb, 2,270 kg st each)
Dimensions: span 26 ft 8 in (8·13 m), length 48 ft $3\frac{3}{4}$ in (14·73 m), height 13 ft $4\frac{1}{2}$ in (4·08 m), wing area 186 sq ft (17·3 m²)
Max level speed: Mach 1·6 at 36,000 ft (11,000 m)
Ceiling: 54,000 ft (16,460 m)
Range: radius with 2 × Sidewinder AAMs 875 miles (1,405 km); radius with near maximum payload 190 miles (305 km)
Weights: 9,588 lb (4,349 kg) empty; 24,080 lb (10,922 kg) maximum
Armament: 2 × 20-mm M39A2 cannon (280 rpg) and 2 × Sidewinder AIM-9 AAMs (on wingtips) up to 7,000 lb of bombs, rockets, missiles (fuselage and wing pylons)

VARIANTS

F-5E standard light tactical fighter.
RF-5E photo-reconnaissance aircraft with four KS-121 cameras in nose.
F-5F two-seat combat/trainer aircraft; length 51 ft 9 in (15·78 m); max speed Mach 1·54; only 1 × 2-mm gun; first flight September 23, 1974.

OPERATIONAL

Brazil, Chile, Greece, Iran, Jordan, South Korea, Malaysia, Morocco, Peru, Philippines, Saudi Arabia, Switzerland, Thailand, United States (Air Force, Navy), Venezuela

Tomcat F-14 Grumman

The F-14 Tomcat is an advanced carrier-based fighter featuring a very high degree of manoeuvrability and a long-range missile system. The two-seat, two-engine aircraft was developed as a replacement for the F-4 Phantom II as the US Navy's standard shipboard fighter. However, budget reductions restrict Navy acquisition to only 18 squadrons with the remaining six carrier fighter squadrons planned for the 1980s to fly the F-18. Planned US procurement is 390 aircraft through 1981. The US Marine Corps decided in mid-1975 to acquire the F-18 in place of the F-14.

The Tomcat's high manoeuvrability is achieved by a variable-geometry wing that operates automatically through an on-board computer to provide the optimum wing sweep as the plane manoeuvres. The TF30 engines and AWG-9/Phoenix weapons system are adapted from the cancelled Navy F-111B variant of the F-111/TFX fighter programme. The Hughes AWG-9 can simultaneously track up to 24 targets and guide up to six Phoenix AAMs to targets more than 50 miles (80 km) from the aircraft. An internal cannon is fitted; four Sidewinder AAMs can be mounted on wing pylons under the fixed portion of the wings and up to 6 × Phoenix AAMs or other weapons can be carried on pallets attached under the fuselage (or 4 × Sparrow AAMs can be carried in place of the pallets).

Status: *Operational.* First flight December 21, 1970; squadron delivery in early 1973. Through Fiscal Year 1975 the US Navy had ordered 234 aircraft and 80 were on order for Iran.

F-14A Tomcat of the US Navy armed with AIM-54 Pheonix and AIM-9 Sidewinder AAMs (US Navy)

SPECIFICATIONS (F-14A)

Crew: 2

Engines: 2 Pratt & Whitney TF30-P-412A turbofan (20,900 lb, 9,480 kg st with afterburners)

Dimensions: span 64 ft 1½ in (19·54 m) extended, 38 ft 2 in (11·63 m) swept, length 61 ft 10½ in (18·86 m), height 16 ft (4·88 m)

Speed: Mach 2·34 at altitude

Ceiling: 60,000 ft (18,300 m)

Range: 2,000 + miles (3,218 km) clean (on internal fuel only)

Weights: 37,500 lb (17,025 kg) empty; 55,000 lb.(24,970 kg) normal take-off; 72,000 lb (32,688 kg) maximum

Armament: 1 × 20-mm M61A1 Vulcan rotary cannon and 4 × Sidewinder AIM-9 AAMs (wing pylons) plus 4 × Sparrow AIM-7 AAMs (recessed in fuselage) or 6 × Phoenix AIM-54 AAMs (fuselage pallets)

VARIANTS

F-14A 12 research and development aircraft plus production aircraft.

F-14B similar to F-14A with P & W F401-PW-400 turbofan engine; first flight September 12, 1973.

F-14C proposed development of F-14B with improved avionics.

F-14D proposed stripped-down aircraft for carrier operation.

F-14X proposed full-capability aircraft except for deletion of Phoenix AAM weapon system.

F-14A Tomcat on the deck of USS Independence *(US Navy)*

OPERATIONAL

Iran, United States (Navy, Marine Corps)

Venom Mk1 of the Swiss Air Force (Alex Reinhard)

Venom de Havilland

The Venom is a single-seat, single-engine fighter developed from the earlier de Havilland Vampire. Formerly flown in large numbers by the Royal Air Force and Royal Navy (Sea Venom) and in lesser numbers by the French, Swiss, and Venezuelan air arms, only Switzerland currently operates Venom fighter bombers.

The Venom retains the twin booms of the Vampire but has a slightly swept wing. Manufactured in France and Switzerland as well as in Great Britain. Armed with four nose cannon with wing pylons for bombs and rockets.

Status: *Operational.* First flight September 1949; squadron delivery in 1952. Approximately 900 Venoms, Sea Venoms, and Aquilons produced.

SPECIFICATIONS

Crew: 1
Engine: 1 de Havilland Ghost 103 turbojet (4,850 lb, 2,200 kg st)
Dimensions: span 41 ft 9 in (12·73 m), length 32 ft 11 in (10·05 m), height 6 ft 2 in (1·88 m)
Max level speed: 640 mph (1,030 km/hr)

Ceiling: 37,000 ft (11,285 m)
Range: 1,000 + miles (1,610 km) with external tanks
Weights: 15,400 lb (6,990 kg) loaded
Armament: 4 × 20-mm Hispano 804 cannon and 2 × 1,000-lb bombs (wing pylons)

VARIANTS

FB.1/4 single-seat fighter aircraft; FB.50 was built under licence in Switzerland; over 350 built primarily for RAF.

NF.2/3 two-seat night fighter aircraft; 189 built.

F.(AW) 20/21/22 two-seat Sea Venom carrier-based aircraft for Royal Navy; F.(AW) 53 was export aircraft flown by Royal Australian Navy; 256 built.

Aquilon modified aircraft built under licence by SNCASE for French Navy carrier operation; first flight October 31, 1952; approx 115 built.

OPERATIONAL

Switzerland

Viggen SAAB-37 SAAB

The Viggen is a multi-mission combat aircraft developed to replace interceptor, attack, and reconnaissance aircraft now in service with the Swedish Air Force. The basic "System 37" aircraft will be produced in all-weather attack (AJ), interceptor (JA), armed reconnaissance (SF), maritime surveillance/attack (SH), and training (SK) variants.

The single-engine Viggen has a canard foreplane and a large, rear-mounted delta wing. Weapons are carried externally on three fuselage attachment points and four underwing hard points except in the interceptor variant (JA) which has instead an internal 30-mm Oerlikon cannon.

Status: *Operational.* First flight February 8, 1967.

SPECIFICATIONS (AJ37)

Saab 37 Viggen of the Swedish Air Force (SAAB)

Crew: 1
Engine: 1 Volvo Flygmotor RM8A turbofan (14,770 lb, 6,705 kg st dry; 26,000 lb, 11,800 kg st with afterburner)
Dimensions: span 34 ft $9\frac{1}{4}$ in (10·60 m), length 53 ft $5\frac{3}{4}$ in (16·30 m) (over nose probe), height 18 ft $4\frac{1}{2}$ in (5·60 m), wing area 495 sq ft (46 m²) (main wings)

Speed: Mach 2 at altitude
Ceiling: 60,000 ft (18,300 m)
Range: tactical radius with external stores 620 miles (1,000 km)
Weight: approx 35,275 lb (16,015 kg) normal loaded
Armament: various combinations of bombs, missiles, 30-mm Aden cannon pods, rockets

VARIANTS

SAAB-37 prototype aircraft; 6 single-seat and 1 two-seat SK-37 prototype built.

AJ 37 production all-weather attack aircraft with interceptor capabilities; first flight February 23, 1971.

JA 37 production fighter-interceptor with attack capabilities; internal 30-mm cannon; Volvo Flygmotor RM8B engine will be used in this variant; first flight of an AJ 37 modified to JA configuration and engine on September 27, 1974.

SF 37 armed photo reconnaissance aircraft; first flight May 21, 1973.

SH 37 maritime reconnaissance/strike aircraft.

SK 37 two-seat trainer; first flight July 1970.

OPERATIONAL

Sweden

Voodoo F-101 McDonnell

The F-101 Voodoo is a swept-wing aircraft originally planned as a long-range penetration fighter to escort strategic bombers. Subsequently developed as a defensive fighter to counter Soviet strategic bombers and as a tactical reconnaissance aircraft. The Voodoo is now flown in the air defence role by the United States and Canada, with the US Air National Guard squadrons phasing out the aircraft, and in the reconnaissance role by Taiwan.

The Voodoo is a twin-engine aircraft with the fighter-interceptor variants being two-seat aircraft and the photo-reconnaissance variants being single seat. The low-slung engine intakes are in the wing roots, well back from the cockpit, with the engine exhaust well forward of the tail structure. Designed with four internal 20-mm cannon, the F-101A production aircraft had one gun deleted to provide space for additional electronic equipment; the F-101A also had two retractable packs holding a total of 12 × 2·75-inch spin-stabilized rockets, and carried three Falcon air-to-air missiles in a rotary weapons bay.

Status: *Operational.* First flight September 29, 1954; squadron delivery May 1957. 808 aircraft produced.

SPECIFICATIONS (F-101B)

Crew: 2

Engines: 2 Pratt & Whitney J57-P-53/-55 turbojets (11,990 lb, 5,443 kg st each dry; 14,990 lb, 6,805 kg st with afterburner)

Dimensions: span 39 ft 8 in (12·09 m); length 67 ft 4¾ in (20·55 m); height 18 ft (5·49 m), wing area 368 sq ft (34·22 m²)

Speed: 1,220 mph (1,963 km/hr) at 40,000 ft (12,200 m) (Mach 1·85); 720 mph (1,158 km/hr) at sea level (Mach 0·95)

Ceiling: 52,000 ft (15,850 m)

CF-101B Voodoo of the Canadian Armed Forces (Canadian Forces)

Range: 1,550 miles (2,495 km)
Weights: 28,000 lb (12,710 kg) empty; 39,900 lb (18,115 kg) loaded; 46,673 lb (21,190 kg) maximum

Armament: 3 × Falcon AIM-4 AAMs or 3 × Falcon AIM-26 AAMs (weapons bay) plus 2 × Genie AIM-2 AAMs (fuselage points)

VARIANTS

XF-88 prototype strategic bomber escort with J34-WE-13 engines; first flight October 20, 1948; 2 built; project cancelled in August 1950.

F-101A revision of XF-88 design for tactical fighter-bomber role; J57-P-13 engines; 29 pre-production aircraft and 50 production aircraft built.

RF-101A reconnaissance version of F-101A with six cameras in place of armament; with J57-P-13 engine; length 69 ft 3 in (21·12 m); YRF-101A prototype first flight May 10, 1956; 35 built.

F-101B air defence interceptor; redesigned forward fuselage with pilot and radar observer in tandem seats; MG-13 fire-control system with missile bay for AAMs; first flight May 27, 1957; 478 built with some configured as TF-101B trainers; 56 F-101B and

10 TF-101B redesignated F-101F for modification/transfer.

F-101C basic F-101A aircraft strengthened for low-altitude bomber missions and in-flight refuelling; 47 built.

RF-101C improved RF-101A aircraft; first flight July 12, 1957; 165 built with 25 subsequently flown by Taiwan.

F-101F 56 F-101B and 10 TF-101B (TF-101F) with nuclear AIR-2A Genie AAMs capability and other modifications for transfer to Canada in 1961; designated CF-101B and CF-101F, respectively, in Canadian service.

RF-101G RF-101A modified for use by US Air National Guard.

RF-101H RF-101C modified for use by US Air National Guard.

OPERATIONAL

Canada, Taiwan, United States (Air National Guard)

Attack

A-10 Fairchild-Hiller

The A-10 is a close-support aircraft designed specifically for that mission and selected for US Air Force service after a competitive fly-off with the Northrop A-9A and LTV A-7D Corsair II. Initial production of 52 A-10 aircraft was approved in July 1974 with a total programme of 733 USAF aircraft currently envisioned with deliveries in 1975–1979. Two prototypes and six R & D aircraft have been built.

The A-10 is a straight-wing aircraft with the cockpit well forward of the wing, the armoured engine pods fixed on pylons on the after fuselage, and twin, widely separated tail fins. There is an internal, seven-barrel 30-mm Gau-8/A cannon firing at rates up to 4,200 rpm, and up to 16,000 lb (7,265 kg) of external stores are carried on one fuselage and 10 wing pylons. A fixed in-flight refuelling probe is fitted in the nose. A two-seat variant is envisioned.

Status: *In production.* First flight May 10, 1972.

SPECIFICATIONS (YA-10)

Crew: 1
Engines: 2 General Electric TF34-GE-100 high bypass ratio turbofans (9,065 lb, 4,115 kg st each)
Dimensions: span 55 ft (16·78 m), length 53 ft 4 in (16·27 m) (over probe), height 14 ft 8½ in (4·5 m), wing area 488 sq ft (45·38 m²)
Speed: 449 mph (722 km/hr) at sea level clean; 443 mph (713 km/hr) at 5,000 ft (1,525 m) with 6 × 500-lb bombs
Ceiling: 20,000 + ft (6,100 m)
Range: 290-mile (465 km) radius with

A-10 of the US Air Force, armed with AGM-65 Maverick ASMs (Fairchild Republic)

9,500 lb (4,315 kg) weapons with 2 hour loiter; 467-mile (750 km) radius in reconnaissance role; 2,650-mile (4,265 km) ferry range
Weights: 18,783 lb (8,527 kg) empty; 44,547 lb (20,225 kg) maximum
Armament: 1 × 30-mm General Electric GAU-8/A rapid-fire cannon (1,350 rpg) and 24 × 500-lb bombs or 16 × 750-lb bombs or 4 × 2,000-lb bombs or 9 × Maverick AGM-65 ASMs plus 2 × Sidewinder AIM-9 AAMs (fuselage and wing pylons)

VARIANTS

YA-10 prototype aircraft; 2 built.
A-10A R & D and production aircraft; span 57 ft 2 in (17·43 m); weight reduced from YA-10.

OPERATIONAL

United States (Air Force)

Advanced Harrier AV-16
Hawker Siddeley/McDonnell Douglas

The Advanced Harrier is an Anglo-American effort to develop an advanced vertical and short take-off and landing (V/STOL) attack aircraft. It would replace the existing Harrier in Royal Air Force service and the A-4 Skyhawk in US Marine Corps service; in addition, the Advanced Harrier could be flown from US and Royal Navy ships.

The Advanced Harrier would be a development of the existing Hawker Siddeley Harrier, retaining some of the present aircraft's features. An under-fuselage gun could be fitted and four or six wing pylons could be provided. The proposed variants are listed below by user.

Status: *Proposal.*

Artist's impression of the AV-16 Advanced Harrier

SPECIFICATIONS (tentative)

Crew: 1
Engine: 1 Rolls-Royce Pegasus 15 turbofan (24,500 lb, 11,125 kg st)
Dimensions: span 30 ft 3½ in (9·23 m), length 46 ft 6 in (14·18 m), height 12 ft (3·66 m), wing area 230 sq ft (21·39 m²)
Speed: 720 mph (1,158 km/hr)
Range: 345-mile (555 km) radius with vertical take-off and 2,000-lb (910 kg) payload; 345-mile (555 km) radius with short take-off and 4,000-lb (1,820 kg) payload
Weights: 21,100 lb (9,580 kg) maximum vertical take-off; 28,000 lb (12,710 kg) maximum
Armament: see variants

VARIANTS

USMC integrated weapons delivery system (IWDS); 20-mm cannon under fuselage; 4 wing pylons.
RAF undernose sensor; 30-mm Aden cannon; 6 wing pylons.
RN/USN fitted for Sidewinder AIM-9 or Sparrow AIM-7 AAMs plus ASMs; for shipboard operation.

Alpha Jet Dassault-Breguet/Dornier

The Alpha Jet is a subsonic trainer developed jointly by France and Germany for their armed forces. The two-seat, twin-turbofan aircraft was designed from the outset to have the dual capability of close support and battlefield reconnaissance to meet German military requirements. Four prototypes have been built and an estimated 200 aircraft will be produced for each nation.

The Alpha Jet has a high, swept wing design with the engines mounted in large nacelles faired into the fuselage under the wings. Various gun combinations can be carried in pods attached to the lower fuselage and four wing pylons can be fitted for a total of 4,850 lb (2,200 kg) of weapons on the five stations.

Status: *Development.* First flight October 26, 1973; squadron delivery late in 1976.

SPECIFICATIONS

Crew: 2
Engines: 2 SNECMA/Turboméca Larzac 04 turbofans (2,976 lb, 1,350 kg st each)
Dimensions: span 29 ft 11 in (9·12 m), length 40 ft 3¾ in (12·29 m), height 13 ft 9 in (4·19 m), wing area 188½ sq ft (17·53 m²)
Max level speed: Mach 0·85 at high altitude
Ceiling: 49,200 ft (15,000 m)
Range: 1,240 miles (2,000 km) ferry range
Weights: 6,944 lb (3,150 kg) empty; 9,920 lb (4,500 kg) normal; 15,432 lb (7,000 kg) maximum
Armament: 1 × 30-mm DEFA cannon or 1 × 27-mm Mauser cannon or 2 × 0·50-cal machineguns (250 rpg) (fuselage pod) and various combinations of bombs and rockets (wing pylons)

Two views of the Franco-German Alpha jet in German Air Force markings (Dassault)

Beagle Il-28 Ilyushin

The Il-28 *Beagle* was the first jet-propelled bomber to be mass produced in the Soviet Union and, although the basic aircraft has been operational for 25 years, continues to be flown in large numbers by the Soviet Union and a number of other nations. Although a light bomber, the Beagle was considered a strategic offensive weapon when the Soviets transported several to Cuba in October 1962, helping to precipitate the Cuban missile crisis. The aircraft is flown in light bomber, tactical reconnaissance, anti-ship torpedo, training, and target-tow roles.

The Il-28 has a simple design with straight wings but a swept tail configuration; large turbojet nacelles are mounted on the wings, and a glazed nose is provided. A nominal bomb load of 4,400 lb (2,000 kg) is carried in an internal weapons bay (although Soviet statements have referred to a three-ton bomb load). Two cannon are fixed in the nose and two more in a prominent tail turret, with the latter visually directed. Camera and ground-mapping radar are normally installed; wingtip fuel tanks are sometimes fitted.

Status: *Operational.* First flight August 8, 1948; squadron delivery 1949–1950; approx 10,000 built including approx 500 aircraft transferred to China beginning in late 1952 (some of which reached Pakistan) and about 300 to other nations.

SPECIFICATIONS

Crew: 3 (1 pilot, 1 navigator/bombardier, 1 radio operator/gunner)
Engines: 2 Klimov VK-1 turbojets (5,952 lb, 2,700 kg each)
Dimensions: span 70 ft 4¾ in (21·45 m), length 57 ft 10¾ in (17·65 m), height 21 ft 11¾ in (6·68 m), wing area 654½ sq ft (60·87 m²)
Speed: 559 mph (900 km/hr) at 14,765 ft (4,500 m); 497 mph (800 km/hr) at sea level

Ceiling: 41,000 ft (12,500 m)
Range: 685-mile (1,100 km) radius with 4,400 lb (2,000 kg) bombs; 2,200-mile (3,550 km) ferry range
Weights: 28,417 lb (12,900 kg) empty; 40,565 (18,415 kg) loaded; 46,297 lb (21,000 kg) maximum
Armament: 4 × 23-mm NR-23 cannon (85 rpg in forward guns) and 12 × 550-lb bombs
or 4 × 1,100-lb bombs (weapons bay)

VARIANTS

Il-28 production light bomber aircraft; 3 prototypes built with RD-45 engines (Rolls-Royce Nene derivative); subsequent aircraft as above.

Il-28R tactical reconnaissance aircraft with ventral radomes; optical or electronic reconnaissance packs fitted in weapons bay.

Il-28T naval strike aircraft fitted to carry 2 × "short" torpedoes; modified avionics.

Il-28U *Mascot*; trainer with raised second (tandem) cockpit; no guns.

Il-20 unarmed aircraft flown by *Aeroflot*.

OPERATIONAL

Afghanistan, Algeria, Bulgaria, China, Czechoslovakia, Egypt, Indonesia, Nigeria, North Korea, Poland, Romania, Somalia, Syria, North Vietnam, North Yemen, South Yemen

The ubiquitous Il-28 Beagle which, although more than twenty-five years old, continues to be flown by sixteen air forces

Brewer Yak-28 Yakovlev
Firebar Yak-28P

This series of Soviet aircraft was developed from the Yak-25 *Flashlight* fighter series. The *Brewer* is a light bomber with Soviet Frontal Aviation and the *Firebar* is an all-weather fighter with Soviet Air Defence of the Homeland. The *Maestro* is a trainer derivative of the design.

The basic Yak-28 configuration is a swept-wing design with large turbojets housed in nacelles under the wing. The *Brewer* is distinguished by its glazed nose while the *Firebar* has a solid nose housing air search radar; the *Maestro* has an additional blister canopy forward of and below the main cockpit and a large nose radome. The *Brewer* has an internal weapons bay and two wing pylons.

Status: *Operational.* First flight early in 1960; *Brewer* squadron delivery in 1961–1962 and *Firebar* squadron delivery in 1962–1963.

SPECIFICATIONS *(Brewer)*

Crew: 2
Engines: 2 Tumansky TDR R37F turbojets (13,120 lb, 5,950 kg st each with afterburner)
Dimensions: span 42 ft 6 in (12·95 m), length 68 ft 6 in (20·89 m), height 15 ft (4·58 m)
Speed: 735 mph (1,180 km/hr) at 35,000 ft (10,670 m) (Mach 1·1); 725 mph (1,165 km/hr) at sea level (Mach 0·95)

Ceiling: 55,770 ft (17,000 m)
Range: 1,500 miles (2,415 km)
Weights: 35,000 lb (15,875 kg) empty; 41,880 lb (19,000 kg) maximum
Armament: 1 or 2 × 30-mm cannon and up to 4,410 lb of bombs and missiles

VARIANTS

Brewer light attack variant; originally known as *Firebar*-C and subsequently *Bassard* for a short period.

Firebar two-seat all-weather fighter; armed with 2 × *Anab* AAMs on wing pylons; no guns; originally known as *Firebar*-B.

Firebar-A tactical reconnaissance version; possibly retains cannon armament.

Maestro trainer version.

OPERATIONAL

Yak-28 Brewer-D, *originally known as* Firebar-C

Soviet Union (*Brewer* in FA, *Firebar* in PVO)

Buccaneer Hawker Siddeley

The Buccaneer was developed as a high-subsonic strike aircraft for operation from British aircraft carriers. A squadron still operates from the *Ark Royal*, Britain's single remaining aircraft carrier, and variants are flown by the Royal Air Force and South Africa. Originally developed as the Blackburn N.A.39, the Buccaneer was intended to counter the Soviet *Sverdlov*-class cruisers and other surface warships constructed in the 1950s. The aircraft has a sophisticated night/all-weather weapons delivery capability, a relatively long range, and can carry conventional or nuclear weapons, or can be fitted as a reconnaissance aircraft.

The swept-wing Buccaneer has two turbofan engines housed in large nacelles on both sides of the fuselage; an internal weapons bay has a rotating door that can hold bombs or a reconnaissance pack for seven cameras; four wing pylons can carry additional ordnance or fuel tanks for a total 16,000-lb (7,265 kg) payload of fuel tanks and ordnance; a detachable refuelling probe is fitted in the S.2; and wings and tail fairing fold for carrier operation.

Status: *Operational.* First flight April 30, 1958; squadron delivery July 1962.

SPECIFICATIONS (S.2A/B)

Crew: 2

Engines: 2 Rolls-Royce RB.168-1A Spey Mk 101 turbofans (11,000 lb, 5,035 kg st each)

Dimensions: span 44 ft (13·41 m) length 63 ft 5 in (19·33 m), height 16 ft 3 in (4·96 m), wing area 514$\frac{3}{4}$ sq ft (47·87 m²)

Speed: 645 mph (1,038 km/hr) at 200 ft (60 m) (Mach 0·85)

Range: 2,300 miles (3,700 km) with weapons

Weight: 62,000 lb (28,148 kg) maximum

Armament: 4 × 1,000-lb bombs (weapons bay) plus 4 × 1,000-lb bombs (wing pylons) or 4 × Bullpup AGM-12 ASMs or 3 × Martel AS.37 ASMs (wing pylons)

VARIANTS

S.1 development and production strike aircraft with Bristol Siddeley Gyron Junior D.GJ.1 turbojet engines (development) and Gyron Junior 101 turbojet engines (production); distinguished by small engine intakes; 20 development and 50 production aircraft built for Royal Navy.

S.2 production strike aircraft with Rolls-Royce Spey engine; first flight June 5, 1964; 84 originally built for Royal Navy and 16 for South Africa (S.50); most Navy aircraft transferred to RAF and redesignated S.2A or, when fitted for Martel ASM, S.2B with all to be brought up to S.2B standard; remaining Navy aircraft are redesignated S.2C or S.2D, latter with Martel ASM; additionally 43 S.2B aircraft built for RAF and 3 S.2B aircraft for Royal Aircraft Establishment for test programmes.

OPERATIONAL

Great Britain (RAF, Navy), South Africa

Buccaneer S.2 of the Royal Navy on board HMS Ark Royal (Ministry of Defence)

Buccaneer S.2 armed with Bullpup ASMs and rocket pods (Hawker Siddeley)

Canberra B-57 English Electric/Martin

The Canberra was Britain's first jet-propelled bomber. Subsequently manufactured continuously for 12 consecutive years, the Canberra has served 11 nations in several roles. A few special-mission Canberras are flown with US markings and the Royal Air Force operates a number in the photo-reconnaissance configuration. Several other air forces fly strike variants of the aircraft. In addition to the combat aircraft listed below, there have been several trainer and target-tow variants.

*RB-57B Canberra
of the US Air
Force (Martin)*

The basic Canberra configuration features a low aspect ratio wing to provide maximum fuel economy at the highest possible cruising altitude. Twin turbojets with small centre cones are mounted in the wings. The Martin-built RB-57F is a strategic reconnaissance aircraft with extended wings and two auxiliary turbojet pods on wing pylons. In the early bomber variants the pilot's seat was on the port side of the cockpit and the navigator and bomb-aimer were seated side-by-side behind the pilot. Some later bomber variants have a glazed nose position for the bombardier.

Status: *Operational.* First flight May 13, 1949; squadron delivery May 1951. English Electric produced 926 Canberras, the Government Aircraft Factory in Australia produced 49, and Martin produced 403 in the United States designated B-57.

SPECIFICATIONS (B.8)

Crew: 2 (1 pilot, 1 bombardier-navigator)
Engines: 2 Rolls-Royce Avon 109 turbojets (7,400 lb, 3,355 kg each)
Dimensions: span 63 ft 11½ in (19·50 m), length 65 ft 6 in (19·96 m), height 15 ft 7 in (4·76 m), wing area 960 sq ft (89·28 m²)
Speed: 580 mph (930 km/hr) at 30,000 ft (9,145 m) (Mach 0·83); 518 mph (833 km/hr) at sea level (Mach 0·68)

Ceiling: 48,000 ft (14,640 m)
Range: 400-mile (645 km) combat radius; 3,630-mile (5,840 km) ferry range (with wingtip fuel tanks)
Weights: 23,173 lb (10,520 kg) empty; 50,992 lb (23,150 kg) loaded; 56,250 lb (25,340 kg) maximum
Armament: 4 × 20-mm cannon (detachable weapons bay pack), 3 × 1,000-lb bombs (weapons bay) and 2 × 1,000-lb bombs (wing pylons)

VARIANTS

B.1 two-seat prototype aircraft with (3) Rolls-Royce Avon or (1) Nene engines; 4 built.

B.2 initial production aircraft with Rolls-Royce Avon 101 engines; three crew; glazed nose; first flight April 23, 1950; 203 built by English Electric, 75 by A. V. Roe, 65 by Handley Page, 76 by Short Brothers, 49 by Government Aircraft Factory in Australia (B.20); flown by RAF, Australia, Rhodesia, Venezuela; refurbished aircraft subsequently transferred to Peru (B.72), Venezuela (B.82); 1 provided to USA as B-57 pattern.

PR.3 three-seat photo reconnaissance variant of B.2 aircraft with Avon 101 engines; 7 cameras fitted; first flight July 31, 1952; 36 built; refurbished aircraft subsequently transferred to Venezuela (PR.82).

B.5 "target-marking" bomber aircraft with Avon 109 engines; fitted with special radar; 1 built.

B.6 three-seat bomber aircraft with Avon 109 engines; first flight January 26, 1954; 88 built by English Electric, 30 by Short Brothers; flown by RAF, Ecuador, France (6 aircraft for support of French missile development programmes).

PR.7 three-seat photo reconnaissance aircraft with Avon 109 engines; increased fuel capacity; 7 cameras fitted; first flight October 28, 1953; 74 built; flown by RAF and India; some modified to T.22 for Royal Navy.

B.8 two-seat bomber aircraft with glazed nose position for bombardier; first flight July 23, 1954; 75 built; flown by RAF, India (B.58), New Zealand (B.12), Peru, South Africa (B.58); refurbished aircraft subsequently transferred to Peru (B.78), Venezuela (B.88).

PR.9 high-altitude strategic reconnaissance aircraft with Avon 206 engines; ceiling 50,000 + ft (15,250 m); first flight July 8, 1955 (converted PR.7; first flight PR.9 July 27, 1958); 45 built by Short Brothers for RAF.

B.15 updated B.6 bomber aircraft with improved electronics and weapons capability for RAF; 38 converted.

B.16 updated B.6 bomber aircraft with improved electronics and weapons capability for RAF; 20 converted.

B-57A two-seat B.2 variant with J65-W-5 engines; 8 built by Martin.

RB-57A two-seat photo reconnaissance aircraft with J65-W-5 engines; limited strike capability; 67 built by Martin.

B-57B two-seat tactical bomber with J65-W-5/-5B/J65-B-5/-5B engines; armed with 8 × ·50-cal MG in wings and rotary weapons bay; 202 built; 30 transferred to Pakistan, also flown by South Vietnam.

EB-57B B-57B modified for electronic countermeasures (ECM) capability.

RB-57B B-57B modified for reconnaissance.

B-57C similar to B-57B with dual controls for training purposes; combat capabilities retained; first flight December 30, 1954; 38 built.

RB-57C B-57C modified for reconnaissance.

TB-57C B-57B modified for training; 3 crew.

WB-57C B-57C modified for weather reconnaissance; 2 crew.

EB-57D ECM aircraft with J57-P-37A engines.

RB-57D strategic reconnaissance aircraft with J57-P-37A engines; span 106 ft (32·33 m); 1 or 2 (6 aircraft) crew; 20 built; 2 transferred to Taiwan.

B-57E tactical bomber with J65-W-5/-5B/J65-B-5/-5B engines; 68 built.

EB-57E B-57E modified for ECM role.

RB-57E B-57E modified for reconnaissance.

TB-57E B-57E modified for training.

RB-57F strategic reconnaissance aircraft with TF-33-P-11A turbofan engines in wing nacelles and two J60-P-9 turbojet pods; span 122 ft

(37·21 m), length 68 ft 10 in (20·98 m); ceiling approx 75,000 ft (22,875 m); range 4,000 + miles (6,435 km); 2 crew; at least 12 converted from B-57B.

WB-57F RB-57F modified for weather reconnaissance.

B-57G similar to B-57B; modified for night attacks against ground targets with laser guided bombs; fitted with self-contained adverse weather/night attack (SCANA) system.

OPERATIONAL

Argentina, Ecuador, Ethiopia, Great Britain (RAF, Navy), India, Peru, Rhodesia, South Africa, United States

(Air Force, Air National Guard) Venezuela

Corsair II A-7 LTV

The A-7 Corsair II is an attack aircraft developed by the US Navy for carrier operation and subsequently flown by the US Navy and Air Force. Initially configured as a visual attack aircraft, in the A-7D/E variants the Corsair II has a night/all-weather attack and navigation capability. The US Air Force and Air National Guard fly the A-7D in large numbers; Greece and Indonesia also fly the Corsair II.

The Corsair II has a high, swept-wing configuration which closely resembles the F-8 Crusader fighter from which the attack aircraft was derived. The A-7 was designed as the replacement for the McDonnell Douglas A-4 Skyhawk. Although the Corsair II replaced the Skyhawk aboard US Navy carriers, it has not had the wide foreign acceptance of the older aircraft. The Corsair II cockpit is relatively far forward, immediately behind the small nose radome, and is faired into the fuselage. The single turbofan has a chin-position air intake. The integrated navigation-attack system of the A-7D/E is built around an IBM digital computer (ASN-91); APG-126 forward-looking radar is fitted. There is an internal cannon, two fuselage cheek-position pylons for air-to-air missiles or rockets, and six wing pylons for an aggregate of 15,000 lb (6,810 kg) of external stores. Fitted for in-flight refuelling with a retractable probe; wings fold for carrier operation. The Roman numeral II in the name was to avoid confusion with the F4U Corsair piston fighter produced by Chance-Vought, predecessor of LTV.

A-7D Corsair II of the US Air Force (US Air Force)

A-7 Corsair II of the US Navy on board USS Ranger (US Navy

Status: *Operational.* First flight September 27, 1965 (A-7A); squadron delivery October 1966.

SPECIFICATIONS (A-7D)

Crew: 1

Engine: 1 Allison TF41-A-1 (Rolls-Royce Spey 168-62) turbofan (14,250 lb, 6,465 kg)

Dimensions: span 38 ft 9 in (11·80 m), length 46 ft 1½ in (14·06 m), height 16 ft ¾ in (4·90 m), wing area 375 sq ft (34·83 m²)

Speed: 700 mph (1,126 km/hr) at sea level

Range: approx 700-mile (1,126 km) radius with 4,000 lb (1,815 kg) ordnance; 3,000-mile (4,825 km) range without external stores; 4,100-mile (6,600 km) ferry range with external fuel tanks

Weights: 19,781 lb (8,972 kg) empty; 42,000 lb (19,050 kg) maximum

Armament: 1 × 20-mm M61-A1 General Electric Vulcan cannon (1,000 rpg) and 4 × Sidewinder AIM-9 AAMs (fuselage pylons) plus 15 × 750-lb bombs or 10 × 1,000-lb bombs or 4 × 3,100-lb bombs or 4 × Maverick AGM-65 ASMs (wing pylons)

VARIANTS

A-7A initial attack aircraft produced for US Navy with TF30-P-6 engine; fitted with 2 × 20-mm Mk-12 cannon (250 rpg); 199 built (including prototypes).

A-7B similar to A-7A with TF30-P-8/-403 engine; first flight February 6, 1968; 196 built for US Navy.

A-7C designation applied in late 1971 to 67 A-7E aircraft with TF-30-P-8 engine.

TA-7C two-seat trainer retaining full weapons capability; 40 converted from A-7B and 41 from A-7C from 1971 to 1976 for US Navy.

A-7D production aircraft for US Air Force with TF41-A-1 engine (except two aircraft with TF30-P-8); armed with 1 × 20-mm M61-A1 cannon; improved avionics and inertial navigation for night/all-weather operation; first flight April 5, 1968; 435 built for US Air Force.

A-7DER proposed close support aircraft; lengthened fuselage, different engine; 1 × 30-mm GAU-8/A cannon (A-10 procured instead).

A-7E production aircraft for US Navy with TF30-P-8 engine in 67 aircraft (redesignated A-7C) and Allison TF41-

A-2 (Spey) in subsequent; 1 × 20-mm M61-A1 cannon; avionics similar to A-7D; being fitted with forward-looking infra-red (FLIR) target designator; first flight November 25, 1968; over 666 planned for US Navy with 506 procured through FY 1975.

RA-7E proposed reconnaissance aircraft fitted with sensor pods to replace RA-5C Vigilante aboard US Navy carriers in late 1970s.

KA-7F proposed carrier-based tanker aircraft based on A-7A/B with 18,600 lb (8,445 kg) internal fuel capacity plus 4 × 450-US gallon external wing tanks (KA-6D procured instead).

A-7G proposed aircraft for foreign procurement.

YA-7H two-seat modified A-7E with TF41-A-2 engine; length 48 ft 2 in (14·69 m); first flight August 29, 1972; 1 converted for test.

A-7H two-seat production aircraft; length 48 ft 2 in (14·69 m); approx 60 being built for Greece.

OPERATIONAL

Greece, Indonesia, United States (Air Force, Navy)

Dragonfly A-37 Cessna

The A-37 Dragonfly is a militarized version of the T-37 turbojet trainer which has been in wide use by the US Air Force since the latter 1950s. The T-37 was adapted for the counterinsurgency (COIN) role for use in the Vietnam War; subsequently redesignated AT-37 and then A-37, the aircraft has been used by the US Air Force for COIN training and by Guatemala, Thailand, and South Vietnam.

The A-37 configuration has straight wings with twin turbojets housed in the wing roots. The cockpit has side-by-side seating; external armament is carried on eight wing pylons for a maximum weapons payload of 4,855 lb (2,205 kg) for the A-37A and 5,600 lb (2,540 kg) for the A-37B; in addition, the A-37B has a single, nose-mounted 7·62-mm minigun. The A-37B introduced an in-flight refuelling capability to the aircraft; wingtip tanks are fitted.

A-37B Dragonfly of the US Air Force (US Air Force)

Status: *Operational.* First flight October 22, 1963 (YAT-37D); squadron delivery May 1967.

SPECIFICATIONS (A-37B)

Crew: 2
Engines: 2 General Electric J85-GE-17A turbojets (2,850 lb, 1,293 kg st each)
Dimensions: span 35 ft 10½ in (10·93 m), length 29 ft 3 in (8·92 m), height 8 ft 10½ in (2·70 m), wing area 184 sq ft (17·09 m²)
Max level speed: 507 mph (816 km/hr) at 16,000 ft (4,875 m)
Ceiling: 41,765 ft (12,730 m)

Range: 460-mile (740 km) range with 4,100-lb (1,860 kg) weapons load; 1,000-mile (1,625 km) range with external fuel tanks
Weights: 6,211 lb (2,817 kg) empty; 14,000 lb (6,350 kg) maximum
Armament: 1 × 7·62-mm General Electric GAU-2B/A minigun (1,500 rpg), 4 × 870-lb bombs, 2 × 600-lb bombs and 2 × 500-lb bombs (wing pylons)

VARIANTS

YA-37A formerly YAT-37D; T-37B airframe converted to prototype COIN configuration with J85-GE-5 engines; 2 converted.

A-37A formerly AT-37D; T-37B trainers converted to COIN role with J85-GE-17A engines; no gun; 39 converted with most transferred to South Vietnam.

A-37B production COIN aircraft; differs from A-37A with increased thrust to provide greater payload, higher ceiling; self-sealing fuel tanks; over 400 built.

OPERATIONAL

Chile, Ecuador, Guatemala, United States (Air Force Rescue, Air National Guard), Thailand

Dragon Ship AC-47 Douglas

The AC-47 Dragon Ship is the armed version of the venerable DC-3 transport aircraft. First flying as a commercial airliner in 1935, the military cargo/transport versions of the aircraft are known as the Skytrain or Dakota, and popularly referred to as the "Gooney Bird". Few survive in military service. Listed below are the "attack" or gunship variants of the aircraft, a configuration developed during the Vietnam War for strafing Communist ground troops.

A subsequent listing in this edition describes the electronic (EC-47) and reconnaissance (RC-47) configurations of the aircraft.

The 7·62-mm General Electric miniguns of the AC-47 are mounted in pods firing out the window and door openings on the port side of the aircraft. Each gun pod has a rate of fire of 6,000 rounds-per-minute and holds 1,500 rounds. The pods can be reloaded in flight with 15,000 to 18,000 rounds being carried on a mission. Night gunship operations are conducted by the

*AC-47 Dragon-
ship, armed
version of the
venerable DC-3
(US Air Force)*

light of flares dispensed by the aircraft. Normal attack altitude is 3,500 ft
(1,065 m), beyond the range of most small arms fire. The name Dragon Ship
is derived from the nickname "Puff the Magic Dragon", the title of a popular
song in the 1960s. These aircraft were unofficially designated FC-47 (for
"fighter") during evaluation.

SPECIFICATIONS (basic C-47D)

Crew: 3 (flight crew)
Engines: 2 Pratt & Whitney R-1830-
  90D radial piston; 1,200 hp each
Dimensions: span 95 ft (29 m), length
  64 ft 4 in (19 62 m), height 16 ft 10
  in (5·12 m)

Speed: 230 mph (370 km/hr)
Ceiling: 24,000 + ft (7,320 m)
Weight: 29,000 lb (13,165 kg) loaded
  (in AC-47D configuration)
Armament: AC-47D has 3 × 7·62-mm
  miniguns (5,000 to 6,000 rpg)

VARIANTS

prototypes C-47D aircraft modified
in 1965 with various combinations of
·30-cal MG and 7·62-mm MG to
determine gunship configuration; 5
converted; subsequently brought to
standard AC-47D configuration

(originally referred to as FC-47D for
"fighter").
  AC-47D C-47D aircraft modified for
gunship operation; 25 believed
converted (including prototypes).

OPERATIONAL

Laos

Enforcer Mustang } F-51 North American/Cavalier

The F-51 (initially P-51) Mustang was one of the outstanding Allied fighter
aircraft of the Second World War and subsequently served with distinction

early in the Korean War. F-51D Mustangs in their original configuration continue in service with several countries as well as the revitalized Cavalier F-51D/TF-51D "Enforcer". The latter aircraft, produced by the Cavalier Aircraft Corporation, were assembled from existing and new component parts. These "new" Mustangs are flown by Bolivia and El Salvador, while the other countries listed below fly "original" Mustangs.

The Mustang has an in-line piston engine, streamlined shape, bubble canopy, and a distinctive radiator scoop faired into the fuselage bottom. Over 14,000 Mustangs were delivered during the Second World War plus 73 two-fuselage F-82 Twin Mustangs just after the war, all produced by North American. Beginning in 1967, the Cavalier firm has rebuilt a small number of aircraft to the improved Mustang or Enforcer configuration, and one aircraft to the Mustang III variant with a Rolls-Royce Dart turboprop engine providing a dash speed of approximately 540 mph (869 km/hr).

Status: *Operational.* First flight October 26, 1940 (NA39/XP-51).

SPECIFICATIONS (Cavalier F-51D)

Crew: 1 or 2
Engine: 1 Rolls-Royce Merlin 620 in-line piston; 1,760 hp
Dimensions: span 37 ft $\frac{1}{2}$ in (11·28 m), length 32 ft $2\frac{1}{2}$ in (9·82 m)
Speed: 457 mph (735 km/hr)

Range: 1,980 miles (3,185 km)
Weights: 12,500 lb loaded (5,675 kg)
Armament: 6 × ·50-calibre machine-guns and 2 × 1,000-lb bombs plus 6 × rocket pods (wing pylons)

VARIANTS

basic F-51D production aircraft with Packard (Rolls-Royce Merlin) V-1650-7 piston engine; major production variant (7,966 built including 10 two-place TP-51Ds).

Cavalier F-51D rebuilt F-51D; most two-seat aircraft with a few one-seat; some with permanent wingtip fuel tanks.
Cavalier TF-51D rebuilt F-51D with dual controls.

Piper Enforcer, a much modified version of the Second World War Mustang

FS-T2-KAI Mitsubishi

The FS-T2-KAI is a single-seat, turbofan close-support aircraft developed from the T-2 trainer. The combat aircraft is being developed specifically to replace the F-86F Sabres flown by the Japanese Air Self-Defence Force. Current planning provides for the eventual delivery of 68 FS-T2-KAI aircraft to the ASDF, although budget limitations have delayed delivery schedules.

The basic T-2 trainer is the first supersonic aircraft to be developed by the Japanese aircraft industry. It is a two-seat, twin-engine, swept-wing aircraft with air intakes aft of the cockpit and faired under the wing roots. The basic tail configuration resembles that of the F-4 Phantom and there are two small, ventral fins under the rear fuselage. The FS version will carry bombs, rockets, and missiles on wing pylons in addition to an internal cannon.

Status: *Development*. First flight July 20, 1971 (XT-2).

SPECIFICATIONS

Crew: 1
Engines: 2 Rolls-Royce/Turboméca Adour turbofans (7,140 lb, 3,238 kg st with afterburner)
Dimensions: span 25 ft 10 in (7·87 m), length 58 ft 7 in (17·86 m), height 14 ft 7 in (4·45 m), wing area 228 sq ft (21·18 m²)

Speed: Mach 1·6 at altitude
Ceiling: 50,025 ft (15,250 m)
Range: 350-mile (565 km) radius with 4,000 lb (1,815 kg) weapons
Weight: approx 31,000 lb (14,075 kg) loaded
Armament: 1 × 20-mm cannon and 12 × 500-lb bombs (wing pylons)

Prototype T-2 which is being developed as a single-seat close-support aircraft (Mitsubishi)

Harrier AV-8 Hawker Siddeley

The Harrier is the West's first fully operational combat aircraft capable of vertical and short take-off and landing (V/STOL). The swept-wing Harrier is a light attack aircraft with a limited intercept capability. Now in service with the Royal Air Force and US Marine Corps, the aircraft is expected to be operational in the near future with Iran and Spain, with a number of other nations expressing interest in the Harrier for ship-based V/STOL operations. The Royal Navy will operate Harriers from its forthcoming *Invincible*-class light aircraft carriers (neé through-deck cruisers) with about five aircraft being assigned to each carrier in addition to Sea King helicopters; 25 maritime Harriers have been approved for RN development.

Developed from the Hawker Siddeley P.1127 Kestrel, the Harrier is powered by a vectored-thrust turbofan engine that exhausts through rotating nozzles. The nozzles are rotated for vertical or short-run take-offs and landings. There are four wing pylons and one fuselage pylon for carrying external stores, with up to 8,000 lb (3,630 kg) being carried, although normal loading of bombs, rockets, reconnaissance pods, and external fuel tanks is limited to just over 5,000 lb (2,270 kg) (with maximum loads of 2,000 lb (908 kg) on centre three pylons and 650 lb (295 kg) on the outer wing pylons). In addition, two gun pods can be fitted under the fuselage. The AV-8A/TAV-8A are fitted to carry Sidewinder air-to-air missiles. One-seat and two-seat aircraft, the latter with near full combat capability, are in service.

Status: *Operational.* First flight December 28, 1967; squadron delivery April 1969 (GR.1 with RAF) and November 1972 (AV-8A with US Marine Corps).

SPECIFICATIONS (GR.3/AV-8A)

Crew: 1

Engine: 1 Rolls-Royce Pegasus Mk 103 vectored-thrust turbofan (21,500 lb, 9,752 kg st)

Dimensions: span 25 ft 3 in (7·70 m), length 45 ft 6 in (13·87 m), height 11 ft 3 in (3·43 m), wing area 201 sq ft (18·69 m²)

Speed: 737 mph (1,186 km/hr) at 1,000 ft (305 m) (Mach 0·95)

Ceiling: 50,000 + ft (15,250 m)

Range: 200-mile (320 km) radius with 2,500 lb (1,135 kg) external weapons; 400-mile (645 km) radius and 1 hr loiter with 2 × Sidewinder AAMs (400 lb)

Weights: 12,200 lb (5,538 kg) empty; 17,500 lb (7,945 kg) gross for vertical take-off; 21,489 lb (9,755 kg) for short-run take-off; 25,000 + lb (11,350 kg) maximum

Armament: 2 × 30-mm Aden cannon (fuselage fairings in RAF variants) plus 3 × 1,000-lb bombs and 2 × rocket pods (wing and fuselage pylons)

VARIANTS

Gr.1/1A.3 initial production aircraft initially with Pegasus 101 engine; refitted with Pegasus 102 engine (GR.1A) and subsequently with Pegasus 103 engine (GR.3); 92 built for RAF.

T.2/2A/4 two-seat aircraft with Pegasus 101/102/103 engines; respectively; length 55 ft 9½ in (17·00 m), height 13 ft 8 in (4·18 m); combat capability retained with some loss of payload; first flight April 24, 1969; 15 aircraft built for RAF.

AV-8A close-support and tactical reconnaissance aircraft similar to GR.3 for US Marine Corps; first 10 aircraft initially delivered with Pegasus 102 engine; produced by Hawker Siddeley as GR.50; fitted for 2 × Sidewinder AIM-9 AAMs on outer wing pylons; 102 built for USMC; 6 ordered for Spain.

TAV-8A two-seat aircraft with Pegasus 103 engine for US Marine

Corps; produced by Hawker Siddeley as GR.54; 8 built for USMC; 2 ordered for Spain.

AV-8B proposed aircraft with uprated Pegasus engine and advanced wing design.

Mk.52 demonstration aircraft similar to T.4 with Pegasus 103 engine; first flight September 16, 1971; 1 built.

FRS.1 single-seat Sea Harrier for Royal Navy; first flight in 1977; 24 planned.

OPERATIONAL

Great Britain (RAF, Navy planned), Iran (planned), Spain, United States

(Marine Corps)

AV-8A Harriers of the US Marine Corps (Hawker Siddeley)

AV-8A Harrier landing on USS Guam (US Navy)

Hawk Hawker Siddeley

The Hawk is a two-seat, turbofan training aircraft with a built-in close-support combat capability. It is planned to replace the Gnat, Hunter, and Jet Provost trainers in the Royal Air Force.

The aircraft has a streamlined configuration with a low, swept wing and small air intakes faired into the fuselage. A cannon pack can be mounted under the fuselage centreline; in RAF service two wing pylons normally will be fitted with the capability of replacing the gun pack and adding two additional wing pylons for a total of five, each with a capacity of 1,000 lb (454 kg). The company designation is HS.1182.

Status: *On order.* First flight August 21, 1974; squadron delivery in late 1976.

SPECIFICATIONS

Crew: 2
Engine: 1 Rolls-Royce/Turboméca RT. 172-06-11 Adour 151 turbofan (5,340 lb, 2,422 kg st)
Dimensions: span 30 ft 10 in (9.40 m), length 39 ft 2½ in (11.95 m), height 13 ft 5 in (4.10 m), wing area 180 sq ft (16.74 m²)
Speed: 595 mph (1,102 km/hr) at 36,000 ft (11,000 m) (Mach 0.9)

Range: approx 1,725 miles (2,780 km) ferry
Weights: 7,450 lb (3,380 kg) empty; 10,250 lb (4,655 kg) loaded clean; approx 16,500 lb (7,490 kg) max
Armament: 1 × 30-mm Aden cannon (fuselage fairing) plus 4 × 1,000-lb bombs (wing pylons)

VARIANTS

T.1 1 pre-production and 175 production aircraft ordered for RAF.

Hawk of the Royal Air Force (Hawker Siddeley)

Hercules AC-130 Lockheed

The basic C-130 Hercules is a turboprop transport aircraft developed to US Air Force specifications. Various models are in commercial cargo use and are flown in a number of variants by the US armed forces and more than a score of foreign military services. Listed below are the "attack" or gunship variants of the Hercules. The AC-130 was developed to replace the earlier AC-47 Dragon Ship and AC-119 Packet gunships.

A subsequent listing in this edition describes the electronic (EC-130) and reconnaissance (RC-130) configurations of the aircraft. Maximum payload of the basic C-130E Hercules is 45,000 lb (20,430 kg). During special tests C-130 aircraft have operated from a large US aircraft carrier without the assistance of catapults or arresting wires.

SPECIFICATIONS (basic C-130E)

Crew: 4 (flight crew)
Engines: 4 Allison T56-A-7 turboprops; 3,755 ehp each
Dimensions: span 132 ft 7 in (40·41 m), length 97 ft 9 in (29·78 m), height 38 ft 3 in (11·66 m), wing area 1,745 sq ft (162·12 m²)
Max level speed: 384 mph (618 km/hr)

Ceiling: 23,000 ft (loaded) (7,015 m)
Range: 4,700 miles (7,560 km) (50% payload with external fuel tanks)
Weights: 72,892 lb (33,090 kg) empty; 155,000 lb (70,370 kg) loaded; 175,000 lb (79,450 kg) maximum overload
Armaments: nil except AC-130 (see below)

VARIANTS

AC-130A gunship with T56-A-1A/9 engines.

AC-130E gunship with T56-A-7 engines; armed with 4 × 20-mm Vulcan multi-barrel cannon, 4 × 7·62-mm miniguns; fitted with searchlight, infrared, and other sensors.

AC-130H gunship with T56-A-15 engines; armed with 1 × 105-mm howitzer, 2 × 20-mm cannon, 2 × 7·62-mm miniguns; fitted with forward-looking infrared (FLIR), low-light-level television (LLLTV), and laser target designator.

OPERATIONAL

United States (Air Force)

AC-130H Hercules gunship of the US Air Force (US Air Force)

Hunter Hawker Siddeley

The Hunter is a multi-purpose combat aircraft that remains in wide use after more than two decades of service. The single-seat, swept-wing aircraft has been one of the most successful British designs of the jet era.

The aircraft has most attractive lines with engine intakes buried in the wing roots. A carrier-capable variant has been operated by the Royal Navy as a ground-attack trainer. Built under licence in Belgium and the Netherlands.

Status: *Operational.* First flight June 20, 1951; squadron delivery in 1954; approximately 2,200 aircraft of all Hunter variants produced through 1974. In addition to the fighter, ground attack, and reconnaissance variants listed below, there have been several trainer variants.

SPECIFICATIONS (FGA.9)

Crew: 1
Engine: 1 Rolls-Royce Avon 207 turbojet (10,150 lb, 4,608 kg st)
Dimensions: span 33 ft 8 in (10·26 m), length 45 ft 10½ in (13·98 m), height 13 ft 2 in (4·01 m)
Speed: 710 mph (1,142 km/hr) at sea level (Mach 0·94); 627 mph (1,008 km/hr) at 36,000 ft (11,000 m) (Mach 0·95)
Ceiling: 53,400 ft (16,290 m)

Range: 350-mile (560 km) combat radius; 1,850-mile (2,975 km) ferry range
Weights: 14,400 lb (6,540 kg) empty; 17,750 lb (8,058 kg) loaded (clean); 24,600 lb (11,170 kg) maximum
Armament: 4 × 30-mm Aden cannon (150 rpg) and 2 × 500-lb bombs or 2 × 1,000-lb bombs plus 24 × 3-in rockets (wing pylons)

VARIANTS

P.1067 series designation during development; powered by Avon and Sapphire engines; 3 built.

P.1099 prototype for F.6 variant; first flight January 22, 1954.

P.1101 prototype for two-seat aircraft with Avon 113 engine; 2 built to basic F.4 and F.6 configurations.

F.1 initial production day fighter aircraft with Avon 113 engine; first flight May 16, 1953; 139 built for Royal Air Force.

F.2 similar to F.1 with Sapphire 101 engine; first flight October 14, 1953; 45

Hunter F.58 of the Swiss Air Force (M Fricke)

built for Royal Air Force.

F.4 similar to F.1 with additional fuel; first flight October 20, 1954; 365 built for RAF, 120 for Sweden (F.50 designated J-34 by Swedes), 30 for Denmark (F.51); 16 original RAF aircraft modified for Peru (F.52).

F.5 similar to F.2 with additional fuel capacity; first flight October 19, 1954; 105 built for RAF.

F.6 production aircraft with Avon 203 engine; first flight March 25, 1955; 382 built for RAF, 15 for Iraq, 12 for Jordan, 12 for Lebanon, 160 for India (F.56), 12 for Switzerland (F.58); Avions Fairey and SABCA built 192 under licence for Belgium; Fokker and Aviolanda built 268 for the Netherlands; 18 former Belgian aircraft modified for Iraq (F.59).

FGA.9 ground attack aircraft with Avon 207 engine; first flight July 3, 1959; 50 built for RAF, 12 for Rhodesia, 4 for Kuwait (F.57); 88 for Switzerland (F.58); also built for Chile (FGA.71), Jordan (FGA.73), Singapore (FGA.74), Abu Dhabi (FGA.76), Qatar (FGA.78).

FR.10 reconnaissance aircraft with Avon 207 engine; fitted with 4 × 30-mm cannon and 3 cameras; first flight November 7, 1958; built for RAF with 4 modified for Singapore (FR.74).

GA.11 F.4 aircraft converted to single-seat ground attack trainer with Avon 122 engine; no guns; fitted for Bullpup AGM-12 air-to-surface missile; replaceable 3-camera nose structure; first flight March 3, 1958; 18 converted for Royal Navy plus 10 aircraft built to this configuration for Royal Navy (all T.8).

OPERATIONAL

Abu Dhabi, Chile, Great Britain (RAF), India, Iraq, Jordan, Kenya, Kuwait, Lebanon, Peru, Qatar, Singapore, Switzerland.

Intruder A-6 Grumman

The Intruder is the world's first fully all-weather/night attack aircraft capable of detecting and identifying tactical or strategic targets and delivering conventional or nuclear weapons on them under zero-visibility conditions. The aircraft was developed in response to a US Navy requirement for a carrier-based strike aircraft to keep station over target areas around-the-clock. All of the larger US aircraft carriers operate an attack squadron of Intruders as well as a tanker detachment; the US Marine Corps flies the attack and electronic variants of the Intruder. The basic Intruder is a two-seat, twin-turbojet aircraft; tactical electronic warfare (EA-6A) and tanker (KA-6D) variants are in service; listed separately is the EA-6B Prowler.

The Intruder is an ungainly aircraft with a wide-diameter fuselage with twin air intakes forward of the swept, mid-wing; there is a large nose radome; the after fuselage tapers considerably to a conventional tail configuration; a refuelling probe projects from just ahead of the cockpit which seats a pilot on the port side and a bombardier/navigator on the starboard side, slightly lower and behind the pilot. Weapons are carried externally on five wing and fuselage pylons, each with a 3,200-lb (1,450 kg) capacity. An onboard computer supports the sophisticated digital integrated attack navigation equipment (DIANE). The wings fold for carrier operation.

Status: *Operational.* First flight April 19, 1960; squadron delivery February 1963.

SPECIFICATIONS (A-6E)

Crew: 2 (1 pilot, 1 bombardier/navigator)

Engines: 2 Pratt & Whitney J52-P-8A/-8B turbojets (9,300 lb, 4,220 kg st each)

Dimensions: span 53 ft (16·15 m), length 54 ft 7 in (16·67 m), height 16 ft 2 in (4·92 m), wing area 529 sq ft (49·2 m²)

Speed: 685 mph (1,100 km/hr) at sea level (Mach 0·9; 482 mph (775 km/hr) cruise

Ceiling: 44,600 ft (13,600 m)

Weights: 25,630 lb (11,635 kg) empty; 60,400 lb (27,420 kg) maximum

Armament: 4 × Bullpup AGM-12 ASMs
or 20 + × 500-lb bombs
or 13 + × 1,000-lb bombs
or 5 × 2,000-lb bombs (wing and fuselage pylons)

A-6E Intruder of the US Navy (Grumman)

EA-6A Intruder of the US Marine Corps (US Marine Corps)

VARIANTS

A-6A formerly A2F-1; initial production aircraft with J52-P-6A/-6B/-8A/-8B engines; 482 built including 8 development aircraft; 6 modified to electronic configuration (EA-6A), 19 fitted to carry Standard-ARM AGM-78 anti-radiation missile (A-6B), 12 fitted forward-looking infra-red (FLIR), low-light-level television (LLLTV), and other sensors for night attack (A-6C), 54 modified to tanker configuration (KA-6D), 192 modified with advanced weapons system (A-6E).

EA-6A formerly A2F-1H; electronic warfare aircraft equipped to identify and jam enemy radars for anti-aircraft suppression; J52-P-8A/-8B engines; 2 crew; 6 modified from A-6A, 21 built as EA-6A, all for US Marine Corps.

KA-6D tanker aircraft with J52-P-6A/-8A engines; fitted with drogue refuelling system in rear fuselage; improved navigation equipment; can transfer 21,000 + lb (9,535 kg) fuel immediately after take-off or 15,000 lb (6,810 kg) at a distance of 288 miles (460 km) from carrier; 2 crew; limited visual attack capability retained; first flight of modified A-6A on May 23, 1966; 54 modified from A-6A aircraft.

A-6E production aircraft with J52-P-8A/-8B engines; improved avionics and weapons delivery system with IBM ASQ-133 solid-state, digital computer; some fitted with target recognition attack multi-sensor (TRAM) with electro-optical package including infra-red and laser components; 192 modified from A-6A plus 82 new production procured through Fiscal Year 1975 for USN and USMC.

OPERATIONAL

United States (Navy, Marine Corps)

Invader B-26 Douglas

The B-26 Invader is a piston-engine light bomber that saw extensive combat in the closing months of the Second World War as the A-26 and in the Korean War after being redesignated B-26. Subsequently modified for counterinsurgency operations, the aircraft was the last piston-engine bomber flown by the US Air Force and is still flown by several nations. Some of these aircraft, again with the designation A-26A, were flown by the USAF into the 1960s; subsequently the USAF briefly used the B-26K variant.

The B-26 is a straight-wing aircraft incorporating many features of the earlier and widely used A-20 Havoc. The radial piston engines are wing-mounted in large nacelles. There is side-by-side seating for the pilot and navigator-bombardier with a radio operator-gunner sometimes seated aft of the weapons bay. Most of the aircraft now flying are B-26K variants with eight wing pylons for 8,000 lb (3,630 kg) of weapons in addition to the internal weapons bay with a capacity of 4,000 lb (1,815 kg). Up to 8 × ·50-cal machineguns are fitted in the nose, 8 × ·50-cal MG in the wings, and 2 × ·50-cal MG in a remote-controlled dorsal turret. During the 1960s the

*B-26 Invader.
This aircraft now
serves principally
with South
American air
forces (US Air
Force)*

On Mark Engineering Company remanufactured existing airframes for the counterinsurgency role, fitting wing weapon pylons, more powerful engines, and a reconnaissance camera. The YB-26K flew in early 1963 and 40 additional aircraft were converted to the B-26K configuration.

Status: *Operational.* First flight July 10, 1942 (XA-26). Production totalled 1,091 aircraft.

SPECIFICATIONS (B-26K)

Crew: 2
Engines: 2 Pratt & Whitney R-2800-PW-103W radial pistons (2,500 hp each)
Dimensions: span 70 ft (21·35 m), length 51 ft 3 in (15·63 m), height 18 ft 5 in (5·63 m)

Speed: 360 mph (580 km/hr)
Ceiling: 20,000 + ft (6,100 m)
Weight: 43,380 lb (1,970 kg) maximum
Armament: 8 or 10 × ·50-cal machineguns and up to 12,000 lb of conventional bombs and rockets

OPERATIONAL

Argentina, Brazil, Chile, Dominican Republic, El Salvador, Guatemala,

Indonesia, Nicaragua, Peru, Portugal

Jaguar SEPECAT

The Jaguar is a light attack aircraft developed under a joint Anglo-French effort to build an advanced trainer and close support aircraft. The swept-wing, twin-turbofan aircraft is being produced in single-and two-seat versions for both British and French service, and for an active foreign marketing programme. Derived from the Breguet Br.121 project, the Jaguar is produced by

SEPECAT (*Société Européenne de Production de l'avion*) a co-operative venture of British Aircraft Corporation and Avions Marcel Dassault/Breguet Aviation.

The Jaguar has a "squared-off" look from some angles, an illusion caused by the flat-bottom fuselage and large, square air intakes for the twin turbofan engines which are faired into the lower portion of the after fuselage. There are one- and two-seat variants, the latter being fitted with dual controls for use as an advanced trainer. There is a long, centreline pylon and four wing pylons for a maximum of 10,000 lb (4,540 kg) of external stores; in addition, there is provision for internal gun armament. Wings folded for carrier operation on the variant developed for naval use.

Status: *Operational.* First flight September 8, 1968 (Jaguar E-01); squadron delivery June 1973. Agreements provide for at least 200 aircraft to be produced for Britain and 200 for France.

SPECIFICATIONS

Crew: 1 in Jaguar-A/K/M/S
2 in Jaguar-B/E

Engines: 2 Rolls-Royce/Turboméca Adour turbofan engines (5,115 lb, 2,320 kg st each; 7,304 lb, 3,315 kg st with afterburners)

Dimensions: span 28 ft 6 in (8·69 m), length 50 ft 11 in (15·52 m) for Jaguar-A/K/M/S; 53 ft 11 in (16·44 m) for Jaguar-B/E, height 16 ft 1¾ in (4·91 m), wing area 258⅓ sq ft (24·02 m)

Speed: 990 mph (1,590 km/hr) at 36,000 ft (11,000 m) (Mach 1·5); 840 mph (1,350 km/hr) at sea level (Mach 1·1)

Range: 500-mile (800 km) combat radius with internal fuel only; 800-mile (1,290 km) combat radius with external fuel tanks; 2,200-mile (3,540 km) ferry range

Weights: 24,000 lb (10,900 kg) normal; 34,000 lb (15,440 kg) maximum

Armament: 1 or 2 × 30-mm cannon and reconnaissance pack
or 1 × Martel AS.37 ASM
or 6 × 250-lb bombs
or 2 × 1,000-lb bombs (centreline pylon) plus 18 × 250-lb bombs
or 6 × 1,000-lb bombs (wing pylons)

Two-seat Jaguar B of the Royal Air Force (BAC)

VARIANTS

Jaguar-A single-seat tactical support aircraft for France; 2 × 30-mm DEFA 553 cannon; first flight March 29, 1969; 80 ordered including prototypes A-03 and A-04.

Jaguar-B two-seat operational training aircraft for RAF (designated Jaguar T.2); 1 × 30-mm Aden cannon; first flight August 30, 1971; 37 ordered including prototype B-08.

Jaguar-E two-seat advanced training aircraft for France; 2 × 30-mm DEFA 553 cannon; 40 ordered including prototypes E-01 and E-02.

Jaguar-K planned export version of Jaguar-A.

Jaguar-M single-seat naval strike aircraft for France; 2 × 30-mm DEFA 533 cannon; designed for carrier operation; project cancelled in 1973.

Jaguar-S single-seat tactical support aircraft for RAF (designated Jaguar GR.1); 2 × 30-mm Aden cannon; fitted with advanced navigation and weapons control system incorporating Elliott MCS 290M digital computer, laser rangefinder, and electronic sensor on tail fin; first flight October 12, 1969; 212 ordered including prototypes S-06 and S-07.

OPERATIONAL

France, Great Britain (RAF)

Jastreb J-1 Soko

The Jastreb (Hawk) is a single-seat, turbojet light attack aircraft developed from the similar Galeb (Seagull) two-seat trainer of the Yugoslavian Air Force. Like the contemporary Jet Provost and Macchi MB.326, the Jastreb/Galeb aircraft are powered by a Rolls-Royce engine. Apart from its use within Yugoslavia, the aircraft has been exported in small numbers to two African states.

Jastreb light attack aircraft, a derivative of the two-seat Galeb trainer

The Jastreb/Galeb design features a straight-wing configuration with small air intakes faired into the fuselage just forward of the wing leading edges. Wingtip tanks are fitted. The Jastreb has three fixed machineguns in the nose (one or two MG in the Galeb) and external stores can be fitted on eight wing attachment points.

Status: *Operational.* First flight May 1961 (Galeb).

SPECIFICATIONS

Crew: 1
Engine: 1 Rolls-Royce Bristol Viper 531 turbojet (3,000 lb, 1,360 kg st)
Dimensions: span 34 ft 8 in (10·56 m), length 35 ft 1½ in (10·71 m), height 11 ft 1½ in (3·64 m), wing area 209 sq ft (19·44 m²)
Speed: 510 mph (820 km/hr) at 19,680 ft (6,000 m)

Ceiling: 39,375 ft (12,000 m)
Range: 945 miles (1,520 km) with tip tanks
Weights: 6,217 lb (2,820 kg) empty; 10,287 lb (4,660 kg) maximum
Armament: 3 × ·50-cal Colt-Browning machineguns (135 rpg) and 4 × 113 lb plus 6 × 127-mm rockets

OPERATIONAL

Tanzania, Yugoslavia, Zambia

Jet Provost BAC (BAC-145)

The Jet Provost counterinsurgency aircraft is an armed configuration of the two-seat, turbojet-powered Jet Provost trainer. The last two production T.4 trainers were modified to the armed T.5 variant to serve as prototypes for a low-cost, easily maintained COIN aircraft. In addition, some armed variants of early Jet Provosts are flown by Rhodesia and South Yemen.

The Jet Provost is a small straight-wing aircraft with small air intakes on either side of the cockpit which has side by side seating. Small wingtip tanks are fitted. There is an internal gun armament and eight wing hardpoints for external stores. The aircraft has the company designation BAC-145.

Jet Provost T.5 of the Royal Air Force

Status: *Operational.* First flight February 28, 1967 (T.5).

SPECIFICATIONS (T.5)

Crew: 2
Engine: 1 Rolls-Royce Bristol Viper
202 turbojet (2,500 lb, 1,135 kg st)
Dimensions: span 35 ft 4 in (10·76
m), length 34 ft (10·37 m), height
10 ft 2 in (3·10 m), wing area
213¾ ft (19·88 m²)
Speed: 440 mph (708 km/hr) at
25,000 ft (7,625 m)

Ceiling: 36,750 ft (11,205 m)
Range: 900 miles (1,450 km)
Weight: 9,200 lb (4,175 kg)
maximum
Armament: 2 × 7·62-mm FN
machineguns (550 rpg) and up to
3,000 lb of bombs, rockets (wing
hardpoints)

VARIANTS

T.5 two-seat armed counter-insurgency aircraft developed from Jet Provost T.4; 110 built for RAF plus 2 prototypes; 5 built for Sudan (designated T.55).

T.51 armed version of Jet Provost T.3 for Kuwait, Sudan, Sri Lanka.
T.52 armed version of Jet Provost T.4 for Iraq, Sudan, Venezuela, South Yemen.

OPERATIONAL

Great Britain (RAF), Iraq, Kuwait, Rhodesia, South Yemen, Sri Lanka,

Sudan, Venezuela

Kraguj Soko

The P-2 Kraguj is a lightweight, piston-engine, close-support aircraft flown by the Yugoslav Air Force. It features ease of handling and simple maintenance.

The aircraft has a low, straight-wing configuration with a bubble cockpit and an air-cooled engine with a large spinner. The main landing gear retracts and there is a fixed tailwheel. A single machinegun is fitted in each wing

Soko Kraguj of the Yugoslav Air Force

outboard of the propeller disc, and two small bombs or rocket pods can be carried on two inboard wing pylons, and rockets on four outboard wing pylons.

Status: *Operational.* First flight in 1966; squadron delivery in 1968.

SPECIFICATIONS

Crew: 1

Engine: 1 Lycoming GSO-480-BiA6 air-cooled in-line piston (340 hp)

Dimensions: span 34 ft 11 in (10·64 m), length 26 ft $\frac{1}{4}$ in (7·93 m), height 9 ft 10 in (3·10 m), wing area 183 sq ft (17·02 m²)

Max level speed: 183 mph (295 km/hr) at 5,000 ft (1,500 m); 171 mph (275 km/hr) at sea level

Range: 500 miles (805 km)

Weights: 2,491 lb (1,130 kg) empty; 3,580 lb (1,625 kg) maximum

Armament: 2 × 7·7-mm machineguns (650 rpg) and 2 × 220-lb bombs plus 4 × 57-mm rockets or 4 × 127-mm rockets (wing pylons)

OPERATIONAL

Yugoslavia

Lansen SAAB-32 SAAB

The Lansen (Lance) is a single-seat, swept-wing, multi-purpose aircraft flown exclusively by the Swedish Air Force. In service since the mid-1950s, the Lansen's replacement by the Viggen began in 1971; however, the Lansen can be expected to remain in first-line service as well as supplementary roles through the 1970s.

The single-engine aircraft has small air intakes in the "cheek" position just forward of the wing leading edges. Internal 20-mm or 30-mm cannon are provided and multiple racks in A and C variants permit carrying bombs or air-to-air and air-to-surface missiles. The aircraft can reach Mach 1 in a shallow dive.

Status: *Operational.* First flight November 3, 1952; approximately 450 aircraft produced from 1953 to 1960.

A32A Lansens of the Swedish Air Force, armed with Rb.04 ASMs

SPECIFICATIONS (A32A)

Crew: 1

Engine: 1 Svenska Flygmotor RM6A Rolls-Royce RB.90 Jk. 47A Avon) (11,025 lb, 5,005 kg st dry; 14,030 lb 6,370 kg st with afterburner)

Dimensions: span 42 ft 7¾ in (13·00 m), length 49 ft ¼ in (14·95 m), height 15 ft 3 in (4·65 m), wing area 402½ sq ft (37·43 m²)

Speed: 710 mph (1,142 km/hr) at sea level (Mach 0·93); 630 mph (1,015 km/hr) at 36,000 ft (11,000 m) (Mach 0·95)

Ceiling: 52,490 ft (16,000 m)

Range: approx 1,000 miles (1,600 km) with AAMs and external fuel

Weights: 16,535 lb (7,507 kg) empty; 24,680 lb (11,205 kg) loaded clean; 29,760 lb (13,510 kg) max loaded

Armament: 4 × 30-mm Aden M/55 cannon
or 2 × RB.04 ASMs
or 24 × rockets (wing racks)

VARIANTS

SAAB-32 prototype aircraft; 4 built.

A 32A all-weather attack variant with RM5A2 (Avon 100) engine; armed with 4 × 20-mm Hispano cannon and 2 × 1,323-lb bombs or 3 × 1,100-lb bombs or 4 × 550-lb bombs; also air-to-surface missiles; approx 260 built 1953–1958.

A 32B night and all-weather fighter variant; first flight January 7, 1957;

approx 150 built through 1960.

A 32C photo-electronic reconnaissance variant with RM 5A (Avon 100) engine; cannon deleted; fitted with 5 OMERA cameras (side oblique and vertical) and Saturnus electronic equipment; wing ordnance racks retained; first flight March 26, 1957; limited number built through 1960.

OPERATIONAL

Sweden

Magister Potez/Aérospatiale (CM. 170/175)
Super Magister

The Magister is an armed turbojet trainer that has been employed in the attack role by Algeria, Israel, Morocco, and Uganda, in addition to being flown by several other air arms in the training role. The Super Magister is essentially the same aircraft with more powerful engines and is flown in the attack role by Eire.

The Magister has slightly swept wings with wingtip tanks, a large bubble canopy, and a distinctive V-shaped tail configuration with the surfaces set at an angle of 110 degrees. Fouga, the original manufacturer, became the Potez group and then part of Sud-Aviation, and subsequently Aérospatiale. The aircraft has been produced under licence by Valmet of Finland and Israel

Aircraft Industries. The company designation was CM. 170 for the Magister and Super Magister, while 32 modified for carrier operation by the French Navy were designated CM. 175 Zephyrs.

Status: *Operational.* First flight July 23, 1952.

SPECIFICATIONS (CM.170-1)

Crew: 2
Engines: 2 Turboméca Marboré IIA turbojets (880 lb, 400 kg st each)
Dimensions: span 39 ft 10 in (12·17 m), length 33 ft (10·07 m), height 9 ft 2 in (2·79 m), wing area 186 sq ft (17·30 m²)
Speed: 444 mph (714 km/hr) at 30,000 ft (11,000 m); 400 mph (644 km/hr) at sea level

Ceiling: 36,000 ft (10,980 m)
Range: approx 600 miles (965 km)
Weights: 4,740 lb (2,150 kg) empty; 7,055 lb (3,200 kg) loaded
Armament: 2 × 7·62 machineguns (200 rpg) and 2 × 110-lb bombs or 2 × Nord AS.11 ASMs (wing racks)

VARIANTS

prototypes 3 built.
CM. 170-1 production aircraft with Marboré IIA engines; first flight July 7, 1954; built for Algeria, Belgium, Brazil, Cambodia, France, Lebanon, Libya, Morocco; licence built in Finland and Israel for El Salvador, Finland, Israel, and Uganda.

CM. 170-2 Super Magister; production aircraft with Marboré VI engines; 130 built for Brazil, Eire, France.
CM. 175 Zephyr; carrier-based trainer; first flight May 30, 1959; 32 built for French Navy.

OPERATIONAL (attack role)

Algeria, Eire, El Salvador, Israel, Morocco, Uganda

Magister of the Israeli Defence Force (Israeli Defence Force)

Zephyr of the French Navy (French Armed Forces)

Marut HF-24 Hindustan Aeronautics Ltd

The HF-24 Marut (Wind Spirit) is a ground attack aircraft which has the distinction of being India's first indigenous combat aircraft. The Marut is a swept-wing aircraft with two turbojet engines. The aircraft is in squadron service with the Indian Air Force and was most successfully employed in the December 1971 war against Pakistan.

The swept-wing Marut has air intakes for the two jet engines forward of the wing leading edges and alongside the cockpit, with half-cone centrebodies projecting from the intakes. Four cannon are mounted in the nose and there is a retractable rocket pack aft of the nosewheel housing. External weapon stores can be carried on four wing pylons.

Status: *Operational.* First flight June 17, 1961; squadron delivery May 1964.

SPECIFICATIONS (HF-24 Mk.I)

Crew: 1
Engines: 2 HAL-built Rolls-Royce Bristol Orpheus 703 turbojets (4,850 lb, 2,200 kg st each)
Dimensions: span 29 ft $6\frac{1}{4}$ in (9·00 m), length 52 ft $\frac{3}{4}$ in (15·87 m), height 11 ft $9\frac{3}{4}$ in (3·59 m), wing area $301\frac{1}{2}$ sq ft (28·04 m²)
Speed: 673 mph (1,083 km/hr) at 40,000 ft (12,200 m) (Mach 1·02)
Ceiling: approx 60,000 ft (18,300 m)
Weights: 13,658 lb (6,200 kg) empty; 19,734 lb (8,960 kg) loaded clean; 24,085 lb (10,935 kg) maximum
Armament: 4 × 30-mm Aden Mk 2 (130 rpg), 50 × 58-mm SNEB AARs (retractable fuselage pack) and 4 × 1,000-lb bombs (wing pylons)

VARIANTS

Mk.1 pre-production and production fighter-attack aircraft (including 2 prototypes).

Mk.IA pre-production Mk.I fitted with afterburner.

Mk.IT two-seat trainer; rocket pack removed; first flight April 30, 1970; 2 prototypes plus limited production.

Mk.II pre-production fighter-attack aircraft with afterburner; 4 built.

Mk.III design study of redesigned aircraft fitted with 2 Turbo-Union R.B.199 turbofan engines; to be capable of Mach 2.

OPERATIONAL

India

HF.24 Marut Mk.1 of the Indian Air Force

M.B.326 Aermacchi

The M.B.326 was developed to meet Italian Air Force requirements for a basic jet trainer and has subsequently been adopted for counterinsurgency by several nations. The M.B.326 is an essentially straight-wing, single-engine aircraft and has replaced older, dual-role aircraft such as the T-6 Texan, T-28 Trojan, and T-33 Shooting Star.

The M.B.326 air intakes are in the wing roots with the wing leading edges having a slight sweep; the tail fin is set forward of the horizontal tail surfaces and wingtip tanks are fitted. The later M.B.326K variant has the second crew position deleted and 2 × 30-mm cannon are provided in the lower front fuselage. Earlier variants armed with gun pods and other external weapons. Up to 4,000 lb (1,815 kg) of external weapon stores can be carried on six wing pylons.

M.B.326K single-seat version of the MB.326 (Aermacchi)

M.B.326H of the Royal Australian Navy (Royal Australian Navy)

Status: *Operational.* First flight December 10, 1957. Approx 600 aircraft built including licenced production by Atlas Aircraft in South Africa, Commonwealth Aircraft Corp in Australia, and EMBRAER in Brazil.

SPECIFICATIONS (M.B.326K)

Crew: 1

Engine: 1 Rolls-Royce Bristol Viper Mk 632-43 turbojet (4,000 lb, 1,815 kg st)

Dimensions: span 35 ft 7 in (10·85 m), length 34 ft 11¼ in (10·65 m), height 12 ft 2 in (3·69 m), wing area 208⅓ sq. ft (19·37 m²)

Max level speed: 576 mph (925 km/hr) at sea level (clean); 426 mph (685 km/hr) at 30,000 ft (11,000 m)

Ceiling: 39,000 ft (11,900 m)

Range: 165-mile (265 km) radius with 2,822 lb (1,280 kg) weapons and internal fuel; 645-mile (1,038 km) radius with camera pod and external fuel tanks; 1,323-mile (2,128 km) ferry range

Weights: 6,240 lb (2,833 kg) empty; 9,680 lb (4,395 kg) normal clean; 12,500 lb (5,675 kg) maximum

Armament: 2 × 30-mm DEFA cannon (125 rpg) or 4 × 500-lb bombs plus 2 × 750-lb bombs (wing pylons)

VARIANTS

prototypes prototype aircraft with Rolls-Royce Bristol Viper 8 engine and Piaggio-built Viper 11 engines; 2 built.

M.B.326/326D two-seat basic trainer with Bristol Viper 11 engine; first flight October 5, 1960; 100 built for Italian Air Force and 4 with modified avionics for *Alitalia* (M.B.326D).

M.B.326B/F/M two-seat trainer/ground attack aircraft with Viper 11 engine; 8 built for Tunisia (M.B.326B), 7 for Ghana (M.B.326F); built by Atlas in South Africa (M.B.326M).

M.B.326G two-seat trainer/ground attack aircraft with Viper 20 Mk 540 engine; 8 built for Argentina, 17 for Zaïre, 20 for Zambia; 112 assembled in Brazil by EMBRAER (designated AT-26 Xavante) for Brazil and 18 for Bolivia.

M.B.326H two-seat trainer aircraft with Bristol Viper 11 engine; built by Commonwealth Aircraft Corp; 97 built for Australia.

M.B.326K single-seat operational trainer/attack aircraft with Bristol Viper 632 engine (initial prototype flew with Viper 540 engine); fixed gun armament; first flight August 22, 1970; in production for Italy and possibly South Africa.

OPERATIONAL

Argentina, Australia; Bolivia, Brazil, Congo, Ghana, Italy, South Africa, Tunisia, Zaïre, Zambia

Mirage 5 Dassault

The Mirage 5 is a ground-attack aircraft with a secondary intercept capability based on the Mirage III-E airframe and engine. Slightly longer and heavier than its predecessor, this single-seat, single-engine, delta-wing aircraft has

Mirage 5-C of the Colombian Air Force (Dassault)

Mirage 5-DV of the Venezuelan Air Force (Dassault)

the same speed as the Mirage III but can carry more fuel and ordnance, and can operate from rough airfields.

Internal cannon are provided and ordnance can be carried on seven external store points which have a maximum aggregate capacity of some 8,000 lb (3,630 kg). A development of the Mirage 5 is an aircraft fitted with so-called "moustaches", which are two small, retractable foreplane surfaces installed in the nose that extend to improve performance during take-off and landing.

Status: *Operational.* First flight May 19, 1967; squadron delivery in May 1968. More than 400 aircraft produced with assembly by SABCA in Belgium.

SPECIFICATIONS

Crew: 1 or 2 (see variants)

Engine: 1 SNECMA Atar 9C turbojet (13,670 lb, 6,200 kg st with afterburner)

Dimensions: span 27 ft (8·22 m), length 51 ft $\frac{1}{4}$ in (15·55 m), height 13 ft 11 in (4·24 m)

Speed: 1,460 mph (2,350 km/hr) at 40,000 ft (12,000 m) (Mach 2·1) (clean); maximum stabilized speed 1,188 mph (1,910 km/hr) (Mach 1·8)

Ceiling: 55,775 ft (17,000 m)

Range: 800-mile (650 km) combat radius with 2,000-lb (910 kg) external ordnance; 2,500-mile (4,020 km) ferry range

Weights: 14,550 lb (6,605 kg) empty; 29,760 lb (13,500 kg) loaded

Armament: 2 × 30-mm DEFA cannon (125 rpg) and 10 × 500-lb bombs or 2 × 1,000-lb bombs plus 1 × AS.30 ASM or 4 × 1,000-lb bombs plus 2 × Sidewinder AIM-9 AAMs (wing and fuselage pylons)

VARIANTS

5-A series single-seat (5-AD/5-RAD) and two-seat (5-DAD) aircraft flown by Abu Dhabi.

5-B series single-seat aircraft with advanced navigation equipment (5-BA), two-seat aircraft (5-BD), and photo reconnaissance aircraft with 5 Vinten 300 cameras (5-BR) flown by Belgium; first flight March 6, 1970 (5-BA).

5-C series single-seat (5-COA/5-COR) and two-seat (5-COD) aircraft flown by Colombia.

5-D series single-seat (5-D/5-DE/5-DR) and two-seat (5-DD) aircraft flown by Libya.

5-J series aircraft produced for Israel but retained by France; 50 built.

5-M series single-seat (5-M) and two-seat (5-DM) aircraft flown by Zaïre.

5-P series single-seat (5-P) and two-seat (5-DP) aircraft flown by Peru.

5-PA series single-seat aircraft flown by Pakistan.

5-S series single-seat (5-SDE) and two-seat (5-SDD) aircraft flown by Saudi Arabia.

5-V series single-seat (5-V) and two-seat (5-DV) aircraft flown by Venezuela.

M5-F French designation of 5-J.

OPERATIONAL

Abu Dhabi, Belgium, Colombia, France, Libya, Pakistan, Peru, Saudi Arabia, Venezuela, Zaïre

Peacemaker AU-23 Fairchild

The US Air Force purchased 15 Fairchild Porter aircraft for counterinsurgency operations, most of which have subsequently been transferred to Thailand. An estimated additional 20 Peacemaker aircraft were ordered for Thailand. Peacemaker is a Fairchild designation while AU-23A is the USAF nomenclature for the aircraft which were acquired for evaluation in competition with the Helio AU-24A under the Credible Chase programme.

The single-engine, short take-off-and-landing (STOL) aircraft is produced by Fairchild Industries under licence from Pilatus Flugzeugwerke AG of Switzerland. The aircraft has a high straight-wing configuration with squared off wingtips, vertical tail surfaces, and tail fin. Also prominent are the large propeller spinner and fixed landing gear. The aircraft is armed with a 20-mm gun manually fired through the aircraft's portside cabin doorway. It can carry minigun pods, rocket launchers, broadcasting speaker pods, camera pods, flare dispensers, or 250 lb (115 kg) bombs on one fuselage hardpoint which can hold 590 lb (270 kg) of stores, two wing pylons for 590 lb (270 kg) each and two for 350 lb (160 kg) each. Eight troops or 1,156 lb (525 kg) of cargo can be carried internally when weapons are not loaded.

Status: *Operational.* First flight May 4, 1959 (Pilatus PC-6).

AU-23A Peace-maker, operated by Thailand

SPECIFICATIONS

Crew: 3 (2 pilots, 1 gunner) + 8 troops
Engines: 1 AiResearch TPE331-1-101F turboprop (575 shp)
Dimensions: span 49 ft 10½ in (15·22 m), length 35 ft 9 in (10·90 m), height 10 ft 6 in (3·20 m), wing area 310 sq ft (28·83 m²)
Speed: 174 mph (280 km/hr)

Ceiling: 27,875 ft (8,500 m)
Range: 863 miles (1,388 km)
Weights: 2,612 lb (1,185 kg) empty; 4,850 lb (2,200 kg) loaded
Armament: 1 × 20-mm XM-197 cannon and up to 2,000 lb (908 kg) of external stores

VARIANTS

AU-23A militarized version acquired by US Air Force; 15 built with 13 transferred to Thailand (1 previously lost); 20 additional aircraft ordered for Thailand.

OPERATIONAL

Thailand

Pucará IA-58 FMA (Argentina)

The IA.58 Pucará is a counterinsurgency aircraft developed to the specifications of the Argentine Air Force. The twin turboprop aircraft was originally known as Dolphin. About 70 are planned for procurement by Argentina.

The Pucará has a distinctive design with the tandem cockpit forward of the straight wings, comparatively small wing-mounted engine nacelles, and the vertical tail surfaces mounted almost at the top of the fin, giving a T-shape

*IA.58 Pucará
of the Argentine
Air Force*

appearance. The aircraft has six internal guns with one pylon under the fuse-lage and two under the outer wing sections for external weapon stores.

Status: *Operational.* First flight September 1958 (AX-01): squadron delivery 1975.

SPECIFICATIONS

Crew: 2
Engines: 2 Turboméca Astazou XVIG turboprops (1,022 ehp each)
Dimensions: span 47 ft 6¾ in (14·50 m), length 46 ft 3 in (14·10 m), height 17 ft 7 in (17·55 m), wing area 326 sq ft (30·32 m²)
Speed: 466 mph (750 km/hr)

Ceiling: 27,165 ft (8,280 m)
Range: 1,890 miles (3,042 km)
Weights: 8,900 lb (4,040 kg) empty; 14,300 lb (6,490 kg) maximum
Armament: 2 × 20-mm Hispano cannon, 4 × 7·62-mm FN machine-guns and up to 2,200 lb of rockets, gun pods (fuselage and wing pylons)

VARIANTS

AX-01 prototype with AiResearch TPE 331 engines.
AX-02 prototype with Turboméca

Astazou XVIG engine; first flight September 6, 1970.

OPERATIONAL

Argentina

SAAB-105 SAAB

The SAAB-105 is a two-seat, twin-turbojet aircraft intended primarily for close support and training. The aircraft, developed as a private venture, is

SAAB 105OE for the Austrian Air Force (SAAB)

designated SK 60 in the Swedish Air Force and is also flown by the Austrian Air Force.

The SAAB-105 has a high wing with turbojet nacelles at the wing roots in the "shoulder" position. The cockpit is forward of the slightly swept wings with normal side-by-side seating; the standard ejection seats can be replaced by four fixed seats. The aircraft has a T-tail configuration. Armament is carried on four wing pylons capable of lifting 992 lb (450 kg) and two pylons for 606 lb (275 kg) with a maximum external load of 5,180 lb (2,350 kg); with full internal fuel up to 3,748 lb (1,700 kg) can be carried externally. A nose camera can be fitted for reconnaissance missions (retaining full weapons capability) or camera pods can be fitted on wing pylons.

Status: *Operational.* First flight June 29, 1963; squadron delivery early 1966.

SPECIFICATIONS (SAAB-105G)

Crew: 2

Engines: 2 General Electric J85-GE-17B turbojets (2,850 lb, 1,293 kg each)

Dimensions: span 31 ft 2 in (9·50 m), length 35 ft 5$\frac{1}{4}$ in (10·80 m), height 8 ft 10 in (2·70 m), wing area 175 sq ft (16·28 m²)

Speed: 597 mph (960 km/hr) clean at sea level; 547 mph (880 km/hr) loaded at sea level; 541 mph (870 km/hr) clean at 32,800 ft (10,000 m)

Ceiling: 42,650 ft (13,000 m)

Range: 430-mile (690 km) radius with 3,000 lb (1,362 kg) weapons; 620-mile (997 km) radius with 2,000 lb (908 kg) weapons; 1,700-mile (2,735 km) ferry range

Weights: 6,834 lb (3,100 kg) empty; 10,714 lb (4,864 kg) loaded clean; 14,330 lb (6,505 kg) maximum

Armament: 6 × 500-lb bombs or 4 × 750-lb bombs plus 2 × Sidewinder AIM-9 AAMs or 4 × 1,000-lb bombs plus 2 × Sidewinder AIM-9 AAMs

VARIANTS

SAAB-105 prototype aircraft; 2 built.

SK 60A production training and liaison aircraft with Turboméca Aubsique turbofans; first flight August 27, 1965; 150 built for Sweden (including SK 60B/C variants).

SK 60B SK 60A modified for attack capability with six wing pylons for 1,543 lb (700 kg) of external stores.

SK 60C SK 60B modified for reconnaissance with permanent nose camera installation; SK 60B weapons capability retained; first flight January 18, 1967.

SAAB-105XT prototype improved attack and training aircraft derived from SK 60B with J85-GE-17B turbojets;

4,410 lb (2,000 kg) external weapons capability; increased internal fuel; first flight April 29, 1967.

SAAB-105XH proposed development of SAAB-105XT for Sweden with internal 30-mm Aden cannon; small fixed wingtip tanks; project cancelled.

SAAB-105Ö production attack and training aircraft based on SAAB-105XT with additional fuel, improved instruments; 40 built for Austria.

SAAB-105G production attack and training aircraft developed from SAAB-105Ö; 5,180 lb (2,350 kg) external weapons capability; improved avionics; increased manoeuvrability; first flight May 26, 1972.

OPERATIONAL

Austria, Sweden

Saeta
Super Saeta } HA-200/HA-220 Hispano

This light, turbojet-powered aircraft is flown by Spain and Egypt in the advanced trainer and ground attack roles. The design has undergone a number of modifications, with the later configurations known as the Super Saeta.

The Saeta has an unusual configuration in that intakes for the twin turbojets are located side-by-side in the nose; the wings are essentially straight with wingtip tanks fitted, a distinctively large "greenhouse" canopy, and the horizontal tail surfaces mounted part way up the fin. One or two guns are fitted in the upper nose fairing, and two fuselage attachment points and four wing pylons can carry a variety of external weapons. Licence production undertaken by Helwan Air Works in Egypt.

Status: *Operational*. First flight August 12, 1955.

SPECIFICATIONS (HA-220)

Crew: 1 (2 in HA-200 variants)
Engines: 2 Turboméca Marboré VI turbojets (1,058 lb, 480 kg each)

Dimensions: span 34 ft 2 in (10·42 m), length 29 ft 5 in (8·97 m), height 9 ft 4 in (2·85 m), wing area $187\frac{1}{4}$ ft (17·41 m²)

Speed: 429 mph (690 km/hr) at 23,000 ft (7,015 m); 413 mph (665 km/hr) at sea level
Ceiling: 42,650 ft (13,008 m)
Range: 930 miles (1,496 km)
Weights: 4,453 lb (2,020 kg) normal; 7,937 lb (3,603 kg) maximum
Armament: 2 × 7·7-mm machineguns and various combinations of bombs and rockets (fuselage hardpoints and wing pylons)

VARIANTS

HA-200 initial design; 2 prototypes and 5 pre-production aircraft built.

HA-200A initial production aircraft with Turboméca Marboré IIA turbojets; 30 built.

HA-200B developed for Egypt; armed with 1 × 20-mm cannon in place of MG; first flight July 21, 1960; 10 built by Hispano and 90 by Helwan (named Al-Kahira), all for Egypt.

HA-200D improved production aircraft; 55 built for Spanish Air Force.

HA-200E Super Saeta advanced trainer with Turboméca Marboré VI turbojets; only prototype built.

HA-220 Super Saeta advanced ground attack aircraft developed from HA-200E; 25 built for Spanish Air Force.

OPERATIONAL

Egypt, Spain

HA-200E Super Saeta of the Spanish Air Force

Shooting Star F-80/T-33 Lockheed

The single-seat, straight-wing F-80 Shooting Star was the first operational US jet-propelled fighter. Developed too late to see combat in the Second World War, an F-80 won history's first jet-versus-jet dogfight, destroying a MiG-15 over North Korea on November 8, 1950. The aircraft was flown extensively by US forces prior to the availability of swept-wing aircraft. Only Uruguay now flies the F-80 in a "combat" role although numerous two-place T-33 variants are in service in more than a dozen countries.

The F-80 design provided for an attractive, low-wing configuration with small engine intakes forward of the wing leading edges. The design readily facilitated adaption to a two-seat aircraft (T-33) and more of the latter were

*T-33 Shooting
Star*

built than the F-80 variants, with some two-seat aircraft being given a limited ground attack capability (AT-33) and reconnaissance capability (RT-33). The T-33 was three feet longer than the basic F-80 aircraft. (Designation changed from P-80 to F-80 in 1947.)

Status: *Operational.* First flight January 9, 1944 (XP-80); squadron delivery in February 1945; 1,751 built plus 5,819 two-seat T-33 aircraft.

SPECIFICATIONS (T-33)

Crew: 2
Engine: 1 Allison J33-A-35 turbojet (5,200 lb, 2,360 kg st)
Dimensions: span 38 ft 10½ in (11·86 m), length 37 ft 6 in (11·44 m), height 11 ft 7 in (3·53 m)
Speed: 600 mph (965 km/hr)

Ceiling: 45,000 + ft (13,725 m)
Range: 1,350 miles (2,172 km)
Weight: 16,000 + lb (7,265 kg) maximum
Armament: 6 × ·50-cal machineguns and 2 × 1,000-lb bombs (wing attachment points)

VARIANTS

XP-80 experimental aircraft with de Havilland Goblin H-1b engine; 1 built.

XP-80A experimental aircraft with General Electric I-40 engine; first flight June 10, 1944; 2 built.

YP-80A production prototypes with Allison J-33 engine; first flight September 13, 1944; 13 built.

P-80A production aircraft with J33-A-11 engine; 677 built through 1947; some subsequently modified to RF-80A photo reconnaissance role or to P-80B configuration; 3 flown by US Navy as P-80A.

P-80B P-80 with J33-A-21 engine

with water-alcohol injection; improved guns; first flight in March 1947; 240 built to P-80B configuration and additional P-80A aircraft modified.

F-80C major production variant with J33-A-23 engine; fitted for air combat and ground attack; first flight March 1, 1948; 798 built through June 1950 with some configured as RF-80C for photo reconnaissance; flown by US Air Force, Navy, and Marine Corps, Brazil, Chile, Ecuador, Peru, Uruguay.

XF-80R high-speed variant (624 mph, 1,004 km/hr) with J33-A-23 engine; 1 built.

T-33A/B two-seat trainer variant with J33-A-23 (T-33A) or J33-A-35 (T-33B) engine; 5,819 built; flown by US Air Force, Navy, Marine Corps, and numerous other nations; RT-33A modified for photo reconnaissance; AT-33A for ground attack role; DT-33A drone control aircraft; QT-33A radio drone.

TV-1 formerly TO-1; F-80C aircraft used by US Navy and Marine Corps as operational trainers; 50 acquired.

TV-2 formerly TO-2; T-33A aircraft used by US Navy and Marine Corps; 699 acquired.

OPERATIONAL (all T-33 variants except Uruguay with both F-80C and T-33)

Brazil, Burma, Bolivia, Ethiopia, Guatemala, Honduras, Mexico,

Nicaragua, Peru, Pakistan, Thailand, Uruguay, Yugoslavia

Skyhawk A-4 McDonnell Douglas

Originally designed to deliver a single nuclear weapon under visual flight conditions from an aircraft carrier against targets in the Soviet Union, the A-4 Skyhawk has become one of the most successful and versatile light attack aircraft ever produced. More than 2,600 Skyhawks have been built since the aircraft entered US Navy service in 1954 with production continuing to the present time. During the 1960s all US aircraft carriers had two or three Skyhawk squadrons; now only the soon-to-be-retired carrier *Hancock* operates the aircraft. However, the Skyhawk remains in US Navy service as a training aircraft and in first-line service with the US Marine Corps as well as Argentina, Australia, Israel, Kuwait, New Zealand, and Singapore.

The Skyhawk was developed in an effort to counter the growing weight and complexity of jet-propelled aircraft. The diminutive aircraft was initially a single-seat aircraft with a single engine and a delta-wing configuration; subsequently, a number of two-seat variants have entered service. The air intakes are above the wing and behind the cockpit; normally 2 × 20-mm cannon are fitted in the wing roots although one gun is sometimes replaced by electronic equipment; three wing and fuselage pylons in the early aircraft increased to five in the A-4E; refuelling probe fitted along the starboard side beginning with the A-4B; dorsal "hump" for additional electronic equipment aft of cockpit in A-4F and later aircraft. The Skyhawk wings are too small to require folding for carrier operation (the AV-8 Harrier is the only other fixed-wing US carrier aircraft with non-folding wings).

Status: *Operational.* First flight June 22, 1954; squadron delivery October 1956.

A-4F Skyhawk of the US Navy (US Navy)

EA-4F Skyhawk, two-seat modification of the TA-4F (US Navy)

SPECIFICATIONS (A-4M/N)

Crew: 1 (2 in TA-4 variants)
Engine: 1 Pratt & Whitney J52-P-408A turbojet (11,200 lb, 5,085 kg st)
Dimensions: span 27 ft 6 in (8·38 m), length 40 ft 3½ in (12·27 m), height 15 ft (4·58 m), wing area 260 sq ft (24·18 m²)
Max level speed: 670 mph (1,078 km/hr) clean at sea level (Mach 0·94); 645 mph (1,038 km/hr) with 4,000 lb (1,816 kg) external weapons
Range: 335-mile (540 km) radius with 4,000 lb (1,816 kg) weapons; 2,055-mile (3,307 km) ferry range
Weights: 10,465 lb (4,750 kg) empty; 24,500 lb (11,123 kg) normal maximum

Armament: 2 × 20-mm Mk-12 cannon (200 rpg) and 4 × Bullpup AGM-12 ASMs
or 3 × 2,000-lb bombs

or 6 × 500-lb bombs plus 12 × 250-lb bombs plus 2 × Bullpup AGM-12 ASMs (wing and fuselage pylons)

VARIANTS

XA4D-1 prototype aircraft with Wright J65-W-2 (Armstrong Siddeley Sapphire) engine; 2 built.

A-4A formerly A4D-1; production aircraft with J65-W-4/-4B engine; span 27 ft 6 in (8·38 m), length 39 ft 4 in (12·00 m); 3 pylons with 5,000 lb (2,270 kg) capacity; 8,400 lb (3,814 kg) empty, 22,000 lb (9,988 kg) maximum; 165 built.

A-4B formerly A4D-2; production aircraft with J65-W-16A/-20 engine; Bullpup AGM-12 ASM capability; first flight March 26, 1956; 542 built for US Navy, and Marine Corps; 30 refurbished for transfer to Thailand, approx 45 for Argentine Air Force (A-4P), approx 15 for Argentine Navy (A-4Q), 40 for Singapore (A-4S) with 2 × 30-mm Aden cannon.

TA-4B noncombat A-4B used for training.

A-4C formerly A4D-2N; production aircraft with J65-W-16A/20 engine; improved avionics; length 42 ft 10¾ in (13·08 m); first flight August 21, 1959; 638 built for US Navy, US Marine Corps; subsequently refurbished for US Naval Reserve (A-4L).

A-4D formerly A4D-3; planned aircraft with J52-P-2 engine; 4 ordered but programme cancelled.

A-4E formerly A-4E; production aircraft with Pratt & Whitney J52-P-6A/-8A/-8B engine; 5 pylons with 8,200 lb (3,722 kg) capacity; 9,853 lb (4,473 kg) empty, 24,500 lb (11,123 kg) maximum; first flight July 12, 1961; 500 built for US Navy, US Marine Corps; 70 A-4E/F built for Israel

(A-4H) with 2 × 30-mm DEFA cannon (150 rpg).

TA-4E prototype two-seat trainer retaining combat capability; length 45 ft 3 in (13·80 m); first flight June 30, 1965; subsequently redesignated TA-4F; 2 built.

A-4F production aircraft with J52-P-8A/-8B engine; improved avionics; first flight August 31, 1966; 146 built for US Navy, US Marine Corps; 8 built for Australia with Sidewinder AIM-9 AAM capability (A-4G); 10 built for New Zealand (A-4K).

EA-4F two-seat modification of TA-4F for electronic warfare training.

TA-4F production two-seat trainer retaining combat capability with J52-P-6A/-6B/-8A engine; length 42 ft 7¼ in (12·99 m); 146 built for US Navy, US Marine Corps plus approx 185 with simplified electronics (TA-4J); 2 built for Australia (TA-4G), 3 built for Israel (TA-4H), 4 built for New Zealand (TA-4K), 6 built for Kuwait (TA-4KU).

A-4M/N production aircraft for US Navy and Marine Corps, respectively, with J52-P-408A engine providing improved performance (except range) over previous Skyhawks; 5 pylons with 9,155 lb (4,156 kg) capacity; first flight April 10, 1970; over 150 built plus 30 A-4M ordered for Kuwait.

Mongoose designation applied to four A-4E aircraft with J52-P-8 engine flown by the US Navy to simulate advanced Soviet fighter aircraft; "Mongoose" is a play on the system of designating Soviet training aircraft with "M" names.

OPERATIONAL

Argentina, Australia, Israel, Kuwait, New Zealand, Singapore, United

States (Navy, Marine Corps)

Skyraider A-1 Douglas

The A-1 Skyraider represented the ultimate in piston-engine attack aircraft and was in first-line service on US Navy aircraft carriers from 1946 into the late 1960s. It was used extensively in combat during the Korean and Vietnam Wars. The Skyraider was flown in a variety of roles by the US and British navies, the US Marine Corps, French Air Force, and Vietnamese Air Force. It is now flown by only two central African states.

A low-wing, wide-fuselage aircraft, the Skyraider has a single radial piston engine and is a one-seat aircraft in the straight attack configuration. A total of 28 variants have been developed, including airborne early warning, night attack, nuclear attack, electronic countermeasures, and photo reconnaissance. The aircraft that remain in service are the survivors of A-1D variants previously flown by France and transferred to the former colonies. Eighty-eight A-1D (AD-4) aircraft were provided to France in 1959 for use in Algeria; some also were retransferred to Cambodia.

Status: *Operational.* First flight March 18, 1945 (XBT2D-1); squadron delivery December 1946; 3,180 built through 1957.

SPECIFICATIONS (A-1J)

Crew: 1
Engine: 1 Wright R-3350-26WB radial piston (3,050 hp)
Dimensions: span 50 ft 9 in (15·41 m) length, 38 ft 10 in (11·84 m), height 15 ft 10 in (4·85 m)
Speed: 318 mph (512 km/hr)

Range: 3,000 miles (4,825 km) with external tanks
Weight: 25,000 lb (11,350 kg) maximum
Armament: 4 × 20-mm cannon and up to 8,000 lb (3,632 kg) external weapons

OPERATIONAL

Central African Republic, Chad

A-1 Skyraider of the French Air Force

Stallion AU-24 Helio

The Stallion AU-24A is a counterinsurgency aircraft developed for the US Air Force in competition with the Fairchild AU-23 Peacemaker under the Credible Chase programme. Designated Stallion by Helio (a division of General Aircraft Corp.), the aircraft was purchased by the USAF for operation by Cambodia.

The Stallion is a single-engine, short-take-off-and-landing (STOL) aircraft with a high, square-tipped wing and swept-back tail fin. Other distinguishing features are the fixed landing gear (with distinctive rear-inclined main legs) and a large propeller spinner. A 20-mm gun is fired manually through the portside cabin doorway and various combinations of miniguns, rocket launchers, broadcasting speaker pods, camera pods, flare dispensers, and small bombs are carried on a fuselage hardpoint (600 lb (272 kg) capacity) and four wing pylons (2 × 500-lb and 2 × 600-lb capacity). Eight troops can be carried.

Status: *Operational.* First flight June 5, 1964 (Helio Stallion Model H-550).

SPECIFICATIONS

Crew: 3 (2 pilots, 1 gunner) + 8 troops without external stores
Engine: 1 United Aircraft of Canada (Pratt & Whitney) PT6A-27 turboprop (680 shp)
Dimensions: span 41 ft (12·51 m), length 39 ft 7 in (12·08 m), height 9 ft 3 in (2·82 m), wing area 242 sq ft (22·51 m²)

Speed: 218 mph (350 km/hr)
Ceiling: 25,000 ft (7,625 m)
Range: 445 miles (716 km)
Weights: 2,860 lb (1,298 kg) empty; 6,300 lb (2,860 kg) loaded
Armament: 1 × 20-mm XM-197 cannon and up to 2,000 lb (1,044 kg) of external stores

VARIANTS

AU-24A militarized version acquired by US Air Force; 14 built and transferred

OPERATIONAL

Cambodia

AU-24A Stallion of the US Air Force (Helio)

Strikemaster BAC (BAC-167)

The BAC 167 Strikemaster, derived from the Jet Provost trainer, has been optimized for the counterinsurgency role while retaining a capability for pilot training. The small, essentially straight-wing aircraft is turbojet powered with small fuselage air intakes just forward of the wing roots, side-by-side seating, and the tail fin set forward of the horizontal tail surfaces. Wingtip tanks are fitted. Armed with internal machineguns and up to 3,000 lb (1,362 kg) of external weapons can be carried on four wing pylons. All aircraft produced have been for export and it is flown by several air forces.

Status: *Operational.* First flight October 26, 1967. Approximately 140 built or on order.

SPECIFICATIONS

Crew: 2

Engine: 1 Rolls-Royce Bristol Viper Mk 535 turbojet (3,410 lb, 1,547 kg st)

Dimensions: span 36 ft 10 in (11·25 m), length 33 ft 8½ in (10·27 m), height 10 ft 11½ in (3·34 m), wing area 213¾ sq ft (19·88 m²)

Speed: 472 mph (760 km/hr)

Range: 247-mile (397 km) radius with 3,000 lb (1,362 kg) of weapons; 408-mile (656 km) radius with 2,000 lb (908 kg) of weapons; 575-mile (925 km) radius with 1,000 lb (454 kg) of weapons; 1,670-mile (2,687-km) ferry range

Weight: 11,500 lb (5,215 kg) maximum

Armament: 2 × 7·62-mm FN machineguns (550 rpg) and 4 × 750-lb bombs (wing pylons)

VARIANTS

Mk.80/80A aircraft for Saudi Arabia; 25 Mk.80 and 10 Mk.80A built.

Mk.81 aircraft for South Yemen; 4 built.

Mk.82/82A aircraft for Oman; 12 Mk.82 and Mk.82A.

Mk.83 aircraft for Kuwait; 18 built.

Mk.84 aircraft for Singapore; 16 built.

Mk.87 aircraft for Kenya; 6 built.

Mk.88 aircraft for New Zealand; 16 built.

Mk.89 aircraft for Ecuador; 12 built.

OPERATIONAL

Ecuador, Kenya, Kuwait, New Zealand, Oman, Saudi Arabia, Singapore

Strikemaster Mk.80 of the Royal Saudi Air Force (BAC)

Texan } T-6 North American
Harvard

This venerable aircraft survives as a trainer with a large number of air arms
and is flown by a half-dozen nations in the attack and counterinsurgency
roles. More than 10,000 were built in the United States, Australia, and
Canada from 1938 to 1954, being known in Britain and Canada as the
Harvard, and as the Texan in the United States. The US service designations
were AT-6 and then T-6 for the Army and Air Force, and SNJ and then T-6
for the Navy. During 1949–1950 a total of 2,068 earlier aircraft were remanufactured to the T-6G configuration with those now flying in the attack/
COIN roles being of this variant.

The Harvard/Texan is a two-seat, straight-wing, piston-engine aircraft
with a large "greenhouse" canopy. The armed aircraft carry light bombs and
rockets on wing attachment points.

Status: *Operational.*

SPECIFICATIONS (T-6G)

Crew: 2
Engine: 1 Pratt & Whitney R-1340-
  AN-1 radial (550 hp)
Dimensions: span 42 ft (12·81 m),
  length 29 ft 6 in (9·00 m), wing area
  253¾ sq ft (25·60 m²)

Speed: 215 mph (345 km/hr)
Ceiling: 21,500 ft (6,557 m)
Range: 870 miles (1,400 km)
Weight: 5,617 lb (2,550 kg) loaded
Armament: bombs, rockets

OPERATIONAL (attack/COIN roles)

Brazil, Mexico, Paraguay, Portugal, Thailand, Zaïre

*T-6 Texan
(Ronaldo S Olive)*

Trojan T-28 North American

The T-28 Trojan is a piston-engine trainer in service with US air forces since 1950 and flown by several countries in the light attack/counterinsurgency role. The aircraft was originally flown by the US Air Force and then by the US Navy from 1952 following the decision to standardize USAF and US Navy training aircraft. It is no longer flown by the US Air Force although the Navy uses it for basic flight training.

The T-28 bears a strong resemblance to some Second World War fighter aircraft with a radial piston engine, low-mounted wing, and bubble cockpit with tandem seating. The armed variants were modified from USAF trainers, fitted with larger engines, machineguns carried in underwing pods, self-sealing fuel tanks, armour plate, and improved communications equipment. Six wing pylons were added for carrying up to 3,500 lb (1,590 kg) of bombs, rockets, or gun pods. In addition to the T-28D/AT-28D modifications undertaken by North American, 130 similar modifications of T-28A aircraft were undertaken in France. The counterinsurgency T-28 aircraft were flown by the US Air Force in Vietnam. Also manufactured by Sud-Aviation in France as the Fennec.

Status: *Operational.* First flight September 26, 1949; squadron delivery 1950.

SPECIFICATIONS (T-28D)

Crew: 2 (1 pilot, 1 observer)
Engine: 1 Wright R-1820-86A radial piston (1,425 hp)
Dimensions: span 40 ft 7 in (12·38 m), length 33 ft (10·07 m), height 12 ft 8 in (3·86 m)
Speed: 352 mph (566 km/hr) at 18,000 ft (5,490 m); 298 mph (480 km/hr) at sea level

Ceiling: approx 35,000 ft (10,675 m)
Range: approx 1,200 miles (1,930 km)
Weight: approx 12,000 lb (5,448 kg) maximum
Armament: 2 × ·50-cal Browning M-3 MG pods, 2 × 750-lb bombs and 2 × 8-tube 2·75-in rocket launchers (wing pylons)

T-28 Trojan of the Royal Moroccan Air Force

VARIANTS

T-28A production trainer with R-1300-1A/1B engine; 1,194 built for US Air Force.

T-28B production trainer with R-1820-86A engine; 489 built for US Navy; some modified to drone control of target aircraft (redesigned T-28BD and then DT-28B).

T-28C production trainer similar to T-28B with reduced propeller diameter, arresting hook, and other features for carrier operation; 299 built for US Navy.

T-28D T-28A aircraft modified with R-1820-86/86A engine; fitted for counterinsurgency operations.

AT-28D T-28A or T-28B aircraft modified with R-1820-86/86A engine; fitted for counterinsurgency operations with 2 × ·50-cal MG in pods.

YAT-28E proposed two-seat counterinsurgency aircraft with Lycoming YT55-L-9 turboprop engine; taller fin and ejection seats; 3 built; programme cancelled.

OPERATIONAL (armed variants)

Argentina, Bolivia, Cambodia, Laos, Thailand, Zaïre

Bombers

B-1 Rockwell International

The B-1 is a variable-geometry bomber being developed to supplement and then replace the Boeing B-52 Stratofortress, primary strategic bomber of the US Air Force. Four prototype B-1A aircraft are being built and flight tested by the US Air Force. A decision for 241 production aircraft was to be made late in 1976. The new aircraft is lighter than the B-52 with a greater weapons capability, shorter take-off run, improved avionics, and reduced infra-red signature and radar cross section to enhance penetration to defended targets. The stand-off SRAM (Short Range Attack Missile) will be the primary B-1 weapon, although conventional or nuclear gravity bombs can be accommodated.

The B-1 wings sweep from 15 degrees when fully extended for take-off, cruise, and landing, to 67·5 degrees when retracted for supersonic flight. The wings "blend" into the body with the four engines in pairs inboard under the wings and adjacent to the fuselage. The tail configuration is swept but of conventional design. There are three internal weapon bays which normally will be fitted with rotary SRAM launchers, each carrying eight missiles. Eight additional SRAMs or up to 40,000 lb (18,160 kg) of conventional weapons can be carried on wing pylons. The B-1 is fitted with advanced avionics including the APQ-144 (Mod) forward-looking radar and can be refuelled in flight. During conception the B-1 was known as the Advanced Manned Strategic Aircraft (AMSA).

Left and overleaf: *Three views of the prototype B-1A variable-geometry bomber being developed to replace B-52s of the US Air Force (US Air Force)*

Status: *Development*. First flight December 23, 1974 (B-1A); squadron delivery in 1980 if procurred.

SPECIFICATIONS

Crew: 4 (2 pilots, 2 systems operators)

Engines: 4 General Electric F101-GE-F100 turbofans (30,000 lb, 13,620 kg st each with afterburner).

Dimensions: span 137 ft (41·79 m), length 143 ft (43·62 m), height 34 ft (10·37 m)

Speed: designed Mach 2·2 at altitude; but limited to Mach 1·6 by inlet modification; Mach 0·85 cruise

Ceiling: 60,000 ft (18,300 m)

Range: 6,100 miles (9,815 km) with minimum weapons

Weight: 395,000 lb (179,330 kg) maximum

Armament: 24 × SRAM AGM-69 ASMs or up to 50,000 lb (22,700 kg) of nuclear or conventional bombs (weapons bays) plus 8 × SRAM AGM-69 ASMs (wing pylons)

Backfire Tupolev

The *Backfire* is a variable-geometry bomber entering service with Soviet Long-Range Aviation (LRA) and Naval Aviation. The exact role of the aircraft is not definite; it will probably replace the older *Badger* aircraft in strike and naval roles, but with inflight refuelling will have an intercontinental attack capability. Over 50 Backfire-B aircraft produced through early 1976.

The outer portions of the *Backfire* wings extend for landing, take-off, and cruise flight, and swing back for high-speed flight. The two identified variants differ in wing and landing gear receptacle configuration; the aircraft has a conventional tail with a single tail fin. The two large turbofan engines have large, square air intakes and are believed to be based on the NK-144 turbofans that power the Tu-144 supersonic transport. The *Backfire* has a fixed refuelling probe in the nose. In the strike role the *Backfire* will probably carry long-range, air-to-surface missiles including the AS-6. According to US defence officials, with in-flight refuelling and staged from Arctic bases, the *Backfire* could cover all of the United States on two-way, subsonic missions with low-altitude penetration; staging from the Chukotsk peninsula (Siberia), the unrefuelled radius would cover the western United States in an arc from San Diego to Chicago. On one-way missions, the *Backfire* could deliver nuclear weapons anywhere in the United States without refuelling (possibly landing in Cuba). The aircraft is smaller than the contemporary Rockwell International B-1 bomber.

Status: *Operational.* Squadron delivery in 1975.

SPECIFICATIONS

Crew: 2 to 4
Engines: 2 Kuznetsov turbofans (40,000 + lb, (18,160 kg) with afterburner)
Dimensions: span 70 ft (21·35 m), length 130 ft (39·65 m)
Speed: Mach 2·0–2·5 at altitude

Ceiling: 50,000 ft (15,250 m)
Range: 2,750–3,570-mile (4,425–5,744 km) combat radius
Weights: 270,000 + lb (122,580 kg) maximum
Armament: air-to-surface missiles

VARIANTS

Backfire-A probably initial development aircraft; large landing gear pods.

Backfire-B probably production aircraft; smaller landing gear pods modified wingtips and air intakes.

OPERATIONAL

Soviet Union (LRA, Navy)

Badger Tu-16 Tupolev

The Tu-16 *Badger* is a turbojet-powered medium bomber which has been in wide use by the Soviet Union for two decades and continues to serve in the conventional bomber, anti-ship missile, strategic and maritime reconnaissance, and tanker roles. Soviet Long-Range Aviation (LRA) and Naval Aviation fly large numbers of *Badgers* and the aircraft is used by China, Egypt, Indonesia, Iraq.

The *Badger* has a swept-wing with large turbojet engines housed in large nacelles faired into the fuselage at the wing roots. During the aircraft's long production run the turbojets have been updated, culminating in the engines listed below. When employed in the tanker role the *Badger* has weapons bay fuel tanks and trails a drogue from the starboard wing-tip; receiving probe is in the port wingtip. Up to 19,800 lb (8,989 kg) of bombs can be carried in

Tu-16 Badger-*A*
of the Egyptian
Air Force (US
Navy)

Tu-16 Badger-
B/G. Note the
wing hard points
for ASMs

Tu-16 Badger-*F.*
Wing pods con-
tain ECM equip-
ment

the internal weapons bay or air-to-surface missiles can be carried under the fuselage or on wing pylons. Most aircraft have 2 × 23-mm cannon in dorsal, ventral, and tail mounts, and 1 × 23-mm cannon on the starboard side of the nose. The *Badger* resembles the now-discarded Boeing B-47 Stratojet bomber in size, role, and performance although the US bomber had a greater range. The Tu-104 *Camel* civil airliner was adapted from the *Badger*; the design designation of the *Badger* was Tu-88.

Status:. *Operational.* First flight 1952; squadron delivery 1954–1955. Approximately 2,000 *Badgers* built in the Soviet Union and about 60 by China, with Soviet and Chinese production continuing into the early 1970s.

SPECIFICATIONS

Crew: approx 7

Engines: 2 Mikulin RD-3M (AM-3M) turbojets (19,180 lb, 8,708 kg st each)

Dimensions: span 110 ft (33·50 m), length 121 ft (36·91 m) (*Badger*-C length 126 ft (38·43 m)), height 35 ft 6 in (10·83 m), wing area approx 1,820 sq ft (169·26 m²)

Speed: 587 mph (945 km/hr) at 35,000 ft (10,675 m)

Ceiling: 42,650 ft (13,008 m)

Range: 3,000 miles (4,827 km) with full payload; 4,000 miles (6,435 km) with 6,600 lb (3,000 kg) bombs

Weight: 158,600 lb (72,000 kg) maximum

Armament: 7 × 23-mm cannon (except 6 × 23-mm cannon *Badger*-C/D) and 19,800 lb bombs (*Badger*-A; weapons bay)
or 2 × *Kennel* AS-1 ASMs (*Badger*-B)
or 1 × *Kipper* AS-2 ASM (*Badger*-C)
or 1 × *Kelt* AS-5 ASM (*Badger*-G)
or 1 × AS-6 ASM (*Badger* G)

VARIANTS

Badger-A bomber aircraft with glazed nose; flown by Soviet LRA, Iraq, Egypt (all 20 destroyed in June 1967).

Badger-B bomber aircraft with glazed nose; ASM capability; flown by Soviet LRA, Soviet Navy, Indonesia

Badger-C bomber aircraft with nose radome; also used in maritime and strategic reconnaissance roles; ASM capability; flown by Soviet LRA, Soviet Navy.

Badger-D maritime reconnaissance aircraft with nose radome; small electronics blisters under fuselage; flown by Soviet Navy.

Badger-E reconnaissance aircraft similar to *Badger*-A with glazed nose; cameras fitted in weapons bay.

Badger-F reconnaissance aircraft similar to *Badger*-E with glazed nose; electronic pods fitted on wing pylons.

Badger-G bomber aircraft with glazed nose; ASM capability; flown by Soviet Navy, Egypt.

Badger-H/J/K reconnaissance aircraft.

OPERATIONAL

China, Egypt, Indonesia, Iraq, Soviet Union (LRA, Navy)

Bear Tu-20/Tu-95 Tupolev

The *Bear* is the only turboprop-propelled strategic bomber to enter operational service with any air force. The *Bear* aircraft, a Soviet contemporary of the US B-52 Stratofortress, comprises about two-thirds of Soviet Long-Range Aviation (approximately 110 aircraft) and provides the Soviet Navy with some 50 long-range reconnaissance aircraft and a few anti-submarine aircraft.

The *Bear* is a swept-wing aircraft with four wing-mounted turboprop engines turning counter-rotating propellers. The aircraft is rated as the fastest propeller-driven aircraft to enter service. The Tu-114 *Cleat* transport aircraft was derived from the *Bear*. Tu-20 is the Soviet military designation of the aircraft with the Tupolev Tu-95 bureau number also being used in the West along with the NATO designation *Bear*.

Status: *Operational.* First flight in 1954; squadron delivery in 1957. An estimated 250 to 300 *Bear* aircraft were produced with production continuing into the early 1970s.

Tu-20 Bear-*D, maritime reconnaissance variant, flown by Soviet Naval Aviation (US Navy)*

Tu-20 Bear-*E, fitted for reconnaissance (US Navy)*

SPECIFICATIONS *(Bear-B)*

Crew: approx 5

Engines: 4 Kuznetsov NK-12 turboprops (14,795 ehp each (as uprated))

Dimensions: span 159 ft (48·50 m), length 155 ft 10 in (over probe) (47·50 m), height 40 ft (12·19 m), wing area 3,000 sq ft (279 m²)

Speed: 550 mph (885 km/hr) at 36,000 ft (11,000 m) (Mach 0·83); long-range cruise 440 mph (708 km/hr) at 36,000 ft (11,000 m) (Mach 0·67)

Ceiling: 45,000 ft (13,715 m)

Range: 7,800 miles (12,555 km) with 25,000 lb (13,338 kg) weapons carried to target; up to 9,000 miles (14,480 km) in reconnaissance role

Weight: 340,000 lb (154,360 kg) maximum

Armament: 1 × 20-mm or 23-mm cannon optional (nose mounting), up to 6 × 23-mm cannon (twin dorsal, ventral, tail turrets) and 25,000 lb (11,350 kg) nuclear or conventional bombs (weapons bay) or 1 × *Kangaroo* AS-3 ASM (external)

VARIANTS

Bear-A strategic bomber with glazed nose for bombardier; full gun armament.

Bear-B strategic bomber with radome under nose and faired blister on starboard side of after fuselage; in-flight refuelling capability; *Kangaroo* missile carried.

Bear-C reconnaissance variant of *Bear*-B with faired blisters on both sides of after fuselage.

Bear-D maritime reconnaissance variant with large belly radome; fitted for missile guidance; approx 8 crew; operational since 1965.

Bear-E reconnaissance variant of *Bear*-A with glazed nose, fixed refuelling probe, and camera openings in weapons bay position.

Bear-F maritime reconnaissance/anti-submarine aircraft; lengthened engine nacelles.

OPERATIONAL

Soviet Union (LRA, Navy)

Bison Mya-4 Myasischev

The Mya-4 *Bison* is the only four-engine Soviet turbojet bomber to be flown in significant numbers. The aircraft was considered unsuccessful for the strategic bombing role for which it was developed but remains in limited service with Soviet Long-Range Aviation (LRA). Currently some 50 are configured as tankers, about 35 as long-range bombers, and a few as strategic reconnaissance aircraft. The *Bison* was first observed in 1954.

The *Bison* is a large, swept-wing aircraft with four turbojet engines in the wing roots. It is fitted with small wingtip pods, two internal weapons bays, and 1 × 23-mm cannon on starboard side of nose in some aircraft with most having 6 to 10 × 23-mm cannon in twin mounts above and below the forward fuselage and in the tail. All apparently fitted for inflight refuelling with the

Bison-B and -C having fixed refuelling probes. The aircraft is slightly smaller than the contemporary Boeing B-52 Stratofortress. The aircraft also has been identified by the design designations M-4 and 201-M as well as the Soviet military designation Mya-4.

Status: *Operational*. Squadron delivery in 1955–1956. Approx 200–300 aircraft built.

SPECIFICATIONS

Crew: approx 8
Engines: 4 Mikulin AM-3D turbojets (19,180 lb, 8,690 kg st each)
Dimensions: span 165 ft 7$\frac{1}{2}$ in (51·13 m), length 154 ft 10 in (47·22 m) (*Bison*-B/C approx 162 ft (49·37 m) over nose probe), height 50 ft (15·25 m)
Speed: 620 mph (1,000 km/hr) at 10,000 ft (3,050 m); 560 mph (901 km/hr) at 36,000 ft (11,000 m)
Ceiling: 45,000 ft (13,725 m)
Range: 3,500-mile (5,630 km) combat bomber configuration
Weight: 352,000 + lb (159,800 kg) maximum
Armament: 6 to 10 × 23-mm cannon and 10,000 lb (4,540 kg) bombs (weapons bay)

VARIANTS

Bison-A bomber aircraft with glazed nose in early aircraft; most apparently refitted as tankers.

Bison-B reconnaissance aircraft with rounded nose radome; fixed refuelling probe; 6 × 23-mm guns; numerous blisters for electronic equipment.

Bison-C bomber aircraft with pointed nose radome tapering into fixed refuelling probe.

OPERATIONAL

Soviet Union (LRA)

Mya-4 Bison-*C*
(US Navy)

Blinder Tu-22 Tupolev

The Tu-22 *Blinder* is a supersonic medium bomber flown by Soviet Long-Range Aviation (LRA) and Naval Aviation in the conventional bomber, anti-ship missile, maritime reconnaissance, and training roles. Although possibly intended as a successor to the *Badger,* only some 200 *Blinders* were built, most of which remain in service. The aircraft was first observed in June 1961.

The *Blinder* is a swept-wing aircraft with turbojet engines mounted in pods at the base of the tail fin; most aircraft have a partially retractable refuelling probe in the nose, a nose radome with small windows behind them in the lower fuselage, tandem seating for a three-man crew, fuel tanks faired into the wing trailing edges, and small wingtip pods. *Blinder*-A carries a bombload of possibly up to 22,000 lb (9,988 kg) in tandem weapon bays; *Blinder*-B carries an air-to-surface missile semi-recessed in the weapons bay; *Blinder*-C has cameras installed in the weapons bay; and *Blinder*-D is a trainer with an additional cockpit stepped up behind the standard cockpit. The aircraft is comparable to the now-discarded Convair B-58 Hustler; the US aircraft was smaller and significantly faster (Mach 2.1 at altitude).

Status: *Operational.* First flight in 1957–1958.

SPECIFICATIONS (estimated)

Crew: 3 or 4

Engines: 2 turbojets (26,000 lb, 11,800 kg st each with afterburning)

Dimensions: span 90 ft 10½ in (27·70 m), length 132 ft 11½ in (40·53 m), height 17 ft (5·19 m)

Speed: 920 mph (1,480 km/hr) at 40,000 ft (12,200 m) (Mach 1·4)

Ceiling: 60,000 ft (18,300 m)

Range: 1,250–1,350 miles (2,010–2,175 km) (later variants)

Weight: 185,000 lb (84,000 kg) maximum

Armament: 1 × 23-mm cannon (tail position) and 22,000 lb (9,988 kg) bombs (*Blinder*-A) or 1 × *Kitchen* AS-4 ASM (*Blinder*-B)

VARIANTS

Blinder-A limited production bomber/reconnaissance aircraft

Blinder-B bomber aircraft with ASM capability; enlarged nose radome.

Blinder-C maritime reconnaissance aircraft; 6 cameras fitted in weapons bay; presumably configured for electronic intelligence (ELINT).

Blinder-D Tu-22U; trainer with additional cockpit.

OPERATIONAL

Iraq (presumably flown by Russians), Soviet Union (LRA, Navy)

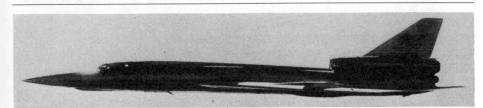

Tu-22 Blinder-*A*

FB-111 General Dynamics

The FB-111 is a variable-geometry aircraft that serves with the B-52 Strato-fortress as the strategic bomber force of the US Air Force. The FB-111A is a derivative of the F-111A fighter. The Air Force originally planned 210 FB-111 aircraft to replace the older B-52C/F and General Dynamics B-58 Hustler bombers; however, production was halted at 76 aircraft because of budgeting considerations.

Stretched FB-111 configurations are being proposed as a substitute for the B-1 manned bomber.

The aircraft's wings sweep from a fully extended position (16-degree sweep) for landing, take-off, and cruise, to a swept-back position (72·5 degrees) for high-speed flight. The aircraft has twin engines and side-by-side crew seating; differs from F-111 in having greater wingspan and sophisticated Mk IIB avionics; fitted with ALQ-94 deceptive electronic countermeasures (ECM). The FB-111 has an internal weapons bay that can accommodate two gravity nuclear weapons or two Short Range Attack Missiles (SRAM) and four gravity weapons or four SRAMs can be carried on four wing pylons. Two additional pylons can be attached to outer wing sections for subsonic flight. Fitted for in-flight refuelling.

Status: *Operational.* First flight July 30, 1967; squadron delivery October 1969; 76 aircraft built through 1971.

SPECIFICATIONS (FB-111A)

Crew: 2 (1 pilot, 1 navigator)
Engines: 2 Pratt & Whitney TF30-P-7 turbofans (20,350 lb, 9,240 kg st each with afterburners)
Dimensions: span 70 ft (21·34 m) spread, 33 ft 11 in (10·34 m) fully swept, length 73 ft 6 in (22·40 m), height 17 ft 1½ in (5·22 m)
Speed: Mach 2·2

Ceiling: 60,000 + ft (18,300 m)
Range: 4,000 + miles (6,435 km)
Weight: approx 110,000 lb (49,940 kg) loaded
Armament: 2 × SRAM AGM-69 ASMs (weapons bay) plus 4 × SRAM AGM-69 ASMs or 42 × 750-lb bombs (wing pylons)

FB-111A strategic bomber of the US Air Force (General Dynamics)

VARIANTS

FB-111A production strategic bomber aircraft.

FB-111G "stretched" bomber aircraft with increased range and weapons payload proposed by General Dynamics as an alternative to the B-1A

bomber; could carry 4 SRAMs internally and 4 SRAMs on wing pylons.

FB-111H "stretched" bomber; could carry up to 12 SRAMs.

OPERATIONAL

United States (Air Force)

Mirage IV-A Dassault

The Mirage IV-A is a turbojet, delta-wing strategic bomber flown by the French Air Force. The aircraft is the first-generation French strategic weapon system and is being succeeded in the strategic role by land-based Intermediate Range Ballistic Missiles (IRBM) and Submarine Launched Ballistic Missiles (SLBM).

The Mirage IV-A can deliver a free-falling nuclear weapon after penetrating to the target in supersonic low-level flight. The 2,200-lb (1,000-kg) nuclear weapon is carried semi-recessed under the fuselage. In the conventional strike role the Mirage IV-A can carry up to 16,000 lb (7,265 kg) of bombs on wing and fuselage attachment points. Fitted for in-flight refuelling.

Status: *Operational.* First flight June 17, 1959 (Mirage IV-01); squadron delivery in 1964.

Mirage IV A strategic bomber of the French Air Force. Note the RATO bottles under the wing roots (M Fricke)

SPECIFICATIONS

Crew: 2 (1 pilot, 1 navigator)

Engines: 2 SNECMA Atar 09K-50 turbojets (10,360 lb, 4,700 kg st each; 15,430 lb, 7,000 kg st with afterburners)

Dimensions: span 38 ft $10\frac{1}{2}$ in (11·85 m), length 77 ft $1\frac{1}{4}$ in (23·50 m), height 18 ft $6\frac{1}{2}$ in (5·65 m), wing area $839\frac{1}{2}$ sq ft (78 m²)

Speed: 1,454 mph (2,340 km/hr) at 36,000 ft (11,000 m) (Mach 2·2); max stabilized speed 1,122 mph (1,805 km/hr) at 60,000 ft (18,300 m) (Mach 1·7)

Ceiling: 65,600 ft (20,000 m)

Range: 770-mile (1,240 km) radius with nuclear weapon

Weights: 31,967 lb (14,510 kg) empty; 69,665 lb (31,600 kg) loaded; 73,800 lb (33,500 kg) maximum

Armament: 1 × 50-kiloton nuclear weapon (fuselage).
or 4 × Martel AS.37 anti-radiation missiles
or 16 × 1,000-lb bombs (wing pylons)

VARIANTS

Mirage IV-01 diminutive experimental aircraft.

Mirage IV-02/03/04 pre-production aircraft; first flight October 12, 1961; 3 built.

Mirage IV-A production aircraft; first flight December 7, 1963; 62 built.

OPERATIONAL

France

Stratofortress B-52 Boeing

The B-52 Stratofortress is a large, eight-engine, swept-wing aircraft that serves as the primary strategic bomber of the US Air Force (currently supplemented by 74 smaller FB-111A aircraft). Operational B-52 strength reached a peak of 640 aircraft in 1962, subsequently declining to the current strength of some 400 aircraft. Designed specifically to carry four thermo-nuclear gravity bombs internally, the later B-52s are fitted with air-to-surface missiles under their wings and during the Vietnam War they were employed in a conventional bombing role. The USAF plans to supplement and then replace the B-52s with the supersonic B-1 bomber beginning in 1980.

The B-52 has a distinctive configuration, with a blunt-nose fuselage and large, high-mounted, swept-back wings. Eight turbofan engines turbojet in A through G models are paired in pods mounted in pylons forward of the wing leading edges. The tall tail fin in the early models has a narrow flat top but gave an almost pointed appearance with the tailplanes having an almost triangular shape; the B-52G/H have shorter tail fins for improved stability in high-speed, low-level flight. The earlier aircraft also had a tail gunner position

*B-52H Strato-
fortress, now
obsolescent
strategic bomber
flown by US Air
Force (US Air
Force)*

with 4 × ·50-calibre MG in a tail turret; in the B-52G the gunner is in the
forward crew compartment and the guns remotely controlled; the B-52H has
1 × 20-mm ASG-21 multi-barrel cannon in the tail. Internal weapons bays
can hold up to 27,000 lb (12,258 kg) of nuclear gravity bombs or over 40,000
lb (18,160 kg) when modified for conventional bombing. Two air-to-surface
missiles can be carried under the wings of the B-52D and later aircraft or
18,000 lb (8,170 kg) of conventional bombs when modified. Fitted for
in-flight refuelling.

Status: *Operational.* First flight April 15, 1952 (YB-52); squadron delivery
June 1955. 744 produced through June 1962.

SPECIFICATIONS (B-52H)

Crew: 6 (2 pilots, 1 navigator, 1 radar operator, 1 electronic warfare operator, 1 gunner)

Engines: 8 Pratt & Whitney TF33-P-3 turbofans (17,000 lb, 7,718 kg st each)

Dimensions: span 185 ft (56·39 m), length 157 ft 7 in (48·03 m), height 40 ft 8 in (12·40 m), wing area approx 4,000 sq ft (372 m²)

Speed: 630 mph (1,015 km/hr) at 40,000 ft (12,200 m) (Mach 0·95), 645 mph (1,035 km/hr) at sea level (Mach 0·85), 565 mph (910 km/hr) at 36,000 ft (11,000 m) cruise

Ceiling: 55,000 ft (16,775 m)

Range: approx 10,000 miles (16,090 km)

Weight: 488,000 lb (221,350 km) maximum

Armament: 1 × 20-mm ASG-21 multi-barrel cannon and 27,000 lb (12,260 kg) of bombs (unmodified weapons bay)
or 85 × 500-lb bombs
or 42 × 750-lb bombs (modified weapons bay) plus 2 × Hound Dog AGM-28 ASMs
or 24 × 750-lb bombs (wing pylons)

VARIANTS

XB-52 prototype aircraft with pilots seated in tandem under bubble canopy; length 153 ft (46·67 m); first flight October 2, 1952 (after YB-52); 1 built.

YB-52 prototype aircraft with pilots seated in tandem under bubble canopy; length 153 ft (46·67 m); 1 built.

B-52A development aircraft with J57-P-19W turbojets; side-by-side pilot seating; length 156 ft (47·58 m) (through B-52F); 4 × 0·50-cal MG in tail (through B-52G); outboard wing tanks on pylons (in all subsequent aircraft); 6 crew; first flight August 5, 1954; 3 built.

NB-52A B-52A modified as airborne launch platform for NASA research aircraft; 2 modified.

B-52B/RB-52B production aircraft with J57-P-19W/29WA or J57-F-19W/-29WA engines; RB-52B fitted with weapons bay camera/electronics reconnaissance pack; 8 crew in B-52B, 2 crew in RB-52B; 50 built.

B-52C/D production aircraft with J57-P-19W/-29WA or J57-F-19W/-29WA engines; increased wing fuel tanks; 6 crew; first flight March 9, 1956; 35 B-52C and 170 B-52D built.

B-52E production aircraft with J57-P-19W/-29WA or J57-F-19W/-29WA engines; improved navigation and bombing system; 6 crew; first flight October 3, 1957; 100 built.

B-52F production aircraft with J57-P-43WA/-43WB or J57-F-43WA/-43WB engines; modified wing and engine pod design; 6 crew; first flight May 6, 1958; 88 built.

B-52G production aircraft with J57-P-43WB or J57-F-43WB engines; redesigned structure with increased fuel capacity, shorter tail fin, tail crew position deleted; length 157 ft (47·89 m); fitted for 2 × ASMs on wing pylons; 6 crew; first flight September 26, 1958; 193 built.

B-52H production aircraft with TF-33-P-3 turbofan engines; 1 × 20-mm gun in tail; designed for 4 × Skybolt GAM-77 ASMs (programme cancelled); 6 crew; 102 built.

B-52 I unofficial designation of "improved" B-52G/H refitted with large commercial turbofan engines for improved performance.

OPERATIONAL

United States (Air Force)

Vulcan Avro (Hawker Siddeley)

The Vulcan is a delta-wing, high subsonic bomber flown by the Royal Air Force in the strike and strategic reconnaissance roles. The aircraft was the final strategic bomber produced in Britain and has been displaced in the quick-response nuclear commitment by Britain's four nuclear-propelled submarines armed with Polaris missiles. The Vulcan is expected to be replaced in the strike role by the Panavia MRCA beginning in the late 1970s.

The Vulcan has a large delta wing and no horizontal tail surfaces; there is an electronic sensor on the top of the tail fin, giving it a squared-off appearance. The aircraft's four turbojet engines are housed in the wing roots. An in-flight refuelling probe extends from the aircraft's nose.

Status: *Operational.* First flight August 30, 1952; squadron delivery May 1957. Approximately 120 aircraft built through 1964.

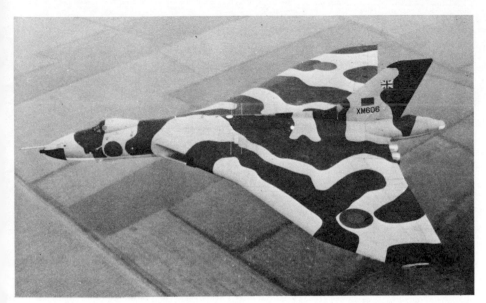

*Vulcan B.2 of the
Royal Air Force
(Ministry of
Defence)*

SPECIFICATIONS (B.2)

Crew: 5
Engines: 4 Bristol Siddeley Olympus
Mk.301 turbojets (20,000 lb, 9,080 kg
st each)
Dimensions: span 111 ft (33·83 m),
length 99 ft 11 in (30·45 m), height
27 ft 2 in (8·29 m), wing area 3,964
sq ft (369 m²)
Speed: 645 mph (1,038 km/hr) at
40,000 ft (12,200 m) (Mach 0·98)

Ceiling: 55,000 ft (16,775 m)
Range: 1,700-mile (2,735 km) radius
for low-level penetration of target;
2,300-mile (3,700 km) radius for
high-level penetration
Weight: 200,000 lb (90,800 kg)
maximum
Armament: 21 × 1,000-lb bombs
(weapons bay)

VARIANTS

prototypes 1 built; originally fitted
with Rolls-Royce Avon engines; refitted
with Bristol Siddeley Sapphires and later
Rolls-Royce Conways.

B.1 initial production aircraft
successively fitted with Olympus 101,
102, and 104 engines; span 99 ft
(30·20 m), length 97 ft 1 in (29·62 m);
first flight February 4, 1955; 45 built.

B.1A B.1 aircraft fitted with
improved avionics and electronic
countermeasures (ECM).

B.1B B.1 with weapons bay
configured to carry 21 × 1,000-lb
bombs.

B.2 production aircraft successively
fitted with Olympus 201 and 301
engines; designed to carry 1 × Blue
Steel ASM stand-off weapon semi-
recessed in fuselage; all modified to
carry 21 × 1,000-lb bombs; first flight
August 19, 1958; 75 built.

SR.2 B.2 aircraft refitted for strategic
reconnaissance.

OPERATIONAL

Great Britain (RAF)

Reconnaissance and ECM

Aero Commander RU-9 Aero Commander

The US Air Force and Army fly a number of Aero Commander light transport aircraft in the VIP transport liaison and roles, designated U-4 and U-9, respectively, according to service. In addition, the Army operates reconnaissance-configured Aero Commanders.

The Aero Commander is a high-wing aircraft with wing-mounted, air-cooled engines, a retractable tricycle landing gear, and seating for five in the standard configuration. Fitted with side-looking aircraft radar (SLAR) in the RU-9D variant.

Status: *Operational.*

SPECIFICATIONS

Crew: 5
Engines: 2 Lycoming IGO-540-A1A fuel-injection air cooled in-line piston engines (350 hp each)
Dimensions: span 49 ft 6 in (15·10 m), length 35 ft 1½ in (10·73 m), height 14 ft 6 in (4·42 m), wing area 255 sq ft (7·4 m²)

Speed: 250 mph (400 km/hr) at sea level; 232 mph (373 km/hr) cruise
Ceiling: 21,900 ft (6,680 m)
Range: 1,800 miles (2,896 km)
Weights: approx 4,650 lb (2,110 kg) empty; 7,500 lb (3,405 kg) maximum
Armament: nil

U-9 Aero Commander of the US Army

VARIANTS (reconnaissance)

RU-9D formerly RL-26D; similar to
U-9B/C aircraft but fitted for reconnaissance.

OPERATIONAL (reconnaissance variants)

United States (Army) United States (Navy)

Blackbird SR-71 Lockheed

This high-flying, Mach 3 aircraft was developed as a strategic reconnaissance aircraft to succeed the famed Lockheed U-2 "spy plane". Existence of the SR-71 was first acknowledged by the US Government on February 29, 1964, when then-President Johnson announced that the aircraft had already been tested at speeds of more than 2,000 mph and at altitudes in excess of 70,000 ft. This performance is greater than that acknowledged for any other fully operational aircraft. Although developed for strategic reconnaissance, the initial aircraft had a fighter configuration (YF-12A). The interceptor variant was not developed because of the decision not to develop an advanced bomber defence system for the United States. The surviving YF-12A variants subsequently have been employed for research by the National Aeronautics and Space Administration (NASA). The SR-71 has been employed in the "tactical" reconnaissance role within its performance constraints (e.g., 90-mile turning radius at Mach 3 speed).

The Blackbird is a delta-wing aircraft with a long, slender fuselage and long, wing-mounted turbojets with extended centre cones. The one- or two-seat cockpit is faired into the forward fuselage. The fuselage has distinctive "chine" fairings that blend into the wings and extend forward to act as a fixed canard to reduce trim drag, provide additional lift area, and improve directional stability. On the YF-12A the chine is cut back from the nose to reduce interference with intercept radar. The aircraft has highly automated flight controls to assist handling in the difficult high-altitude flight region; construction is largely titanium; fitted for in-flight refuelling; and surfaces are painted with high-heat-emissive black paint to help retard the approximately 450- to 1,100-degree F. skin temperatures of sustained supersonic flight in a "standard" atmosphere of −56 degrees F. at 80,000 ft. The name "Blackbird" is derived from the paint scheme as well as the clandestine mission.

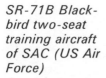

SR-71B Blackbird two-seat training aircraft of SAC (US Air Force)

Photographic equipment in the SR-71 variants can survey 100,000 square miles of the earth's surface in one hour. The YF-12s were designed with the Hughes ASG-18 pulse-doppler fire control radar in a nose radome, infra-red sensors, and two missile bays which could each accommodate 2 × Falcon AIM-47A air-to-air missiles.

Status: *Operational.* First flight April 26, 1962 (YF-12A); squadron delivery January 1966 (SR-71A); 3 aircraft built to YF-12 configurations and about 30 to SR-71 configurations.

SPECIFICATIONS (SR-71A)

Crew: 2 (1 pilot, 1 reconnaissance systems officer—RSO)

Engines: 2 Pratt & Whitney JT11D-20B (J58) high by-pass turbojets (turboramjets) (approx 23,000 lb, 10,440 kg each; 32,500 lb, 14,755 kg st each with afterburner)

Dimensions: span 55 ft 7 in (16·95 m), length 107 ft 5 in (32·74 m), height 18 ft 6 in (5·64 m), wing area 1,800 sq ft (167·4 m²)

Speed: 1,980 mph (3,186 km/hr) at 78,740 ft (24,000 m) (Mach 3)

maximum level speed; 1,320 mph (2,124 km/hr) at 30,000 ft (9,150 m) (Mach 2)

Ceiling: 80,000 + ft (24,400 m)

Range: 1,200-mile (1,930 km) radius; approx 3,000 miles (4,025 km) at Mach 3 at altitude

Weights: 60,000 lb (27,240 kg) empty; 170,000 lb (77,180 kg) maximum (including 80,000 + lb (36,320 kg) fuel)

Armament: nil

SR-71A Black-bird of US Air Force Strategic Air Command (US Air Force)

VARIANTS

YF-12A prototype aircraft completed to fighter-interceptor configuration; length 101 ft (30·81 m); 140,000 lb (63,560 kg) max; pilot only; 3 built (1 crashed June 24, 1971); survivors flown by NASA in Advanced Supersonic Technology programme.

YF-12C prototype aircraft completed to SR-71 configuration; redesignated YF-12C after loss of YF-12A prototype; flown by NASA in Advanced Supersonic Technology programme.

SR-71A strategic photo and electronic reconnaissance aircraft; developed from YF-12A prototypes via YF-12C; first flight December 22, 1964; estimated 25 to 30 built, several of which are in storage.

SR-71B two-seat training aircraft with elevated second cockpit; reportedly 2 built (1 crashed).

SR-71C two-seat training aircraft; 1 modified from SR-71A after loss of SR-71B.

OPERATIONAL

United States (Air Force, NASA)

Bronco OV-10 Rockwell International

The OV-10 Bronco is a multi-purpose, light attack aircraft initiated by the US Navy-Marine Corps as a counterinsurgency (COIN) aircraft. Normally powered by twin turboprops, some Bronco variants are fitted with an auxiliary turbojet mounted above the fuselage. Design criteria for the aircraft include mission versatility, rough field operation and simplified maintenance. Broncos have carried out carrier landings and take-offs without the assistance of arresting wires or catapults.

The Bronco has a high-wing, twin-boom configuration, with a high tailplane to facilitate rear loading of the fuselage in the cargo or medical evacuation roles. The rear seat can be removed to provide space for 3,200 lb (1,453 kg) of cargo or five paratroopers or two stretchers with attendant. Four weapon attachment points are provided on the small fuselage sponsons and a fifth point is provided under the fuselage; two Sidewinder air-to-air missiles or rockets can be carried on two wing attachment points; and two machine-guns are normally mounted in the sponsons. Up to 3,600 lb (1,635 kg) of weapons can be carried. The night observation gunship system (NOGS) provides for a turret with 2 × 20-mm XM-197 cannon under the fuselage in place of the sponsons.

Status: *Operational.* First flight July 16, 1965 (YOV-10A). Approximately 370 aircraft built.

SPECIFICATIONS

Crew: 2 (1 pilot, 1 observer)
Engines: 2 AiResearch T76-G-10/-10A-12/-12A turboprops (715 shp each)
Dimensions: span 40 ft (12·19 m), length 41 ft 7 in (12·67 m), height 15 ft 2 in (4·63 m), wing area 291 sq ft (27·1 m²)
Speed: 281 mph (452 km/hr) at sea level clean

Range: 228-mile (367 km) radius in attack role; 1,430-mile (2,300 km) ferry range
Weights: 6,969 lb (3,164 kg) empty; 9,908 lb (4,499 kg) loaded; 14,466 lb (6,568 kg) maximum
Armament: 2 × 7·62-mm machineguns 1 × 1,200-lb bomb (centreline) 4 × 600-lb bombs (sponsons)

VARIANTS

YOV-10A prototype aircraft with T76 engines or (one aircraft) T74/PT6A engines; details differed; 7 built.

OV-10A production aircraft; first flight August 6, 1967; flown by US Air Force, Marine Corps, Navy, Indonesia; 15 modified under USAF Pave Nail programme for night air control and target designation role.

OV-10B target tow aircraft with T76-G-410A/-411A/-412/-413 engines; 6 built for West Germany.

OV-10B(Z) target tow aircraft similar to OV-10B with auxiliary J85-GE-4 turbojet mounted atop fuselage; first flight September 21, 1970; 12 built for West Germany.

OV-10C similar to OV-10A for Thailand; 32 built.

YOV-10D modified OV-10A to test NOGS concept; armed with 2 × 20-mm cannon in fuselage turret; fitted with forward looking infra-red (FLIR) sensor under nose; 2 converted for US Marine Corps.

OV-10D OV-10A aircraft modified to NOGS configuration fitted with uprated T76 engines (1,000 ehp) and increased fuel capacity; 24 converted for US Marine Corps.

OV-10E similar to OV-10A for Venezuela; 16 built.

OPERATIONAL

West Germany
Indonesia
Thailand

United States (Air Force, Marine Corps)
Venezuela

*OV-10A of the
US Navy (US
Navy)*

Constellation } EC-121 Lockheed
Warning Star

The Constellation/Warning Star aircraft are an airborne early warning (AEW) modification of the civilian Super Constellation airliner. During the Second World War the US armed forces began flying Constellations in the transport role; subsequently, in 1949, the Navy modified two Constellation L-747 aircraft to PO-1W, later WV-1, radar picket aircraft. The success of these aircraft led the Navy and Air Force to procure L-1049 "stretched" Constellations for use in the AEW role to give warning of Soviet bomber attacks against the United States. The Air Force variants (initially RC-121 and then EC-121) retained the commercial aircraft name while the Navy variants (initially WV-2/-3 and then EC-121/WC-121) were named Warning Star. Only limited numbers of these aircraft remain in service, with the Air Force E-3A planned as a replacement for the AEW role and the Navy already flying specialized P-3 Orions in the electronic and weather reconnaissance roles.

The Lockheed Constellation first flew in January 1943 as a military transport, not being produced in a purely civil version until 1946. The streamlined "Connie" has a distinctive appearance, with straight wings, a circular-section fuselage, and a three-fin tail (a holdover from the 1930s design concept that distinguished many British bombers and US aircraft such as the B-25 Mitchell, B-24 Liberator, and PBM Mariner). Four piston engines are mounted on the low wing. The standard EC-121 aircraft carry search radar in a "guppy" radome under the fuselage, height-finding radar in a vertical radome atop the fuselage, and extensive communications equipment linking the aircraft with ground control centres and for the direction of interceptor aircraft. Some 12,000 to 14,000 lb (5,450 to 6,355 kg) of electronic equipment are installed.

*EC-121D
Constellation of
the US Air Force
(US Air Force)*

*EC-121K
Warning Star of
the US Navy (US
Navy)*

Status: *Operational.* First flight in 1949 (PO-1W).

SPECIFICATIONS (EC-121K)

Crew: 26

Engines: 4 Wright R-3350-34/-42
radial pistons (3,400 hp each)

Dimensions: span 126 ft 2 in (38·48
m) (123 ft (37·52 m) without
wingtip tanks), length 116 ft 2 in
(35·43 m), height 27 ft (8·24 m)
(over dorsal radome), wing area
1,654 sq ft (153·8 m²)

Speed: 321 mph (516 km/hr) at
20,000 ft (6,100 m)

Ceiling: 20,600 ft (6,283 m)

Range: 4,600 miles (7,400 km)

Weights: 80,611 lb (36,600 kg)
empty; 143,000 lb (64,920 kg)
loaded

Armament: nil

VARIANTS

EC-121C formerly RC-121C; Air Force AEW aircraft with R-3350-34 engines.

EC-121D formerly RC-121D; Air Force AEW aircraft with R-3350-93 engines; wingtip tanks; 16 crew.

EC-121H Air Force AEW aircraft with R-3350-93 engines; 13 crew.

EC-121K formerly WV-2/PO-2W; Navy AEW aircraft with R-3350-34/-42 engines; wingtip tanks; 26 crew; 142 built; 8 modified to WV-3/WC-121N for Navy weather reconnaissance.

EC-121L formerly WV-2E; modified AEW aircraft with rotating UHF radome in dorsal position; wingtip tanks; 26 crew; 1 modified from EC-121K for test and evaluation.

EC-121M formerly WV-2Q; Navy electronic countermeasure (ECM) aircraft; 26 crew; modified from EC-121K.

EC-121P Navy surveillance/submarine detection aircraft; 26 crew; modified from EC-121K.

EC-121Q Air Force aircraft fitted for special project; modified from EC-121D.

EC-121R Navy aircraft fitted as relay for ground sensors in Vietnam War (Project Igloo White); modified EC-121K/P.

EC-121ST Air Force aircraft fitted with special electronics.

OPERATIONAL

United States (Air Force, Navy)

Cub An-12 Antonov

Several Soviet An-12 *Cub* military transports have been configured for electronic intelligence (ELINT) operations. The basic *Cub* is a four-turboprop transport in wide use with the Soviet armed forces and generally similar in size and to some extent appearance to the Lockheed C-130 Hercules. The ELINT-configured *Cub*-C retains the glazed nose and chin radome associated with the transport variants but is distinguished by a solid tail housing electronic equipment (vice tail guns position) and electronic pods are faired into the forward fuselage and ventral surfaces of the aircraft.

The An-12 initially was a militarized version of the An-10 *Cat* transport, with a high-wing mounting four underslung, turboprop engines, a sharply upswept rear fuselage incorporating a flat, underside loading ramp/door, and a tail gun position above the horizontal tail surfaces. The An-12 has become the standard Soviet Air Forces transport and is flown by a number of other nations. Subsequently, a civilianized version of the An-12 has entered service with *Aeroflot* and some foreign airlines. Maximum payload of the basic An-12 is 44,090 lb (20,015 kg), approximately the same as the C-130E Hercules.

SPECIFICATIONS (basic An-12)

Crew: 5 (flight crew: 2 pilots, 1 engineer, 1 radio operator, 1 navigator)

Engines: 4 Ivchenko AI-20K turboprops (4,000 ehp each)

Dimensions: span 124 ft 8 in (38·02 m), length 121 ft $4\frac{1}{2}$ in (37·02 m), height 32 ft 3 in (9·84 m), wing area 1,286 sq ft (119·6 m²)

Speed: 482 mph (776 km/hr); 416 mph (669 km/hr) max cruise

Ceiling: 33,500 ft (10,218 m)

Range: 2,236 miles (3,598 km) with full payload; 3,550-mile (5,710 km) ferry range

Weights: 61,730 lb (28,025 kg) empty; 121, 475 lb (55,150 kg) normal

Armament: removed from ELINT variants (normally 2 × 23-mm NR-23 cannon)

OPERATIONAL (*Cub*-C ELINT variant)

Egypt (presumably flown by Russians)
Soviet Union (Air Forces, Navy)

An-12 Cub-*C configured for electronic intelligence (ELINT) operations, flown by the Egyptian Air Force*

E-3 AWACS Boeing

The planned E-3/Airborne Warning and Control System (AWACS) provides for the development of Boeing model 707-320B aircraft to control aircraft in nuclear or conventional combat operations. The AWACS requirement was proposed by the US Air Force in 1963, with initial planning for up to 64 aircraft to provide Continental US air defence against Soviet bomber attacks as well as to support overseas tactical operations. Subsequently, the CONUS air defence requirement was deleted and current planning provides for 34 aircraft to maintain an estimated six airborne surveillance stations in tactical situations. The programme has been questioned because of increasing costs.

Three Boeing 707-320B aircraft have been modified to serve as test platforms in the E-3/AWACS programme. These aircraft are designated EC-137D. The planned E-3A operational aircraft was to have eight TF34-GE-2 turbofan engines paired on wing pylons; however, in a cost reduction move the decision was made to power the E-3A with four TF33-PW-100/100A turbofans with a $2\frac{1}{2}$-hour reduction in mission time. The E-3A will be distinguished by a 30-foot radar rotodome mounted 14 feet above the after fuselage, providing radar surveillance of an area some 460 miles in diameter while on station at an altitude of approximately 30,000 feet. The E-3A will carry a crew of 17 with nine radar consoles. The aircraft will be fitted for in-flight refuelling to extend the normal $11\frac{1}{2}$-hour flight endurance.

Status: *Development.* First flight February 9, 1972 (EC-137D).

SPECIFICATIONS (E-3A)

Crew: 17 (2 pilots, 1 navigator, 1 flight engineer, 1 battle commander, 1 senior director, 4 maintenance personnel, 7 systems operators)
Engines: 4 Pratt & Whitney TF33-PW-100/100A turbofans (21,000 lb, 9,535 kg st each)
Dimensions: span 145 ft 9 in (44·4 m), length 152 ft 11 in (46·64 m), height 41 ft 4 in (12·61 m)
Speed: 530 mph (853 km/hr); approx 415 mph (668 km/hr) on station
Ceiling: approx 35,000 ft (10,675 m)
Range: approx 1,200-mile (1,930 km) radius with 5 hours on station
Weight: 325,000 lb (147,000 kg) maximum
Armament: nil

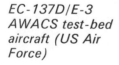

EC-137D/E-3 AWACS test-bed aircraft (US Air Force)

VARIANTS

EC-137D Boeing 707-320 aircraft modified to serve as airborne test platforms for AWACS with Pratt & Whitney JT3D-3B turbofan engines; 3 aircraft modified (to be brought up to full E-3A standards after test programme is completed).

E-3A planned production AWACS aircraft; 10 funded through Fiscal Year 1976 with 31 planned; first flight February 1975.

E-4 AABNCP Boeing

The E-4 Advanced Airborne National Command Post (AABNCP) provides an airborne operations centre for the National Command Authority (i.e., President or his successor) or the Commander Strategic Air Command. The E-4/AABNCP aircraft are developed from Boeing model 747-200B aircraft. Several aircraft are planned under the AABNCP programme to replace EC-135 aircraft (modified Boeing 707) now used in this role. (The Soviet Union flies the Ilushin Il-62 *Classic* and Il-76 *Candid* in the airborne national command post role.)

Three operational E-4A aircraft and one E-4B test aircraft are being procured for the AABNCP role. The operational aircraft are being configured with conference, briefing, operations, and sleeping rooms, and are fitted with advanced communications and display systems. When fully converted the E-4 aircraft will be distinguished from conventional 747 airliners by the SHF and UHF radomes behind the raised flight deck (in addition to the markings "United States of America"). The E-4 will carry a payload of approximately 100,000 lb (45,400 kg) and have 3,000 sq ft of floor space available. The E-4B differs from the E-4A with modified avionics and an in-flight refuelling capability. These are the largest aircraft flown by the US armed services.

Status: *Development.* First flight February 9, 1972; squadron delivery December 1974.

E-4 Advanced Airborne National Command Post (AABNCP) aircraft, developed from the commercial Boeing 747

SPECIFICATIONS (E-4A)

Engines: 4 Pratt & Whitney F-105-PW-100 high by-pass turbofans (approx 47,000 lb, 21,338 kg st each)	**Speed:** approx 600 mph (965 km/hr)
	Ceiling: 45,000 + ft (13,725 m)
	Range: 12 + hour endurance
Dimensions: span 198 ft 8 in (60·59 m), length 231 ft 4 in (70·56 m), height 63 ft 5 in (19·34 m)	**Weight:** 798,000 lb (362,300 kg) maximum
	Armament: nil

VARIANTS

E-4A initial operational AABNCP aircraft; 3 planned.

E-4B modified AABNCP aircraft; 1 planned.

Gannet Fairey

The Gannet is the Royal Navy's carrier-based airborne early warning (AEW) aircraft employed in the surveillance and electronic countermeasure (ECM) roles from HMS *Ark Royal*, the surviving British aircraft carrier. The aircraft evolved from the Gannet anti-submarine aircraft flown by the Royal Navy as well as Germany and Indonesia. Subsequently, 38 of the AEW.3 variants were built from 1958 to 1961 to replace the former US Navy AD-4W/AEW.1 Skyraiders used aboard British carriers.

The Gannet is a straight-wing aircraft powered by essentially two engines which separately turn contra-rotating propellers on the same axis. The fuselage and tail fin are totally redesigned from the Gannet AS series; there is a large, "guppy" radome under the fuselage and ECM pods or fuel tanks are carried on two wing pylons; the pilot sits in a high, bubble canopy with two radar operators seated side-by-side below and behind the pilot. The wings fold with a double break for carrier operation.

Status: *Operational.* First flight August 20, 1958.

Gannet AEW-3 of the Royal Navy landing on HMS Ark Royal *(Ministry of Defence)*

SPECIFICATIONS

Crew: 3 (1 pilot, 2 radar operators)
Engine: 1 Bristol Siddeley Double Mamba 102 turboprop (contra-rotating propellers) (3,875 ehp)
Dimensions: span 54 ft 6 in (16·61 m), length 44 ft (13·41 m), height 16 ft 10 in (5·14 m), wing area

$482\frac{3}{4}$ sq ft (44·9 m²)
Speed: 250 mph (402 km/hr) at 5,000 ft (1,525 m)
Range: approx 800 miles (1,285 km)
Weight: 24,000 lb (10,885 kg) loaded
Armament: nil

OPERATIONAL

Great Britain (Navy)

Hawkeye E-2 Grumman

The Hawkeye is a large, carrier-based airborne early warning (AEW) aircraft which provides long-range surveillance and aircraft control. Developed by the US Navy, the aircraft is now operational with four-aircraft squadrons aboard several carriers. The Hawkeye is replacing the older E-1B Tracer, with about 70 aircraft required to provide four aircraft for the 12 carriers planned for operation in the 1980s. The Hawkeye's surveillance radar can track over 300 aircraft simultaneously over an area more than 400 miles in diameter from an altitude of 30,000 ft. The E-2C has been proposed as a possible alternative to the E-3/AWACS (Airborne Warning and Control System) for some applications. Although in some respects less capable than the E-3/AWACS, the E-2C could provide an already proven, in production, cost-competitive alternative for attaining an overland AWACS capability.

The Hawkeye has a straight-wing configuration with two turboprop engines. The most distinctive feature is the 24-ft diameter, saucer-like radome for the APS-120 UHF radar. The radome revolves in the free airstream at the rate of six revolutions per minute. It furnishes sufficient lift to offset its own weight in flight and can be lowered to facilitate housing the aircraft in a carrier hangar deck. The Hawkeye has an onboard Litton L-304 computer to support the airborne tactical data system (ATDS) which collects, stores, collates, and relays information to co-ordinate air operations and pass data to surface forces. Special equipment includes the ALR-59 passive detection system and a secure UHF and HF data link. The total weight of installed avionics is approximately 10,000 lb (4,540 kg). A four-fin tail structure provides stability without exceeding hangar deck clearances as would be necessary for a single fin. The wings fold for carrier operations.

Status: *Operational.* First flight April 19, 1961; squadron delivery January 1964.

SPECIFICATIONS (E-2C)

Crew: 5 (2 pilots, 1 combat information centre [CIC] officer, 1 air control officer, 1 radar operator or technician)
Engines: 2 Allison T56-A-422 turboprops (4,591 shp each)
Dimensions: span 80 ft 7 in (24·58 m), length 57 ft 7 in (17·56 m), height 18 ft 4 in (5·59 m), wing area 700 sq ft (65·1 m²)
Speed: 375 mph (603 km/hr); 310 mph (499 km/hr) cruise
Ceiling: 30,800 ft (9,395 m)
Range: 1,600-mile (2,575 km) ferry range; 5- to 6-hour patrol endurance
Weights: 37,678 lb (17,105 kg) empty; 51,569 lb (23,412 kg) max
Armament: nil

VARIANTS

E-2A formerly W2F-1; initial production aircraft with T56-A-8/-8A/-8B engines; 59 built; some updated to E-2B configuration.

TE-2A E-2A with ATDS and other avionics removed for use as trainer.

E-2B improved E-2A with Litton L-304 computer; first flight February 20, 1969; all E-2A updated to E-2B configuration; no additional aircraft built.

E-2C improved aircraft with advanced radar capable of detecting aircraft against ground clutter, passive detection equipment, and simplified maintenance; first flight January 20, 1971; 2 prototypes plus 34 production aircraft built for delivery through 1975.

OPERATIONAL

United States (Navy)

E-2C Hawkeye of the US Navy (US Navy)

Hercules EC-130/RC-130 Lockheed

Listed below are the electronic (EC-130) and reconnaissance (RC-130) variants of the C-130 Hercules transport/cargo aircraft. Basic specifications and notes are provided in an earlier section of this edition under the attack (AC-130) configuration of the Hercules. The Navy aircraft are used for back-up radio relay to strategic missile submarines; the term TACAMO for this programme comes from the expression "Take charge and move out"; 14 aircraft are planned in the TACAMO programme.

VARIANTS

RC-130A modified C-130A with T56-A-9 engines; fitted for electronic geodetic surveying and photogrammetric mapping; 7 flight crew and 4 technicians; flown by US Air Force.

EC-130E modified C-130E with T56-A-7 engines; fitted with additional radio operator for calibration of LORAN electronic navigation system; 1 flown by US Coast Guard.

EC-130G modified C-130E with T56-A-16 engines; fitted with TACAMO III or IVB airborne communications system; 8 flight crew and 6 communications personnel; flown by US Navy.

EC-130Q similar to EC-130G; flown by US Navy.

RC-130S modified C-130A with T56-A-9 engines; employed in special reconnaissance role; flown by US Air Force.

OPERATIONAL (EC-130/RC-130)

United States (Air Force, Navy, Coast Guard)

RC-130 Hercules of the US Air Force (US Air Force)

Mohawk OV-1 Grumman

The Mohawk is a battlefield surveillance aircraft developed for the US Army to provide ground commanders with rapid-response, day/night observation and reconnaissance. Four Mohawks normally are assigned to each Army division, the only fixed-wing aircraft at that level of command. Originally fitted only for visual and photo reconnaissance, later models have a variety of sensors. It is also flown in small numbers by Israel.

The Mohawk is a two-seat, twin-turboprop aircraft capable of operation from short, unimproved airfields, with considerable in-flight manoeuvrability. The aircraft has a bulbous canopy with side-by-side seating, straight wings, two underwing pylons for auxiliary fuel tanks, flare dispensers, and a three-fin tail configuration. The aircraft is capable of being armed (see JOV-1A variant), but a 1965 decision by the Department of Defence prohibits Army fixed-wing aircraft from carrying weapons to avoid conflicting with the US Air Force in the close support role. The US Marine Corps participated in the Mohawk development, but has not operated the aircraft.

Status: *Operational.* First flight April 14, 1959 (YOV-1A); squadron delivery in 1962. Over 375 built through December 1970.

SPECIFICATIONS (OV-1D)

Crew: 2 (1 pilot, 1 systems operator)
Engines: 2 Lycoming T53-L-701 turboprops (1,400 shp each)
Dimensions: span 48 ft (14·63 m), length 41 ft (12·50 m), height 12 ft 8 in (3·86 m), wing area 360 sq ft (33·5 m²)
Speed: 305 mph (491 km/hr) at 5,000 ft (1,525 m) without SLAR; 290 mph (465 km/hr) at 5,000 ft (1,525 m) with SLAR; 207 mph (333 km/hr) cruise

Ceiling: 25,000 ft (7,620 m)
Range: 1,010 miles (1,627 km) without SLAR; 945 miles (1,520 km) with SLAR
Weights: 12,054 lb (5,473 kg) empty; 15,741 lb (7,146 kg) loaded with SLAR; 18,109 lb (8,221 kg) maximum with SLAR
Armament: nil

OV-1D Mohawk of the US Army, fitted with long-range tanks on wing hard points and carrying SLAR under the forward fuselage (Grumman)

VARIANTS

YOV-1A formerly YAO-1A (designated OF-1 by US Marine Corps); development aircraft with T53-L-3 engines: 9 built.

OV-1A formerly AO-1A; production aircraft with T53-L-3 engines; span 42 ft (12·81 m); 9,937 lb (4,511 kg) empty, 15,031 lb (6,824 kg) maximum; fitted for day-night visual and photo reconnaissance with internal camera; dual controls (2 pilots).

JOV-1A armed reconnaissance aircraft similar to the OV-1A with gunsight and four 500-lb capacity pylons for 2·75-inch rocket pods and ·50-calibre MG pods.

OV-1B formerly AO-1B; production aircraft with T53-L-7 engines; span 48 ft (14·64 m); 11,067 lb (5,024 kg) empty, 19,230 lb (8,730 kg maximum; fitted with APS-94 side-looking airborne radar (SLAR) in 18-ft fibreglass pod attached to starboard side of fuselage and internal camera with in-flight processor; dual controls deleted; 82 built; some converted to OV-1D.

OV-1C formerly AO-1C; production aircraft with T53-L-3 engines; span 42 ft (12·81 m); 10,400 lb (4,722 kg) empty, 19,230 lb (8,730 kg) maximum; fitted with AAS-24 infra-red (IR) sensor and internal camera; 115 built; some converted to OV-1D.

RV-1C OV-1C permanently modified for electronic reconnaissance.

OV-1D similar to OV-1B with T53-L-7 series engines and side-loading doors to accept pallet with SLAR, IR, or other sensors; 86 converted from OV-1C/D.

RV-1D OV-1D permanently modified for electronic reconnaissance.

EV-1 OV-1B converted to special electronic configuration in Quick Look II programme.

OPERATIONAL

United States (Army), Israel

Moss Tu-126 Tupolev

Moss is the US/NATO name for a Soviet airborne warning and control system (AWACS) fitted in the Tu-114 airframe. The aircraft is designed to provide area surveillance for the warning of hostile aircraft intruders and to direct interceptors. In the United States the AWACS mission is carried out by the E-2 Hawkeye and E-3. The Soviet AWACS is based on the Tu-114 Rossiya airframe (US-NATO code name *Cleat*), a commercial turboprop airliner which first flew in 1957. At the time it was the world's largest and heaviest airliner, capable of carrying 170 to 220 passengers on short-distance flights. The *Moss* was first observed in 1968.

The *Moss* retains the swept-wing, and long, cylindrical fuselage of the basic Tu-114. The four wing-mounted turboprop engines have contra-rotating propellers with large spinners. There is a large, 36-ft diameter radome mounted on a single pylon atop the after fuselage and small radomes are faired after fuselage, one on each side and two below the fuselage; a small ventral fin has been added to improve stability; and the tail is capped with an avionics pod. A refuelling probe is fitted forward of the cockpit.

Status: *Operational.*

Tu-126 Moss
AEW aircraft
flown by the
Soviet Navy
(US Navy)

SPECIFICATIONS

Crew: not known
Engines: 4 Kuznetsov NK-12 series
  turboprops (contra-rotating
  propellers) (approx 15,000 ehp each)
Dimensions: span 167 ft 7¾ in (51·13
  m), length approx 185 ft (56·43 m),
  height approx 50 ft 10 in (15·51 m),

wing area 3,348½ sq ft (311 m²)
Speed: 500 + mph (805 km/hr);
  approx 475 mph (764 km/hr) cruise
Ceiling: approx 40,000 ft (12,200 m)
Weight: 375,000 + lb (170,250 kg)
  maximum
Armament: nil

OPERATIONAL

Soviet Union (PVO)

Prowler EA-6B Grumman

The EA-6B Prowler is a US Navy electronic warfare aircraft designed specific
ally to locate, identify, and jam enemy radars. The airframe is based on the
A-6 Intruder attack aircraft but has been lengthened to accommodate addi
tional electronic equipment and a four-man crew. About 50 of the currently
planned 77 aircraft were delivered through 1975. The 77 aircraft will permi
four to be deployed on each of 12 aircraft carriers and provide aircraft fo
training, pipeline, and attrition.

   The Prowler resembles the A-6 Intruder with a lengthened forward
fuselage; several antennas are faired into the tail fin which is topped by ar
electronics pod. Five additional electronic jamming pods are carried on the
wing and fuselage pylons, each tuned to a different frequency. The principa
jamming devices are the ALQ-92 and ALQ-99, the latter also being installed
in the US Air Force EF-111A.

Status: *Operational*. First flight May 25, 1968.

*EA-6B Prowler of
the US Navy
(US Navy)*

SPECIFICATIONS

Crew: 4 (1 pilot, 3 systems operators)
Engines: 2 Pratt & Whitney J52-P-8A/-8B/-408 turbojets (9,300 lb, 4,218 kg st each)
Dimensions: span 53 ft (16·15 m), length 59 ft 5 in (18·11 m), wing area 529 ft (49 m²)

Max level speed: 685 mph (1,100 km/hr) at sea level
Ceiling: 44,600 ft (13,595 m)
Range: 2,164 miles (3,482 km)
Weights: 34,581 lb (15,700 kg) empty; 58,500 lb (26,560 kg) maximum
Armament: nil

VARIANTS

EA-6B 1 development aircraft, 4 pre-production aircraft, plus production aircraft.

OPERATIONAL

United States (Navy)

Seminole RU-8 Beech Aircraft

The US Army flies some 200 militarized Beechcraft Twin-Bonanza aircraft in the VIP transport and liaison roles with the designation U-8 and the name Seminole. Thirty aircraft have been equipped with radar reconnaissance systems.

The Twin-Bonanza was the first American light twin-engine aircraft of post-Second World War design. The aircraft has a low-wing configuration with wing-mounted engines in streamlined nacelles. The standard cabin accommodation is for six or seven persons.

Status: *Operational.*

RU-8D Seminole fitted with UPD-1 radar flown by the US Army (Beech)

SPECIFICATIONS

Crew: 3
Engines: 2 Lycoming GO-480-1 six-cylinder air cooled piston engines (285 hp each)
Dimensions: span 45 ft 11½ in (14·00 m), length 31 ft 6½ in (9·61 m), height 11 ft 4 in (3·46 m), wing area 277 sq ft (25·8 m²)

Speed: 214 mph (344 km/hr) at 2,500 ft (760 m); 203 mph (327 km/hr) cruise at 7,000 ft (2,135 m)
Ceiling: 20,300 ft (6,192 m)
Range: 1,650 miles (2,655 m)
Weights: 4,100 lb (1,861 kg) empty; 6,300 lb (2,860 kg) maximum
Armament: nil

VARIANTS (reconnaissance)

RU-8D formerly RL-23D; similar to U-8D aircraft but fitted for reconnaissance with UPD-1 radar in under-fuselage "canoe" for side-looking airborne radar (SLAR).

OPERATIONAL (reconnaissance variants)

United States (Army)

Skytrain Dakota } **EC-47/RC-47** Douglas (DC-3)

The electronic (EC-47) and reconnaissance (RC-47) variants of the C-47 Skytrain or Dakota are listed below. The basic specifications and notes are provided in an earlier listing for the Dragon Ship (AC-47) configuration of the aircraft.

EC-47 of the US Air Force (Stephen Peltz)

VARIANTS

RC-47A C-47A configured for photo or electronic reconnaissance; R-1830-90C/-90D/-92 engines; flown by South Vietnam.

EC-47D C-47D configured for airborne early warning (AEW); R-1830-90D engines.

EC-47H/J C-47H/J configured for electronic countermeasures (ECM) training; R-1830-90C/-90D/-92

engines; 3 crew, 1 instructor, 11 students; flown by US Navy.

EC-47N/P C-47A/D configured for electronic reconnaissance; R-1830-90D/-92 engines.

EC-47Q C-47A/D configured for special electronic missions; R-2000-4 engines to provide increased performance.

OPERATIONAL

United States (Air Force, Navy)

Skywarrior EA-3/EKA-3/RA-3 Douglas

Developed as a carrier-based, nuclear strike aircraft for the US Navy, the Skywarrior remains in service in electronic, tanker, photo reconnaissance, and executive transport variants. The swept-wing, twin-turbojet Skywarrior had the distinction of being the first all-jet strike aircraft to operate from carriers and the heaviest aircraft to regularly operate from carriers. Few remain in active Navy service; several are flown by Naval Air Rescue.

The Skywarrior is a high-wing aircraft with twin turbojet pods suspended from the wings. The nose section houses radar and the three-seat cockpit is located relatively far forward. The A-3B variants have a long, fixed refuelling probe extending from the port side. As built all "straight" A-3A and A-3B aircraft had 2 × 20-mm cannon in a remote/radar-controlled tail turret; subsequently replaced by electronic countermeasure (ECM) equipment. In

EKA-3B tanker/ EW aircraft of the US Navy (US Navy)

RA-3B reconnais- sance variant, also flown by the US Navy (US Navy)

the bomber role an internal weapons bay could hold up to 12,800 lb (5,810 kg) of nuclear or conventional weapons (including mines in the A-3B series). Wings and tail fin fold for carrier operation. An extensively modified Skywarrior design flew with the US Air Force with the popular name Destroyer in the B-66/EB-66/RB-66/WB-66 configurations.

Status: *Operational.* First flight October 22, 1952; squadron delivery April 1956; 282 Skywarriors of all variants produced through January 1961.

SPECIFICATIONS (A-3B)

Crew: 3 in A-3B (1 pilot, 1 bombardier-navigator, 1 engineer), 7 in EA-3B, 5 in RA-3B, 8 in TA-3B (1 pilot, I instructor, 6 students)

Engines: 2 Pratt & Whitney J57-P-10 turbojets (10,500 lb, 4,767 kg st each; 12,400 lb, 5,630 kg st each with water injection)

Dimensions: span 72 ft 6 in (22·11 m), length 76 ft 4 in (23·28 m), height 22 ft 9½ in (6·94 m), wing area 812 sq ft (75·5 m²)

Speed: 610 mph (980 km/hr) at 10,000 ft (3,050 m) (Mach 0·83); 560 mph (900 km/hr) at 36,000 ft (10,980 m) (Mach 0·85)

Ceiling: 41,000 ft (12,505 m)

Range: 1,000-mile (1,609 km) tactical radius; 2,900-mile (4,666 km) range with auxiliary fuel tanks in weapons bay

Weights: 39,409 lb (17,890 kg) empty; 73,000 lb (33,142 kg) loaded; 82,000–84,000 lb (37,228–38,136 kg) max take-off

Armament: none in EA-3/RA-3/TA-3 configurations

VARIANTS

XA3D-1 prototypes with XJ40-WE-3 engines; 2 built.

A-3A formerly A3D-1; limited production strike aircraft with P & W J57-P-6 engines; first flight (YA3D-1) September 16, 1953; 50 built (including YA3D-1); some subsequently converted to 7-seat electronic countermeasure aircraft (A3D-1Q/EA-3A) and photo reconnaissance (A3D-1P/RA-3A).

A-3B formerly A3D-2; standard US Navy heavy attack aircraft with J57-P-10 engines; 168 built with survivors in late 1960s converted to executive transports (A3D 2Z/VA 3B), tanker aircraft (KA-3B), and electronic countermeasure-tanker aircraft (EKA-3B); normal KA-3B gross weight up to 78,000 lb (35,412 kg) including 34,178 lb (15,517 kg) fuel (5,026 US gallons) of which about two-thirds could be transferred to other aircraft.

EA-3B formerly A3D-2Q; electronic countermeasures aircraft with forward- and side-looking radars, infra-red sensors, special ECM equipment, etc.; first flight December 10, 1958; 24 built.

RA-3B formerly A3D-2P; photo reconnaissance aircraft with up to 12 cameras fitted in fuselage; first flight (YRA-3B) July 22, 1958; 31 built.

TA-3B formerly A3D-2T; bombardier/navigator training aircraft; first flight August 29, 1959; 12 built for operational training.

VA-3B VIP configuration.

OPERATIONAL

United States (Navy)

Stratolifter EC-135/RC-135 Boeing

The C-135 aircraft is the military designation of the widely used Boeing 707 commercial aircraft. The US Air Force flies more than 600 KC-135 tanker aircraft plus a few transports and the special configuration aircraft listed below; the French Air Force flies 11 KC-135F tankers to support its strategic

RC-135 recon-naissance aircraft of the US Air Force (US Air Force)

bombers. Payload for the basic C-135 aircraft is 87,000 lb (39,500 kg) or 126 passengers; the KC-135 stratotanker can carry more than 31,000 gallons of fuel plus a limited amount of cargo.

SPECIFICATIONS (basic C-135A)

Crew: 4 (flight crew)
Engines: 4 Pratt & Whitney J57-P-59W turbojets (13,750 lb, 6,243 kg st each)
Dimensions: span 130 ft 10 in (39·91 m), length 134 ft 6 in (41·02 m), height 41 ft 8 in (12·71 m)
Speed: 600 mph (965 km/hr)

Ceiling: 50,000 + ft (15,250 m)
Range: 5,000 + miles (8,045 km); ferry range 8,000 + miles (12,870 km)
Weight: 277,000 lb (125·750 kg) maximum
Armament: nil

VARIANTS

EC-135A modified KC-135A with J57-P/F-59W engines; fitted for use as Airborne Command Post (ACP) and communications relay station.

RC-135A modified C-135A with J57-P/F-59W engines; fitted for photographic mapping; 4 crew.

EC-135C formerly KC-135B; modified KC-135A with TF33-P-9 engines; fitted for use as Airborne Command Post and communications relay.

RC-135C modified EC-135C with TF33-P-9 engines; fitted for electronic reconnaissance; in-flight refuelling capability, 18 crew.

RC-135D/R/T J57-P/F-59W engines; modified for special reconnaissance; formerly KC-135A.

EC-135G/H/K/P J57-P/F-59W engines; fitted for use as Airborne Command Post; formerly EC-135A.

EC-135J TF33-P-9 engines; fitted for use as Airborne Command Post; formerly KC-135B.

RC-135M TF33-P-5 engines; fitted for special reconnaissance; formerly C-135B.

EC-135N J57-P/F-59W engines; fitted for electronic range instrumentation in support of the Apollo Space programme.

RC-135S TF33-P-5 engines; fitted for special reconnaissance; formerly RC-135D.

RC-135U TF33-P-9 engines; fitted for special reconnaissance; formerly RC-135C.

OPERATIONAL (EC-135/RC-135)

United States (Air Force)

Tracer E-1 Grumman

The E-1 Tracer is a carrier-based, airborne early warning (AEW) aircraft developed from the S-2 Tracker anti-submarine aircraft. Now replaced aboard most US aircraft carriers by the E-2 Hawkeye, the aircraft provides detection of approaching aircraft and has a limited fighter-direction capability. The Tracer is a twin-engine aircraft distinguished by a saucer-type radome.

The Tracer has the basic Grumman Tracker configuration with an elliptical radome 32-ft long and 20-ft wide housing a $17\frac{1}{2}$-ft antenna for the APS-82 search radar which rotates six times per minute. In addition, the E-1 has a twin-fin tail configuration with folding wings for carrier operation. The aircraft is popularly known as the "Willy Fudd", a name derived from the earlier WF designation.

Status: *Operational.* First flight March 1, 1957; squadron delivery February 1958.

SPECIFICATIONS (E-1B)

Crew: 4 (2 pilots, 1 airborne intercept controller, 1 avionic technician)
Engines: 2 Wright R-1820-82A/-82WA radial pistons (1,525 hp each)
Dimensions: span 72 ft 4 in (22·06 m), length 45 ft 4 in (13·83 m), height 16 ft 10 in (5·14 m), wing area 506 sq ft (47 m²)
Speed: 250 mph (402 km/hr)
Weights: 21,024 lb (9,545 kg) empty; 26,966 lb (12,243 kg) loaded
Armament: nil.

VARIANTS

XWF-1 prototype design study; replaced by XTF-1W.
E-1A formerly WF-1; pre-production aircraft; 2 built.
E-1B production aircraft; 88 built.

OPERATIONAL

United States (Navy)

E-1B Tracer of the US Navy, now replaced on board most US aircraft carriers by the E-2 Hawkeye (US Navy)

U-2 Lockheed

The U-2 is a high-altitude, low-speed strategic reconnaissance aircraft developed specifically for flights over the Soviet Union. The aircraft has been replaced in the strategic reconnaissance role by the SR-71 Blackbird, but is still flown in secondary roles by the United States and in the reconnaissance role by Taiwan. US-flown aircraft made photographic flights over the Soviet Union from 1956 until May 1, 1960, when a U-2B (piloted by Francis Gary Powers) was shot down by a Soviet surface-to-air missile. The aircraft also was employed over Cuba in October 1962 with one (piloted by Major Rudolf Anderson, Jr.) shot down by Soviet SAMs. Subsequently, they have flown over Mainland China, piloted by Taiwan and possibly US fliers, with some of the former being shot down.

The U-2 has a glider-like appearance with a long, straight wingspan and large wing area to provide lift with minimum drag in the thin air of the stratosphere. There is a single centreline main landing gear and a tailwheel; outriggers provide lateral support on the ground and are jettisoned after take-off. Wingtip slides protect the wings during landing. The early U-2A variant had a range of 2,200 miles; "slipper" tanks built into the wings extended the range to 2,600 miles, with "wet wings" further extending the range. Reconnaissance equipment consists of long-focus cameras in the fuselage.

Status: *Operational.* First flight in 1955; squadron delivery in June 1957; 55 aircraft built.

U-2 flown by US Air Force Strategic Air Command (US Air Force)

SPECIFICATIONS (U-2D)

Crew: 1 (2 in U-2D/WU-2D)
Engine: 1 Pratt & Whitney J75-P-13 turbojet (approx 17,000 lb, 7,718 kg st)
Dimensions: span 80 ft (24·4 m), length 49 ft 7 in (15·13 m), height 13 ft (3·97 m), wing area approx 565 sq ft (52·5 m²)

Speed: approx 500 mph (805 km/hr) at cruise altitude; 460 mph (740 km/hr) cruise
Ceiling: 70,000 + ft (21,350 m)
Range: 3,000 + miles (4,827 km)
Weight: 17,00 + lb (7,718 kg) loaded
Armament: nil

VARIANTS

U-2A initial production aircraft with J57-P-37A engine.

WU-2A U-2A modified for high-altitude research and weather reconnaissance.

U-2B production aircraft with J75-P-13 engine.

U-2C modified U-2A with dorsal equipment structure.

U-2CT two-place training aircraft.

U-2D two-place aircraft with J75-P-13 engine; 5 built.

WU-2D two-seat U-2D modified for high-altitude research and weather reconnaissance.

U-2 EPX proposed Navy ocean surveillance aircraft (Electronics-Patrol-Experimental) with APS-116 radar; programme cancelled.

OPERATIONAL

Taiwan, United States (Air Force, NASA)

Ute RU-21 Beechcraft

The US Army has a number of reconnaissance variants of the Ute U-21 utility aircraft, the militarized version of a Beechcraft twin engine light transport. Most RU-21 aircraft are flown by the Army Security Agency (ASA) and employed in electronic intercept operations.

The aircraft has a low, straight-wing configuration with wing-mounted turbo-prop engines, and a retractable tricycle landing gear. Various electronic antennas are fitted on the wings and fuselage. Most are being updated under the GUARDRAIL airborne signal intelligence project.

Status: *Operational.* First flight March 1967 (U-21A); 46 built to reconnaissance configuration through 1974.

SPECIFICATIONS (RU-21E)

Crew: 4 (2 pilots, 2 electronic systems operators)
Engines: 2 United Aircraft of Canada (Pratt & Whitney) PT6A-20 turbo-props (500 shp each)
Dimensions: span 45 ft 10½ in (13·98 m), length 35 ft 6 in (10·83 m), height 14 ft 2½ in (4·33 m), wing

area 279¾ sq ft (26 m²)
Speed: approx 250 mph (402 km/hr)
Ceiling: approx 26,000 ft (7,930 m)
Range: 1,160 miles (1,866 km)
Weight: 9,650 lb (4,380 kg) maximum
Armament: nil

RU-21D Ute of the US Army (Beech)

RU-21J Ute developed for the US Army's Cefly Lancer programme (Beech)

VARIANTS (reconnaissance)

RU-21A PT6A-20 engines; U-21A fitted with ASA electronic intercept equipment; 4 built.

RU-21B PT6A-29 engines; U-21A fitted with ASA electronic intercept equipment; 3 built.

RU-21C PT6A-29 engines; similar to RU-21B with different antenna array; 2 built.

RU-21D PT6A-20 engines; similar to RU-21A with modified controls; 18 built.

RU-21E PT6A-2D engines; U-21A fitted for electronic intercept in the combat zone; 4 built.

RU-21H PT6A-20 engines; similar to RU-21E with structural modifications and 10,200-lb (4,630 kg) maximum take-off weight; 12 built.

RU-21J reconnaissance variant with improved engines and T-tail combination; 3 built.

OPERATIONAL (reconnaissance variants)

United States (Army)

Victor SR Handley Page

The strategic/maritime reconnaissance variant of the Victor is configured for high-altitude ocean photography. The Victor SR.2 is a modification of the Victor B.2 strategic bomber, a swept-wing, transonic medium bomber that was in Royal Air Force service from the mid-1950s through the 1960s. Tankers and strategic reconnaissance aircraft (the latter to be replaced by the Vulcan SR.2) are the only Victors now flying.

The Victor has a unique "crescent" wing planform and a high, swept-T tail configuration. Four turbofan engines are fitted in the wing roots, providing high subsonic speeds. The SR variant carries a "camera crate" in the weapons bay with cameras for day, night, and survey operations; flash cannisters or auxiliary fuel tanks also are carried in the weapons bay. Radar mapping equipment is fitted. In-flight refuelling probe is provided above the canopy. The SR.2 aircraft initially was known as the Victor B(SR).2.

Status: *Operational.* First flight December 24, 1952; squadron delivery in 1958.

SPECIFICATIONS

Crew: 5

Engines: 4 Rolls-Royce Conway R.Co.17 Mk.201 turbofans (19,750 lb, 8,966 kg st each)

Dimensions: span 120 ft (36·60 m), length 114 ft 11 in (35·04 m), height 30 ft 1½ in (9·20 m), wing area, 2,597 sq ft (241·5 m²)

Speed: 630 mph (1,014 km/hr) at 36,000–50,000 ft (11,340–15,250 m) (Mach 0·95); 560 mph (901 km/hr) at 40,000 ft (12,200 m) (Mach 0·92) cruise

Ceiling: 55,000 ft (16,775 m)

Range: approx 5,000 miles (8,045 km)

Weight: approx 200,000 lb (90,800 kg) loaded

Armament: nil

Victor SR.2 strategic/ maritime recon- naissance aircraft (Ministry of Defence)

VARIANTS

Prototypes

B.1 initial production bomber aircraft with Sapphire 202 turbojet engines; span 110 ft (33·6 m); first flight February 1, 1956; 66 built; several updated to B.1A with additional electronic countermeasures (ECM).

K.1A B.1A modified to tanker aircraft; up to 52,860 lb (24,000 kg) of transferable fuel carried; first flight in 1964.

B.2 production bomber aircraft with Conway R.Co.11 engine (Conway R.Co.17 engine in later aircraft); fitted to carry Blue Steel ASM; first flight February 20, 1959.

SR.2 strategic/maritime reconnaissance variant.

OPERATIONAL

Great Britain (RAF)

Vigilante RA-5C North American

The RA-5C Vigilante is derived from the A-5 nuclear strike aircraft, the only supersonic attack aircraft developed for carrier operation. Now in service with the US Navy only in the tactical reconnaissance configuration, the Vigilante can fly all-weather and night missions employing a variety of sensors. A secondary nuclear strike capability is retained.

The Vigilante is a sleek-looking, swept-wing aircraft with large, squared air intakes for the twin turbojet engines which are housed in large nacelles that extend along the fuselage from just behind the two-place, tandem cockpit to the tail. In the original attack configuration the Vigilante had a tunnel-like, linear weapons bay in the fuselage. The nuclear weapon was rigidly linked to a pair of 275 US gallon fuel tanks that were all ejected from the rear of the aircraft. This arrangement limited weapons flexibility. Subsequently the weapons bay has housed reconnaissance equipment and fixed fuel tanks; side-looking aircraft radar (SLAR) is fitted in an elongated pod ("canoe") fitted to the bottom of the aircraft. Photographic, infra-red, active and passive electronic countermeasure (ECM) sensors are fitted. Pods containing chaff, strobe flashers, fuel, or weapons can be carried on four wing pylons, each of which has a 2,500-lb (1,135 kg) capacity. The aircraft has REINS (radar equipped inertial navigation system) for all-weather navigation and an in-flight refuelling receptacle. Wings fold for carrier operation.

Status: *Operational.* First flight August 31, 1958 (YA3J-1); squadron delivery June 1961; approx 150 built through 1970.

Two views of the RA-5C Vigilante reconnaissance aircraft flown by the US Navy (US Navy)

SPECIFICATIONS (RA-5C)

Crew: 2 (1 pilot, 1 navigator/systems operator)

Engines: 2 General Electric J79-GE-8A/8B turbojets (10,900 lb, 4,949 kg st each; 17,000 lb, 7,718 kg st each with afterburner)

Dimensions: span 53 ft (16·17 m), length 73 ft 2½ in (22·33 m), height 19 ft 4¾ in (5·92 m), wing area 700 sq ft (65 m²)

Speed: 1,385 mph (2,228 km/hr) at 40,000 ft (12,200 m) (Mach 2·1); 1,254 mph (2,003 km/hr) (Mach 1·9) maximum stabilized (clean); 560 mph (901 km/hr) at 40,000 ft (12,200 m) (Mach 0·85) cruise

Ceiling: 64,000 ft (19,520 m)

Range: 3,000 miles (4,827 km)

Weight: 61,730 lb (28,025 kg) loaded

Armament: 4 × Bullpup AGM-12 ASMs

or 4 × 2,000-lb bombs (wing pylons in attack configuration)

VARIANTS

YA3J-1 prototypes with YJ70-GE-2 engines; 2 built.

A-5A formerly A3J-1; initial produc-tion attack aircraft with J79-GE-8A/8-B engines; configured for nuclear strike with 2 wing pylons and internal weapons bay; 55 built.

A-5B formerly A3J-2; planned attack aircraft with increased fuel capacity in fuselage "hump" aft of cockpit; boundary layer wing control; 4 wing pylons; first flight April 29, 1962; production aircraft completed to RA-5C configuration.

RA-5C formerly A3J-3P; reconnaissance aircraft; fitted with advanced sensors; first flight June 30, 1962; approx 100 built to RA-5C configuration plus conversion of earlier aircraft.

OPERATIONAL

United States (NAVY)

Anti-Submarine/Maritime Patrol

Albatross HU-16 Grumman

The Albatross is a twin-engine amphibian operational in a number of air arms in the search and rescue (SAR) role with a few employed in the maritime reconnaissance/anti-submarine role. Originally designated as SA-16 when it first entered US Navy service in 1949, the aircraft subsequently was redesignated HU-16. In the anti-submarine role the Albatross has an enlarged nose radome, a retractable magnetic anomaly detector (MAD) boom in the rear fuselage, and an electronic pod and searchlight on the wings along with pylons for depth charges. Only the anti-submarine aircraft are described below. No Albatross variants currently are flown by US armed forces; the US Coast Guard flies the HU-16E in the SAR role.

Status: *Operational.* First flight October 24, 1947 (XJR2F-1).

SPECIFICATIONS (basic HU-16B)

Crew: approx 5

Engines: 2 Wright R-1820-76A radial pistons (1,275 hp each)

Dimensions: span 96 ft 8 in (29·48 m), length 62 ft 10 in (19·17 m), height 25 ft 10 in (7·88 m), wing area 1,035 sq ft (96·3 m²)

Speed: 236 mph (380 km/hr); 224 mph (360 km/hr) cruise

Range: 2,850 miles (4,585 km) (with 20 minutes over target)

Weights: 22,883 lb (10,389 kg) empty; 30,353 lb (13,780 kg) loaded; 37,500 lb (17,025 kg) maximum

Armament: depth charges or anti-submarine torpedoes (wing pylons)

HU-16 Albatross (Grumman)

VARIANTS (ASW variants)

HU-16B formerly SA-16B; improvement of earlier HU-16A(SA-16A); some fitted for ASW. HU-16C formerly SA-16C/Navy	UF-1; original US Navy variant; subsequently modified for ASW for foreign use.

OPERATIONAL (ASW variants)

Chile, Greece, Peru, Spain, Thailand

Alizé Breguet (Br.1050)

The Alizé (Tradewind) is a three-seat, anti-submarine aircraft flown from French and Indian aircraft carriers. The aircraft has a limited capability against modern submarines and will be phased out of service in the near future.

Developed from the experimental Vultur Br.960 carrier-based strike aircraft, the Alizé is a straight-wing aircraft with a single turboprop engine, a large, retractable radome in the rear fuselage, and dummy wing nacelles containing droppable sonobuoys. There is an internal weapons bay and six underwing pylons for some 2,000 lb (910 kg) of anti-submarine or air-to-surface weapons. The wings fold outboard of the nacelles for carrier operation.

Status: *Operational.* First flight October 6, 1956. The basic configuration was retained through 3 prototype aircraft, 2 pre-production aircraft, 75 models built for *Aéronavale*, and 12 produced for the Indian naval air arm.

SPECIFICATIONS

Crew: 3 (1 pilot, 2 systems operators)
Engine: 1 Rolls-Royce Dart R.Da.7 Mk.21 turboprop (2,020 eshp)
Dimensions: span 51 ft 2 in (15·61 m), length 45 ft 6 in (13·88 m), height 15 ft 7 in (4·76 m), wing area $387\frac{1}{2}$ sq ft. (36 m²)
Speed: 285 mph (459 km/hr) at sea level; 290 mph (467 km/hr) at 10,000 ft (3,050 m); 144 mph (232 km/hr) patrol speed
Ceiling: 20,500 ft (6,253 m)
Range: 1,785-mile (2,872 km) ferry range; patrol endurance up to $7\frac{1}{2}$ hours
Weights: 12,566 lb (5,705 kg) empty; 18,100 lb (8,217 kg) loaded

Alizé of the French Navy on board the sea control ship Arromanches (French Armed Forces)

Armament: 3 × 353-lb depth charges   bay) plus 2 × Nord AS.12 ASMs
or 1 × anti-submarine torpedo (weapons   or 6 × 5-inch rockets (wing pylons)

OPERATIONAL

France, India

Argus CP-107 Canadair (CL-28)

The Argus set the trend for post-Second World War maritime patrol aircraft by adopting a commercial airliner design. The four-engine, straight-wing Argus is based on the Britannia airliner, produced by Canadair as the CL-28 (military designation CP-107). The Argus is used exclusively by the Maritime Command of Canadian Forces in the land-based maritime patrol/anti-submarine role. The aircraft will be replaced by the Lockheed P-3 Orion.

The Argus has the Britannia's straight wing and a conventional tail structure. The fuselage was redesigned to meet military requirements and US-developed turbo-compound engines were provided for sustained flight at low levels during search operations. The aircraft features a radome in the "chin" position, internal weapon bays forward and aft of the wing, and a fixed magnetic anomaly detection (MAD) boom in the tail. A 70-million candle-power searchlight is fitted in the starboard wing. Some 4,000 lb (1,815 kg) of ordnance can be carried in each weapons bay and up to 7,600 lb (3,450 kg) on wing pylons.

Status: *Operational.* First flight March 28, 1957; squadron delivery May 1958.

CP-107 Argus Mk.2 of the Canadian Armed Forces (Canadian Forces)

SPECIFICATIONS

Crew: 15 (3 pilots, 3 navigators, 2 flight engineers, 7 communications personnel and systems operators)
Engines: 4 Wright R-3350 (TC18-EA-1) turbo-compounds (3,700 hp each)
Dimensions: span 142 ft 3½ in (43·40 m), length 132 ft 4½ in (40·38 m), height 36 ft 8 in (11·18 m)
Speed: 315 mph (507 km/hr) at 20,000 ft (6,100 m); 190 mph (306 km/hr) cruise at sea level
Range: 4,040 miles (6,500 km) in patrol configuration; 5,900 miles (9,493 km) maximum
Weight: 157,000 lb (71,278 kg) loaded
Armament: various combinations of depth charges, anti-submarine torpedoes, bombs up to 15,600 lb (7,082 kg)

VARIANTS

Mk.1 initial aircraft with APS-20 search radar in large "chin" radome; 1 prototype and 12 production aircraft built.

Mk.2 improved electronics including British-developed radar in smaller "chin" radome; 20 built.

OPERATIONAL

Canada

Atlantic Breguet (Br.1150)

The Atlantic is a long-range maritime patrol/anti-submarine aircraft designed and built to fulfil a NATO requirement for a successor to the American P2V/P-2 Neptune. The Breguet 1150 design was for a twin-turboprop aircraft with production aircraft being the product of a British-Dutch-French-German-Italian consortium under the overall leadership of Breguet. It is the only twin-engine aircraft of the current generation of maritime patrol aircraft.

The Atlantic features a conventional, straight-wing design with a retractable CSF radome under the forward fuselage, a single internal weapons bay, a fixed magnetic anomaly detection (MAD) boom in the tail, and an electronic countermeasures (ECM) pod at the top of the tail fin. The prototype aircraft had wingtip fuel tanks; these are not now standard but provision for them remains on production aircraft. Two underwing pylons can carry rockets or Nord AS.12 air-to-surface missiles.

Status: *Operational.* First flight October 21, 1961; squadron delivery December 10, 1965 (French Navy); 87 built to Mk.I configuration.

SPECIFICATIONS

Crew: 12 (2 pilots, 1 navigator, 1 tactical co-ordinator, 3 observers, 5 systems operators); provision for 12 additional crewmen for long-duration missions
Engines: 2 SNECMA Rolls-Royce Tyne RTy.20 Mk.21 turboprops (6,106 ehp each)
Dimensions: span 119 ft 1 in (36·30 m), length 104 ft 2 in (31·75 m), height 37 ft 2 in (11·34 m), wing area 1,295 sq ft (120 m²)
Speed: 409 mph (658 km/hr) at altitude; 354 mph (570 km/hr) cruise
Ceiling: 32,800 ft (10,000 m)
Range: 3,500 miles (5,632 km) in patrol configuration at 195 mph (314 km/hr); 5,600 miles (9,010 km) maximum
Weight: 95,900 lb (43,539 kg) maximum
Armament: various combinations of depth charges, anti-submarine torpedoes, bombs, air-to-surface missiles (weapon bays and wing pylons)

VARIANTS

Mk.I 2 prototypes (101 ft, 30·81 m long), 2 pre-production aircraft, and production aircraft for France, West Germany, Italy, and Netherlands (designated SP-13A); second prototype first flew on February 23, 1962, and crashed on April 19, 1962.

Mk.II/IIB under development; advanced avionics; prototype converted from Mk.1 04 aircraft with first flight in 1976.

OPERATIONAL

France, West Germany, Italy, Netherlands, Pakistan

Atlantic of the German Navy (Bundesministerium der Verteidigung)

Atlantic of the French Navy (French Armed Forces)

PBY Catalina of the Brazilian Air Force (Ronaldo S Olive)

PBY Catalina of the Brazilian Air Force (Ronaldo S Olive)

Catalina PBY Convair

The PBY Catalina is an ungainly flying boat that first saw service with the US Navy in the late 1930s. Several of the PBY-5A variants still serve with Central and South American air forces, primarily in the search-and-rescue (SAR) role.

The Catalina's square-tipped wing is supported above the fuselage by a pylon with radial engines fitted into the wing leading edges. The PBY-5A featured a fully retractable landing gear for operations from runways and floats that retract to form wingtips. As built the PBY-5A had ·50-cal machine-guns mounted in the nose and two side blisters, and a ·30-cal MG in a hull tunnel; bombs, depth charges, or torpedoes could be carried under the wings.

Status: *Operational.* First flight in 1939 (XPBY-5A modified from PBY-4). Some 4,000 aircraft of the Catalina design were built with production undertaken by Boeing and the Naval Aircraft Factory, and in Canada and the Soviet Union. The last operational US Navy Catalina (a PBY-6A) was retired in January 1957.

SPECIFICATIONS (PBY-5A)

Crew: 5 to 9

Engines: 2 Pratt & Whitney R-1830-92 Twin Wasp radial pistons (1,200 hp each)

Dimensions: span 104 ft (31·72 m), length 63 ft 10½ in (19·49 m), height 20 ft 2 in (6·15 m), wing area 1,400 sq ft (130 m²)

Speed: 180 mph (290 km/hr) at 7,000 ft (2,135 m)

Ceiling: 14,700 ft (4,484 m)

Range: 2,500 miles (4,023 km); 1,800 miles (2,896 km) with 2,000 lb (908 kg) weapons

Weights: 20,910 lb (9,493 kg) empty; 33,975 lb (15,425 kg) loaded; 35,500 lb (15,890 kg) maximum

Armament: small bombs or depth charges on wing attachment points

OPERATIONAL

Brazil, Chile, Dominican Republic, Mexico

Harpoon PV-2 Lockheed

The Harpoon is a long-based, anti-submarine patrol aircraft developed by the US Navy during the Second World War. Evolved from the Lockheed twin-engine Hudson bomber, in turn developed from the Ventura/Vega series, the Harpoon was used extensively by the US Navy in the later stages of the war and subsequently by several other air arms. Peru and Portugal still fly the aircraft in the maritime patrol role, with the latter nation's Harpoons also having been employed in general bombing missions in Angola.

The Harpoon's twin radial engines are mounted well forward in the mid-wing. There is an internal weapons bay, with a tunnel gun position aft, firing under the twin tail fins. As built most Harpoons had 5 × ·50-cal MG in the solid nose and 2 × ·50-cal MG in the dorsal turret plus 2 × ·30-cal MG in the tunnel position.

Status: *Operational* First flight in 1944.

SPECIFICATIONS

Crew: 5

Engines: 2 Pratt & Whitney R-2800-31 radial pistons (2,000 hp each)

Dimensions: span 75 ft (22·88 m), length 52 ft 1 in (15·88 m), height 13 ft 3 in (4·04 m), wing area 686 sq ft (63·8 m²)

Speed: 282 mph (454 km/hr) at 13,700 ft (4,180 m); 270 mph (434 km/hr) at sea level

Ceiling: 23,900 ft (7,290 m)

Range: 1,790 miles (2,880 km) with 2,000 lb (908 kg) of weapons; 2,900-mile (4,666 km) ferry range

Weights: 21,028 lb (9,547 kg) empty; 33,638 lb (15,272 kg) loaded; 36,000 lb (16,344 kg) maximum

Armament: various combinations of bombs and depth charges up to 2,000 lb (908 kg) (internal weapons bay)

OPERATIONAL

Peru, Portugal

PV-2 Harpoon, now flown only by Peru and Portugal (Flight International)

Madge Be-6 Beriev

The *Madge* is a piston-engine amphibian employed by the Soviet Navy in the maritime patrol role during the 1950s and 1960s. The aircraft remains in service with the Chinese Navy, having been transferred from the USSR in the 1950s.

The *Madge* was a post-war design of Georgi Mikhailovich Beriev, developer of Russian seaplanes since the early 1930s. The large aircraft has a high gull-wing and twin tail fins similar to the US Navy PBM Mariner while the Shvetsov engines are based on American Wright R-3350s (the design for which was obtained from US B-29s forced to land in Soviet Siberia late in the Second World War). Weapons are carried on wing attachment points. Some later variants have a magnetic anomaly detection (MAD) boom fitted in the tail and retractable radome under the after fuselage; some are fitted with additional electronic detection equipment. Stripped aircraft have been employed as transports and for air-sea rescue.

Status: *Operational.* First flight in 1949.

SPECIFICATIONS

Crew: 8
Engines: 2 Shvetsov ASh-73TK radial pistons (2,400 hp each)
Dimensions: span 108 ft 3¼ in (33·03 m), length 77 ft 3 in (23·56 m), height 25 ft 1 in (7·65 m)
Speed: 258 mph (415 km/hr) at 7,875 ft (2,400 m); 210–225 mph (338–362 km/hr) cruise

Range: 3,045 miles (4,900 km)
Weight: 51,588 lb (23,420 kg) loaded
Armament: 3 or 4 × 20-mm cannon (nose, dorsal, tail turrets) and various combinations of depth charges, torpedoes, bombs, mines up to approx 4,000–6,000 lb (1,816–2,724 kg)

OPERATIONAL

Be-6 Madge *of the Soviet Navy*

China

Mail Be-12 Beriev

The *Mail* is a twin turboprop-powered amphibian flown by the Soviet naval air arm. The Russian name for the aircraft is *Tchaika* (Seagull) and the designation is Be-12 or M-12, although the NATO code name *Mail* is common in Western usage. The *Mail* was the direct successor of the Be-6 *Madge* in the Soviet naval air arm; the intermediate, jet-propelled Be-10 *Mallow* flying boat did not enter squadron service in the same manner as the contemporary Martin P6M Seamaster did not achieve US operational status. The *Mail* is slowly being replaced in service by the Il-38 *May*.

Developed from the *Madge* amphibian, the *Mail* has a glazed nose under a protruding nose radome, a gull-wing configuration, and twin tail fins, and a protruding magnetic anomaly detection (MAD) boom. A fully retractable undercarriage is provided for operation from land bases. There are four underwing pylons for weapons in addition to the internal weapons bay aft of the hull step. The aircraft has lifted payloads of 20,000 lb (9,080 kg) on test flights.

Status: *Operational.* First flight about 1960; squadron delivery about 1965.

SPECIFICATIONS

Crew: 6 to 10
Engines: 2 Ivchenko AI-20D turbo-props (4,190 shp each)
Dimensions: span 97 ft 6 in (29·70 m), length 99 ft (30·20 m), height 22 ft 11½ in (6·98 m)
Speed: 379 mph (610 km/hr) at 10,000 ft (3,050 m); 200–250 mph (322–402 km/hr) cruise

Ceiling: 37,000 ft (11,285 m)
Range: 2,500 miles (4,023 km)
Weight: 65,035 lb (29,525 kg) maximum
Armament: various combinations of depth charges, torpedoes, mines, bombs (weapons bay and wing pylons)

OPERATIONAL

Soviet Union (Navy)

Be-12 Mail *flown by the Soviet Navy*

Be-12 Mail

May II-38 Ilyushin

The *May* is a four-turboprop maritime reconnaissance/anti-submarine aircraft being used in increasing numbers by the Soviet naval air arm. The *May* is a modification of the II-18 *Coot* commercial airliner, an approach to maritime patrol aircraft similar to the US Orion, British Nimrod, and Canadian Argus. The *May* ends a long-line of Beriev flying boats employed in this role by the Soviet Navy. *Mays* have flown from Egyptian bases with Russian crews but with UAR markings.

The *May* has a longer fuselage than the *Coot* with a fixed radome under the nose, an internal weapons bay, and magnetic anomaly detector (MAD) boom fixed in the tail. An onboard computer is provided to perform tactical calculations.

Status: *Operational.* First flight about 1969.

Two views of the II-38 May *flown by Soviet Naval Aviation*

SPECIFICATIONS

Crew: approx 12
Engines: 4 Ivchenko AI-20M
    turboprops (4,250 shp each)
Dimensions: span 122 ft 8½ in (37·40
    m), length 129 ft 10 in (39·28 m),
    height 33 ft 4 in (10·17 m)
Speed: 400 mph (644 km/hr) at sea
    level

Ceiling: 35,500 ft (10,828 m)
Range: 4,500 miles (7,240 km)
Armament: various combinations of
    depth charges, torpedoes, bombs
    (weapons bay)

OPERATIONAL

India (planned), Soviet Union (Navy)

Neptune P-2 Lockheed

The P-2 Neptune is a land-based maritime patrol/anti-submarine aircraft of Second World War design powered in its current configuration by two piston engines and two jet pods, the latter for take-offs and for dash speeds to reach submarine contacts. The Neptune has been produced in larger numbers and has been flown by more air forces than any other post-war maritime patrol aircraft. The Neptune has been replaced in active US Navy patrol squadrons by the P-3 Orion and will be replaced in the US Naval Reserve by 1980.

The Neptune was developed during the Second World War, but did not see service in that conflict. The aircraft has a conventional straight-wing configuration and the early variants had a glazed nose (subsequently reintroduced) and carried a heavy gun armament. The internal weapons bay contained electronic equipment in some early specialized configurations, with most later aircraft having an extended magnetic anomaly detection (MAD) tail boom. Wingtip tanks are fitted in most models with the starboard tank housing a searchlight. Early Neptunes were launched from US aircraft carriers to demonstrate nuclear attack capability and the P2V-3C variant was designed specifically for carrier launching although no hooks were fitted and no landings were attempted.

Status: *Operational.* First flight May 15, 1945; squadron delivery in March 1947. Between 1945 and April 1962, Lockheed produced 1,099 Neptunes and an additional 89 were built under licence in Japan by Kawasaki.

Two views of the SP-2H Neptune flown by the US Navy (US Navy)

SPECIFICATIONS (P-2H)

Crew: 7 (2 pilots, 1 navigator, 1 engineer, 3 observers and systems operators)

Engines: 2 Wright R-3550-32W radial piston (3,500 hp each) and 2 Westinghouse J34-WF-32W turbojets (3,400 lb, 1,540 kg st each)

Dimensions: span 103 ft 11 in (31·65 m), length 91 ft 8 in (27·94 m), height 29 ft 3½ in (8·94 m), wing area 1,000 sq ft (93 m²)

Speed: 356 mph (573 km/hr) at 10,000 ft (3,050 m) (piston engines only); 173 mph (278 km/hr) patrol at 980 ft (300 m)

Ceiling: 22,000 ft (6,710 m)

Range: 2,200 miles (3,540 km) in patrol configuration; 3,685 miles (5,930 km) maximum

Weights: 49,935 lb (22,670 kg) empty; 79,895 lb (36,272 kg) maximum

Armament: 2 × 2,165-lb anti-submarine torpedoes
or 2 × 2,000-lb Mk-55 mines
or 8 × 1,000-lb Mk-52 mines
or 12 × 325-lb depth charges
or 8 × 1,000-lb bombs
or 4 × 2,000-lb bombs (weapons bay) plus 16 × 5-inch rockets (wing pylons)

VARIANTS

XP2V-1 prototype with two R-3350-8 engines; glazed nose; 7 crew; armed with 6 × ·50-cal MG in twin nose, dorsal, tail positions; 2 built.

P2V-1 initial production aircraft; 1 stripped for long-distance flight (*Truculent Turtle*); 15 built.

P2V-2 powered by two R-3350-24W engines; solid nose with 6 × 20-mm cannon plus 4 × ·50-cal MG in early aircraft; subsequently armed with 20-mm in dorsal and tail positions; first flight (XP2V-2) January 7, 1947; 81 built.

P2V-3 powered by two R-3350-26W engines; improved ASW systems; solid nose; only dorsal and tail guns fitted; first flight August 6, 1948; 83 built including 12 as P2V-3C for carrier-launched nuclear weapons delivery; 2 as P2V-3Z armoured transport, and 30 as P2V-3W with APS-20 radar in large belly radome.

P-2D formerly P2V-4; powered by two R-3350-30W turbo-compound engines; improved electronics and APS-20 radar; solid nose; first flight November 14, 1949; 52 built.

P-2E formerly P2V-5; powered by R-3350-30W engines; originally armed with 2 × 20-mm in solid nose plus 2 × ·50-cal MG in dorsal position and 2 × 20-mm in tail; solid nose subsequently replaced by glazed nose and MAD boom fitted in tail; two Westing-house J-34-WE-34 turbojets fitted in underwing pods (P2V-5F); most refitted with advanced avionics (P2V-5FE/EP-2E) or Jezebel passive detector (P2V-5FS/SP-2E); some fitted for drone aircraft control (P2V-5FD/DP-2E); some fitted for tactical recon-naissance over Vietnam (AP-2E/OP-2E); first flight December 29, 1950; 424 built with 36 provided to Royal Air Force (of which 12 subsequently transferred to Portugal); 6 transferred to Argentina, 14 transferred to Brazil.

P-2F formerly P2V-6; similar to P-2E; modified electronic equipment and minelaying capability; with J-34-WE-36 jet pods redesignated P-2G; redesignated P2V-6M/MP-2F when employed in minelaying or to carry Petrel AUM-N-2 ASMs; redesignated P2V-6T/TP-2F in training role; first flight October 16, 1952; 83 built with several transferred to France.

P-2G P-2F fitted with jet pods (see above).

P-2H formerly P2V-7; ultimate Lockheed production Neptune with

R-3350-32W engines and J34-WE-36 jet pods in original configuration; bulged cockpit canopy; initially fitted with 2 × ·50-cal MG in dorsal position which was replaced by 2 × 20-mm guns and finally deleted; aircraft for Netherlands delivered with solid nose housing 4 × 20-mm guns refitted with glazed nose; large radome under forward fuselage and MAD boom; redesignated P2V-7S/SP-2H when fitted with Jezebel/Julie equipment; some fitted for low-level ground and coastal interdiction in Vietnam (AP-2H); few fitted for Arctic photo reconnaissance (P2V-7LP/LP-2J); first flight (YP-2H) April 26, 1954; 359 built by Lockheed and 48 by Kawasaki with 16 Lockheed aircraft transferred to Japan, 25 to Canada, 15 to Netherlands, and several to France; 7 provided to US Air Force for electronic test/training activities (P2V-7U/RB-69A) One modified by USN with UHF telemetry equipment and ASW equipment removed (EP-2H).

P-2J Kawasaki-built variant with two GE T64-IHI-10 turboprop and two Ishikawajima-Harima J3-IHI-7C turbojet pods; span 97 ft 8$\frac{1}{2}$ in (29·80 m), length 95 ft 10$\frac{3}{4}$ in (29·25 m); 42,500 lb (19,295 kg) empty; 75,000 lb (34,050 kg) maximum; first flight July 21, 1966; 89 built.

OPERATIONAL

Argentina, Brazil, France, Japan, Netherlands, Portugal, United States (Naval Reserve)

Nimrod Hawker Siddeley (HS.801)

The Nimrod was the first all jet-powered aircraft to be adapted to the maritime patrol/anti-submarine role. (The only other aircraft currently in this category is the Lockheed S-3 Viking.) The swept-wing, turbofan-powered Nimrod, like its US and Soviet contemporaries, is based on a commercial airliner airframe, in this case the Comet 4C. The Nimrod is flown only by the Strike Command of the Royal Air Force, but is being put forward as a replacement for the Canadian Argus and for service in the Australian and South African air forces.

Resembling the Comet 4C aircraft from which it was adopted, the Nimrod has a swept-wing configuration with four turbojet engines nested in the wing roots. The protruding lower nose houses an ASV-21D search radar; a long (approximately 50-foot) shallow weapons bay and two double wing pylons can hold a variety of weapons; a magnetic anomaly detection (MAD) boom is fitted aft, and an electronic pod tops the tail fin; fuel tanks are faired into the wings with the forward end of the starboard tank housing a searchlight. The company designation is HS.801.

Status: *Operational.* First flight May 23, 1967; squadron delivery in 1970.

Nimrod MR.1 of the Royal Air Force (Ministry of Defence)

SPECIFICATIONS

Crew: 12 (2 pilots, 1 flight engineer; 1 navigator; 1 tactical navigator; 1 radio operator; 1 radar operator; 2 observers; 3 systems operators)

Engines: 4 Rolls-Royce RB.163-20 Spey Mk 250 turbofans (12,160 lb, 5,520 kg st each)

Dimensions: span 114 ft 10 in (35·00 m), length 126 ft 9 in (38·63 m), height 29 ft 8½ in (9·06 m), wing area 2,121 sq ft (197 m²)

Speed: 575 mph (926 km/hr); 490 mph (788 km/hr) cruise

Range: 5,755-mile (9,260 km) ferry range; 12-hour patrol endurance

Weights: 177,500 lb (80,585 kg) loaded; 192,000 lb (87,168 kg) maximum

Armament: various combinations of depth charges, anti-submarine torpedoes, bombs or mines (weapons bay), plus 4 × Nord AS.12 ASMs (wing pylons)

VARIANTS

Prototypes 2 Comet 4C airframes modified; one to serve as aerodynamic test bed for Nimrod (RB.163-20 engines) and one to serve as electronics test bed for Nimrod (Avon engines).

MR.1 production aircraft; first flight June 28, 1968; 46 built.

R.1 aircraft configured for electronic reconnaissance; MAD boom deleted; 3 built.

MR.2 under development; improved avionics and Elliott 920A7C computer for tactical data processing which will be back-fitted to MR.1 aircraft.

OPERATIONAL

Great Britain (RAF)

Orion P-3 Lockheed

The P-3 Orion is a four-engine, land-based maritime patrol/anti-submarine aircraft operated in large numbers by the US Navy and several other air forces. Like its British and Soviet contemporaries, the Orion is based on the airframe of a commercial airliner, in this case the Lockheed Electra. The Orion replaced the P2V/P-2 Neptune and P5M/P-5 Marlin as the US Navy's standard patrol aircraft. In addition, several specialized variants are in service.

The Orion is a straight wing aircraft powered by four turboprop engines; the fuselage is 7 ft 4 in shorter than the Electra; up to 15,000 lb (6,810 kg) of weapons can be carried in the large internal weapons bay and on ten wing pylons (six outboard and four inboard), with one starboard pylon normally mounting a searchlight; it has the distinctive magnetic anomaly detection (MAD) tail boom associated with ASW aircraft. The P-3C variant, now standard in US Navy patrol squadrons, has the computer-driven A-NEW avionics system to provide rapid solutions to tactical ASW problems. A total of 241 P-3C aircraft are planned for active Navy patrol squadrons with older Orion variants in 12 reserve patrol squadrons by about 1980.

Status: *Operational.* First flight August 19, 1958; squadron delivery July 1962; over 400 of all variants produced.

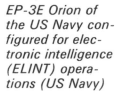

EP-3E Orion of the US Navy configured for electronic intelligence (ELINT) operations (US Navy)

SPECIFICATIONS (P-3C)

Crew: 10 to 12

Engines: 4 Allison T56-A-14 turboprops (4,910 ehp each)

Dimensions: span 99 ft 8 in (30·37
m), length 116 ft 10 in (35·61 m),
height 33 ft 8½ in (10·28 m), wing
area 1,300 sq ft (121 m²)

Speed: 473 mph (761 km/hr) at
15,000 ft (4,570 m); 378 mph (608
km/hr) cruise at 25,000 ft (7,625 m);
237 mph (381 km/hr); patrol at
1,500 ft (458 m)

Ceiling: 28,300 ft (8,632 m)

Range: 2,380 miles (3,830 km) in
patrol configuration; 17 hour patrol
endurance

Weights: 61,491 lb (27,917 kg)
empty; 135,000 lb (61,290 kg)
loaded; 142,000 lb (64,468 kg)
maximum

Armament: 1 × 2,000-lb mine
or 3 × 1,000-lb mine
or 4 × anti-submarine torpedoes
(weapons bay) plus 4 × 2,000-lb
mines
or 4 × anti-submarine torpedoes
(inboard wing pylons) plus 2 × 2,000-
lb mines and 2 × 1,000-lb mines and
1 × 500-lb mine (outboard pylons)

VARIANTS

Prototype Electra airframe modified
to serve as aerodynamic test bed.

YP-3A formerly YP3V-1; second
Electra airframe modified as test bed;
first flight November 25, 1959.

P-3A formerly P3V-1; initial
production aircraft with T56-A-10W/
-10WA engines; first flight April 15,
1961; 3 subsequently transferred to
Spain.

RP-3A P-3A aircraft modified for
special reconnaissance; 1 for Project
Outpost Seascan, a worldwide
environmental survey (named *El
Coyote*); 1 for Project Birdseye, an
arctic environmental survey (*Arctic Fox*).

WP-3A P-3A aircraft modified for
weather reconnaissance.

P-3B production aircraft with
T56-A-14 engines (weights same as
P-3C); US aircraft fitted to carry Bullpup
ASMs; 10 built for Australia, 5 for
Norway, 5 for New Zealand.

EP-3B P-3B aircraft modified for
electronic reconnaissance.

YP-3C P-3B fitted for evaluation of
A-NEW avionics and other improvements.

P-3C production aircraft with
A-NEWS; 142 ordered through Fiscal
Year 1975.

RP-3D P-3C aircraft modified for
Project Magnet, a worldwide magnetic
survey (named *Roadrunner).*

WP-3D modified aircraft for weather
research; 2 flown by National Oceanic
and Atmospheric Administration (US
Dept. of Commerce); 4 crew and 12
scientists.

EP-3E electronic reconnaissance
variant; fitted with T56-A-14 engines;
large radar pods faired into upper and
lower fuselage, large radome under
forward fuselage; 10 converted from
P-3A and 2 from EP-3B; 15 crew.

P-3F modified P-3C for Iran;
primarily ocean surveillance aircraft with
some avionics deleted; fitted for ASMs;
6 built.

OPERATIONAL

Australia, Iran, New Zealand, Norway,
Spain, United States (Navy, National

Oceanic and Atmospheric Administration), Canada (on order)

PS-1 Shin Meiwa

The PS-1 is the only military flying boat currently in production. Designed specifically to meet Japanese requirements for maritime patrol/anti-submarine operations in territorial waters, the PS-1 has a high, straight-wing configuration with four turboprop engines. The general external design resembles the late Martin P-5/P5M Marlin, the US Navy's last operational patrol seaplane. The flying boat configuration of the PS-1 marks a radical departure from contemporary US, British, Soviet, and NATO approaches to maritime patrol aircraft.

Features of the PS-1 include the protruding radome nose housing an APS-80J radar, retractable undercarriage for land operations, HQS-101 "dipping" sonar which can be lowered while the aircraft is on the water, Jezebel/Julie and other anti-submarine detection equipment, a magnetic anomaly detection (MAD) tail boom, a high "T" tail, and twin underwing "pods" for anti-submarine torpedoes. The company designation is SS-2.

Status: *Operational.* First flight October 5, 1967.

SPECIFICATIONS (PS-1)

Crew: 10 (2 pilots, 1 tactical co-ordinator, 1 flight engineer, 1 navigator, 1 radar operator, 1 radio operator, 3 systems operators)

Engines: 4 Ishikawajima-Harima (General Electric) T64-IHI-10 turbo-props (3,060 ehp)

Dimensions: span 108 ft 8¾ in (33·14 m), length 109 ft 11 in (33·52 m), height 31 ft 10½ in (9·73 m), wing area 1,462 sq ft (136 m²)

Speed: 340 mph (547 km/hr) at 5,000 ft (1,525 m); 196–265 mph (315– 426 km/hr) cruise at 5,000 ft (1,525 m)

Ceiling: 29,500 ft (9,000 m)

Range: 1,347 miles (2,168 km)

Weights: 56,128 lb (25,482 kg) empty; 79,365 lb (36,030 kg) max sea operation; 99,200 lb (45,037 kg) max land operation

Armament: 4 × 330-lb bombs (weapons bay), 4 × anti-submarine torpedoes (wing pods) and 6 × 5-in rockets (wingtip launchers)

PS-7 of the Japanese Maritime Self-Defence Force (Shin Meiwa)

VARIANTS

Prototypes 2 built.
PS-1 production aircraft; 21 built or programmed.

US-1 search-and-rescue variant; up to 12 crew plus 12 passengers plus 12 stretchers; first flight October 16, 1974; 3 built.

OPERATIONAL

Japan

Shackleton Avro

The Shackleton is a land-based, maritime patrol aircraft developed from the Lancaster/Lincoln bombers of the Second World War. After serving as Britain's only aircraft in this role from the mid-1950s to 1970, when the Nimrod became operational, the Shackleton remains in RAF operation as an airborne early warning aircraft and continues in the maritime patrol role with South Africa.

The Shackleton has an ungainly design with four in-line wing-mounted, piston engines, an extremely large weapons bay extending about half the length of the fuselage, and twin tail fins. The initial Shackleton MR.1 carried 2 × 20-mm cannon in a dorsal turret, 2 × ·50-cal MG in the tail position, and was distinguished by a large radome in the chin position; the MR 2 is more streamlined without the chin radome, with 2 × 20-mm guns in the nose, a semi-retractable radome under the after fuselage, and a glazed tail cone (with MG deleted). The MR.3 added habitability features, wingtip fuel tanks, turbojets for take-offs in outboard nacelle extensions, and deleted the guns.

Status: *Operational.* First flight March 9, 1949; squadron delivery in 1951; 191 aircraft built.

Shackleton AEW.2 of the Royal Air Force (Ministry of Defence)

SPECIFICATIONS (MR.3)

Crew: 10
Engines: 4 Rolls-Royce Griffon 57A in-line (liquid-cooled) piston (2,450 hp each) and 2 Bristol Siddeley Viper B.S.V.11 turbojets (2,500 lb, 1,135 kg st each)
Dimensions: span 119 ft 10 in (36·52 m), length 92 ft 6 in (28·21 m), height 23 ft 4 in (7·12 m), wing area 1,458 sq ft (135·5 m²)
Speed: 302 mph (486 km/hr) at 12,000 ft (3,660 m); 200–253 mph

(322–407 km/hr) cruise
Ceiling: 19,200 ft (5,856 m)
Range: 3,660 miles (5,889 km) in patrol configuration; 4,215 miles (6,782 km) maximum
Weights: 57,800 lb (26,240 kg) empty; 85,000 lb (38,590 kg) loaded; 100,000 lb (45,400 kg) maximum
Armament: 3 × anti-submarine torpedoes
or 9 × depth charges
or 12 × 1,000-lb bombs (weapons bay)

VARIANTS

Prototypes 3 built.

MR.1/1A initial production aircraft; first flight October 24, 1950; 77 built.

MR.2/2C streamlined configuration; ventral radar in place of chin radome; all modernized with avionics and anti-submarine equipment brought up to MR.3 standards (redesignated MR.2C); 69 built.

MR.3 nosewheel undercarriage, wingtip tanks, improved avionics and anti-submarine equipment; subsequently updated to "phase 3" configuration with turbojet pods for supplementary power during take-off; first flight September 2, 1955; 34 built for Royal Air Force and 8 for South Africa.

AEW.2 airborne early warning (AEW) aircraft converted from MR.2 aircraft; anti-submarine equipment deleted and large radome fitted under forward fuselage; first flight on September 30, 1971; 12 converted.

OPERATIONAL

Great Britain (RAF), South Africa

Tracker S-2 Grumman

The Tracker is a long-serving, widely used anti-submarine aircraft originally developed for US Navy carrier operation. The aircraft was one of the first to combine advanced search and attack capabilities in a single airframe, resulting in a relatively large aircraft for its time. However, the versatility of the twin-engine, four-place aircraft has led to its use from carriers and shore bases by ten nations. The tracker is now being replaced in US Navy squadrons by the S-3 Viking. It also will be phased out of the US Naval Air Reserve in the near future.

S-2E Tracker of the US Navy with MAD boom extended (US Navy)

The Tracker has a high-wing, twin-engine configuration, giving a compact appearance, with the pilots' cockpit relatively far forward. Features include an internal weapons bay, retractable APS-88 radome under the rear fuselage, a retractable magnetic anomaly detection (MAD) boom in the tail, and a searchlight mounted in the starboard wing. Eight expendable sonobuoys are housed in the rear of each engine nacelle. The wings fold for carrier operation. Derivatives are WF/E-1 Tracer airborne early warning aircraft (AEW), listed separately, and TF/C-1 Trader carrier on-board delivery (COD) cargo aircraft.

Status: *Operational.* First flight December 4, 1952; squadron delivery February 1954; over 1,000 built by Grumman plus 100 built under licence in Canada by de Havilland.

SPECIFICATIONS (S-2E)

Crew: 4 (1 pilot, 1 co-pilot/navigator, 2 systems operators)

Engines: 2 Wright R-1820-82A radial piston (1,525 hp each)

Dimensions: span 72 ft 7 in (22·13 m), length 43 ft 6 in (13·26 m), height 17 ft 6 in (5·34 m), wing area 499 sq ft (46·4 m²)

Speed: 280 mph (450 km/hr) at sea level; 150 mph (241 km/hr) patrol at 1,500 ft (458 m)

Ceiling: 23,000 ft (7,015 m)

Range: 1,352 miles (2,175 km) in patrol configuration

Weights: 18,315 lb (8,315 kg) empty; 24,500 lb (11,123 kg) loaded; 26,147 lb (11,870 kg) maximum

Armament: 2 × anti-submarine torpedoes or 4 × 385-lb depth charges (weapons bay) plus 6 × 5-inch rockets or 6 × 250-lb bombs (wing pylons)

VARIANTS

XS2F-1 prototype with R-1820-82 engines; 1 built.

S-2A formerly S2F-1; initial production aircraft with R-1820-82 engines; span 69 ft 8 in (21·25 m), length 42 ft (12·81 m), height 16 ft 3½ in (4·97 m); 17,357 lb (7,880 kg) empty, 24,500 lb (11,123 kg) loaded, 26,300 lb (11,940 kg) max; approx 500 built by Grumman including 6 for Argentina, 48 for Italy, 60 for Japan, 24 for Netherlands; 60 built by de Havilland Canada including 13 for Brazil, 17 for Netherlands (Canadian-built aircraft initially designated CS2F-1; modified to -2 and -3 with improved equipment; subsequently changed to CP-121).

TS-2A formerly S2F-1T; S-2A used in training role.

US-2A S-2A modified for target tow.

S-2B formerly S2F-1S; S-2A modified with installation of Julie anti-submarine detection equipment.

US-2B S-2B with some equipment removed and five passenger seats fitted; used in utility role.

S-2C formerly S2F-2; S-2A with enlarged weapons bay; 60 built; most modified to RS-2C or US-2C configuration.

RS-2C formerly S2F-2P; S-2C modified for photo reconnaissance; 4 crew.

US-2C formerly S2F-2U; S-2C modified for target tow.

S-2D formerly S2F-3; improved anti-submarine aircraft with R-1820-82A/-82WA engines; span 72 ft 7 in (22·14 m), length 43 ft 6 in (13·27 m), height 17 ft 6 in (5·34 m); increased fuel capacity; improved anti-submarine equipment; first flight May 21, 1959; 215 built.

YAS-2D S-2D modified to prototype night attack configuration for US Air Force.

AS-2D final S-2D configuration for night attack for US Air Force.

S-2E final production aircraft; fitted with improved anti-submarine equipment; 14 transferred to Australia.

S-2F S-2B fitted with final Julie/Jezebel submarine detection equipment.

YS-2G S-2E modified for anti-submarine avionics development.

OPERATIONAL

Argentina, Australia, Brazil, Canada, Italy, Japan, Taiwan, Thailand, United States (Naval Reserve), Uruguay

Viking S-3 Lockheed

The S-3 Viking is an advanced anti-submarine aircraft powered by twin turbo-fan engines intended to replace the venerable S-2 Tracker aboard US Navy aircraft carriers. The compact Viking was developed to counter the more sophisticated Soviet submarines that have exceeded the growth potential of the 20-year-old Tracker. The US Navy plans to operate one 10-aircraft squadron of Vikings from each of the 12 large carriers in service during the 1980s.

Two views of the S-3A Viking (US Navy)

Developed from the VSX competition of the 1960s, the winning Lockheed design provided an aircraft of about the Tracker dimensions, but considerably heavier, faster, and carrying more advanced anti-submarine equipment. The cockpit is located relatively far forward, a retractable refuelling probe is installed on the top of the fuselage, an internal weapons bay can accommodate 2,400 lb of ordnance, and an ASQ-81 magnetic anomaly detection (MAD) boom retracts into the tail. Other sensors include APS-116 high-resolution radar, a retractable forward-looking infra-red (FLIR) scanner, electronic countermeasure (ECM) pods on the wingtips, and 60 sonobuoys carried in fuselage tubes. A Sperry Univac 1832A (AYK-10) computer is provided for solving tactical problems. The turbofan engines are on wing pylons (in the manner of the A-3 Skywarrior). The wings and tail fin fold for carrier operation.

Status: *Operational*. First flight January 21, 1972; squadron delivery February 1974; 187 aircraft planned of which 138 funded through Fiscal Year 1975.

SPECIFICATIONS (S-3A)

Crew: 4 (2 pilots, 1 tactical co-ordinator, 1 systems operator)

Engines: 2 General Electric TF34-GE-2 high by-pass ratio turbofans (9,275 lb, 4,210 kg st each)

Dimensions: span 68 ft 8 in (20·93 m), length 53 ft 4 in (16·26 m), height 22 ft 9 in (6·94 m), wing area 598 sq ft (55·6 m²)

Speed: 506 mph (814 km/hr) at sea level; 400 + mph (644 km/hr) cruise; 184 mph (296 km/hr) loiter

Ceiling: 40,000 ft (12,200 m)

Range: 2,300+ miles (3,700 km) in patrol configuration; 3,500-mile (5,632 km) ferry range

Weights: 26,600 lb (12,076 kg) empty; 42,500 lb (19,295 kg) loaded

Armament: 4 × Mk-46 anti-submarine torpedoes or combinations of bombs, mines, depth charges (weapons bay) plus bombs, rocket pods (wing pylons)

VARIANTS

Prototypes S-3A aircraft assigned to test programme; 8 built.

S-3A production aircraft.

US-3A carrier on-board delivery (COD) configuration of Viking; length increased to 59 ft 2 in (18·04 m); 50,273 lb (22,824 kg) maximum; up to 23 passengers; first flight planned for 1977; 24 aircraft planned.

ES-3 proposed electronic warfare aircraft fitted with tactical airborne signal exploitation systems (TASES) to replace EA-3B Skywarrior.

OPERATIONAL

United States (Navy)

Helicopters

A.106 Agusta

An original Agusta design, the A.106 was produced to fulfil an Italian Navy requirement for a light-weight ASW helicopter, and to compete on the international market as a light-weight armed scout helicopter. Twenty-three A.106s were built for operation from Italian Navy guided missile destroyers, these being equipped with all-weather avionics, sonobuoys, and Julie acoustic gear. The A.106 programme was terminated after delivery of this initial order.

Status: *Operational.* First flight in November 1965; squadron delivery in 1972.

SPECIFICATIONS

Crew: 1
Engine: 1 Turboméca-Agusta TAA 230 turboshaft (300 shp)
Dimensions: overall length 36 ft (10·98 m); fuselage length 26 ft 3 in (8·01 m); height 8 ft 2½ in (2·50 m); main rotor diameter 31 ft 2 in (9·50 m)
Speed: 109 mph (175 km/hr); 104 mph (167 km/hr) cruise
Ceiling: 9,850 ft (3,004 m) hovering in ground effect
Range: 150 miles (241 km); 460 miles (740 km) ferry
Weights: 1,300 lb (590 kg) empty; 3,086 lb (1,401 kg) maximum
Armament: 2 × Mk-44 ASW torpedoes

OPERATIONAL

Italy

A-106 lightweight ASW helicopter of the Italian Navy

Alouette II Aérospatiale

The Alouette II utility helicopter has proved to be one of the world's most popular helicopters, with almost 1,000 in service in 37 countries. Missions for the Alouette II have included anti-submarine warfare, observation, photography, casualty evacuation, rescue, light transport, liaison, training, close support, crop dusting, and flying crane duties. The designer of the Alouette II, Sud-Est, merged with another company in 1957 to form Sud-Aviation, which in turn, was absorbed by Aérospatiale in 1970. The designations of the Alouette variants therefore progress from SE to SA prefixes.

The Alouette II has a conventional main rotor/tail rotor configuration with an open, latticework tailboom and small horizontal stabilizer. Landing gear can be of either the skid or wheeled type, or pneumatic floats.

Status: *Operational.* First flight March 12, 1955; squadron delivery in 1957. Approximately 1,000 built.

SPECIFICATIONS (SA-318C)

Crew: 1 + 4 troops

Engines: 1 Turboméca Astazou IIA turboshaft (530 shp)

Dimensions: overall length 39 ft 8½ in (12·11 m); fuselage length 31 ft 11¾ in (9·74 m); height 9 ft (2·75 m); main rotor diameter 33 ft 5⅝ in (10·21 m)

Speed: 127 mph (204 km/hr); 112 mph (180 km/hr) cruise

Ceiling: 10,800 ft (3,294 m); 5,085 ft (1,550 m) hovering in ground effect

Range: 450 miles (724 km)

Weights: 1,961 lb (890 kg) empty; 3,630 lb (1,648 kg) maximum

Armament: experimentally fitted with Nord AS.10 or AS.11 ASMs; homing torpedoes carried in ASW variants

Alouette II of the French Navy (French Armed Forces)

VARIANTS

SE-3120 prototypes with Salmson 9 piston engine; developed for crop spraying; 2 built.

SE-313B formerly SE-3130; Turboméca Artouste IIC6 turboshaft; production version.

SA-315 formerly SE-3150; Artouste turboshaft; predecessor of Alouette III; flown by India as Lama.

SA-318C formerly SA-3180; engine and rotor drive of Alouette III (described separately).

OPERATIONAL

Algeria, Belgium, Cambodia, Cameroun, Central African Republic, Chad, Dominican Republic, Finland, France, West Germany, Great Britain, India, Indonesia, Israel, Ivory Coast, Laos,

Lebanon, Libya, Mexico, Morocco, Netherlands, Nigeria, Peru, Portugal, South Africa, Sweden, Switzerland, Tunisia

Alouette III Aérospatiale (SA-316/319)

The Alouette III, developed from the earlier Alouette II, has greater cabin capacity, a more powerful turbine engine, updated equipment, and greater performance than its predecessor. This helicopter has had even greater success on the international market than its predecessor, having been flown by more than 60 countries. Licence production of the Alouette III is carried out in three of those countries: India, Romania, and Switzerland.

The cabin of the Alouette III is more enclosed than that of its predecessor, and can accommodate up to six passengers in addition to the pilot. All seats are removable to permit an unobstructed cargo area for internal loads, while sling attachment points are provided for external loads exceeding 1,500 lb (680 kg). Military variants are flown in a variety of roles, the two most popular being as an assault helicopter with a variety of anti-personnel and anti-armour weapons, and a naval configuration with anti-submarine sensors and weapons.

Alouette III of the French Navy (Aérospatiale)

Status: *Operational.* First flown February 28, 1959; squadron delivery in 1962. Over 1,200 built.

SPECIFICATIONS

Crew: 1 + 6 troops
Engine: 1 Turboméca Artouste IIIB turboshaft (870 shp)
Dimensions: overall length 42 ft 1$\frac{1}{2}$ in (12·84 m); fuselage length 32 ft 10$\frac{3}{4}$ in (10·03 m); height 9 ft 10 in (2·99 m); main rotor diameter 36 ft 1$\frac{3}{4}$ in (11·02 m)
Speed: 130 mph (209 km/hr); 115 mph cruise (185 km/hr)
Ceiling: 10,500 ft (3,203 m) service; 9,450 ft (2,882 m) hovering in ground effect
Range: 335 miles (540 km)
Weights: 2,474 lb (1,123 kg) empty; 4,850 lb (2,202 kg) maximum
Armament: 1 × 7·62-mm MG or 1 × 20-mm cannon or 4 × AS.11 ASMs or 2 × AS.12 ASMs or 2 × 68-mm rocket pods or 2 × Mk-44 anti-submarine torpedoes

VARIANTS

SE-3160 initial production variant; produced through 1969.
SA-316B uprated engine, strengthened transmission.
SA-319B Astazou XIV turboshaft with 25% reduction in fuel consumption.

OPERATIONAL

Abu Dhabi, Argentina, Austria, Bangladesh, Belgium, Burma, Cambodia, Denmark, Dominican Republic, Ecuador, Eire, Ethiopia, France, Ghana, India, Indonesia, Iraq, Israel, Jordan, Laos, Lebanon, Libya, Malaysia, Mexico, Netherlands, Pakistan Peru, Portugal, Rhodesia, Romania, Saudi Arabia, Singapore, South Africa, Switzerland, Tunisia, Venezuela, Yugoslavia, Zaïre, Zambia

Bö.105 Messerschmitt-Bölkow-Blohm

Designed by Bölkow prior to its being subsumed under Messerschmitt Bölkow-Blohm, the Bö.105 is a light, five-seat helicopter, used primarily in a utility role, but capable of operating as a light, armed scout with missiles and/or machineguns. West Germany operates a fleet of Bö.105s as casualty evacuation ambulances under its *Katastrophenschutz* programme. Boeing Vertol has US licence rights to the Bö.105 and has offered a version of it to the US Navy for its LAMPS III requirement to succeed the SH-2D/F helicopters.

Bö.105 of the West German Army armed with TOW anti-tank weapons

The Bö.105 possesses a commodious cabin seating five (including the pilot), with access to cargo space behind the rear bench seat through a pair of clamshell doors in the rear of the fuselage. Landing gear is of the skid type, with optional flotation gear available.

Status: *Operational.* First flight February 16, 1967.

SPECIFICATIONS

Crew: 1 + 4 troops

Engines: 2 Allison 250-C20 turboshafts (400 shp each)

Dimensions: length 28 ft $\frac{1}{2}$ in (8·56 m); height 9 ft $9\frac{3}{8}$ in (2·99 m); main rotor diameter 32 ft $2\frac{3}{4}$ in (9·83 m)

Speed: 165 mph (265 km/hr); 145 mph (233 km/hr) cruise

Ceiling: 16,500 ft service (5,032 m); 8,900 ft (2,715 m) hovering in ground effect

Range: 400 miles (644 km)

Weights: 2,447 lb (1,110 kg) empty; 5,070 lb (2,300 kg) maximum

Armament: variety of missiles, cannon, machineguns

OPERATIONAL

West Germany, Netherlands, Nigeria, Philippines

Cayuse OH-6A Hughes (Model 500)

Developed for a US Army Light Observation Helicopter (LOH) competition in 1961, the OH-6 (originally HO-6) was intended to perform the functions of several helicopters already in the Army inventory. It was to perform observation, photo reconnaissance, utility transport, casualty evacuation, and light air support functions. The Spanish Navy flies the Cayuse in the anti-submarine role. A remarkably successful design, the Model 500 set 23

Hughes 500M international version of the OH-6A, of the Italian Army (Hughes)

international records in 1966 for helicopter performance.

Civilian and military export versions of the OH-6A are designated Model 500E, 500S, and 500M, with the last being the military variant. An advanced version of the currently produced civilian model is under development, and Hughes has offered a military version (designated OH-6D) to the US Army in fulfilment of its "Advanced Scout" requirement. The aircraft has a "bubble" fuselage, and a high tailboom with two vertical fins and a horizontal fin opposite the small, anti-torque rotor. A skid landing gear is fitted.

Status: *Operational.* First flight February 27, 1963; squadron delivery in 1966; 1,434 built.

SPECIFICATIONS (OH-6A)

Crew: 2 (1 pilot, 1 observer) + 4 troops
Engine: 1 Allison T63-A-5A turboshaft (317 shp)
Dimensions: overall length 30 ft 3¾ in (9·24 m); fuselage length 23 ft (7·02 m); height 8 ft 1½ in (2·48 m); main rotor diameter 26 ft 4 in (8·03 m)
Speed: 150 mph (241 km/hr); 134 mph (216 km/hr) cruise

Ceiling: 15,800 ft (4,820 m); 11,800 ft (3,600 m) hovering in ground effect
Range: 380 miles (611 km)
Weights: 1,176 lb (534 kg) empty; 2,700 lb (1,225 kg) maximum
Armament: 1 × 7·62-mm XM-27 machinegun
or 1 × 40-mm XM-75 grenade launcher

VARIANTS

OH-6A formerly HO-6; 1,434 built for US Army.
OH-6C experimental model with Allison 250–C20 turboshaft engines.

Model 500M military export variant with uprated engine; Spanish ASW variant carries MAD gear, 2 × Mk 44 ASW torpedoes.

OPERATIONAL

Argentina, Bolivia, Brazil, Colombia, Denmark, Dominican Republic, Japan,

Mexico, Nicaragua, Philippines, Spain, Taiwan, United States (Army)

Chickasaw H-19 Sikorsky (S-55)
Whirlwind Westland

Designed in the late 1940s for the US Air Force, the Sikorsky H-19 series of radial-engine, multi-purpose helicopters has been one of the longest-lived helicopter designs. Approximately 1,700 of all variants were built by four different manufacturers over a 20-year period for the military air arms of some 30 nations. They have flown in the anti-submarine, troop transport, casualty evacuation, search and rescue, and utility roles.

Characterized by its high, horizontal tailboom faired into the fuselage with a triangular fillet, the S-55 series has been built by Sikorsky, Westland Helicopters of Great Britain (which converted the basic design to turboshaft power), Mitsubishi of Japan, and SNCA du Sud-Est of France.

Status: *Operational.* First flight November 10, 1949; squadron delivery in 1950. 1,281 built by Sikorsky, almost 500 by licencees.

H-19 Chickasaw of the US Army (US Army)

Whirlwind HAS.7 of the Royal Navy (Ministry of Defence)

SPECIFICATIONS (CH-19E)

Crew: 1 + 8 troops
Engine: 1 Wright R-1300-3D radial piston (800 hp)
Dimensions: fuselage length 42 ft 3 in (12·8 m); height 13 ft 4 in (4·07 m); main rotor diameter 53 ft (16·17 m)

Speed: 112 mph (180 km/hr)
Ceiling: 12,900 ft (3,935 m)
Range: 360 miles (579 km)
Weight: 7,900 lb (3,587 kg) maximum
Armament: nil

VARIANTS

YH-19 prototype; 5 built for USAF.

UH-19A formerly H-19A; first production variant with Pratt & Whitney R-1340-57 radial engine; 2 crew + 10 troops; 50 built for USAF; flown by US Army as UH-19C (formerly H-19C); 10 built for US Navy as HO4S-1; 60 built for US Marine Corps as HRS-1.

UH-19B formerly H-19B; Wright R-1300-3 series radial engine; 270 built for US Air Force; search and rescue (SAR) variant designated HH-19B (formerly SH-19B); 338 built for USA as UH-19D (formerly H-19D).

CH-19E formerly HO4S-2 and HRS-2; similar to UH-19B; 1 crew + 8 troops; 91 built for USN and USMC; 10 built for SAR role for RN (HAR.21).

UH-19F formerly HO4S-3 and HRS-3; similar to CH-19E; 145 built for USN and USMC; 30 converted to SAR role designated HH-19G (formerly HO4S-3G) for US Coast Guard; 15 built with ASW equipment for RN (designated HAS.22).

HAR.1 Westland-built similar to UH-19A; 10 built for RN; 10 built for British Army and RAF (designated HAR.2).

HAR.3 Westland-built similar to UH-19F/HAR.22; flown by RN.

HAR.4 Westland-built similar to CH-19E/HAR.21; flown by British Army and RAF.

HAR.5 similar to HAR.1 with Alvis Leonides Major radial piston engine; first flight August 28, 1955; designated HAS.7 in anti-submarine role; designated HCC.8 in VIP configuration for 4 to 7 passengers.

HAR.9 converted HAS.7 with Rolls-Royce Gnome turboshaft; first flight February 28, 1959; designated HAR.10 with provision for 4 × Nord SS.11 ASMs; designated HCC.12 in VIP configuration for 4 to 7 passengers.

OPERATIONAL

Great Britain (RAF, Navy), Greece, Guatemala, Honduras, South Korea, Kuwait, Nigeria, Pakistan, Philippines, Qatar, Taiwan, Thailand, Venezuela, Yugoslavia

Chinook CH-47 Boeing Vertol (Model 114)

The CH-47 Chinook was designed to meet a 1959 US Army requirement for a turbine-powered, medium-lift transport helicopter that could carry two tons internally or eight tons externally on a sling. The US Army has used the Chinook in troop transport, aircraft recovery, and casualty evacuation roles.

Generally similar in appearance to the CH-46 Sea Knight operated by the US Navy and Marine Corps, the CH-47 is a great deal larger. It is a twin-

*CH-47 Chinook
of the US Army
(US Army)*

*CH-147 Chinook
of the Canadian
Armed Forces
(Canadian
Forces)*

engine, tandem-rotor helicopter with quadricycle landing gear, watertight fuselage, all-weather flight capabilities, dual controls, and a rear loading ramp.

Planning is underway to modernize the US Army's 200 CN-47A/B helicopters.

Status: *Operational.* First flight September 21, 1961; squadron delivery in 1962. Over 800 built.

SPECIFICATIONS (CH-47C)

Crew: 3 + 44 troops
Engines: 2 Lycoming T55-L-11A turboshafts (3,750 shp each)
Dimensions: overall length 99 ft; (30·20 m) fuselage length 51 ft (15·56 m); height 18 ft 7 in (5·67 m), main rotor diameters 60 ft (18·3 m)
Speed: 180 mph (290 km/hr); 160 mph (257 km/hr) cruise

Ceiling: 10,200 ft (3,111 m) service; 10,200 ft (3,111 m) hovering in ground effect
Range: 230 miles (370 km); 1,400-mile (2,252 km) ferry range
Weights: 20,616 lb (9,360 kg) empty; 46,000 lb (20,884 kg) maximum
Armament: nil

VARIANTS

YCH-47A formerly YHC-1B; T55-L-5 turboshafts; 5 built.

CH-47A initial production version with T55-L-7 turboshafts; 49 transferred to South Vietnam in 1971.

ACH-47A similar to CH-47A with experimental armament; 4 built.

CH-47B similar to CH-47A with T55-L-7C turboshafts.

CH-47C production variant with T55-L-11A turboshafts; strengthened transmission, increased internal fuel; all early model Chinooks scheduled to be uprated to this configuration.

CH-147 similar to CH-47C with T55-L-11C turboshafts; 8 built for Canada (1 crashed during delivery flight).

OPERATIONAL

Australia, Canada, Iran, Israel, Spain, Thailand, United States (Air Force, Army)

Choctaw
Seahorse } **H-34** Sikorsky (S-58)
Seabat

In 1952 Sikorsky received a developmental contract from the US Navy to produce an anti-submarine helicopter to succeed the firm's own H-19 series. The resultant design bore a family resemblance to the earlier Sikorsky models, but the performance was greatly increased over its predecessor. Variants were developed for use by the US armed forces, as well as numerous foreign nations. The S-58 was known as the Choctaw by the US Air Force and Army, the Seahorse by the US Marine Corps, and Seabat by the US Navy. Westland-built variants (all turboshaft-powered) were known as Wessex (covered separately).

Status: *Operational.* First flight March 8, 1954; squadron delivery in 1955. Approximately 2,000 built.

SPECIFICATIONS (CH-34A)

Crew: 2 + 16 to 18 troops
Engine: 1 Wright R-1820-84C radial piston (1,525 hp)
Dimensions: overall length 56 ft 8¼ in (17·29 m); fuselage length 46 ft 9 in (14·26 m); height 15 ft 11 in (4·86 m); main rotor diameter 56 ft (17·08 m)

Speed: 122 mph (196 km/hr); 97 mph (156 km/hr) cruise
Ceiling: 9,500 ft (2,898 km); 4,900 ft (1,495 m) hovering in ground effect
Range: 247 miles (397 km)
Weights: 7,750 lb (3,519 kg) empty; 14,000 lb (6,356 kg) maximum
Armament: nil

*H-34 Choctaw of
the Israeli
Defence Force
(Israeli Defence
Force)*

VARIANTS

XHSS-1 prototype; 1 built for US
Navy.

CH-34A Choctaw; formerly H-34A;
transport and general purpose variant,
equipped to carry external sling loads;
flown by US Army.

CH-34C Choctaw; formerly H-34C;
similar to CH-34A with automatic
stabilization equipment; flown by USA
and USAF; VH-34C similar with VIP
configuration.

UH-34D Seahorse; formerly HUS-1;
similar to CH-34A; flown by USN and
USAF; designated VH-34D (formerly
HUS-1Z) in VIP configuration.

LH-34D Seahorse; formerly HSS-1L;
similar to UH-34E; modified for
Antarctic operations.

UH-34E Seahorse; formerly HUS-1A;
similar to UH-34D with external fuel
tanks, flotation gear.

HH-34F search and rescue (SAR)
variant; 6 built for US Coast Guard.

SH-34G Seabat; formerly HSS-1;
original production ASW variant; 4
crew; flown by USN and subsequently
transferred to other navies; redesignated
UH-34G when ASW equipment
removed for utility role.

SH-34J Seabat; formerly HSS-1N;
development of SH-34G with automatic
stabilization, night flight capability;
flown by US Navy; redesignated
UH-34J with ASW equipment removed
for utility role.

OPERATIONAL

Argentina, Haiti, Indonesia, Italy, Japan,
Laos, Philippines, Taiwan, Thailand,

United States (Air Force, Army, Marine
Corps, Navy)

Gazelle Aérospatiale (SA.341)
Westland

Designed to replace the Alouette II series in the Aérospatiale product line, the
SA.341 Gazelle has the same transmission as its predecessor coupled to an

uprated Astazou turboshaft engine. Although the Gazelle was designe exclusively by its parent company, it is produced jointly with Westlan Helicopters in Great Britain and also built under licence in Yugoslav Operators include the armed forces of both Britain and France, and milita and civilian owners in over a dozen countries.

Basically a five-seat light utility helicopter, the Gazelle has a convention main/tail rotor layout and normally comes equipped with skid-landing ge although floats or skis are available. The tail rotor is somewhat unusual in th it has 13 blades enclosed in a shrouded vertical stabilizer, the unit bein dubbed "fan-in-fin".

Status: *Operational.* First flight April 7, 1967; squadron delivery in 1971.

SPECIFICATIONS

Crew: 1 + 4 troops
Engine: 1 Turboméca Astazou IIIA turboshaft (590 shp)
Dimensions: overall length 39 ft 3$\frac{5}{16}$ in (11·98 m); fuselage length 31 ft 3$\frac{3}{16}$ in (9·54 m); height 10 ft 2$\frac{5}{8}$ in (3·11 m); main rotor diameter 34 ft 5$\frac{1}{2}$ in (10·51 m)
Speed: 190 mph (306 km/hr); 165 mph (265 km/hr) cruise
Ceiling: 16,400 ft (5,000 m) service;

9,350 ft (2,850 m) hovering in ground effect
Range: 415 miles (668 km)
Weights: 2,000 lb (908 kg) empty; 3,970 lb (1,802 kg) maximum
Armament: 2 × 7·62-mm machinegu and 2 × 36-mm rocket pods
or 4 × AS.11 ASMs
or 2 × AS.12 ASMs
or 4 × anti-tank missiles

VARIANTS

SA.340 prototype; 2 built.
SA.341 pre-production test machines; 4 built.
SA.341B Gazelle AH.1 for British Army with Astazou IIIN turboshaft.
SA.341C HT.2 trainer for Royal Navy.
SA.341D HT.3 trainer for Royal Air Force.

SA.341E HCC.4 transport for Royal Air Force.
SA.341F Astazou IIIC turboshaft; flown by French Army.
SA.341G Astazou IIIA; civilian variant.
SA.341H Astazou IIIB; military export variant.

OPERATIONAL

France, Great Britain (RAF, Army), Kuwait, Yugoslavia

Gazelle HT.2 of the Royal Navy (Ministry of Defence)

OH-5A Fairchild Hiller (FH-1100)

Designed by Hiller prior to its takeover by Fairchild Industries, the Model 1100 was intended as a competitor to the Hughes OH-6 and Bell OH-4A in the US Army's 1962–1963 Light Observation Helicopter competition. The winner of that decision was the Hughes entry, but both of the other entrants successfully marketed variants of their products in first the civilian sector and later in military variants. The FH-1100 is a refinement of the original OH-5A, suitable for a wide variety of civilian and military applications including duties as an ambulance, observation platform, and border patrol helicopter. The FH-1100 was produced with two fuselage configurations, permitting accommodation for the pilot and either three or four passengers.

Status: *Operational.* First flight January 26, 1963; approx 250 built.

SPECIFICATIONS

Crew: 1 + 3 or 4 passengers
Engine: 1 Allison 250-C18 turboshaft (317 shp)
Dimensions: overall length 39 ft 9½ in (12·14 m); fuselage length 29 ft 9½ in (9·09 m); height 9 ft 3½ in (2·84 m); main rotor diameter 35 ft 4¾ in (10·80 m)

Speed: 127 mph (204 km/hr)
Ceiling: 14,200 ft (4,330 m); 13,400 ft (4,087 m) hovering in ground effect
Range: 350 miles (563 km)
Weights: 1,396 lb (633 kg) empty; 2,750 lb (1,249 kg) maximum
Armament: nil

OPERATIONAL

Argentina, Ecuador, El Salvador, Philippines, Thailand

OH-5A flown by Argentina (Alex Reinhard)

HH-52 Sikorsky (S-62)

Designed in the late 1950s as a turbine-powered commercial helicopter, th
Sikorsky S-62 was adapted to the US Coast Guard requirement for a searc
and rescue helicopter. Using the transmission and rotor system of the earli
H-19 series, the HH-52 has an entirely new watertight fuselage and singl
turbine power. Specialized equipment includes an automatic stabilizatic
device, towing gear, and a rescue platform that extends over the water to a
in rescue operations. The US Coast Guard-flown HH-52As do not have a
official name assigned.

Status: *Operational.* First flight May 14, 1958 (S-62); US Coast Gua
delivery in 1963. Over 100 built for military or police service with son
assembled by Mitsubishi in Japan.

SPECIFICATIONS

Crew: 3 + 11 troops

Engine: 1 General Electric T58-GE-8B
turboshaft (1,250 shp)

Dimensions: overall length 45 ft $5\frac{1}{2}$ in
(13·87 m); fuselage length 44 ft $6\frac{1}{2}$ in
(13·59 m); height 16 ft (4·88 m);
main rotor diameter 53 ft (16·17 m)

Speed: 109 mph (175 km/hr); 98 mph

(158 km/hr) cruise

Ceiling: 11,200 ft (3,416 m) service,
12,200 ft (3,720 m) hovering in
ground effect

Range: 475 miles (764 km)

Weights: 5,083 lb (2,308 kg) empty;
8,100 lb (3,677 kg) maximum

Armament: nil

OPERATIONAL

India, Japan, Taiwan, Thailand, United States (Coast Guard)

*HH-52A of the
US Coast Guard
(US Coast Guard)*

YUH-60A Sikorsky (S-70)

The YUH-60A is Sikorsky's entrant in the US Army's UTTAS (Utility Tactical Transport Aircraft System) competition, vying for a multi-million dollar contract as successor to the ubiquitous UH-1 Iroquois/Huey with Boeing Vertol's YUH-61A. The total planned UTTAS buy is 1,100 helicopters commencing in 1978. The prototype phase of the competition requires delivery of four aircraft from Boeing Vertol and four from Sikorsky for evaluation.

The YUH-60A is a twin-turbine helicopter with a four-bladed main rotor and a canted four-bladed anti-torque tail rotor. The main landing gear is retractable with a fixed tailwheel. Stability is enhanced through the use of a highly swept horizontal stabilizer.

Status: *Development.* First flight October 17, 1974.

SPECIFICATIONS

Crew: 3 + 11 troops
Engines: 2 General Electric T700-GE-700 turboshafts (1,500 shp each)
Dimensions: main rotor diameter 53 ft (16·17 m)

Speed: 185 mph cruise (298 km/hr)
Weight: 22,000 lb (9,988 kg) maximum
Armament: variety of machineguns and cannon

YUH-60 Utility Tactical Transport Aircraft System (UTTAS) prototype (Sikorsky)

YUH-61 UTTAS prototype (US Army)

YUH-61A Boeing Vertol (Model 179)

The Boeing Vertol YUH-61A is competing with the Sikorsky YUH-60A for the US Army's UTTAS (Utility Tactical Transport Aircraft System) contract which is for a purchase of 1,100 aircraft over an eight-year period.

Equipped with a tricycle undercarriage, four-bladed main and anti-torque tail rotors, and a highly swept horizontal stabilizer much like its YUH-60A competitor, the YUH-61A is powered by the same engines as the other UTTAS entrant. The Boeing Model 179 is a commercialized variant of the YUH 61A designed to transport 20 passengers in airline style comfort.

Status: *Development.* First flight November 29, 1974.

SPECIFICATIONS

Crew: 3 + 11 troops
Engines: 2 General Electric T700-GE-700 turboshafts (1,500 shp each)

Armament: variety of machineguns and cannon

Hare Mi-1 Mil
WSK-Swidnik

A general utility helicopter that entered service in the Soviet Union in 1951, the *Hare* performs as a civilian and military transport, ambulance, crop duster, forestry patrol vehicle, mail carrier, and geological exploration vehicle. The first of a long series of Soviet-developed rotorcraft, the *Hare* has served with the armed forces of most Eastern bloc nations, as well as those Third-World nations to which the Soviet Union has provided assistance.

The *Hare's* single main rotor and small anti-torque tail rotor provide the layout to which most Mil designs have conformed. Its primary variant is four-seat (including the pilot). Built under licence in Poland as the SM-1.

Status: *Operational.* First flight in September 1948.

SPECIFICATIONS

Crew: 1 + 3 passengers
Engine: 1 AI-26V radial piston (575 hp)
Dimensions: fuselage length 39 ft 8½ in (12·11 m); height 10 ft 10 in (3·30 m); main rotor diameter 47 ft 1 in (14·36 m)

Speed: 96 mph (154 km/hr)
Ceiling: 9,843 ft (3,002 m) service
Range: 375 miles (603 km)
Weight: 5,204 lb (2,363 kg) maximum
Armament: nil

Mi-1 Hare
*general purpose
helicopter*

VARIANTS

Mi-1 basic four-seat helicopter; SM-1 similar.

Mi-1T three-seat variant.

Mi-1NKh multi-purpose variant fitted with external stretcher containers, fuel tanks, or chemical spray tanks;

Polish-built variants are mission-designated as SM-1W/WS with stretcher containers, SM-1WZ with agricultural spraying or dusting equipment, and SM-1WSZ as dual-control trainer.

OPERATIONAL

Afghanistan, Albania, Algeria, Cuba, Czechoslovakia, East Germany, Iraq,

Mongolia

Harke Mi-10 Mil

The Mi-10 *Harke* is a flying crane derivative of the Mi-6 heavy lift helicopter. It is distinguished by a stalky quadricycle undercarriage supporting a long, flat fuselage which can carry up to 28 passengers in addition to cargo slung beneath the aircraft. Several different wheeled cargo platforms are designed to be positioned under the *Harke* and attached flush against the fuselage. Up to 17,600 lb (7,990 kg) of cargo can be carried externally. Closed circuit television monitors the cargo while in flight.

Mechanically, the *Harke* is almost identical to the earlier Mi-6 *Hook*. The power plant, transmission system, main and tail rotors as well as most of the rest of the aircraft's equipment are, in fact, interchangeable between the two helicopters.

Mi-10 Harke
flying crane

Status: *Operational.* First flight in 1960.

SPECIFICATIONS

Crew: 3 + 28 troops
Engines: 2 Soloviev D-25V turboshafts
(5,500 shp each)
Dimensions: overall length 137 ft $5\frac{1}{2}$ in
(41·93 m); fuselage length 107 ft $9\frac{3}{4}$
in (32·88 m); height 32 ft 2 in
(9·81 m); main rotor diameter 114 ft
10 in (35·02 m)

Speed: 124 mph (200 km/hr); 112
mph (180 km/hr) cruise
Ceiling: 9,850 ft (3,004 m) service
Range: 155 miles (249 km)
Weights: 60,185 lb (27,323 kg)
empty; 96,340 lb (43,738 kg)
maximum
Armament: nil

OPERATIONAL

Soviet Union (VVS)

Hind Mi-24 Mil

The *Hind* is a relatively new Soviet helicopter being deployed in support of Soviet Ground Forces in the gunship and troop lift roles. Eight to ten troops can be carried and stub wings are fitted with pylons for air-to-ground weapons.

A twin-turboshaft powered helicopter, the *Hind* has a streamline appearance with its fully retractable landing gear. It has a conventional, five-blade

Mi-24 Hind-*B*
gunship/troop
lift helicopter

main rotor and anti-torque tail rotor. The high-mounted stub wings differ in
the *Hind*-A and B variants, with the former having four weapon pylons and
the latter six pylons. Rocket pods or *Sagger* anti-tank missiles can be fitted.
In addition, there is an internal, forward-firing machinegun.

Status: *Operational.* First flight 1971–1972; squadron delivery 1973.

SPECIFICATIONS

Crew: 2 + 8 to 10 troops
Engines: 2 Isotov TV2-117 turboshafts
  (1,500 shp each)
Dimensions: overall length 55 ft 9 in
  (17·00 m); height 14 ft (4·27 m);

main rotor diameter 55 ft 9 in
  (17·00 m)
Armament: 1 × 12·7-mm MG and
  rocket pods and Sagger anti-tank
  missiles

VARIANTS

Hind-A anhedral stub wings with six
stores stations.

Hind-B no anhedral or dihedral to
stub wings; four stores stations.

OPERATIONAL

Soviet Union (VVS)

Hip Mi-8 Mil (V-8)

The *Hip* is a medium transport helicopter based upon the earlier Mi-4 *Hound* design. The military versions of the aircraft have portholes whereas the civilian helicopters have larger, square windows. The *Hip* has become the standard troop-lift helicopter for the Soviet armed forces. Up to 24 troops can be lifted internally with their heavy weapons carried on racks over the wheels. Alternatively, the racks can be used to hold stretchers for medical evacuation. Rocket pods can be mounted on either side of the main cabin. The Soviet Navy apparently flies a few *Hip* helicopters configured for aerial minesweeping, some of which have operated from the helicopter carrier *Leningrad* during the 1974 mine clearing of the Suez Canal.

While its overall dimensions are similar to those of the *Hound*, the *Hip*'s powerplant differs not only in type (turbine versus the *Hound*'s piston), but also in location (above the fuselage). Early *Hip* helicopters had the *Hound*'s four-bladed rotor system, but later versions, particularly those in the military configuration, have a newer, five-bladed rotor. Clam-shell rear doors are provided to facilitate cargo handling, total load capacity being 8,800 lb (3,995 kg). Approximately 1,200 built for military and civilian use.

Status: *Operational.* First flight in 1961; squadron delivery in 1967.

SPECIFICATIONS

Crew: 3 + 24 troops
Engines: 2 Isotov TV2-117A turboshafts (1,500 shp each)
Dimensions: overall length 82 ft 9¾ in (25·25 m); fuselage length 60 ft ¾ in (18·30 m); height 18 ft 6½ in (5·65 m); main rotor diameter 69 ft 10¼ in (21·30 m)
Speed: 160 mph (257 km/hr); 140 mph (225 km/hr) cruise

Ceiling: 14,760 ft (4,500 m) service; 6,233 ft (1,900 m) hovering in ground effect
Range: 300 miles (483 km); 745-mile (1,200 km) ferry range
Weights: 15,026 (6,820 kg) empty; 26,455 lb (12,010 kg) maximum
Armament: rocket and gun pods on 8 external store stations

Mi-8 Hip-C medium-lift helicopter, based on the earlier Mi-4 Hound

VARIANTS

Hip-A single Soloviev turboshaft (2,700 shp) with four-blade rotor.

Hip-B two turboshafts with four-blade rotor.

Hip-C two turboshafts (upgraded to 1,500 shp each) with five-blade rotor.

OPERATIONAL

Afghanistan, Bangladesh, Czechoslovakia, Egypt, Ethiopia, Finland, East Germany, Hungary, India, Iraq, Pakistan, Peru, Poland, Romania, Somalia, Soviet Union (VVS, Navy), Sudan, Syria, South Yemen, Yugoslavia

Homer Mi-12 Mil (V-12)

The Mi-12 *Homer* is the world's largest helicopter, developed in response to a Soviet requirement for a heavy lift helicopter that could carry the same loads as the An-22 *Cock* cargo aircraft. The aircraft has a highly distinctive appearance with its large fuselage and turboshaft engines mounted in twin pods at the extremity of the craft's oddly tapered wings. In addition to its military use, the *Homer* is flown by *Aeroflot* in support of oil and natural gas exploration and production in remote areas.

There is a large rotor mounted atop each of the *Homer*'s engine pods, each of which holds two turboshafts. The high-mounted wings have an inverse taper, narrowing at the fuselage and extending at the engine pods. The twin main rotor arrangement alleviates the requirement for an anti-torque rotor. Up to 55,000 lb (24,970 kg) can be lifted in the vertical take-off mode and up to 76,000 lb (34,505 kg) with a take-off run.

Status: *Operational.* First flight 1968.

Mi-12 Homer *heavy-lift helicopter. Version in this picture is in* Aeroflot *colours*

SPECIFICATIONS

Crew: 6 (1 pilot, 1 co-pilot, 1 flight engineer, 1 navigator, 1 radio operator, 1 electrician) + 50 troops
Engines: 4 Soloviev D-25VF turboshafts (6,500 shp each)
Dimensions: fuselage length 121 ft $4\frac{1}{2}$ in (37·02 m); height 41 ft (12·51 m); wingspan 219 ft 10 in (67·05 m) (over rotor tips); rotor diameter 114 ft 10 in (35·02 m) each
Speed: 160 mph (257 km/hr); 150 mph (241 km/hr) cruise
Ceiling: 11,500 ft (3,508 m) service
Range: 310 miles (500 km)
Weight: 231,500 lb (105,100 kg) maximum
Armament: nil

OPERATIONAL

Soviet Union

Hoodlum Ka-26 Kamov

The *Hoodlum* is a light, twin-engine helicopter first observed by Western sources in 1964. It is used for ambulance, personnel and cargo transport, agricultural spraying, firefighting, mineral prospecting, and pipeline work. Interchangeable pods are positioned behind the crew's cockpit to perform the variety of roles of which the *Hoodlum* is capable. It is not now used in the military role by the Soviet armed forces.

Like other Kamov designs, the *Hoodlum* has the three-bladed, co-axial rotor arrangement, although the engines are mounted alongside the fuselage instead of atop the fuselage. It boasts a quadricycle landing gear and twin tailbooms like its larger contemporary, the *Hormone*. A passenger pod can be fitted to carry six persons. It is flown by military services in Hungary and Sri Lanka.

Status: *Operational.*

SPECIFICATIONS

Crew: 2
Engines: 2 Vedeneev M-14V-26 radial pistons (325 hp each)
Dimensions: fuselage length 25 ft 5 in (7·75 m); height 13 ft $3\frac{1}{2}$ in (4·06 m); main rotor diameter 42 ft 8 in (13·01 m) each
Speed: 105 mph (170 km/hr); 93 mph (150 km/hr) cruise
Ceiling: 9,840 ft (3,000 m) service; 4,265 ft (1,300 m) hovering in ground effect
Range: 248 miles (400 km); 745-mile (1,200 km) ferry
Weights: 4,300 lb (1,950 kg) empty (no pod); 7,165 lb (3,252 kg) maximum
Armament: nil

Ka-26 Hoodlum.
*Now used
operationally
only by Hungary
and Sri Lanka
(Flight Inter-
national)*

OPERATIONAL

Hungary, Sri Lanka

Hook Mi-6 Mil

When first flown in the mid-1950s and for ten years thereafter the Mi-6 *Hook* was the largest helicopter in the world. Cargo capacity is rated at just over 26,000 lb (11,805 kg). As is common with most Soviet helicopters, the *Hook* was produced in both civil and military variants to fulfil a variety of roles, among which are troop and equipment transport, flying crane duties, and firefighting.

With a conventional single main rotor and small anti-torque tail rotor, the *Hook* was the first turbine powered helicopter to be produced in the Soviet Union. Small wings are fitted to ease the strain on the rotor in forward flight, but these are removed to increase the lift capabilities of the aircraft when large external loads are carried.

Status: *Operational.* Squadron delivery in 1957–1958.

SPECIFICATIONS

Crew: 5 + 65 troops
Engines: 2 Soloviev TV-2BM turboshafts (5,500 shp each)
Dimensions: overall length 136 ft 11½ in (41·75 m); fuselage length 108 ft 10½ in (33·21 m); height 32 ft 4 in (9·86 m); wing span 50 ft 2½ in (15·31 m); main rotor diameter 114 ft 10 in (35·04 m)

Speed: 186 mph (300 km/hr); 155 mph (250 km/hr) cruise
Ceiling: 14,750 ft (5,000 m)
Range: 404 miles (650 km); 900-mile (1,450 km) ferry range
Weights: 60,055 lb (27,264 kg) empty; 93,700 lb (42,540 kg) maximum
Armament: nil

Mi-6 Hook *heavy lift helicopter. Seen here in* Aeroflot *colours,* Hook *is operated by five other countries*

OPERATIONAL

Egypt, Indonesia, Iraq, Peru, Soviet Union (VVS), North Vietnam

Hoplite Mi-2 Mil (V-2)
WSK-Swidnik

The Mi-2 *Hoplite* is a derivative of the earlier Mi-1 *Hare*, employing two light-weight turbines to increase the load-carrying capability. The roles of the *Hoplite* are identical to those of the *Hare*, which it replaced in the Soviet military and civilian inventories starting in 1964.

Mi-2 Hoplite, *a derivative of the earlier Mi-1* Hare

The basic Mi-2 can accommodate up to eight passengers, while the ambulance variant carries four stretchers and a medical attendant. Cargo is carried either internally or externally on a sling. Produced exclusively by WSK-Swidnik in Poland since the original Mil prototype completed testing.

Status: *Operational.* First flight in 1961.

SPECIFICATIONS

Crew: 1 + 8 passengers
Engines: 2 Isotov GTD-350 turboshafts (437 shp each)
Dimensions: overall length 57 ft 2 in (17·44 m); fuselage length 37 ft 4¾ in (11·39 m); height 12 ft 3½ in (3·75 m); main rotor diameter 47 ft 6¾ in (14·50 m)

Speed: 130 mph (210 km/hr); 124 mph (200 km/hr) cruise
Ceiling: 13,755 ft (4,195 m) service; 6,550 ft (2,000 m) hovering in ground effect
Range: 360 miles (580 kg)
Weights: 5,213 lb (2,366 kg) empty; 8,157 lb (3,703 kg) maximum
Armament: nil

OPERATIONAL

East Germany, Poland, Romania, Soviet Union (VVS)

Hormone Ka-25 Kamov

The Ka-25 *Hormone* is a descendant of the earlier Kamov designed Ka-15/Ka-18 series of piston-engine helicopters employed in large numbers in Soviet military and civilian activities. The *Hormone* is primarily a naval design, with an internal weapons bay for homing torpedoes and extensive ASW equipment. Submarine detection devices include radar in a chin housing, droppable sonobuoys, "dipping" sonar, and an electro-optical sensor in the tail. The *Hormone*-B has additional electronic equipment. Although dummy air-to-surface missiles were seen on an aircraft during a Soviet aviation day flight, no missiles are known to be operationally employed from the helicopter.

A twin-turbine co-axial rotor helicopter, the *Hormone* is used primarily by the Soviet Navy in the anti-submarine variant. Since 1967 it has operated from various Soviet surface ships including the anti-submarine cruisers *Moskva* and *Leningrad,* as well as other cruisers and large destroyers. The utility version can carry 12 passengers.

Status: *Operational.* Squadron delivery in 1961–1962.

Ka-25 Hormone
ASW helicopter
flown by Soviet
Naval Aviation
(US Navy)

SPECIFICATIONS

Crew: 4
Engines: 2 Glushenkov GTD-3
  turboshafts (900 shp each)
Dimensions: overall length 32 ft (9·76
  m); height 17 ft 7½ in (5·37 m);
  main rotor diameters 51 ft 8 in (15·76
  m)

Speed: 137 mph (220 km/hr); 120
  mph (193 km/hr) cruise
Ceiling: 11,500 ft (3,508 m)
Range: 400 miles (644 km)
Weights: 9,700 lb (4,404 kg) empty;
  16,100 lb (7,309 kg) maximum
Armament: 2 × ASW torpedoes
  or nuclear depth charges

VARIANTS

Hormone-A standard utility and
ASW variant.
  Hormone-B special electronics

variant.
  Ka-25K flying crane variant;
rearward-looking control gondola.

OPERATIONAL

Soviet Union (Navy), Syria

Hound Mi-4 Mil

Similar in basic configuration to its Western contemporary, the Sikorsky H-19, the Mi-4 *Hound* is a transport and general purpose helicopter that entered Soviet service in 1953. Since that time, the *Hound* has become the most widely used Soviet rotary-wing aircraft, with several thousand having been built in both the Soviet Union and in China.

Both military and civilian variants of the basic design have been built, with capacity for up to 16 passengers being provided in the high-density *Aeroflot* configuration. It is also used as an ambulance, crop duster and firefighter, as well as in its military duties of troop transport, vehicle/artillery transport, and anti-submarine warfare. About 5,200 lb (2,360 kg) of cargo can be carried in normal operation.

Status: *Operational.* First flight August 1952; squadron delivery in 1953.

SPECIFICATIONS

Crew: 2 + 16 troops
Engine: 1 ASh-82V radial piston (1,700 hp)
Dimensions: fuselage length 55 ft 1 in (16·81 m); height 17 ft (5·19 m); main rotor diameter 68 ft 11 in (21·01 m)
Speed: 130 mph (209 km/hr); 100

mph (161 km/hr) cruise
Ceiling: 18,000 ft (5,490 m) service
Range: 155 miles (250 km)
Weight: 17,200 lb (7,808 kg) maximum
Armament: 1 × MG (in forward fuselage and rockets on fuselage stations

Mi-4 Hound
ASW helicopter
flown by Soviet
Naval Aviation

VARIANTS

Mi-4 basic military variant; under-fuselage gondola for navigator; double clamshell rear loading doors.
Mi-4P *Aeroflot* passenger variant; as

ambulance can carry 8 litters.
Mi-4S agricultural variant with large hopper in cabin.

OPERATIONAL

Afghanistan, Albania, Algeria, China, Cuba, Czechoslovakia, Egypt, Finland, East Germany, Hungary, India, Indonesia, Iraq, North Korea, Mali, Mongolia, Poland, Romania, Somalia, Soviet Union (VVS, Navy), Sudan, Syria, North Vietnam, North Yemen, South Yemen, Yugoslavia

HueyCobra / SeaCobra } AH-1 Bell (Model 209)

The AH-1 HueyCobra is a development of the successful Bell UH-1 Iroquois (Huey) utility helicopter employed extensively in the Vietnam War. During that conflict it was determined that the troop-carrying helicopters required armed escort to suppress ground fire in the vicinity of the landing zones. The AH-1 was developed by Bell to meet this requirement. The original single-engined version was developed for the US Army, while a twin engined model was built for the US Marine Corps, with export orders placed for the latter by the Imperial Iranian Army; also flown by Spanish Navy.

The AH-1 couples a new, slim fuselage with the power plant, transmission and rotor system of the earlier UH-1. The fuselage is only 38 inches wide, presenting a minimal cross-section. Stores are carried under small, stubby wings, and include rockets or miniguns in addition to the built-in armament of machineguns or grenade launchers.

AH-1J Sea Cobra of the US Marine Corps (Bell)

AH-1Q Huey-Cobra of the US Army fitted with TOW anti-tank missiles (Bell)

Status: *Operational.* First flight September 1965; squadron delivery in June 1967.

SPECIFICATIONS (AH-1J SeaCobra)

Crew: 2 (1 pilot and 1 gunner)
Engines: 2 United Aircraft of Canada T-400-CP-400 turboshafts (1,800 shp each)
Dimensions: wing span 10 ft 4 in (3·15 m), length overall 53 ft 4 in (16·27 m), fuselage length 44 ft 7 in (13·60 m), height 13 ft 8 in (4·17 m), main rotor diameter 44 ft (13·42 m)
Speed: 207 mph (333 km/hr)
Ceiling: 10,550 ft (3,218 m) service; 12,450 ft (3,797 m) hovering in ground effect
Range: 360 miles (580 km)
Weights: 6,816 lb (3,094 kg) loaded; 10,000 lb (4,540 kg) maximum
Armament: 1 × 20-mm XM-197 cannon (750 rpg) and 4 × XM-159 rocket packs (19 × 2·75 in rockets per pack)
or 4 × SM-157 rocket packs (7 × rockets per pack)
or 2 × 7·62 mm XM-18E1 minigun pods

VARIANTS

AH-1G initial gunship with 1 Lycoming T53-L-13/-13A/-13B turboshaft engine; overall length 52 ft 11½ in (15·87 m), height 13 ft 5½ in (4·11 m), max weight 9,500 lb (4,313 kg); twin turret-mounted 7·62 mm miniguns, or 2 × 40 mm grenade launchers; standard US Army variant; 1,078 built with 38 to USMC, and 8 to Spain.

TH-1G same as AH-1G except modified to include instructor controls and instruments.

AH-1J standard USMC and Iranian variant; 69 built for USMC and 202 for Iran (latter includes some "improved").

AH-1Q AH-1G modified to fire TOW missiles; 101 modified through 1974; turret mounted 40-mm grenade launcher and 7·62-mm minigun fitted.

AH-1S HS Army AH-1G fitted for TOW missile; 290 planned.

AH-1T uprated engine, extended fuselage, weight 14,000 lb (6,356 kg) maximum, range 430 miles (690 km); fitted for 8 × TOW anti-tank missiles; 57 planned for USMC.

OPERATIONAL

Iran, Spain, United States (Army, Marine Corps), Israel

Huskie H-43 Kaman (Model 600)

The H-43 Huskie series of helicopters was designed in 1950 in response to a US Navy requirement for a liaison and general duty helicopter for service with the Marine Corps. The Huskie was produced for operation by the US Navy, Marine Corps and Air Force, as well as for provision to foreign governments through the military assistance programme. A twin-turbine version of the Huskie was developed by Kaman for evaluation by the US military, but production was never approved.

The Huskie has a distinctive appearance, with a box-like fuselage with twin pylons supporting the contra-rotating rotors. A multiple tail fin is supported by a short boom structure.

Status: *Operational.* First flown September 27, 1956; squadron delivery in 1958. Approximately 320 built.

SPECIFICATIONS (HH-43F)

Crew: 2 + 11 passengers
Engine: 1 Lycoming T53-L-11A turboshaft (1,150 shp)
Dimensions: fuselage length 25 ft 2 in (7·67 m); height 12 ft 7 in (3·84 m); rotor diameter 47 ft (14·34 m) (each)

Speed: 120 mph (193 km/hr)
Ceiling: 25,000 ft (7,625 m)
Range: 500 miles (805 km)
Weight: 7,100 lb (3,223 kg) maximum
Armament: nil

HH-43 Huskie of the US Air Force (US Air Force)

VARIANTS

XHOK-1 prototype with Pratt & Whitney R-1340-52 radial piston; 2 built for US Marine Corps.

HH-43A formerly H-43A; firefighting and rescue variant with R-1340-52 radial piston; 2 crew + 6 passengers; 18 built for US Air Force.

HH-43B formerly H-43B; similar to HH-43A with Lycoming T53-L-1B turboshaft; 2 crew + 8 passengers; 193 built.

UH-43C formerly HUK-1; similar to HH-43 configured for plane guard on aircraft carriers; 2 crew + 2 passengers; flown by US Navy; flown by USMC as OH-43D (formerly HOK-1).

HH-43F similar to IIH-43B with Lycoming T53-L-11 turboshaft; 2 crew + 6 to 11 passengers; for foreign transfer.

QH-43G radio-controlled drone developed for US Navy.

OPERATIONAL

Colombia, Iran, Morocco, Pakistan, Thailand, United States (Air Force)

Iroquois H-1 Bell (Model 204/205)

The Bell H-1 Iroquois utility helicopter is widely employed by the US armed forces and by many other nations. The Bell Model 204 won a 1955 US Army competition for a utility helicopter suitable for casualty evacuation, instrument training, and general utility duties. Since that time, the "Huey" (familiar nickname derived from its original HU-1 designation) has expanded its missions to include close fire support, anti-submarine warfare (ASW), troop transport, electronic countermeasures (ECM), and rescue. Licence-built by Fuji in Japan, Agusta SpA in Italy, Dornier in Germany, and the state factory in Taiwan.

Early versions of the Iroquois had provisions for one pilot and five passengers, with subsequent variants increasing the cabin size to provide additional capacity for up to a total of 14 troops or six litters. All variants have skids in lieu of wheels.

UH-1E Iroquois of the US Marine Corps (US Navy)

Status: *Operational.* First flight October 20, 1956 (XH-40); squadron delivery in 1959; over 9,000 built.

SPECIFICATIONS (UH-1D)

Crew: 1 + 11 troops
Engine: 1 Lycoming T53-L-13 turboshaft (1,400 shp)
Dimensions: length overall 57 ft 1 in (17·42 m), fuselage length 41 ft 10¾ in (12·78 m), height 14 ft 6 in (4·42 m); main rotor diameter 48 ft (14·64 m)
Speed: 127 mph (204 km/hr)
Ceiling: 12,600 ft (3,843 m) service; 13,600 ft (4,148 m) hovering in ground effect

Range: 320 miles (515 km)
Weights: 4,939 lb (2,242 kg) empty; 9,500 lb (4,313 kg) maximum
Armament: 1 × 20-mm Gatling gun or 1 × ·50-calibre machinegun (mounted in doorway) plus 4 × ·50-calibre machineguns or 48 × 2·75-in rockets (fuselage outriggers) or 1 × 40-mm grenade launcher (nose turret)

VARIANTS

XH-40 prototype; 3 built.

YH-40 service test model; 6 built.

UH-1 formerly HU-1; pre-production model; 9 built.

UH-1A formerly designated HU-1A; initial production version; with Lycoming T53-L-1A turboshaft; 1 crew + 5 troops; 13 modified to carry 16 × 2·75-in rockets and 2 × ·30-cal machineguns; remainder unarmed; rotor diameter 44 ft (13·42 m).

YUH-1B formerly XH-40A; prototype for UH-1B; 1 built.

UH-1B formerly HU-1B; T53-L-5/-9/-9A/-11/-11A/-11B/-11C/-11D turboshaft; 2 crew + 7 troops or 3 litters; some armed with rocket packs and machineguns; licence-built in Japan by Fuji.

UH-1C similar to UH-1B except modified with rotor blades of increased chord; T53-L-11 turboshaft; some armed as UH-1B.

UH-1D T53-L-11 turboshaft; relocated fuel cells, increased cabin space; 1 crew + 11 passengers; transferred to Australia, Brazil, Chile and New Zealand; licence-built in Germany by Dornier.

UH-1E similar to UH-1B; rescue hoist, rotor brake; with some armed with two fixed forward-firing 7·62-mm M-60 machineguns, 2 rocket pods; flown by USMC and US Navy (as UH-1L).

UH-1F similar to UH-1B except 48-ft (14·64 m) diameter rotor, modified tail boom and skids; used to provide operational support to ICBM installations and used in Vietnam for classified psychological warfare ops; flown by US Air Force.

TH-1F similar to UH-1F except modified for instrument and hoist training.

UH-1H similar to UH-1D; T53-L-13 turboshaft; licence-built in Taiwan; flown by Canadian forces as CH-118 (formerly CUH-1H).

EH-1H similar to UH-1H except modified for US Army Security Agency electronic warfare missions under projects Quick Fix and Multens.

HH-1H similar to UH-1H except modified for local base rescue; flown by USAF.

HH-1K similar to UH-1E with T53-L-13 turboshaft; flown by US Navy for search and rescue (SAR).

TH-1L similar to UH-1E; T53-L-13 turboshaft; armour and armament deleted; flown by US Navy as trainer.

UH-1M similar to UH-1C; T53-L-13 turboshaft; flown by US Army.

UH-1P similar to UH-1F; modified to perform special missions.

OPERATIONAL

Argentina, Australia, Austria, Brazil, Brunei, Cambodia, Canada, Chile, Colombia, Ethiopia, West Germany, Greece, Guatemala, Indonesia, Iran, Israel, Italy, Japan, South Korea, Kuwait, Morocco, Netherlands, New Zealand, Norway, Oman, Philippines, Saudi Arabia, Spain, Sweden, Taiwan, Thailand, Turkey, Uganda, United States (Air Force, Army, Marine Corps, (Navy), Uruguay, Venezuela, Yugoslavia, Zambia

Iroquois UH-1N } Bell (Model 212/214A)
Huey Plus

A twin-engined development of the Bell Model 205 (UH-1D), the Bell Model 212 UH-1N was originally produced for the Canadian government. Subsequently orders for the Model 212 have been placed for the armed services of the United States and several other countries. A further improvement, the Model 214A, has been procured for the Imperial Iranian Army by the US Army. The planned UH-1N programme is 294 for the US Navy and Marine Corps.

Both models carry up to 16 troops, the major differences being in the

UH-1N twin-engined helicopter of the US Air Force (Bell)

powerplant. The United Aircraft of Canada PT6T turboshaft is used in the Model 212, while the Lycoming LTC4B-8D is used in the 214A. The latter engine permits a 20% increase in capability of the 214A over the UH-1N.

Status: *Operational.* First flight May 1969 (UH-1N) and October 12, 1970 (Model 214); squadron delivery in 1970 (UH-1N) and 1975 (Model 214A).

SPECIFICATIONS (UH-1N)

Crew: 1 + 16 troops
Engines: 2 United Aircraft of Canada PT6 turboshafts (PT6T-3 Turbo Twin Pac) (900 shp each)
Dimensions: length overall 57 ft $3\frac{1}{4}$ in (17·47 m), fuselage length 42 ft $4\frac{3}{4}$ in (12·93 m), height 14 ft $4\frac{3}{4}$ in (4·39 m), main rotor diameter 48 ft $2\frac{1}{4}$ in (14·70 m)
Speed: 126 mph (203 km/hr)

Ceiling: 15,000 ft (4,575 m) service; 12,900 ft (3,935 m) hovering in ground effect
Range: 250 miles (402 km)
Weights: 5,549 lb (2,519 kg) empty; 10,500 lb (4,767 kg) maximum
Armament: various combinations of 7·62-mm machineguns, 40-mm grenade launchers, and 2·75-in rockets

VARIANTS

UH-1N basic production version for US services.
VH-1N executive transport version of UH-1N for US Army; 2 crew + 7 passengers.
CH-135 Canadian Forces variant.

Isfahan Model 214A for Iran with Lycoming LTC4B-8D turboshafts; maximum weight 13,000 lb (5,902 kg), cruise speed 150 mph (241 km/hr), range 300 miles (483 km).

OPERATIONAL

Brunei, Canada, Colombia, Ghana, Iran, Italy, South Korea, Lebanon, Mexico, Peru, Spain, Uganda, United States, (Army, Air Force, Marine Corps, Navy), Zambia

Kiowa OH-58
Sea Ranger TH-57 } Bell (206A Jet Ranger)

The Bell Model 206A is a compact, light observation helicopter used by military services, governmental agencies, and civilian groups throughout the world. In its military variants it is employed as a trainer, forward air control aircraft, gunship, border patrol, and light utility platform.

The model 206A was developed from Bell's losing entry in a 1962 US Army Light Observation Helicopter (LOH) competition. Originally catering exclusively to the civilian market, a militarized variant was offered by Bell for a new LOH competition in 1968, which the Model 206A won. The United States Navy had meanwhile declared the Jet Ranger the winner of a primary trainer competition, procuring 40 TH-57A Sea Rangers. Export orders have followed significant US Army purchases of the OH-58A. Also built under licence in Italy and Australia.

Status: *Operational.* First flight January 10, 1966; squadron delivery in 1969; over 2,500 built.

SPECIFICATIONS (OH-58A)

Crew: 2
Engine: 1 Allison T63-A-700 turboshaft (317 shp)
Dimensions: length overall 40 ft 11¾ in (12·50 m), fuselage length 32 ft 7 in (9·94 m), height overall 9 ft 6½ in (2·91 m), main rotor diameter 35 ft 4 in (10·78 m)

Speed: 138 mph (222 km/hr); 117 mph (188 km/hr) cruise
Ceiling: 18,900 ft (5,765 m) service, 13,600 ft (4,148 m) hovering in ground effect
Range: 300 miles (483 km)
Weights: 1,464 lb (665 kg) empty; 3,000 lb (1,362 kg) maximum
Armament: 1 × 7·62-mm minigun

VARIANTS

TH-57A dual-control trainer: accommodation for 5; 40 built for US Navy.

OH-58A standard production helicopter for US Army and export; 74 built for Canada as COH-58A, later CH-136.

Model 206B-1 similar to OH-58A; licence built in Australia.

CH-136 Kiowa of the Canadian Armed Forces (Bell)

OPERATIONAL

Abu Dhabi, Argentina, Australia, Austria, Brazil, Brunei, Canada, Chile, Dubai, Finland, Iran, Israel, Italy, Mexico, Oman, Saudi Arabia, Spain, Sri Lanka, Sweden, Tanzania, Thailand, Turkey, Uganda, United States (Army, Navy)

Lynx Westland (WG.13)
Aérospatiale

Although designed under the auspices of Westland, the WG.13 Lynx is one of three helicopters covered by an Westland/Aérospatiale collaboration agreement which provides for joint production of those three aircraft (the other two being the SA.330 Puma and the SA.341 Gazelle). Designed as a twin-engined multi-purpose helicopter, the Lynx is being produced in general-purpose, utility, and ASW variants for the armed services of Britain and France, as well as civilian users.

Designed with a conventional layout, the Lynx has an all-weather capability in all variants and the capacity to carry a variety of weapons. ASW variants have in addition search radar and other specialized sensors and carry homing torpedoes.

Status: *Development.* First flight March 21, 1971; squadron delivery in 1976.

Lynx HAS.2 of the French Navy (Aérospatiale)

Lynx AH.1 of the British Army (Westland Helicopters)

SPECIFICATIONS

Crew: 1 + 10 troops (or 2 to 4 crew depending upon mission)
Engines: 2 Rolls-Royce BS.360-07-26 Gem turboshafts (900 shp each)
Dimensions: overall length 49 ft 9 in (15·17 m); fuselage length 39 ft 6⅔ in (12·06 m); height 11 ft 6 in (3·51 m); main rotor diameter 42 ft (12·81 m)

Speed: 205 mph (330 km/hr); 175 mph (282 km/hr) cruise
Ceiling: 12,000+ ft (3,660 m)
Range: 475 miles (764 km)
Weights: 5,641 lb (2,561 kg) empty; 9,250 lb (4,200 kg) maximum
Armament: variety of missiles, cannon, machineguns, or torpedoes

VARIANTS

Prototypes 5 built.
AH.1 British Army utility variant.
HAS.2 ASW variant with search and tracking radar in chin radome; flown by Royal Navy and French Navy.
HT.Mk 3 training variant for Royal Air Force.

Sea Lynx Sikorsky proposal for US Navy LAMPS III requirement (SH-2D/F successor).
Model 606 civilian variants under study include utility and VIP versions.

OPERATIONAL

Argentina, Brazil, France (Navy), Great Britain (Army, Navy)

Osage TH-55A Hughes (Model 200/300)

The TH-55A Osage was initiated in the mid-1950s as a commercial venture under the Hughes designation 269A. In 1958 the US Army ordered five

*TH-55A Osage
of the US Army
(Hughes)*

models for evaluation as a light-weight primary helicopter-trainer. Not until 1964 did the Army place quantity orders for the helicopter. The Army order was for the two-seat Model 269A (changed to Model 200 in 1965), although Hughes also had in production at that time the three-seat Model 269B (changed to Model 300).

An exceptionally light helicopter, the Osage has dual controls, skid landing gear with manoeuvring wheels fitted to their forward ends (floats may be fitted alternatively), and a tubular tailboom with a horizontal stabilizer fitted opposite to the tail rotor. Bredanardi of Italy holds a marketing licence for all models.

Status: *Operational.* First flight October 1956 (Model 269A); squadron delivery in 1964. Over 1,700 built for civilian and military use.

SPECIFICATIONS (TH-55A)

Crew: 2 (1 pilot, 1 student)
Engine: 1 Lycoming H10-360-B1A piston (180 hp)
Dimensions: overall length 28 ft $10\frac{3}{4}$ in (8·81 m); fuselage length 21 ft $11\frac{3}{4}$ in 6·69 m); height 8 ft $2\frac{3}{4}$ in (2·51 m); main rotor diameter 25 ft $3\frac{1}{2}$ in (7·72 m)
Speed: 86 mph (138 km/hr); 75 mph

(121 km/hr) cruise
Ceiling: 11,900 ft (5,403 m) service; 5,500 ft (1,678 m) hovering in ground effect
Range: 204 miles (328 km)
Weights: 1,008 lb (458 kg) empty; 1,670 lb (758 kg) maximum
Armament: nil

VARIANTS

YHO-2HU prototype; 5 built.
TH-55A production version.

OPERATIONAL

Algeria, Brazil, Colombia, Ghana, India,   United States (Army)
Japan, Kenya, Nicaragua, Sweden,

Puma Aérospatiale (SA.330)
     Westland

Developed by Sud-Aviation to meet a French Army requirement for a medium-size tactical transport helicopter capable of all-weather operation, the Puma was also selected in 1967 for the Royal Air Force Tactical Transport Programme.

A twin-engined, conventional, medium-lift helicopter, the SA.330 Puma has a large, four-bladed main rotor, semi-retractable tricycle landing gear, optional emergency flotation units, and accommodation for 16 to 20 troops or 6 litters and 4 seated patients/attendants. It can also be operated as a flying crane, transporting bulky cargo externally. Armament varies with the user and can consist of missiles, cannon and/or machineguns mounted in a variety of positions. Collaboration in production between Sud's successor Aérospatiale and Westland Helicopters of Britain resulted from the joint Anglo/French requirement, a partnership that was extended to include the later SA.341 Gazelle. Several other nations have shown interest in, and placed orders for the Puma, and Romania has entered negotiations to obtain a licence to assemble approximately 100 SA.330s.

*SA.330B Puma
of the French
Army
(Aérospatiale)*

Status: *Operational.* First flight April 15, 1965; squadron delivery in 1969.

SPECIFICATIONS

Crew: 2 + 16 to 20 troops
Engines: 2 Turboméca Turmo IVB turboshafts (1,400 shp each)
Dimensions: overall length 59 ft $6\frac{1}{2}$ in (18·16 m); fuselage length 46 ft $1\frac{1}{2}$ in (14·07 m); height 16 ft $10\frac{1}{2}$ in (5·15 m); main rotor diameter 49 ft $2\frac{1}{2}$ in (15·01 m)
Speed: 170 mph (274 km/hr); 160 mph (257 km/hr) cruise
Ceiling: 15,100 ft (4,606 m) service; 6,890 ft (2,100 m) hovering in ground effect
Range: 365 miles (587 km)
Weights: 7,562 lb (3,433 kg) empty; 14,770 lb (6,706 kg) maximum
Armament: variety of missiles, cannon, and/or machineguns

VARIANTS

SA.330 prototype and pre-production machines; 8 built.
SA.330B Turmo IIIC4 turboshafts; flown by French Army; military export variant is 330C.
SA.330E Puma HC.1 with Turmo IIIC4 engines; 40 built for RAF.

SA.330F 2 Turmo IVA turboshafts; civilian passenger and cargo aircraft.
SA.330G similar to SA.330F with uprated Turmo IVC engines.
SA.330H SA.330C with uprated Turmo IVC engines.

OPERATIONAL

Abu Dhabi, Algeria, Cameroun, Chile, Ecuador, France, Great Britain, Kuwait, Mexico, Portugal, Romania, South Africa, Zaïre, Zambia

Raven H-23 Hiller 12

The Hiller H-23 series of light helicopters was derived from the civilian Hiller Model 12, which had made the first trans-continental United States flight by a helicopter. Examples were tested by the US Army and Navy as light utility helicopters for the former and trainers for the latter service, resulting in production orders from both. Extensively employed in the Korean War, improved versions were developed, incorporating changes indicated by Korean combat conditions.

With a production life stretching from the late 1940s to the mid-1960s, the Hiller 12 series found its way into the inventories of most Western nations. It has been replaced in almost all instances since its utility is limited by modern standards.

Status: *Operational.* First flight in 1948 (Model 12); squadron delivery in 1950. Over 2,000 built.

SPECIFICATIONS (OH-23C)

Crew: 1 + 2 troops
Engine: 1 Franklin 0-335-6B vertically opposed piston (200 hp)
Dimensions: fuselage length 27 ft 6 in (8·39 m); height 9 ft 6 in (2·90 m); main rotor diameter 35 ft (10·68 m)

Speed: 87 mph (140 km/hr)
Ceiling: 10,500 ft (3,203 m)
Range: 135 miles (217 km)
Weight: 2,500 lb (1,135 kg) maximum
Armament: nil

VARIANTS

H-23A original production version for US Army; all metal fuselage with two-bladed main rotor and two-bladed anti-torque rotor mounted on enclosed, tubular tail boom; 100 built for US Army and 5 for evaluation by US Air Force; 16 built for US Navy as HTE-1 trainers.

OH-23B formerly H-23B; uprated engine, dual controls; 273 built for US Army; 35 built for US Navy as HTE-2.

OH-23C similar to OH-23B; bubble canopy; 145 built.

OH-23D similar to OH-23C with Lycoming O-435-23B engine; 483 built.

OH-23F similar to OH-23D with Lycoming O-540-9 engine; 22 built.

OH-23G similar to OH-23D with Lycoming O-540-9 engine; 347 built plus 24 for Canada (CH-112 Nomad); 21 for Great Britain (HT.2).

OPERATIONAL

Chile, Colombia, Dominican Republic, Japan, Mexico

OH-23 Raven of the US Army, now no longer in US Forces inventory

Scout } Westland
Wasp }

The Westland Scout is a light liaison helicopter built for British Army servic
with the Wasp being an anti-submarine derivative developed for use from
destroyers and frigates. The basic design was initiated by Saunders-Roe in the
late 1950s as a follow-on to their earlier Skeeter design, but the new aircraf
was to be powered by a single turboshaft engine in lieu of the Skeeter's piston
In actuality, the new design bore little resemblance to the Skeeter and ha
become even more popular, being ordered by several other nations as well a
by the British armed forces.

A five- or six-seat general purpose helicopter, the Scout/Wasp has a four
bladed main rotor and a two-bladed anti-torque tail rotor. The Scout's landing
gear is of the skid type, while the Wasp has a quadricycle undercarriage to
facilitate handling aboard ship. Although tasked with an anti-submarine
mission, the Wasp is not equipped with any ASW sensors, relying instead
upon the detection equipment of its mother-ship for directions to employ
ASW torpedoes against hostile submarines.

Status: *Operational.* First flight July 20, 1958; squadron delivery in 1963.

SPECIFICATIONS

Crew: 2 + 3 troops (Scout)
Engine: 1 Rolls-Royce Bristol
  Nimbus turboshaft (685 hp (Scout);
  710 hp (Wasp))
Dimensions: overall length 40 ft 4 in
  (12·30 m); fuselage length 30 ft 4 in
  (9·25 m); height 11 ft 8 in (3·56 m);
  main rotor diameter 32 ft 3 in (9·84
  m)

Speed: 131 mph (211 km/hr) (Scout);
  120 mph (193 km/hr) (Wasp)
Ceiling: 13,400 ft (4,087 m) service
  (Scout); 12,200 ft (3,721 m) (Wasp)
Range: 315 miles (507 km) (Scout);
  270 miles (434 km) (Wasp)
Weights: 3,452 lb (1,567 kg) empty;
  5,500 lb (2,497 kg) maximum (Wasp)
Armament: 2 × Mk 44 torpedoes
  (Wasp)

*Wasp HAS.1s of
the Royal Navy
(Ministry of
Defence)*

ARIANTS

Prototypes 325 shp Turmo turbo-
aft; 2 built.

AH.1 Scout; flown by British Army,
ustralian Navy, Jordanian Air Force,
gandan and Bahrein police;
pproximately 150 built.

HAS.1 Wasp; folding tail and
quadricycle landing gear; fitted for
ASW, search and rescue, training; flown
by Royal Navy, South Africa, Brazil,
New Zealand, and Netherlands.

PERATIONAL

ustralia, Bahrein, Brazil, Great Britain
Army, Navy), Jordan, New Zealand,

Netherlands, South Africa, Uganda

ea King H-3 Sikorsky (S-61A/B/D)
ommando Westland

he Sikorsky Sea King series of twin-turbine helicopters was designed initially
o meet a US Navy anti-submarine specification. Since its service debut in
961, the H-3 series has undergone a variety of modifications for virtually all
irborne missions capable of being flown by a helicopter in both military and
ivilian service. Variants have been license-built by Italian, British, and
apanese companies, and serve in the armed forces of over a dozen nations.

All models of the S-61 have an amphibious capability and generous cabin
pace for either ASW gear, passengers or cargo. The S-61L and S-61N
ariants are stretched fuselage commercial helicopters (not covered herein),
vhile the S-61R is an extensively redesigned version listed separately as the
H-3 Sea King/HH-3 Jolly Green Giant. Also built under licence by Westland
n Great Britain and Agusta in Italy.

Status: *Operational.* First flight March 11, 1959 (XHSS-2); squadron
delivery in June 1961.

SPECIFICATIONS (SH-3D)

Crew: 4 (1 pilot, 1 co-pilot, 2 systems
operators)
Engines: 2 General Electric T58-GE-10
turboshafts (1,400 shp each)
Dimensions: overall length 72 ft 8 in
(22·16 m), fuselage length 54 ft 9 in
(16·70 m), height 16 ft 10 in (5·13
m), main rotor diameter 62 ft
(18·91 m)

Speed: 166 mph (267 km/hr); 136
mph (219 km/hr) cruise
Ceiling: 14,700 ft (4,484 m) service;
10,500 ft (3,203 m) hovering in
ground effect
Range: 625 miles (1,006 km)
Weights: 11,865 lb (5,387 kg) empty;
20,500 lb (9,307 kg) maximum
Armament: 840 lb (381 kg) of
weapons, including homing torpedoes

*SH-3H Sea King
ASW helicopter of
the US Navy
(Sikorsky)*

*Sea King HAS.1
of the Royal
Navy (Ministry of
Defence)*

*SH-3A Sea King
ASW helicopter of
the US Navy
lowering Sonar
(US Navy)*

ARIANTS

XHSS-2 prototype; 1 built for US
▪vy evaluation.

YHSS-2 service trials aircraft; 7 built
˙ USN.

SH-3A formerly HSS-2; production
▪craft with T58-GE-8B engines; ASW
▪nfiguration for USN; some updated
▪ SH-3H.

RH-3A SH-3A modified for airborne
▪nesweeping.

VH-3A formerly HSS-2Z; VIP
▪nsport for US President; 10 built with
▪presented to Egypt; flown by US
▪my and US Marine Corps.

HH-3A modified SH-3A with
▪8-GE-8F turboshafts; electronics
▪moved, 2 × 7·62-mm minigun turrets
▪stalled behind sponsons, high-speed
▪fuelling and fuel dumping systems,
▪odified avionics, external auxiliary fuel
▪nks, high-speed rescue hoist, complete
▪mour installed; for USN search and
▪scue.

S-61A export variant of SH-3A with
▪olls-Royce Bristol Gnome H.1200
▪rboshafts or T58 turboshafts;
▪mphibious transport for 26 troops or 15
▪ters or 12 VIP; flown by Denmark and
▪oyal Malaysian Air Force.

CH-3B similar to S-61A; US Air
▪orce utility helicopter; 3 crew, 25

passengers; 6 modified from SH-3A.

CH-124 similar to SH-3A for
Canadian Forces.

SH-3D production ASW helicopter
for USN; also built by Agusta.

VH-3D similar to VH-3A with
SH-3D equipment.

SH-3G SH-3A with ASW gear
removed for utility role; some fitted as
SH-3H.

SH-3H multi-purpose variant of
SH-3D with improved ASW and
electronic equipment.

Sea King similar to SH-3D;
Westland-built ASW variant with Rolls-
Royce Gnome H.1400 turboshafts;
56 built for Royal Navy, 12 for India
(Mk.42), 6 for Pakistan (Mk.45).

Sea King Mk.41 similar to S-61A
for search and rescue; 22 built for
Germany, 10 for Norway (Mk.43), 5 for
Belgium (Mk.48).

Sea King Mk.50 similar to Mk.1
with Gnome H.1400–1 turboshafts for
Australia.

Commando Mk.1 attack/transport
variant with Gnome H.1400–1
turboshafts; 3 crew, 25 troops, 5 built
for Egypt.

Commando Mk.2 similar to Mk.1;
production variant.

PERATIONAL

▪ustralia, Belgium, Brazil, Egypt,
▪est Germany, Great Britain, India,
▪an, Italy, Japan, Malaysia, Norway,

Pakistan, Spain, United States (Air
Force, Army, Marine Corps, Navy)

▪ea King CH-3
▪olly Green Giant HH-3 } Sikorsky (S-61R)
▪elican HH-3F

▪his amphibious transport helicopter was based upon the earlier Sea King
▪eries developed originally for the US Navy anti-submarine mission by
▪ikorsky. The HH-3E Jolly Green Giant variant was used extensively in
▪outheast Asia by the US Air Force to rescue pilots down in hostile territory.

HH-3E Jolly Green Giant of the US Air Force (US Air Force)

These helicopters made deep penetrations of North Vietnamese airspace i the face of heavy groundfire to perform armed rescue and recovery missions

Design changes from the basic Navy SH-3A included deletion of the ASW gear and addition of a rear ramp for loading vehicles, retractable tricycl landing gear, and gas turbine auxiliary power supply. The search and rescu (SAR) variants have armour, self-sealing fuel tanks, defensive guns, an rescue hoist.

Status: *Operational.* First flight June 17, 1963 (S-61R); squadron deliver in 1963.

SPECIFICATIONS (CH-3E)

Crew: 2 + 25 passengers
Engines: 2 General Electric T58-GE-5 turboshafts (1,500 shp each)
Dimensions: overall length 73 ft (22·27 m), fuselage length 57 ft 3 in (17·46 m), height 18 ft 1 in (5·52 m), main rotor diameter 62 ft (18·91 m)

Speed: 162 mph (260 km/hr); 144 mph (232 km/hr) cruise
Ceiling: 11,100 ft (3,386 m) service; 4,100 ft (1,250 m) hovering in ground effect
Range: 465 miles (748 km)
Weights: 13,255 lb (6,018 kg) empty; 22,050 lb (10,010 kg) maximum
Armament: nil

VARIANTS

CH-3C first production version with GE T58-GE-1 turboshafts; 41 built; all later brought up to CH-3E standard.

CH-3E uprated engines; 42 built and 41 modified, of which 50 converted to HH-3E.

HH-3E Jolly Green Giant; 2 × 7·62-mm minigun turrets on each sponson;

armour, self-sealing fuel tanks, retractable inflight refuelling probe, rescue hoist; first helicopter to make non-stop trans-Atlantic crossing.

HH-3F similar to HH-3E with combat equipment removed; 40 built for US Coast Guard; named "Pelican" by that service.

OPERATIONAL

United States (Air Force, Coast Guard, Marine Corps)

Sea Knight H-46 Boeing Vertol (Model 107)

A development of the commercial Model 107-II, the H-46 Sea Knight series initially was evaluated by the US Army to fulfil a medium lift transport helicopter requirement. However, the US Navy and Marine Corps subsequently became the prime users of the Sea Knight. The Navy flies the tandem-rotor helicopter in the vertical replenishment (VERTREP) role, transferring stores, parts, munitions, and personnel from logistic support ships to combatant ships at sea; the Marine Corps employs the Sea Knight as its primary medium troop lift helicopter. Variants have also been supplied to the US Army, the Canadian Forces, and the Royal Swedish Air Force and Navy.

The Sea Knight's tandem-rotor configuration has the twin turboshaft power plants sitting atop the fuselage at the base of the rear rotor mount. This arrangement permits the unobstructed use of the length of the internal fuselage, and allows for a rear cargo ramp to facilitate the loading of troops, cargo, and small vehicles.

Status: *Operational.* First flight April 22, 1958; squadron delivery in 1964. Over 600 built, with production by Kawasaki of Japan as well as Boeing Vertol.

SPECIFICATIONS (CH-46D)

Crew: 3 + 26 troops

Engines: 2 General Electric T58-GE-10 turboshafts (1,400 shp each)

Dimensions: overall length 84 ft 4 in (25·72 m); fuselage length 44 ft 10 in (13·67 m); height 16 ft 8½ in (5·09 m); main rotor diameter 51 ft (15·56 m) (each)

Speed: 166 mph (267 km/hr); 161 mph (259 km/hr) cruise

Ceiling: 14,000 ft (4,270 m); 9,500 ft (2,898 m) hovering in ground effect

Range: 250 miles (402 km)

Weights: 13,067 lb (5,932 kg) empty; 23,000 lb (10,442 kg) maximum

Armament: nil

CH-46D Sea Knight of the US Marine Corps (Boeing Vertol)

UH-46 Sea Knight of the US Navy (US Navy)

VARIANTS

YHC-1A US Army prototype converted from commercial Model 107.

CH-46A formerly HRB-1; production version with two T58-GE-8 turboshafts; flown by US Marine Corps; designated UH-46A when modified for use in vertical replenishment (VERTREP) by US Navy.

RH-46A CH-46A modified for minesweeping for US Navy evaluation; 3 crew.

CH-46C formerly HC-1A; similar to CH-46A for US Army.

CH-46D similar to CH-46A with two T58-GE-10 turboshafts; designated UH-46D when VERTREP modified; designated CH-46E with automatic navigation system, armoured crew's

seats; and designated CH-46F with instrument panel changes.

CH-113 similar to CH-46A for search and rescue (SAR); 6 built for Canada; designated CH-113A as troop transport (12 built).

Hkp-4 export variant with two Bristol-Siddeley Gnome H.1200 turboshafts; 13 built for Swedish Air Force (SAR) and Navy (ASW).

KV-107 Kawasaki licence-built variants; fitted for mine counter-measures, troop transport, search and rescue missions; flown by Japanese Self-Defence Forces.

Hkp-4C Kawasaki-built airframes for Sweden; similar to Hkp-4.

OPERATIONAL

Canada, Japan, Sweden, Thailand, United States (Marine Corps, Navy)

Seasprite H-2 Kaman (Model K-20)

The H-2 Seasprite series was developed to a US Navy requirement for a long-range, all-weather utility helicopter capable of operating from smaller ships with helicopter platforms. It has since evolved into rescue and anti-

*SH-2D Seasprite
of the US Navy
(US Navy)*

submarine variants, the latter role being the US Navy's LAMPS (Light Airborne Multi-Purpose System). The 105 LAMPS I helicopters were converted from earlier model UH-2 search and rescue variants.

Powered by turbines, the H-2 series has one main rotor and an anti-torque rotor opposite a horizontal stabilizer on the tail. The LAMPS variants are equipped with surface search radar, magnetic anomaly detection (MAD), sonobuoys, and data link, and can carry Mk-46 anti-submarine torpedoes.

Status: *Operational.* First flight July 2, 1959; squadron delivery in 1962. 194 built.

SPECIFICATIONS (SH-2D)

Crew: 3 (1 pilot, 1 co-pilot, and 1 systems operator)

Engines: 2 General Electric T58-GE-8F turboshafts (1,350 shp)

Dimensions: overall length 52 ft 7 in (16·04 m); fuselage length 38 ft 4 in (11·69 m); height 15 ft 6 in (4·73 m); main rotor diameter 44 ft (13·42 m)

Speed: 165 mph (265 km/hr); 150 mph (241 km/hr) cruise

Ceiling: 22,500 ft (6,863 m) service; 18,600 ft (5,673 m) hovering in ground effect

Range: 420 miles (676 km)

Weights: 6,953 lb (3,157 kg) empty; 12,800 lb (5,811 kg) maximum

Armament: 2 × Mk 46 ASW torpedoes

VARIANTS

YHU2K-1 prototype with 1 T58-GE-6 turboshaft; 4 built.

UH-2A formerly HU2K-2; 1 T58-GE-8F; general utility helicopter; 2 crew + 2 passengers; 88 built.

UH-2B similar to UH-2A with some instrumentation removed; 102 built.

UH-2C all UH-2A/B converted with 2 T58-GE-8F turboshafts.

HH-2C further conversion of UH-2C for armed search and rescue with increased instrumentation, armour, self-sealing fuel tanks, 1 × 7·62-mm minigun in chin turret, variable speed hoist; 6 converted.

HH-2D similar to HH-2C without armament/armour; 67 converted.

SH-2D similar to HH-2D with ASW gear, interim LAMPS helicopter; 20 converted from HH-2D.

YSH-2E similar to SH-2D with improved radar, new sensors; 2 converted from HH-2D.

SH-2F similar to SH-2D with improved avionics, ASW and ECM gear; new rotor system; 85 converted.

OPERATIONAL

United States (Navy)

Sea Stallion H-53 Sikorsky (S-65)

The H-53 series was developed as a heavy assault transport in response to a US Marine Corps requirement issued in 1962. Subsequent variants have been developed for use as a mine countermeasure aircraft for the US Navy and as a search and rescue helicopter to replace the HH-3 "Jolly Green Giant" in the US Air Force. In this latter guise it is referred to as "Super Jolly". The Israelis fly several in an electronic intelligence (ELINT) collection configuration.

A hybrid development combining an enlarged H-3 Sea King series fuselage with the six-bladed rotor power-train of the CH-54 Skycrane, the H-53 has a watertight body with a rear ramp that provides access for 38 troops and equipment, or 24 litters and 4 attendants, or 8,000 lb (3,630 kg) of cargo. Produced by VFW-Fokker under licence for West Germany. The CH-53E heavy lift derivative is listed separately.

Status: *Operational.* First flight October 14, 1964; squadron delivery in 1966; 265 built for US armed forces; production by VFW-Fokker continues.

SPECIFICATIONS (CH-53D)

Crew: 3 + 37 troops
Engines: 2 General Electric T64-GE-413 turboshafts (3,925 shp each)
Dimensions: overall length 88 ft 3 in (26·92 m); fuselage length 67 ft 2 in (20·48 m); fuselage width 8 ft 10 in (2·69 m); height 24 ft 11 in (7·59 m); main rotor diameter 72 ft 3 in (22·04 m)

Speed: 196 mph (315 km/hr); 173 mph (278 km/hr) cruise
Ceiling: 21,000 ft (6,405 m) service; 13,400 ft (4,087 m) hovering in ground effect
Range: 540 miles (869 km)
Weights: 23,485 lb (10,662 kg) empty; 42,000 lb (19,068 kg) maximum
Armament: nil

*CH-53D Sea
Stallions of the
US Marine Corps
(US Marine
Corps)*

*HH-53C Sea
Stallion of the
US Air Force
(US Air Force)*

VARIANTS

CH-53A initial variant with 2 T64-GE-6B turboshafts; assault cargo transport; first helicopter automatic terrain clearance flight in 1968 experiment.

RH-53A similar to CH-53A with T64-GE-413 turboshafts; fitted for minesweeping for US Navy.

HH-53B similar to CH-53A with T64-GE-3 turboshafts; retractable flight refuelling probe, auxiliary fuel tanks, rescue hoist, improved avionics, armour, 3 × 7·62 mm Miniguns; 8 built.

HH-53C similar to HH-53B with 2 T64-GE-7 turboshafts; 58 built.

CH-53D similar to CH-53A with 2 T64-GE-413 turboshafts.

RH-53D RH-53A retrofitted with 2 T64-GE-415 turboshafts; automatic flight control system, reinforced fuselage, 2 × ·50-cal. MG to detonate surfaced mines; advanced minesweeping gear.

YCH-53E heavy lift variant described separately.

VH-53F VIP transport version of CH-53D

CH-53G similar to CH 53A for West Germany with German-made components; 2 T64-GE-7 turboshafts.

S-65-Ö similar to HH-53C for Austrian Air Force; 2 built.

OPERATIONAL

Austria, West Germany, Israel, United States (Air Force, Marine Corps, Navy)

Super Stallion CH-53E Sikorsky (S-65A)

Chosen in 1973 as the US Navy and Marine Corps heavy lift helicopter, the Sikorsky CH-53E is a three-turbine development of the earlier twin-turbine Sea Stallion series. Flown at gross weights exceeding 70,000 lb (31,780 kg), the Super Stallion's missions include cargo and troop transport, tactical recovery of downed or damaged aircraft, external (sling) transport of heavy, bulky equipment and supplies, and towing of craft and minesweeping devices. It is currently the West's most powerful helicopter. Plans call for an initial order of 30 each for US Navy and Marine Corps plus ten for training and pipeline.

Externally similar to the earlier variants of the H-53 series, the CH-53E differs significantly in the powerplant, the rotor/drive system, and fuselage length.

Status: *Development.* First flight March 1, 1974.

SPECIFICATIONS

Crew: 3 + 56 troops
Engines: 3 General Electric T64-GE-415 turboshafts (4,380 shp each)
Dimensions: overall length 99 ft 6 in (30·35 m); fuselage length 91 ft 7 in (27·94 m); height 27 ft 8 in (8·44 m); overall length 79 ft (24·10 m)

Speed: 196 mph (315 km/hr)
Range: 1,080 miles (1,738 km)
Weights: 31,915 lb (14,490 kg) empty; 70,000 + lb (31,780 kg) maximum
Armament: nil

YCH-53E Super Stallion heavy-lift helicopter of the US Marine Corps (Sikorsky)

Sioux H-13 Bell (Model 47)

Variants of the Bell Model 47 have been in use around the world since 1946. Seeing extensive use with both the US Army and the US Navy in the Korean War, the helicopter continued in production into 1972 and has found employment with the armed forces of over 30 nations. It is no longer flown by US services. The 47G is the last and longest-lived variant of the series.

The H-13 (US military designation of the Model 47) was originally produced with an enclosed cabin, but was soon altered to the distinctive bubble-type or "goldfish bowl" canopy by which the Model 47 has become easily recognizable. Another recognition feature, the open lattice-work tail boom, became standardized in 1949. Further changes were more on the order of refinements, with the basic design being essentially unchanged throughout the remainder of the production runs. Exceptions involved mostly licence-built machines, especially the Model 47J-3 with its four- or five-place cabin and enclosed tail boom built by Agusta for anti-submarine warfare. Agusta in Italy, Westland in Great Britain, and Kawasaki in Japan have contributed to the more than 5,000 examples of the Model 47 produced.

Status: *Operational.* First flight December 8, 1945; squadron delivery in 1946.

SPECIFICATIONS (OH-13S)

Crew: 1 + 1 passenger
Engine: 1 Lycoming TVO-435-25 in-line piston (260 hp)
Dimensions: overall length 42 ft 3½ in (12·90 m); fuselage length 31 ft 7 in (9·64 m); height 9 ft 3 in (2·82 m), main rotor diameter 37 ft 1½ in (11·32 m)

Speed: 105 mph (169 km/hr)
Ceiling: 18,500 ft (5,643 m) service; 18,000 ft (5,490 m) hovering in ground effect
Range: 315 miles (507 km)
Weights: 1,936 lb (879 kg) empty; 2,850 lb (1,294 kg) maximum
Armament: nil

OH-13S Sioux of the US Army (Bell)

VARIANTS

YR-13 prototype for US service evaluation; enclosed cabin; 18 built for US Army and 10 for US Navy (HTL-1).

H-13B Model 47D with Franklin engine; bubble canopy; 65 built for US Army with 16 converted to aerial ambulance (H-13C); 12 built for US Navy (HTL-2).

HTL-3 Model 47E with Franklin engine; 9 built for USN.

H-13D Model 47D-1 with open lattice tailboom; 87 built for US Army and 46 for USN (HTL-4).

OH-13F 3-place helicopter similar to H-13D with dual controls; 490 built plus 36 for USN (HTL-5).

XH-13F Model 201 turbine engine testbed.

OH-13G Model 47G with increased fuel capacity, controllable horizontal stabilizer; 265 built plus 48 for USN (HTL-6), with additional USN units with dual controls designed TH-13M.

OH-13H similar to OH-13G with Lycoming 0-435-23 engine; 452 built plus units for USN (TH-13L).

UH-13J similar to OH-13H with fully enclosed cabin, 4 seats; 2 built for US Air Force plus 28 for USN (UH-13P).

OH-13K fitted with Franklin 6VS-0-335 engine.

TH-13N similar to OH-13G/TH-13M with Lycoming 0-435-6/-6A; flown by US Coast Guard as utility aircraft for icebreakers.

HH-13Q formerly HUL-1G; UH-13P modified for search and rescue (SAR); flown by US Coast Guard.

UH-13R turbine engine testbed.

UH-13S modified OH-13H with turbo supercharger, lengthened tailboom, and modified rotor blades.

TH-13T similar to OH-13S for instrument training with larger cabin; flown by US Army.

AH Mk.1 Model 47G-3B built by Agusta and assembled by Westland for the British Army and Royal Air Force (HT Mk.2).

OPERATIONAL

Argentina, Austria, Brazil, Burma, Colombia, Ecuador, Great Britain (Army, Air Force), Greece, Guinea, India, Italy, Japan, Kenya, Malaysia, Mexico, Morocco, New Zealand, Pakistan, Paraguay, Peru, Spain, Sri Lanka, Taiwan, Tanzania, Turkey, Uruguay, Venezuela, Zaïre, Zambia

Super Frelon Aérospatiale (SA.321)

The SA.321 Super Frelon (Hornet) is a large passenger and utility transport helicopter, with a specialized naval anti-submarine variant. Now produced by Sud-Aviation's successor, Aérospatiale, the Super Frelon is the largest helicopter built in France and is used by the military services of that country as well as those of China, Israel, South Africa, Iran, and Libya. It was originally designed by Sud-Aviation with technical assistance from Sikorsky Aircraft in the late 1950s and early 1960s.

SA-321 Super Frelons of the French Navy (Aérospatiale)

The SA.321 series possesses some typical Sikorsky characteristics such as a water-tight hull for amphibious operations, float-type sponsons housing the main landing gear, and a Sikorsky-designed rotor system. The fuselage has a rear loading ramp, and the extreme aft section of the tailboom (with the tail rotor) folds forward for carrier stowage. The ASW variant is flown only by the French Navy.

Status: *Operational.* First flight (SA.3200) June 10, 1959; squadron delivery in 1966; 77 military variants built.

SPECIFICATIONS (SA.321G)

Crew: 5 (2 pilots, 3 sensor operators)
Engines: 3 Turboméca Turmo IIIC6-70 turboshafts (1,630 shp each)
Dimensions: overall length 75 ft $6\frac{5}{8}$ in (23·06 m); fuselage length 65 ft $10\frac{3}{4}$ in (20·10 m); height 21 ft $10\frac{1}{4}$ in (6·68 m); main rotor diameter 62 ft (18·91 m)
Speed: 170 mph (274 km/hr); 155 mph (249 km/hr) cruise
Ceiling: 10,325 ft (3,150 m) service; 7,120 ft (2,170 m) hovering in ground effect
Range: 510 miles (820 km), 635 miles (1,022 km) ferry
Weights: 14,607 lb (6,632 kg) empty; 28,660 lb (13,012 kg) maximum
Armament: 4 × ASW homing torpedoes

VARIANTS

SA.3200 Frelon prototype; three Turmo IIIB turboshafts; swing-tail cargo loading; 2 crew + 28 troops; 2 built.

SA.3210 Super Frelon prototype; three Turmo IIIC2 turboshafts; Sikorsky-designed rotor system, rear loading ramp; first flight December 7, 1962; 2 built.

SA.321 pre-production machines; 4 built.

SA.321F commercial version for carrying 37 passengers.

SA.321G first production version; ASW variant with radar, IFF, dipping sonar, ASW torpedoes; 24 built for French Navy.

SA.321J utility and commercial transport prototype; first flight July 6, 1967.

SA.321Ja utility and commercial
production aircraft; external load
capability up to 11,000 lb (4,994 kg);

27 passengers; flown by Israel
(SA.321K), South Africa (SA.321L).

OPERATIONAL

China, France, Iran, Israel, Libya, South Africa

Tarhe CH-54 Sikorsky (S-64)

The CH-54 Tarhe—popularly known as the "Flying Crane"—was developed
to meet US military requirements for a heavy lift helicopter to perform in a
variety of roles including field hospital support, troop transport, anti-
submarine warfare, heavy equipment movement, and minesweeping. These
diversified operations could be accomplished through the use of specialized
pods or vans carried beneath the Skycrane's spindly fuselage.

The Skycrane has a cab forward housing the pilot and co-pilot facing
forward with a third pilot facing aft to control the helicopter during loading
and unloading operations. The "backbone" structure houses the engines,
transmission, and rotors. Tricycle landing gear is fitted with the main wheels
on outriggers to straddle bulky cargo, and provision is made for the landing
gear oleos to lower hydraulically permitting the aircraft to "squat down" onto
cargo. Up to 67 troops or 20,000 lb (9,080 kg) of cargo can be van-lifted, including such specialized cargoes as medical vans and other containerized
facilities. Civilian variants have been employed for ship-to-shore movement of
freight containers, passenger shuttle service, and oil drilling support, both
inland and offshore. It is similar in appearance and role to the Mi-10 *Harke*
with the Soviet helicopter having a quadricycle undercarriage while the US
helicopter has a "droop" cabin.

Status: *Operational.* First flight May 9, 1962; squadron delivery in 1964.
Over 100 built.

SPECIFICATIONS (CH-54B)

Crew: 3
Engines: 2 Pratt & Whitney JFTD-12A-
  4A turboshafts (4,500 shp each)
Dimensions: overall length 88 ft 6 in
  (26·99 m); fuselage length 70 ft 3 in
  (21·43 m); height 25 ft 5 in; ground
  clearance under fuselage boom 9 ft
  4 in (2·87 m); main rotor diameter
  72 ft (21·96 m)

Speed: 126 mph (203 km/hr); 105
  mph (169 km/hr) cruise
Ceiling: 9,000 ft (2,745 m) service;
  10,600 ft (3,233 m) hovering in
  ground effect
Range: 230 miles (370 km)
Weights: 19,234 lb (8,732 kg) empty;
  42,000 lb (19,068 kg) maximum
Armament: nil

*Two views of the
CH-54A Tarhe
flying crane
flown by the US
Army (US Army)*

VARIANTS

CH-54A formerly YCH-54A;
Sikorsky Model S-64A with JFTD-12A-
4A turboshafts; approx 60 built.
CH-54B improved CH-54B with
JFTD-12A-5A turboshafts; dual landing
gear wheels, automatic flight
stabilization; 47,000 lb (21,338 kg)
maximum with 25,000-lb (11,350-kg)
lift capacity.

OPERATIONAL

United States (Army)

Wessex Westland

Derived from the Sikorsky S-58, for which Westland had purchased a production licence in 1956, the Wessex differed from its American counterpart in being powered by a turboshaft plant instead of the latter's radial piston engine. Production Wessex models have been used in the ASW role, as assault transports, and as VIP passenger carriers with The Queen's Flight.

Efforts were taken to retain mechanical and dimension compatibility between the Wessex and the Sikorsky S-58 (H-34 series). Therefore, the rotor system, hydraulic and avionics systems are virtually identical, the only differences being those required by the nature of the different power plants.

Status: *Operational.* First flight May 17, 1957 (re-engined Sikorsky S-58); squadron delivery in 1960.

SPECIFICATIONS (HU.5)

Crew: 2+16 troops
Engines: 2 Rolls Royce Gnome turboshafts (1,550 shp combined)
Dimensions: overall length 65 ft 9 in (20.05 m); fuselage length 48 ft 4½ in (14.76 m); height 16 ft 2 in (4.93 m); main rotor diameter 56 ft (17.08 m)
Speed: 132 mph (212 km/hr); 120 mph (193 km/hr) cruise
Ceiling: 14,100 ft (4,300 m) service; 5,900 ft (1,800 m) hovering in ground effect
Range: 475 miles (764 km)
Weights: 8,657 lb (3,930 kg) empty; 13,500 lb (6,129 kg) maximum
Armament: variety of machineguns, rockets, ASMs, torpedoes

Wessex HU.5s of the Royal Navy (Ministry of Defence)

*Wessex HAS.3 of
the Royal Navy
(Westland
Helicopters)*

VARIANTS

HAS.1 SH-34G with one Napier Gazelle 161 turboshaft engine; fitted for anti-submarine warfare; 4 crew; flown by Royal Navy.

HC.2 Transport variant with two Rolls-Royce Gnome turboshafts; 1 crew + 16 troops; flown by Royal Air Force; designated CC.4 in VIP configuration; designated HU.5 in troop lift configuration for Royal Marines (flown by RN);

12 built for Iraq (Mk.52); 3 built for Ghana (Mk.53), 1 built for Brunei (Mk.54).

HAS.3 similar to HAS.1 with one Gazelle 165 turboshaft; fitted with search radar in dorsal dome; flown by RN.

HAS.31 similar to HAS.1 with Gazelle 162 turboshaft; flown by Australia.

OPERATIONAL

Australia, Brunei, Ghana, Great Britain, Iraq

Appendices

Appendix A   Aircraft Designations

GREAT BRITAIN

British military aircraft designations include the basic type name, letters indicating the aircraft's function, and numerals indicating the specific mark or model of the aircraft. For example, Gannet AEW.3 indicates the airborne early warning configuration and the third version of the Gannet. The prefix letters currently in use for British combat aircraft and for helicopters are:

AEW	Airborne Early Warning	**FR**	Fighter/Reconnaissance
AH	Army Helicopter	**G**	Ground Attack (formerly GA)
AL	Army Liaison	**HAR**	Helicopter/Air Rescue
AOP	Air Observation	**HAS**	Helicopter/Anti-Submarine
AS	Anti-Submarine	**HC**	Helicopter/Cargo
B	Bomber	**HR**	Helicopter/Rescue
B(I)	Bomber/Interdictor	**HT**	Helicopter/Training
B(K)	Bomber/Tanker	**HU**	Helicopter/Utility
B(PR)	Bomber/Photographic Reconnaissance	**MR**	Maritime Reconnaissance
		R	Reconnaissance (formerly PR)
F	Fighter	**S**	Strike
FGA	Fighter/Ground Attack	**SR**	Strategic Reconnaissance
FAW	Fighter/All-Weather		
FGR	Fighter/Ground Attack/ Reconnaissance		

The designations **AL, AOP, B, B(.PR), FAW, HU,** and **SR** will not be allocated in the future.

SOVIET UNION

Soviet military aircraft are generally known in the West by their US-NATO reporting names. Based on a system developed by the Air Standards Co-ordinating Committee, these names are assigned with the initial letter indicating the aircraft's primary role. The initial letters are:

B	Bomber	**H**	Helicopter
C	Cargo-transport	**M**	Anti-Submarine, Maritime Patrol, Trainer, and Utility
F	Fighter		

Variations to the basic type are indicated by suffix letters; for example, the *Flagon*-A is the basic fighter aircraft while the *Flagon*-B is the STOL development of the aircraft.

The Soviet Union assigns letter abbreviations based on the design bureau with numerals indicating the sequence in the bureau's projects. Military and bureau numbers sometimes differ, such as Tu-20 being the military designation of the *Bear* aircraft and Tu-95 that of the design bureau. Current bureau designations relevant to combat aircraft and helicopters are:

Be	Beriev	**Mya**	Myasishchev
Il	Ilyushin	**Su**	Sukhoi
Ka	Kamov	**Tu**	Tupolev
Mi	Mil	**Yak**	Yakovlev
MiG	Mikoyan and Gurevich		

The bureau designations have suffix letters for modifications and variations. The most frequently used are "bis" to indicate later variants, "F" for *forsazh* or "boosted", and UTI indicating aircraft adopted for training.

UNITED STATES

All US military aircraft have had a common designation system since September 1962 when Army and Navy aircraft were redesignated in a common system with the US Air Force. This system consists of a basic mission letter and design number, the latter within the basic mission sequence. Because of the high numbers within some mission types (fighters reached F-111), some later aircraft have had low numbers assigned. The current basic mission letters for combat aircraft and helicopters are:

A	Attack	**O**	Observation
B	Bomber	**P**	(Maritime) Patrol
E	Electronic	**S**	Anti-Submarine
F	Fighter	**U**	Utility
H	Helicopter	**V**	VSTOL and STOL

Although not a formal basic mission designation, the letters SR are used to denote Strategic Reconnaissance for the SR-71 Blackbird. (The letters were used only once previously, for the cancelled B-70 strategic bombers which was redesignated SR-70 for Strike-Reconnaissance.)

Prefix and suffix letters are used to indicate status, modified missions, and sequential variants. The principal status prefix letters are:

J	Temporary Special Test (as JC-130)	**X**	Experimental (as XH-51)
		Y	Prototype (as YF-17)
N	Permanent Special Test (as NC-135)	**Z**	Planning (as ZO-4)

The principal modified mission prefix letters are:

A	Attack (as AC-47)	**F**	Fighter (as FV-12)
C	Cargo (as CH-53)	**H**	Search/Rescue (as HH-52)
D	Director (drone control; as DP-2)	**K**	Tanker (as KC-135)
		L	Cold Weather (as LH-34)
E	Special Electronics (as EA-3)		

O	Observation (as OV-10)	T	Trainer (as TB-57)
Q	Drone (as QF-104)	U	Utility (as US-2)
R	Reconnaissance (as RF-4)	V	Staff (VIP; as VA-3)
S	Anti-Submarine (as SH-3)	W	Weather (as WP-3)

Thus, the designation YOV-10D indicates the basic aircraft is the tenth STOL-type aircraft developed by the US services (V-10), with the observation mission (O), the prototype being indicated (Y) of the fourth variant (D). The suffix letters O and I are not used to avoid confusion with numerals.

Appendix B Aircraft Carriers*

* NOTES: Type symbols are based on US Navy system: CV for aircraft carrier capable of operating high-performance aircraft, CVL for light carrier, CH for helicopter ship, CHG for missile-armed helicopter ship, LPH or LHA for amphibious assault helicopter ship, and CVT for training carrier with suffix N indicating nuclear propulsion; displacement is full load; length is overall; troop capacity is indicated for normal operation.

Type	Ship	Launched	Compl.	Displ.	Length	Machinery	Speed	Aircraft (troops)
Argentina								
CVL	25 de Mayo	1943	1945	19,896 tons	693 ft	steam turbines 40,000 shp	24 kts	21 { Tracker / Skyhawk / Sea King
Australia								
CVL	Melbourne	1945	1955	19,966 tons	701½ ft	steam turbines 42,000 shp	23 kts	6 Tracker / 8 Skyhawk / 10 Wessex
Brazil								
CVL	Minas Gerais	1944	1945	19,890 tons	695 ft	steam turbines 40,000 shp	25 kts	20 { Tracker / Sea King
France								
CV CV	Clemenceau Foch	1957 1960	1961 1963	32,780 tons	869¼ ft	steam turbines 126,000 shp	32 kts	40 { Etendard IV / Crusader / Alizé
CHN	(unnamed)	building	1980	18,400 tons	686½ ft	nuclear	28+ kts	20+ { Lynx / Puma / Super Frelon (1,500 troops)
Great Britain								
CV	Ark Royal	1950	1955	50,786 tons	845 ft	steam turbines 152,000 shp	31½ kts	12 Phantom / 12 Buccaneer / 4 Gannet / 6 Sea King
CHG	Invincible	building	1980	20,000 tons	650 ft	gas turbines 112,000 shp	30 kts	20 { Harrier / Sea King

Type	Ship	Launched	Compl.	Displ.	Length	Machinery	Speed	Aircraft (Troops)
LPH	*Hermes*	1953	1959	28,700 tons	744¼ ft	steam turbines 76,000 shp	28 kts	20 { Sea King / Sioux (750 troops)
LPH	*Bulwark*	1948	1954	27,705 tons	737¾ ft	steam turbines	28 kts	20 { Sea King / Sioux (750 troops)
India								
CVL	*Vikrant*	1945	1961	19,500 tons	700 ft	steam turbines 40,000 shp	24 kts	21 { Sea Hawk / Alizé
Soviet Union								
CHG	*Moskva*	1965	1967	18,000 tons	644¾ ft	steam turbines 100,000 shp	30 kts	20 *Hormone*
CHG	*Leningrad*	1966	1968					
CHG	*Kiev*	1973	1975	35,000 tons	925 ft	steam turbines	30 kts	35 { *Freehand* / *Hormone*
CHG	*Minsk*	building						
Spain								
CH	*Dédalo*	1943	1943	15,800 tons	623 ft	steam turbines 100,000 shp	32 kts	20 { Sea King / HueyCobra
United States								
CVT-16	*Lexington*	1942	1943	39,000 tons	894½ ft	steam turbines 150,000 shp	30+ kts	70+ { (non assigned) / Crusader / Skyhawk or Corsair / miscellaneous
CV-19	*Hancock*	1944	1944	44,700 tons	894½ ft			
CV-34	*Oriskany*	1945	1950		890 ft			
CV-41	*Midway*	1945	1945	64,000 tons	979 ft	steam turbines 212,000 shp	33 kts	75+ { Phantom / Corsair / Intruder / miscellaneous
CV-42	*F. D. Roosevelt*	1945	1945					
CV-43	*Coral Sea*	1946	1947					
CV-59	*Forrestal*	1954	1955		1039 ft	steam turbines 280,000 shp	33 kts	85+ { Phantom / Corsair / Intruder / miscellaneous
CV-60	*Saratoga*	1955	1956	78,000 tons	1046½ ft	(*Forrestal* 260,000)	35 kts	
CV-61	*Ranger*	1956	1957					
CV-62	*Independence*	1958	1959					

Type	Ship	Launched	Compl.	Displ.	Length	Machinery	Speed	Aircraft (troops)
CVN-65	*Enterprise*	1960	1961	89,600 tons	1123 ft	nuclear 280,000 shp	35 kts	95 { Tomcat, Corsair, Intruder, miscellaneous
CV-63	*Kitty Hawk*	1960	1961	80,000 tons	1062½ ft	steam turbines 280,000 shp	35 kts	85+ { Phantom, Corsair
CV-64	*Constellation*	1960	1961		1072½ ft			
CV-66	*America*	1964	1965	87,000 tons	1047½ ft			95+ { Intruder, miscellaneous
CVA-67	*John F. Kennedy*	1967	1968		1047½ ft			
CVN-68	*Nimitz*	1972	1975	91,400 tons	1092 ft	nuclear 300,000+ shp	30+ kts	100 { Tomcat, Corsair, Intruder, miscellaneous
CVN-69	*D. D. Eisenhower*	building	1977					
CVN-70	*Carl Vinson*	building	1981					
LPH-2	*Iwo Jima*	1960	1961					
LPH-3	*Okinawa*	1961	1962					
LPH-7	*Guadalcanal*	1963	1963					30 { Iroquois, Sea Knight, Sea Stallion (2,100 troops)
LPH-9	*Guam*	1964	1965	18,300 tons	592 ft	steam turbines 23,000 shp	20 kts	
LPH-10	*Tripoli*	1965	1966					
LPH-11	*New Orleans*	1968	1968					
LPH-12	*Inchon*	1969	1970					
LHA-1	*Tarawa*	1973	1975					
LHA-2	*Saipan*	building	1976					
LHA-3	*Belleau Wood*	building	1976	39,300 tons	820 ft	steam turbines 70,000 shp	22+ kts	30 { Iroquois, Sea Knight, Sea Stallion (1,825 troops)
LHA-4	*Nassau*	building	1977					
LHA-5	*Da Nang*	building	1977					

Index

Index of Countries

Index of Aircraft